To Bernard

With best wishes

Alan Lang

23.1.19.

DIVIDED WE STAND

His Honour Judge Israel Finestein, QC
Photograph by Julian Oster Weinberg

Divided We Stand

A Journey with
Judge Israel Finestein QC

Colin Lang

VALLENTINE MITCHELL
LONDON • PORTLAND, OR

English edition published in 2017 by Vallentine Mitchell

Catalyst House,
720 Centennial Court,
Centennial Park, Elstree WD6 3SY, UK

920 NE 58th Avenue, Suite 300
Portland, Oregon
97213-3786 USA

www.vmbooks.com

British Library Cataloguing in Publication Data:
An entry can be found on request

ISBN 978-1-910383-50-6 (cloth)
ISBN 978-1-910383-51-3 (Ebook)

Library of Congress Cataloging in Publication Data:
An entry can be found on request

Printed by Clays Ltd, Bungay, Suffolk

In memory of my parents

Samuel Lang
1907–1990

Mary Lang (nee Finestein)
1908–2003

Contents

Preface   ix

Acknowledgements   xii

List of Abbreviations   xiv

Introduction by Todd M. Endelman   xv

1. Division   1

2. Emancipation   13

3. Agree to Differ   23

4. The Watchman   33

5. The God Within   43

6. Bleak Landscape   55

7. Holy War   65

8. Helping with Inquiries   76

9. The Mirage of Unity   85

10. In Whose Name?   93

11. The Velvet Revolution   103

12. Women of Worth   112

13. Peoplehood   122

14. Restoration   132

15. Zion   142

16. Secularity   153

17. Justice   162

18. The Board   171

19. Leadership   183

20. London and the Regions   194

21. Robinson Row   203

22. The New Community   213

23. Children of the Ghetto   224

24. In Conclusion   233

Epilogue   240

Glossary   244

General Bibliography   246

Bibliography of Israel Finestein's Work   250

Index   252

Preface

There are no compartments in history. However remote Jewish life in the mid-nineteenth century may appear, we are instantly at home with its problems, attitudes, yearnings and sometimes agony. We detect the beginnings of later issues, and recognise in distant sounds, the unmistakable intimation of things to come.

Israel Finestein[1]

Judge Israel Finestein QC (1921–2009) was one of the most respected of the communal leaders of his generation, a successful lawyer, and a historian of note. He was also my uncle!

This work is part tribute, part retrospective, and part update. His five books, and some twenty-five published articles, represent a body of thought and opinion based on considerable knowledge of the past, revealing the complex nature of the Jewish world and the ideas which have formed and fractured it.

Deep within his narrative, and hopefully in mine, there is to be found an abiding belief in our people, and the principles for which we stand. My hope in writing this book is that his voice may be heard again, the voice of reason and tolerance.

I have taken as my theme the subjects of division and alienation, which have always dominated Jewish life. We Jews will distance ourselves from fellow Jews for the flimsiest of reasons, often without regard to the needs of the institution or community concerned. In the religious sphere, the damage caused by division remains far-reaching on an individual level, and on a communal level looks set to become a serious threat to the cohesion of our people worldwide.

Israel Finestein was only too well aware of Jewish disharmony, which was the subject of one of his earliest articles in print, but rooted in traditional orthodoxy, he did not fear division. His approach was not to strive for an impossible unity, still less for a stultifying uniformity, but always to search for the common ground, and never to dismiss those who thought differently from him. He believed, as I do, that whatever the differences, we should look to the considerable assets and heritage shared by all Jews.

Israel Finestein was well known for his eloquence. His use of language and impeccable prose were immensely accurate and attractive. His speeches were always a joy to hear, as was his ability to find the right word or phrase to encapsulate his thoughts, and our concerns. He often spoke at length without notes, such was his command over the language and the subject involved.

We shared a mutual interest in Jewish history and the institutions and personalities of Anglo-Jewry. We did not agree on everything, but my own thoughts have undoubtedly been influenced by a lifetime of proximity.

Apart from his writing and his professional duties, the extent of his involvement with the community was quite extraordinary, and included the Board of Deputies (BOD) of which he was President (1991–94), the Jewish Historical Society of England (JHSE), the Jewish Museum, Hillel Foundation, Norwood, the World Jewish Congress (WJC), Jews' College, British ORT, Jewish Care, the Jews' Free School (JFS) and the Council of Christians and Jews (CCJ).

I have chosen to write in a series of Essays, rather than Chapters. Numbers 1–10 are chronological. Thereafter I deal with topics on which Israel Finestein has written or spoken, as set out in the Contents. He was extremely supportive of the emergence of Jewish women in public life (No.11). The issue of Nation versus Religion is considered in No.13, and the role of the Board of Deputies is examined in Nos 18/19.

In particular I would draw attention to Israel Finestein's major research into the history of the Jews of Hull where he was born (No 21). Its growth and inner tensions, its achievements and its ultimate decline, will I believe reflect the experience of many other communities.

The thoughts and ideas expressed here are entirely my own, unless directly attributable elsewhere. It is not my intention to put words into my uncle's mouth, and I have ensured that he will speak for himself in the many quotations I have selected. I have tried to be as discreet and objective as he always was. If anything, I am perhaps more impatient with our weaknesses, which he never was.

There are no new facts here. Everything I have written about can be found elsewhere with ease, and with more detail. My work can be no more than an introduction to our unique history and unusual identity, and I hope that it might inspire further interest in these subjects.

Many in the past have sounded the death knell of Anglo-Jewry, but Israel Finestein regarded such obituaries as premature, and today a clear revival is at hand. In his day, he did not flinch from the enormity of the many tasks facing the community.

The Jewish world is now divided primarily between Israel and America, with small communities elsewhere including Anglo-Jewry. Much of what follows is focussed on the Anglo-Jewish experience, with which Israel Finestein was mainly but not exclusively concerned. Within it and the Jewish world at large, there are myriad divisions and subdivisions, which have remained a constant factor in our story.

The expression 'United we stand, divided we fall' does not seem to apply to the Jews! Division is in our genes and we are certainly divided, but incredibly we are still here; because each Jew, orthodox, reform or secular, who acknowledges his or her membership of the Jewish people, helps transcend our differences, and retain the memory of who we are, and what unites us.

Colin Lang
Edgbaston, Birmingham
December 2016

Note

1. Israel Finestein, *Jewish Society in Victorian England* (London and Portland, OR: Vallentine Mitchell, 1993), p.152.

Acknowledgements

Most authors seem to thank their wives last but not least! I wish to thank my wife Elizabeth first and foremost, not only for her patience and understanding during the long process of writing and research, but also for her valuable advice throughout. I also wish to thank my sons Jeremy and Richard for their comments, and their assistance with the technical aspect of the work.

I would like to express my appreciation and gratitude to the following for their advice, comments, and suggestions, having read or discussed all or various parts of the book. Jonathan Arkush; Ann Bennett; Henry Cohn; Howard Cuckle; Ivor Goldwater; Haya Lewi; David Lewis; Marleena Shmool; Karen Skinasi; and Professor Todd Endelman. I am of course solely responsible for the final outcome.

I have used many primary and secondary sources which are all listed or cited where appropriate in the work itself. All were invaluable, and I apologise if any have been omitted.

I have taken the liberty of quoting liberally from the *Jewish Chronicle*, and wish to pay tribute to this important Anglo-Jewish institution as a major source of historical material, now available on the internet. I would also like to thank the Jewish Museum for access to their archives.

I am indebted to Toby Harris and Lisa Hyde of Vallentine Mitchell for guiding me through the publication process, and to my anonymous 'reader' for his/her detailed attention to my work.

I am grateful to Simon Prais for his contribution towards the design of the book jacket and Charles Davis for his photography.

Please note that I have taken the liberty of abbreviating Israel Finestein's name to 'IF' for purpose of the Endnotes, and please note that his list of published articles does not claim to be exhaustive.

I would also like to emphasize that wherever the word 'Jew' appears it includes the word 'Jewess' without any negative imputation of any kind.

Shortly before the final draft of this book was sent to the publishers, my dear friend Fred Barshak passed away. Special thanks are due to him for his interest and encouragement for this project from the outset. He came from Vienna on the Kindertransport, and became widely known and respected as a proud and devoted Jew. He had an unlimited supply of anecdotes, and an unlimited interest in the history of our people. His many friends will miss him, and I am proud to associate his name with this work in memoriam.

Abbreviations

AJA	Anglo-Jewish Association
BOD	Board of Deputies of British Jews
CCJ	Council of Christians and Jews
CST	Communal Security Trust
ECHR	European Convention on Human Rights
EZF	English Zionist Federation
IDF	Israel Defence Forces
IUJF	Inter-University Jewish Federation
JC	*Jewish Chronicle*
JEDT	Jewish Educational Development Trust
JFS	Jews Free School
JHSE	Jewish Historical Society of England
JJS	Jewish Journal of Sociology
JLC	Jewish Leadership Council
JNF	Jewish National Fund
JOFA	Jewish Orthodox Feminist Alliance
JPR	Institute of Jewish Policy Research
JREB	Jewish Religious Educational Board
JRU	Jewish Religious Union
LBJRE	London Board of Jewish Religious Education
LJS	Liberal Jewish Synagogue
UCL	University College, London
UJIA	United Jewish Israel Appeal (formerly JIA)
UJS	Union of Jewish Students (formerly IUJF)
ULPS	Union of Liberal and Progressive Synagogues
UOHC	Union of Orthodox Hebrew Congregations
US	United Synagogue
WJC	World Jewish Congress
WUPJ	World Union of Progressive Judaism
ZF	Zionist Federation of Great Britain

Introduction

Communal discord and dissension are hallmarks of modern Jewish history. From the dawn of the modern period, when the inclusion of Jews into state and society first became a possibility, Jews have debated a cluster of interrelated questions about the character of their integration into the modern world.

They have argued about whether and to what extent they needed to modify their customs and habits to enjoy legal emancipation and social integration. They have wondered whether they should preserve their cultural and social distinctiveness once they became citizens of the states in which they lived and, if so, what steps they should take to remain a people apart. They have clashed over the modernization of Jewish worship, ritual, and belief, including the language and content of the prayer service, the training of rabbis, and observance of the dietary laws.

They have disagreed about how far they needed to bend to demonstrate their loyalty to the states that emancipated them. And they have quarrelled fiercely about identity issues – whether they were a nation, a tribe, a race, an ethnos, or, more narrowly, a religious minority. Overlapping with – and exacerbating – these issues have been conflicts between the rich and the poor, between the native-born and the foreign-born, and among the observant, the not-so-observant, and the non-observant.

Although not always acknowledged, the absence of communal harmony is as characteristic of the history of Jews in Britain as it is of the history of Jews on the Continent or in North America. The existence of long established community-wide institutions –pre-eminently the chief rabbinate and the United Synagogue – has often masked the internal disharmony that frequently embroiled the community. Moreover, spokesmen for Anglo-Jewry have often viewed these institutions as symbols of the wellbeing, virtue, and piety of the community and as enviable achievements that distinguish Anglo-Jewry from less 'successful' communities elsewhere.

In their view, unity, harmony and conformity were highly desirable and whatever threatened them was a danger to Judaism. In particular, they thought it was critical for Anglo-Jewry to present a united front and speak with one voice when addressing the public or lobbying the government. In a recent biography of Chief Rabbi J.H. Hertz, for example, the author deplores the opposition, from critics on both the right (the Ultraorthodox camp) and the left (the Progressive camp), to his middle-of-the-road traditionalism, viewing them almost as acts of treason. On the other hand, Immanuel Jakobovits, Chief Rabbi from 1966 to 1991, accepted that Anglo-Jewry was a patchwork of competing interests and labelled the desire for unity, which he thought was unobtainable, as an 'Anglo-Jewish fetish'.

Truth be told, unity and conformity are often the enemies of creativity and vitality. Homogeneity and centralization more often than not stifle ingenuity, breed complacency, and dampen enthusiasm and dynamism. It is no accident that most of the bold new endeavours that have invigorated Anglo-Jewish life in the last few decades – Limmud, Jewish Book Week, the introduction of Jewish studies into British universities, and the growth of independent *minyanim*, for example – owe nothing to the community's central institutions, which either opposed or were indifferent to them. The resourcefulness of American Jewry in responding to the challenges of the last two centuries, in comparison to the more somnolent performance of British Jewry, highlights the advantages of competition, dissension and decentralization.

The Anglo-Jewish scene appears tranquil, however, only in contrast to the hyperactive turbulence of the American Jewish scene. Intra-communal conflicts and clashes have loomed large in its history and have played a much larger – and more productive – role in it than has often been acknowledged. The cohort of academic Anglo-Jewish historians who began publishing in the 1980s – Geoffrey Alderman, David Feldman, Tony Kushner, and the late David Cesarani, pre-eminently – realized this and have rewritten this history, placing religious, political, and socio-economic conflict at its very centre.

They have thought this neither embarrassing nor threatening. On the contrary, they have found it empowering. Stripping Anglo-Jewish history of its apologetic and consciousness-raising tasks has allowed them to attract readers, academic and lay, who were put off by its previous unwillingness to address the unpleasantness of much human behaviour, Jewish or otherwise. It has also allowed them to rescue Anglo-Jewish history from its island insularity and place it in larger historiographical contexts – modern British and modern Jewish history.

Colin Lang's book *Divided We Stand* is written in this spirit. Its very title proclaims its *Tendenz*. Lang begins with the emancipation debates of the mid-Victorian years, takes the reader through the divisions of the immigrant period and the interwar years, and concludes with accounts of more recent contretemps, including, of course, the Louis Jacobs affair in the early 1960s, which was widely reported in the national press, and the stresses and strains of the chief rabbinate of Jonathan Sacks from 1990 to 2013, which were less well known outside the Jewish community. For Lang, communal dissension is neither an aberration nor a curse. It is an essential element in the unfolding of Anglo-Jewish history, neither to be deplored nor kept out of sight.

Colin Lang's book is also a tribute to and was inspired by the historical writing of his uncle, Israel Finestein (1921–2009). Born into an Orthodox, East European family in Kingston-upon-Hull, Finestein was educated in a local grammar school and at Trinity College, Cambridge, from which he graduated in 1943 with a double first in history. Despite the master of Trinity, G.M. Trevelyan, and his tutor, George Kitson Clark, both eminent historians, encouraging him to pursue graduate work in history, he chose a legal career instead. He was called to the bar in 1953, eventually becoming Queen's Counsel, a Crown Court judge, and a Deputy High Court judge in the family division. He was also a prominent communal leader, taking an active part in the work of the Hillel Foundation, the Council of Christians and Jews, the Board of Deputies, which he served as president, and the Jewish Historical Society of England.

In addition to his professional and communal achievements, Finestein was also a distinguished historian of Anglo-Jewry, best known for his learned articles on the nineteenth and twentieth centuries. Finestein was an 'amateur' historian in the sense that writing history was for him an avocation not a vocation. But he was not an 'amateur' in the sense that many of his contemporaries in the Jewish Historical Society of England were – that is, he was not an antiquarian, burying himself in the archives, delighting in new discoveries, and assembling lists of names and accomplishments. He knew that the writing of serious history required more than gathering facts and telling a story, that it comprehended as well making sense of the story, showing its relevance to other stories, placing it in its larger contexts, and identifying its driving forces. In other words, he well understood that writing history was an intellectual, not just an artisanal, challenge.

Colin Lang refers frequently to Finestein's work and includes generous quotations from it. In this sense it serves as an introduction to his uncle's historical interests. Hopefully, it will also inspire readers to seek out the various volumes in which Finestein's essays were collected. One essay of his, in particular, is essential to understanding Anglo-Jewish history and deserves mention. In 1964, the *Transactions of the Jewish Historical Society of England* published Finestein's article 'Anglo-Jewish Opinion during the Struggle for Emancipation'. Its central argument was that Anglo-Jewry was divided about the value of removing the remaining legal disabilities that blocked full Jewish participation in political life.

Finestein explained that there was widespread Jewish indifference to full emancipation (as well as some explicit opposition to it from traditionalists who feared that further integration would lead to a dilution of Jewish traditions and allegiances). Most importantly, he also explained that the source of this indifference was the already satisfactory legal status of Jews in Britain. Those who were born in Britain were by law already citizens and faced little economic and fiscal discrimination. Most were uninterested in holding political office and hence indifferent to the emancipation campaign, which the communal elite was spearheading.

What emerged from Finestein's article was that 'emancipation' in Britain meant something different from what it did in other European states. Reading this essay for the first time as a graduate student in the mid-1970s opened up for me new ways of thinking about Anglo-Jewish history. Lang's volume highlights this and other insights of Finestein as it explores the mirage of unity in Anglo-Jewish history.

Todd M. Endelman
Professor Emeritus of History and Judaic Studies
University of Michigan

1

Division

Division is no stranger to the Jewish people.

Israel Finestein[1]

With the above opening sentence, the young Israel Finestein, then perhaps only 23 years old, confirmed his arrival on the Anglo-Jewish scene. Already Chairman of the principal student body, the Inter-University Jewish Federation (IUJF) and its representative on the Board of Deputies, he had also served as President of the Cambridge Jewish Society, and Chair of the Universities Zionist Council.

The theme and content of his article in *Academy,* the student periodical published by the IUJF, epitomised his concern for a subject which has always dominated Jewish life. It is clear that throughout history, despite our small numbers, and frequent external dangers, the Jews have a propensity to division which is extremely damaging, and potentially self-destructive.

No better example of the divisive tendency can be found than in modern Israel. With a population of only six million, no less than seventeen political parties contested the General Election held on 17 March 2015. The corresponding UK equivalent (relative to population) would be over 100 parties, which gives a better idea of the scale of division in Israel and Jewish society generally.

Ten Israeli parties succeeded in obtaining sufficient votes for a seat in the Parliament (Knesset) and it is significant that the leading party (Likud) achieved barely 25 per cent of the overall vote. Since the formation of the State, this pattern has resulted in a long series of Government coalitions, with very few surviving the full four-year term provided for in the Constitution.

The power of small parties is disproportionate to their numbers, since they may be needed to maintain the coalition itself in power, and if so, they can hold the ruling party to ransom. This may well encourage them to pursue their own sectional interests, thus distorting the democratic mandate. In December 1944, Dr Chaim Weizmann, leader of the Zionist movement, warned against the danger inherent in a multitude of parties in Palestine.

'They are the result of Jewish individualism', he declared, 'but this is no means of furthering development in the future.'[2]

He was addressing a national conference of the Jewish Labour movement, and urged the need to unify all the creative forces within the new State, and not quarrel over petty things – the greatest obstacle was within, he said. David Ben Gurion, first Prime Minister, saw the potential for instability in a Parliamentary democracy with too many parties, and sought to introduce a constituency system as in Britain, but to no avail.

Division is indeed no stranger. It has dwelt among us since the beginning of time. It is expressly referred to five times in the first chapter of Genesis, and is clearly implied in the complexity of life set in train by creation. Indeed we celebrate its importance at the termination of every Shabbat with a blessing (*Havdalah*) for the distinction made by the Almighty 'between the holy and the profane, between light and darkness, between Israel and the other nations, and between the seventh day and the six working days'.[3]

Praiseworthy as these divisions may be, there are others affecting every-day life which are less so – social divisions as likeminded humans come together in tribal or religious or political groups, and feel themselves superior, or inferior, or envious, or in need of protection from other such groups. The group identifies those who belong to it, and inevitably those who do not are perceived as a threat. This too is an attribute of creation, defining humankind, and imposing upon it the basic obligation to deal with others in a moral way, respecting their rights, views and aspirations.

Division involves boundaries, with which the Jewish people have a special affinity – whether as the walls of a ghetto, or the invisible loosely defined walls of an area where we choose to live among each other, or the highly visible security fence built by the Israeli government along their eastern border. Boundaries are also associated with the separation of the sexes and with the Sabbath. An intangible limit determines how far one may travel on that day, and a tangible boundary (known as an *eruv*) determines the area within which certain restrictions may be relaxed.

Our sense of belonging is determined by such boundaries, and the rationale by which we seek to protect the ideas and customs we most cherish. 'Make a fence round the Torah' said the men of the Great Assembly,[4] significantly using the boundary metaphor. But what if the boundary is transgressed or contested? Preservation of a distinctive identity at all costs can only lead to fragmentation, unless the boundaries involved are flexible, subject to debate and agreement, flexible enough to admit, rather than to exclude.

Division is not always harmful. Awareness of good and evil can be beneficial, and the apparent conflict between science and religion can lead to a greater understanding of both. The existence of rich and poor provides a challenge to those in authority to ensure adequate welfare provision, a fundamental obligation of Judaism.[5] Political parties are by definition divisive, but serve an important purpose in a democratic society under the rule of law. Division and diversity are facts of life. How we deal with them, determines whether they are a blessing or a curse.

The sanctity of life, at the heart of Biblical teaching, clearly points the way, but by contrast, its historical narrative points to a future of disunity, as is obvious from the fratricidal squabbles of Genesis. In this context, who is not pleased at the appearance of the rejected Ishmael at his father's funeral,[6] nor moved by the reunion of Esau and Jacob after years of separation?[7] How eloquent and heart rending is the appeal of Judah for the life of Benjamin[8] whose brother Joseph he had sold into slavery? The message of Genesis however is not one of unity, but of reconciliation, whether in silence at Abraham's funeral,[9] in joy at Jacob's homecoming, or in pathos at the Court of the Pharaoh.[10]

And despite the overwhelming evidence of redemption and deliverance, the Children of Israel were prone to frequent bouts of panic and doubt. Concern over provision of food and water in the wilderness may have been justified but always supplied, and 'your clothes did not wear out on you, nor did your foot swell these forty years'.[11]

Yet they turned to the Golden Calf in the absence of Moses, and the negative report from ten of the twelve spies at a later date produced a direct challenge to his leadership, with the possibility of open rebellion. It is hardly surprising that the generation of the Exodus (with the exception of Joshua and Caleb) was refused entry to the Promised Land towards which it had shown so little faith.[12]

In the ancient world, there were serious differences within the Priesthood among the descendants of Aaron. The concentration of sacrifice in Jerusalem, and the division of the Kingdom, left many priests effectively unemployed and potentially dissident. However they retained a symbolic value, emphasising 'two distinct modes of worship' in our tradition, representing the ritual and ceremonial aspect of life, as against the private and personal 'service of the heart'.[13]

There have indeed been very few periods when the Jewish people have been united. Perhaps unity only ever existed for a brief period under King David, a highly unusual leader: part warrior, part poet, part judge, and part sinner, whose latter days were marked by intrigue, indecision and guilt. 'Wash me thoroughly of my iniquity and purify me … for I recognise my transgressions', he pleaded (Psalm 51), perhaps in reference to when he sent the husband of Bathsheba to certain death so he could marry her.

He had been careful in his youth not to be disloyal to his predecessor, but the followers of King Saul did not see it that way, and perpetuated their resentment. However his capture of 'the stronghold of Zion'[14] enabled the creation of Jerusalem as the centre of Jewish life. He provided a home for the divine presence, to be housed in a Temple built by his son, and thus gave his people a focus, and an identity, which continues to this day.

The new King Solomon, advised by his dying father, was able to suppress opposition to his succession. He consolidated and vastly expanded the Kingdom, with the Temple as its centrepiece, but the people led by Jeroboam (an Ephraimite) grew to resent the excesses of his reign, and his death in 928 BCE precipitated one of the most dramatic of all divisions.[15] His son Rehoboam arrogantly refused to alleviate the heavy taxes imposed by his father, and showed considerable ignorance of the grievances of those who felt they had contributed but not benefitted from the wealth of Solomon's kingdom, controlled as it was by the tribe of Judah.

The secession of the ten northern tribes ('To your tents O Israel!') led to a long period of savage wars between the two kingdoms which 'overshadowed the blood ties that had once united them', as if the ancient struggle between the children of Rachel and Leah had been reignited.[16] Territory acquired by Solomon was soon lost, and in 722 BCE the northern kingdom became easy prey to the Assyrians who deported most of the population. However some fled south to Jerusalem, which expanded considerably in this period, and others fled elsewhere throughout the Middle East.[17]

The loss of Solomon's kingdom was stated to be a punishment for his leaning towards the idolatry of his foreign wives later in life[18] although its severity was reduced 'for David my servant's sake, and for the sake of Jerusalem'. Nevertheless the extent of the subsequent losses and suffering caused by war and deportation seems a heavy price to have paid for the sins of one man. The message of 'Kings' is quite clear: Jewish leaders are accountable. They are not there to accumulate wealth.[19] They cannot please themselves, and bear a heavy responsibility to do what is right.

King Hezekiah (716–687 BCE) had witnessed the Assyrian annexation of the northern kingdom, and invited the remnants of the northern tribes to attend Temple rites in Jerusalem, but few responded. His great grandson, King Josiah (640–609 BCE) also dreamed of reuniting the kingdoms, strongly supported by the prophet Jeremiah. 'Ephraim is my firstborn', he declared,[20] referring to the Northern Kingdom so-called after its largest tribe, and invoking Rachel, mother of Joseph, weeping for her children. But the people rejected his vision of unity based on the shared identity of the sons of Jacob, and 'Because ye have not heard my words', Jeremiah prophesied a 'desolate wasteland' and 'service to the King of Babylonia for seventy years'.[21]

The new experience of exile created a fundamental divergence of view which resonates down the centuries – the silent submissive Jew versus the outspoken defender; when to fight or when to flee; whether in the immortal words of Hamlet 'to suffer the slings and arrows of outrageous fortune, or to take arms against a sea of troubles, and by opposing end them'.[22] There were those who wished to settle in their new home, to adapt to life under foreign rule, and rebuild the Temple 'by the rivers of Babylon'. By contrast there were those who were unable to reconcile themselves to marrying and farming in a foreign land, who dreamt of a return to Zion and restoring the Davidic dynasty.

Jeremiah was always aware of the precarious position of the Kingdom of Judah, squeezed between much larger forces to north and south. He had warned against foreign entanglements, and believed that it was the Almighty who would determine the rise and fall of nations. Meanwhile Babylon was the reigning super power and could not be opposed without disaster.

His warning against rebellion[23] was not defeatist. 'Serve the King of Babylon and live! Why should the city [Jerusalem] be destroyed?' When the opportunity arose to return to Zion, with the defeat of Babylon by Cyrus of Persia, many Jews chose to remain, in due course becoming a unique centre of Jewish learning, and a major Diaspora community for some two thousand years.

The urge to resist foreign domination arose under the Greeks as the Maccabees led the successful revolt against Antiochus (167–161 BCE). However, the legitimacy of the new Hasmonean king-priests was repudiated by the Pharisees, the guardians of holiness, and the dynasty led only to the emergence of competing groups, internal dissension and an absence of spiritual authority. Jerusalem was like 'a great body torn in pieces' according to the historian Josephus.

The urge to resist arose again under increasing Roman provocation. The massacre of some twenty thousand Jews at Caesarea led to a revolt which was understandable, but whose outcome could not be in doubt. Among those who rebelled were the zealots who, according to Rabbi Lau, 'transmitted their fanatic nationalism from one generation to the next, from the days of Shammai until the Destruction of the Temple'.[24]

Yohanan ben Zakkai, a disciple of Hillel, realised that the refusal of the zealots to negotiate made the fall of Jerusalem inevitable, and that the survival of the Jewish people was more important than a futile and pointless war with Rome. He managed to escape the city, and persuade the future Emperor Vespasian to allow him to establish an academy for Torah study at Yavneh.

However, deep divisions of opinion existed among his sages, but faced with many new challenges as well as unresolved issues, a new creative spirit emerged, emphasising reason and practicality over a rigid reliance on traditional thought, so that following the loss of the Temple in 70 CE, 'Judaism floated free from the grave of history. It was to be a perpetual present, endlessly reanimated in memory.'[25]

Even so, there were those who still believed that the Almighty would rescue them from Roman rule. The ill-fated Bar Kochba uprising (132–135 CE) which ended with the fall of Betar, was supported by Rabbi Akiva at the cost of his life. The inevitable defeat by Rome devastated the Jewish community, which was finally left with no alternative but to disperse. However, Jewish society survived for a time in Galilee,[26] where at the Roman city of Tsippori, Yehuda Hanassi (135–217 CE) completed the compilation of the Mishna, a written record of the Oral Law as previously practised.

The Mishna provided a focal point for a Jewish world whose structure would be vastly different from before, and it was perhaps inevitable that Judaism would henceforward concentrate on Torah study. However, Akiva's support for the revolt revealed the notion that 'nationalism was an organic part of Torah',[27] not an alternative, but an inherent component of religious identity, which emphasised the connection between the Jewish people and their land. How to incorporate such aspirations into Jewish religious life was a source of ongoing disagreement, and the national impulse would lay mainly dormant until the modern struggle for Jewish independence.

By 300 CE, some three million Jews had settled in every part of the Roman Empire according to Sir Martin Gilbert,[28] and the dispersion eventually scattered the Jews throughout the world. They can be divided into two main groups depending on whether they initially went north into Europe (Ashkenazim) or south (Sephardim). The latter joined the considerable community already in Egypt, and gradually moved along North Africa and into Spain as far north as Toledo, where they benefitted from Muslim rule as long as it lasted.

The Jews were expelled from Spain in 1492 and from Portugal in 1497. Those that remained were expected to convert to Christianity, and were pitifully pursued by the Inquisition. Many of those expelled moved north into Holland, which successfully rebelled against Spain, and became a place of religious tolerance. It also became a place of great prosperity with Amsterdam for a time one of the wealthiest cities in the world. Ashkenazi Jews were attracted to move there from central Europe, whether for safety or for trade, and thus by entirely different routes the two communities converged, but did not merge, during the Dutch Golden Age in the seventeenth century.

Sephardi merchants were keen to obtain a share of the lucrative trade available in London. Perhaps also influenced by the increasing number of new and unwelcome arrivals from the east, they supported Menasseh ben Israel (1604–57) in his attempt to gain re-admission of the Jews to England. In his book *The Hope of Israel* (1650) he argued that the Messiah would not come until the Jews were scattered throughout the world, and here was England with no Jews (openly practising as such) since the expulsion of 1290.

Oliver Cromwell was not opposed to re-admission, influenced no doubt by the likely economic advantages, but also by his belief in religious liberty, and the Messianic ideas of Menasseh coincided with those held by many English Christians. The Whitehall Conference which Cromwell called in December 1655 was inconclusive, but a tacit acceptance of re-admission seems to have occurred, and was supported by the monarchy when restored in 1660. By the end of that century, an estimated 800 Jews were openly resident in England, mainly Sephardim, but the Ashkenazim followed, and eventually outnumbered them.

Despite only minor differences in pronunciation and liturgy, the two communities have kept apart, undoubtedly influenced by different historical experiences and, for the Sephardim, an intense pride in their Spanish past. Each has maintained its own structures and Chief Rabbi, even in Israel, although intermarriage between the two will surely blur and perhaps even extinguish the differences over time. However, almost one million Sephardim from former Arab countries were initially side-lined to some extent by the mainly ex-European Ashkenazi leadership in Israel.

Menachem Begin (1913–92) leader of the Israeli 'Freedom' party, saw the danger in this division, and also saw an opportunity. He championed their cause, and they rewarded him with office as Prime Minister in 1977, when the founding Labour coalition began to split. As leader of the breakaway underground movement against the British Mandate, he had been in conflict with the fledgling Israel army (Hagannah) but in the opinion of his 1984 biographer, Begin 'fought as hard as anyone to prevent a Jewish civil war'[29] in the early days of the State. However after 1967 his implacable belief in 'Greater Israel', which included the West Bank, put him in conflict with those willing to trade land for peace.

Without the trappings of power to argue about, the focus of division for the Jews in dispersion turned to religion. They carried their traditions with them during the frequent uprooting and migration of communities in every century, and in particular they carried the Torah, which in effect replaced the Temple, as the embodiment of the Divine spirit. It was essential to comply with its requirements, but local custom inevitably varied over time, and interpretations were 'marked by frequent disagreement and tangled debate'.[30]

In order to survive, the Jewish people needed an unambiguous code which all could follow.

Maimonides was born in Cordova in 1138. He was a man of the greatest intellect, who would have excelled in any branch of modern scholarship. He was master of the known sciences of his day and made significant contribution to the knowledge and practice of medicine. He was an outstanding medieval philosopher, an expert on Aristotle, and deeply immersed in Arab culture. His family left Cordova in 1148, and after a period in Morocco, and a brief visit to the Holy Land, he settled in Egypt in 1168. There he was appointed Court physician to the royal family, and became leader of the Jewish community until his death in 1204.

It is difficult to see how he found time to write his monumental work *Mishne Torah* completed in 1180 – a comprehensive and authoritative codification of all Jewish law free from 'Talmudic disagreements, unresolved disputes and minority opinions'.[31] Whilst his views are followed today by most orthodox Jews, deep divisions arose in the immediate aftermath of his death.

There were those who felt that he was wrong to seek an ultimate restatement of Halakhah, as if to supersede the Talmud, although it is not clear that was his intention. To them and others over time, the different opinions recorded and retained in the Talmud were of value; the Halakhah was not a fixed statute, but a living organism, intended for ceaseless debate, and for an ongoing search to ascertain what the Almighty wishes of us.

Maimonides' Thirteen Principles of Faith were even more controversial in his day, although now viewed by some on the 'Right' as the litmus test of orthodoxy. He insisted they were 'binding dogmas that define the boundaries of the Jewish community'[32] and included resurrection, reward and punishment, a concept of God outside time and space, and Torah from heaven in a literal sense.

The ensuing level of theological dissension was so pronounced as to involve Christian clergy, who did not hesitate to take advantage of the opportunity to interpose themselves, leading to the burning of Maimonides' books in Paris in 1233. On the other hand his work on Tort Law with its emphasis on responsibility, and avoidance of damage, would have graced the shelves of any modern Supreme Court. Likewise in his work on slavery, Maimonides referred to the fundamental equality of man, and thus the need to treat both Jewish and non-Jewish slaves in a humanitarian and compassionate manner.[33]

It was Joseph Caro (1488–1575), undoubtedly influenced by his study of Maimonides, who took the process of codification further with his *Shulchan Aruch*. Perhaps it was inevitable that the complex and comprehensive nature of Jewish law would one day need to be simplified. However, the coming of the printing press effectively froze (some might say fossilised) his Code. The orthodox Rabbi Nathan Cardozo of Jerusalem prefers 'embalmed' and regrets the 'loss of personal religious creativity, and devotion'. Codification came at a very high price, and ultimately divided the Jewish world between those who observed the Halakhic code and those for whom it failed to take account of changing circumstances, knowledge or needs – by far the most fundamental fault-line in Jewish society.

At one end of the spectrum was Elijah ben Solomon, known as the Vilna Gaon (1720–97). He was well aware that Enlightenment had begun to challenge the basic premises of tradition, and he introduced a scientific approach to Torah study. He was himself consulted on matters of mathematics and astronomy. His emphasis on Hebrew grammar and textual criticism was of great value to the Jewish enlightenment (the *Haskalah*) which would in due course offer an alternative identity to the traditional, notwithstanding a number of important religious *maskilim*.[34] Furthermore he was forward thinking in his view that the Holy Land was an essential component of Jewish theology, and encouraged his followers to make *aliyah*.

He was without doubt a child prodigy and later acknowledged as among the greatest of sages. His main focus was to preserve the integrity of both Oral and Written Law at all cost, and his authority was such that according to a recent biography[35] he is responsible for the 'intellectual dynamism, social confidence and political assertiveness' of contemporary Jewish orthodoxy. Its revival at the end of the twentieth century and ongoing owes much to his influence, but some might say that his heirs have gone too far, and now only exacerbate religious and indeed social division.

However, the self-contained world of the Gaon was vastly different and a considerable distance from the world of Moses Mendelssohn (1729–1786), his contemporary counterpart in Berlin. His followers wished to embrace the opportunities offered by enlightenment and were prepared to 'sell their souls' in exchange for citizenship. The Jewish masses in Eastern Europe had no such opportunity. In any event, they did not aspire to integrate into Polish society, or to reform Judaism for that purpose. 'Inspired by the Genius of Vilna, they developed their own cultural superstructure.'[36]

Poland and Lithuania effectively ceased to exist following a series of partitions in the eighteenth century, and the largely autonomous Jewish community then found itself belonging to one of three absolutist empires: Russia, Prussia and Austria. The Council of the Four Lands by which the Jews had largely ruled themselves, was abolished in 1764, leading to a period of chaos and upheaval. The Jewish masses became prey to false Messiahs of whom the notorious Shabbetai Zvi was the most divisive, and it was left to another of the Gaon's contemporaries to reach out and provide much needed help.

Israel ben Eleazar, otherwise known as the Baal Shem Tov (1700–60), taught a message of love for God, for the people, and for the Land of Israel. He believed in personal redemption, joy and salvation, and by the time of his death, he had effectively established a revivalist movement, which we know as Chasidism. Without any organized structure, its adherents simply ignored the new political borders, forming independent groups, which coalesced around charismatic rabbis 'whose leadership took Eastern Europe by storm'.[37] Among the most well-known perhaps are Nachman of Bratslav (1772–1810) whose spirituality continues to inspire many to this day, and Shneur Zalman (1745–1812) who founded the Chabad branch of Chasidism.

The Chasidic emphasis on prayer, their somewhat emotional approach to religion, their determination 'to see God in every tree and every rock',[38] their belief in the value of good works, and their criticism of certain existing priorities, inevitably drew opposition from the Gaon and his followers. The opponents of Chasidism (the *Mitnagdim*) campaigned against it, and the Gaon excommunicated it in 1777, creating yet another of our great historical divisions. Efforts to denigrate Chasidism ultimately failed, amid charges and counter-charges pursued in the public domain, at great risk to those concerned.

Judaism was thus ill prepared for the onset of modernity. 'It broke upon the Jews with remarkable suddenness',[39] dividing Jewish society between those with an inward looking, and those with an outward looking view of the world.

The former 'awaited a grand (messianic) dénouement, living predominantly in an enclave if not an actual ghetto, regarding the outside world as alien if not hostile, whatever might be the extent of personal cordiality'.[40] By contrast, there were those who 'emerged into the wider society, with new types of opportunity for personal fulfilment, a society in which the inhibitions of centuries could readily fade, and the pressure to identify with other interests seemed to belong to the natural order of things'.[41]

Sadly, the religion intended to unite the Jewish people around the world, slowly became a source of division, and by the beginning of the nineteenth century, the cry of the Northern tribes was heard again, overburdened this time not by taxes, but by religious minutiae. The result, no less dramatic, was in due course the rejection of the 'Oral Law' by the majority of the Jewish people.

Notes

1. Israel Finestein, *Academy*, Inter-University Jewish Federation, *c*.1944.
2. 'Transition period unavoidable' *JC* 1 December 1944, p. 8.
3. Revd Simeon Singer, *Daily Prayer Book* (London: Eyre & Spottiswoode, 1962, new edn), p.293.
4. Ibid., p. 251. Ethics of the Fathers 1:1.
5. Maimonides, *Mishne Torah*, Gifts to the poor.
6. Genesis 25:9.
7. Genesis 33:4.
8. Genesis 44:18/34.
9. For a fascinating explanation of Ishmael's presence, see Jonathan Sacks, *Not in God's Name: Confronting Religious Violence* (London: Hodder and Stoughton, 2015), p.118.
10. This entire chapter was written before my reading of Sacks, *Not in God's Name*, in which Rabbi Lord Sacks sets out a detailed analysis of sibling rivalry.
11. Deut. 8:4.
12. Numbers 14:30.
13. See Jonathan Sacks, *Exodus, the Book of Redemption* (London: Maggid Books, 2010), p.230.
14. II Samuel 5:7.
15. I Kings Ch. 12.
16. Binyamin Lau, *Jeremiah, The Fate of a Prophet* (Jerusalem: Maggid Books, 2013), p.3.
17. Martin Gilbert, *Atlas of Jewish History* (London: Routledge, 2006, 7th edn), Map 7.
18. I Kings 11:11.
19. Deut. 17:16.
20. Jeremiah 31:8.
21. Jeremiah 25:11.
22. *Hamlet* Act 3 Scene 1.
23. Jeremiah 27:17.
24. Binyamin Lau, *The Sages, Character, Context and Creativity*, Vols I and II (Jerusalem: Maggid Books, 2010 and 2011), Vol. I, p.325.
25. Simon Schama, *The Story of the Jews 1000BCE–1492CE: Finding the Words* (London: The Bodley Head, 2013), Pt 1, p.150.
26. For a detailed account, see Martin Goodman, *State and Society in Roman Galilee AD 132–212* (London and Portland, OR: Vallentine Mitchell, 2000, 2nd edn).
27. Lau, *The Sages*, Vol. II, p.376.
28. Gilbert, *Atlas of Jewish History*, p.17.
29. Eric Silver, *Dateline Jerusalem* (Brighton: Revel Barker Publishing, 2011), p.88.
30. Moshe Halbertal, *Maimonides: Life and Thought* (Princeton, NJ: Princeton University Press, 2014), p.1.
31. Ibid.
32. Ibid., p.136.
33. Ibid., pp.272–4.
34. Such as Rabbi Nachman Krochmal and Rabbi Shlomo Rapoport.
35. Eliyahu Stern, *The Genius: Elijah of Vilna and the Making of Modern Orthodoxy* (London: Yale University Press, 2013), p.171.
36. Ibid.
37. Israel Bartal, *The Jews of Eastern Europe 1772–1881* (Philadelphia, PA: University of Pennsylvania Press, 2002), p.51.

38. Stern, *The Genius*, p.95.
39. IF, *Jewish Society in Victorian England* (London and Portland, OR: Vallentine Mitchell, 1993), p.154.
40. Ibid.
41. Ibid., p.155.

2

Emancipation

No feature of Jewish life impinging upon English society was
left untested by the criterion of its favourable or reverse impact
on Jewish emancipation.

Israel Finestein[1]

'It was not hardship which led the Jews of England to demand their civil
emancipation. Nor was the immediate occasion for initiating the struggle a
specific Jewish issue.'[2] The 'immediate occasion' was the decision of the
House of Lords in 1828 to introduce into legislation 'a deliberate
demarcation between the Christian dissenting bodies and the Jews.'[3] Roman
Catholics were granted further relief in 1829 and this 'strengthened the
resolve of the Jewish emancipationists.'[4] The ensuing struggle was to last for
thirty years.

Nevertheless, the discrimination was on a relatively narrow front,
compared with restrictions placed on Jews in various parts of Europe. Since
the Resettlement in 1656, English Jews had enjoyed freedom of movement,
and to a certain extent, freedom of occupation, although there were limits
as to where Jewish retail trade was permitted. Professing Jews could not be
called to the Bar until 1833, Sir Francis Henry Lyon Goldsmid (1809–78)
being the first Jewish barrister. Professing Jews were able to exercise the
parliamentary franchise, but 'technically this was only by virtue of the Act
of 1835'.[5]

The principal issues which remained were exclusion from municipal
office and from Parliament. There was also exclusion from the ancient
universities until 1854, and some doubt as to ownership of freehold property.
Lionel de Rothschild was repeatedly elected to Parliament, but was repeatedly
refused admission as the oath of abjuration required him to swear it 'on the
faith of a Christian', and he would not do so. A special Act was required for
David Salomons to serve as Sheriff of the City of London without subscribing
to the statutory Christian declaration. There was a succession of Bills before
Parliament for full civic emancipation throughout the period. Some were
passed in the Commons, but not in the Lords until 1858.

On 18 December 1958, Israel Finestein addressed a meeting organised jointly by the Jewish Historical Society of England (JHSE) and the Board of Deputies of British Jews (BOD) to mark the centenary of the passing of the Jewish Relief Act. His address was entitled 'Anglo-Jewish Opinion during the Struggle for Emancipation 1828–58'[6] and as its name implies, he does not deal solely with the events of the campaign, but focuses on the opinions of those involved, which have a surprisingly modern ring. He also looks closely at the Jewish communal history of the period, and revealed that despite favourable circumstances generally, there was 'Jewish hostility or indifference to emancipation which looked like, and in some cases was, a product of the ghetto.'[7] His conclusions may have come as a surprise to those who heard his lecture!

There was in fact little enthusiasm on the part of Chief Rabbi Nathan Adler, who feared that emancipation would have a damaging effect on religious observance. His first pastoral letter in 1845 referred rather apologetically to the need to be 'worthy of the proud position which we now occupy in society', and in 1858, when emancipation was before Parliament for the last time, he felt it necessary to issue a public denial of any opposition on his part.

The mass of poor Jews was not engaged, and the need 'to raise the social and cultural level of the poorer ranks of the Jewish tradesmen and manual workers became something of an obsession with the emancipationists.'[8] The writer and translator Moses Samuel[9] (1795–1860), when wishing to further Jewish literary effort in 1844, castigated the community for their apparent apathy in the 'great cause of our emancipation'.

The perception of Jewish opposition, both religious and secular, seemed to justify the opposition of some like the Archbishop of Canterbury who considered the Jews were under a divine curse. He maintained that the Jewish plight was a punishment for the rejection of Jesus, whilst emphasising his respect, even admiration, for the Jews as individuals and as a people.

It was thus left to the wealthy families such as the Goldsmids, the Salomons and the Rothschilds to pursue the struggle, and they were not disposed to accept piecemeal legislation. They considered that after several generations of honoured prominence, it was 'an affront that they should yet suffer legal discrimination', and were genuinely surprised at the rejection of successive Bills before Parliament. In any event, a citizen's rights ought not to depend on his religion, and they expected equality with other religious groups which dissented from the established Church.

But those other groups were Christian, and as stated by the Duke of Cambridge in May 1848, 'We cannot admit the Jews to a share in the counsels of the State as long as this is a Christian country'.[10] Lord Shaftesbury, an otherwise prominent social reformer, regarded Jewish entry to Parliament as endangering the Christian character of that institution. Likewise for Gladstone, the issue touched upon the connection between Church and State. William Cobbett considered civil emancipation of the Jews meant 'abolishing Christianity in England', and in the Commons (1833) he expressed a particular fear over the prospect of Jewish judges.

The doctrine that Judaism was nothing more than one of a number of non-conformist creeds clearly had its difficulties, and it was suggested by some that the Jews of London had more in sympathy with the Jews of Berlin or Vienna than with the Christians among whom they lived. On the other hand, there were Christian advocates of emancipation who felt that full citizenship would erode the Jewish national characteristic, perhaps with a long term view to the possibility of conversion. In any event, support for the Established Church was a central tenet of the Conservative party, and its leader Lord Salisbury stated in a letter to the JC[11] that he had spoken against the 1858 Bill because he thought the Jews would be necessarily hostile to the Church of England, but he now knew this was far from being the case.[12]

The debate was dogged by the complex question as to what was meant by the Jewish 'nation'. The Jews are 'strangers and sojourners', said Sir Robert Inglis, one of the leading opponents to Jewish emancipation, 'and their highest aspiration is a return to their own land'. Spencer Walpole, an eminent Tory barrister, speaking in the House of Commons said that 'The Jew is of a separate creed and interest. He is not a citizen of this country, but of the world. He has no land he can call his own, save the Land of Promise.'[13]

The problem of nationality was compounded by the aspiration of some Jews to be restored to Palestine, and the ancient messianic nature of this aspiration, which was extremely difficult to reconcile with the demands of the emancipationists. Sir Francis Goldsmid sought to propel such thoughts far into the unknowable future when, according to the Rev. D.W. Marks of the West London Synagogue, 'the tone of society will be changed, and all the nations will be subject to a system of government wholly different from that which obtains today'.[14] And in reply to the contention that the Jews were not Englishmen, but a nation across boundaries, the response was to deny that the Return had any effect on the allegiance of the Jews to the Sovereign.

Emancipationists also emphasised the uniqueness of English power and prestige. The contrast between English constitutional government and foreign autocracy intensified the respect with which English Jews looked upon their country. It was also hoped that Jewish emancipation in England would inhibit oppression of Jews abroad and legislative discrimination by foreign governments.

England was the cradle of liberty, in the first rank among civilised nations. Fair play was an English trait, and Jewish institutions sought to regulate their affairs according to English methods. An English gentleman was a designation worthy of aspiration, and it was felt intolerable by some if a Jew could not achieve that category.

Thomas (later Lord) Macaulay (1800–59), author of his prestigious *History of England*, supported the removal of all civil disabilities for the Jews. He believed that all disabilities on account of religious opinions are indefensible, in that they made for less efficient government and alienated a part of its operative strength. Are we, he asked, to exclude all who wish to anticipate a far-off universal messianic event? The Jews were not alone in this belief. As regards restoration, Macaulay asked rhetorically whether this 'made the Jew insensible to fluctuations in the Stock Exchange'.[15]

Barnard Van Oven (1796-1860), a Fellow of the Royal College of Surgeons and a member of one of the leading Jewish families, put it more simply: 'The restoration of Israel has been delayed 1,800 years, and may be delayed more. It would be absurd to allow the anticipation of such an event to influence our (present) conduct or feelings.'[16] For the purpose of practical citizenship, the Jews must take their fate as they find it, regardless of such a remote possibility. The obligation to remember Jerusalem was not an injunction to return there.

But the reality was to become less remote or unknowable than was supposed. Within barely forty years, Herzl converted a dream into a practical programme, and as Israel Finestein pointed out in his article entitled 'Emancipation Apologetics',[17] the centenary of the Emancipation was also the tenth anniversary of the creation of the Jewish State. Nationhood had become a reality, and meanwhile 'the impulse to divest Judaism of its redemptionist and national features, carried the heirs of the emancipationists into stern anti-Zionism'.

Not surprisingly, Macaulay quickly achieved a status bordering on that of 'patron saint' for the emancipationist movement. He considered that religious differences might affect the fitness of a Jew to be a Bishop, but not to be a cobbler; but what of the fitness of a Jew to be a legislator in a Christian country? To many, Macaulay may have seemed too dogmatic. His argument that separateness might in fact be caused by the host country was controversial, and contrary to Jewish protestations, of which unreserved loyalty was a cardinal principle.

> Macaulay's advocacy had the two-edged quality which demonstrates the unique nature of the debates about Jews. It took place against a background of generations of historical conditioning … in which the

Jew was the irretrievable outsider, the devil's kin, the literate and learned infidel, feared, derided and reviled in the parishes of Christendom.[18]

Thus the emancipationists had also to grapple with the centuries old 'ineradicable animosity' towards the Jews, a general antipathy by which they were portrayed as anti-social, and overly influenced by rabbinic law and money-making. As early as 1823, Charles Lamb did not relish 'the approximation of Jew and Christian which has become so fashionable. The reciprocal endearments have something hypocritical and unnatural in them.'[19]

> The Jews were seen to be, and were, multi-faceted, belonging and not belonging, inspiring at the same time caution, suspicion, perhaps animosity, also respect, wonder and perhaps awe, inward looking and yet possessed of the most far reaching humanistic aims, particularist and yet genuinely professing a proven universalism.[20]

The end result was pragmatic. As long as they exist, the Jews must be accommodated. Ancient prejudices must give way to considerations of policy, principle and humanity. 'The idea of making amends to the Jews gave the conclusion an added welcome and propriety, and in so far as the Jews were part of an ever widening democracy, Jewish emancipation formed a significant part of English history.'[21]

Israel Finestein points out that throughout the period of struggle, about one half of Anglo-Jewry was foreign born, 'retaining the peculiarities from whence they came, peculiarities entirely disconsonant to their English brethren',[22] according to Pastor Mills who was nevertheless a sympathetic observer. The above proportion increased in the 1850s, and with widespread poverty and unemployment, the privileges conferred by emancipation were of limited if any concern to the bulk of the Jewish community. Opponents of emancipation and observers were thus able to point to considerable indifference, even apathy, as to whether a small number of Jews might sit in Parliament.

'Again and again the narrowness of the area of the Jewish community which was likely to feel the benefit of emancipation was pointed out.'[23] And looking back in 1891, Lucien Wolf wrote in his *Essays* that 'the agitation was a struggle for the privileges of the rich men, and the disabilities which were contested did not weigh on the daily rank and file'.[24]

Supporters of emancipation sought to play down the opposition and indifference of the community which they described as a falsity, and later as a 'strange assertion'. Francis Goldsmid pointed to benefits other than access to Parliament. Other supporters pointed to the pride and self-esteem which would flow from the new privileges, even if inevitably limited to the most distinguished members of the Jewish community.

The extremes of wealth and poverty were aggravated through the abandonment by the upper classes of the old areas of residence around the City of London in favour of Marylebone and Mayfair. The new provincial communities were more closely knit, with less social distance between rich and poor, 'but distance there was, and efforts to ally the humbler classes with the aspirations of the wealthy were spasmodic and artificial'. The middle class itself was socially divided, and 'for all the anxiety to draw tighter the bonds of community, the gulfs remained'.[25]

However there were frequent challenges to the 'gilded leaders' of Anglo-Jewry, and to the oligarchic habits of the Elders at Bevis Marks. The rise of the Jewish press provided a transparency and impetus towards a wider democracy, which was slow in coming, and largely ignored by the emancipationists. The *Jewish Chronicle* and *The Voice of Jacob* 'persistently condemned the high-handedness, the arbitrary exercise of power and the closed and proprietary system of government which had for generations prevailed in Anglo-Jewish affairs'.[26]

The pressure for emancipation thus contrasted sharply with the maintenance of such internal restrictive practises within the Jewish community, where for example barely half of the members of the Great Synagogue had the right to vote.[27] 'We shall be able to bestow our undivided attention on our internal and external development', wrote Abraham Benisch, in a 'memorable' editorial on 6 August 1858 shortly after the passing of the Jewish Relief Act.[28] Here was a clear implication that the needs of the community had been neglected during the long campaign, and that there was a need to 'emancipate ourselves from within'.

Between those Jews who were for and those against emancipation, there was a large middle group of those who preferred a step by step approach, dealing with each disqualification as it presented itself, and accepting each concession which might be conceded. This middle group was represented by the Board of Deputies whose long time President from 1835 was Moses Montefiore (1784–1885). Whilst he undoubtedly hoped for full emancipation, he shared with Adler a fear of excessive assimilation, and a consequent challenge to the orthodox tradition.

Regrettably there was a growing divergence between the Board and Goldsmid, who looked for a more robust strategy. Despite prior assurances not to act without consultation with the Board, and despite a constitutional assertion in 1836 that the Board was the sole official medium of communication with the Government, Goldsmid proceeded to institute his own Bills to Parliament, and in 1838 he made it clear that he could not 'possibly entrust my political interests to the charge of Deputies'.[29] When re-elected to the Board by the Great Synagogue in 1839, he refused to serve.

This divergence in the leadership of the community was sadly exposed by two separate deputations to the Prime Minister, Sir Robert Peel, in 1845. He was prepared to grant the abolition of municipal disabilities, which the deputation led by Montefiore was prepared to accept. The other led by Goldsmid wanted full emancipation, which was not on offer at that time. It should be added that active Jewish participation at municipal level began prior to 1845. David Salomons was the first professing Jewish magistrate (Kent) appointed in 1838. Benjamin Cohen was appointed to the Surrey Bench in 1841 and Sir Moses Montefiore was appointed a JP in 1844. There is no record that any of them took a religious oath as was then required.[30]

When eventually granted in July 1858, the Board was criticised for periods of apparent apathy. However, the accusation that the Board was a slow-moving and cumbersome deliberative assembly, unable to respond swiftly to a major challenge (frequently repeated since!) needs to be seen in the context of a representative body which must take care not to prejudice its status as such, and not to outstrip public opinion. Political agitation across Europe in the 1840s also needed to be taken into account, and there were those of a previous generation for whom a high pressure political campaign would have smacked of ingratitude to the host country.

Montefiore was also concerned about the rising tide of Reform Judaism, and the possibility that existing religious forms and privileges might be traded in exchange for emancipation. He was also much engaged with the fate of Jews abroad as highlighted by his personal involvement with the Damascus Affair of 1840, and his various visits to Palestine. He did not wish to prejudice his relations with harassed British Ministers by pressing for political concessions at home. Israel Finestein suggests[31] that for Montefiore the struggle for emancipation was a subsidiary issue, but he approved the comment of Lucien Wolf in his 1884 biography of Montefiore that 'whilst his views were not heroic, they were intelligent and practical'.[32]

The emancipation struggle brought to the fore the growing dichotomy of those Jews for whom the nation and the religion were important with civic rights a privilege, and those Jews who claimed the privileges and status of Englishmen as a right. This contrast extended to other issues, and certainly rumbled on into the twentieth century in one guise or another. The emancipation campaign thus highlighted the question of Jewish identity, and what was to be the response of Jews to the new order of society and its opportunities.

Whether by friend or foe, the Jews were called upon to explain or defend their role, and their expectation of divine fulfilment. Their distinctive existence was their heritage and their problem. Emancipation highlighted their separateness, making it the subject of more intense curiosity and enquiry that ever before.[33]

At the end of the campaign, Lord Derby told the House of Lords in 1857, 'No doubt they discharge their duties as citizens ... but they retain their peculiar customs ... they do not associate freely with their fellow subjects ... though among us, they have interests wholly apart.'[34] Was he so far from the truth? He returned to office as Prime Minister later that year, and Benjamin Disraeli (1804–81) became Chancellor of the Exchequer and Leader of the House.

Disraeli was known to be of Jewish descent, but had previously taken little interest in Jewish issues. His belated espousal of Jewish emancipation has therefore been the subject of much speculation. Cecil Roth rather effusively claimed Disraeli as one of our own. Israel Finestein more cautiously referred to him as an enigma.[35] Professor Harold Fisch[36] of Bar Ilan University, recipient in 2000 of the prestigious Israel Prize for Literature, referred to the 'unconscious dimension of Disraeli's Jewishness' in an essay entitled 'Disraeli's Hebraic Compulsions'.[37] David Cesarani referred to his 'dual identity'.[38] Disraeli referred to himself as the blank page between the two Testaments.

Having arrived near the political summit, the Jewish question might well have become an embarrassment which needed to be resolved. In any event Disraeli was beholden to the Rothschilds, but his position was somewhat ambivalent, and his argument in favour of emancipation took an unusual route. 'The Jews should not be excluded from the legislature, he argued, because their religion was the basis of the Christian state.'[39] Jewish emancipation would therefore reinforce not undermine its Christian character!

He was not concerned with Jewish rights as such, or with religious liberalisation, but sought rather 'to extend the definition of Englishness to include the Jews',[40] and by so doing perhaps make their emancipation more palatable to the Tory party. To this end he made extravagant claims for the Jewish intellect in a speech to Parliament in 1847, which led to the assumption that he believed in Jewish superiority.[41] He may have found support for his case in the high regard of the Sephardi tradition for culture, learning and descent. Or, as succinctly put by Isaiah Berlin, 'Disraeli overcame a serious obstacle to his career, by inflating into it a claim to noble birth'.[42]

Israel Finestein regarded Disraeli's advocacy of Jewish civil emancipation as courageous, and when the opportunity came he devised a compromise by which Jews were allowed to be admitted to the Commons without having to take the offending Christian oath. The Jewish Relief Act of 1858 was finally and grudgingly confirmed in the Lords, and Baron Lionel de Rothschild became the first MP to take advantage of the new legislation as a professing Jew. Sir David Salomons was in fact elected to Parliament earlier in 1851 but had been convicted of having spoken and voted in the House without the necessary oath.[43] His appeal was dismissed!

The 1858 Act heralded for the Anglo-Jewish community a 'golden age, which lasted until threatened by an unprecedented deluge of Jewish immigrants from 1882'.[44] On the religious front, the corrosive effect of emancipation would weaken Judaism, but the emancipationists were not entirely to blame. Judaism had already lost some of its hold as a result of the Enlightenment. The issue which remained to be resolved was then, and still remains, the survival and content of Judaism without the pressure of the ghetto. With emancipation came the question as to what was the object of Jewish distinctiveness, and by what means was it to be sustained.

Notes

1. IF, *Jewish Society in Victorian England* (London and Portland, OR: Vallentine Mitchell, 1993), p.55.
2. Ibid., p.1.
3. Ibid.
4. Ibid.
5. Ibid., p.2.
6. IF, 'Anglo-Jewish Opinion during the Struggle for Emancipation 1828–58', *Jewish Historical Studies*, Vol.20 (1964), pp.113–43.
7. IF, *Jewish Society in Victorian England*, p.3.
8. Ibid., p.16.
9. A clockmaker by trade, and a founder of what became H Samuel Jewellers.
10. IF *Jewish Society in Victorian England*, p. 135.
11. JC, 27 November 1885, p.10.
12. IF, *Studies and Profiles in Anglo-Jewish History: From Picciotto to Bermant* (London and Portland, OR: Vallentine Mitchell, 2008), p.87.
13. IF, *Scenes & Personalities in Anglo-Jewry* (London: Vallentine Mitchell, 2002), p.285.
14. IF, *Jewish Society in Victorian England*, p.9.
15. Ibid., p.94.
16. IF, *Scenes & Personalities*, p.286.
17. IF, 'Emancipation Apologetics', JC, 14 February 1958, p.17.
18. IF, *Jewish Society in Victorian England*, p.97.
19. IF, *Jewish Society in Victorian England*, p.92.
20. Ibid., p.136.

21. Ibid., p.100.
22. Ibid., p.18.
23. Ibid., p.25.
24. Lucien Wolf, *Essays in Jewish History*, ed. Cecil Roth, pp.51–4.
25. Ibid., p.21.
26. IF, *Jewish Society in Victorian England*, p.23.
27. Ibid.
28. Ibid., pp.24–5.
29. Ibid., p.30.
30. Ann Ebner, 'The First Jewish Magistrates', *Jewish Historical Studies*, Vol.38, p.51.
31. IF, *Jewish Society in Victorian England*, p.32.
32. Ibid., p.50, n.66.
33. Ibid., p.143.
34. Ibid., p.167.
35. Ibid., p.175.
36. For an appreciation see IF, *Studies and Profiles in Anglo-Jewish History*, Ch.14.
37. IF, H.J. Zimmels & J. Rabbinowitz (eds), *Essays Presented to Chief Rabbi Israel Brodie* (London: Soncino Press, 1968), pp.81–3.
38. David Cesarani, *Disraeli, the Novel Politician* (London: Yale University Press, 2016), p.232.
39. Todd M. Endelman and Tony Kushner (eds), *Disraeli's Jewishness* (London and Portland, OR: Vallentine Mitchell, 2002), p.80.
40. Ibid., p.81.
41. See IF, *Anglo-Jewry in Changing Times, Studies in Diversity 1840–1914* (London and Portland, OR: Vallentine Mitchell, 1999), p.157.
42. Presidential address, JHSE 1967.
43. IF, *Jewish Society in Victorian England*, p.115.
44. Arie M. Dubnov, *Isaiah Berlin: The Journey of a Jewish Liberal* (New York: Palgrave Macmillan, 2012), pp.37–8.

3

Agree to Differ

The issues raised by the emancipation and by the new Jewish learning were not transitory or superficial. They touched upon Jewish identity, and upon the rationale for distinctive Jewish survival.

Israel Finestein[1]

The spectre of reform or the urge to reform, depending on one's viewpoint, was a motif throughout nineteenth-century Anglo-Jewry, and in Western Europe, traditional Jewish observance was seen as a barrier to taking advantage of the new freedom and emancipation available.

Reform Judaism began as early as 1810 in Seesen, Germany, and the first explicitly reform 'Temple' was established in Hamburg in 1818. The service was conducted in German, with a choir and an organ, and a sermon in German – all contrary to the then existing practise, and Hebrew prayers of great antiquity were abandoned. In Frankfurt, one of Europe's oldest Jewish communities, a Reform congregation was set up in the 1840s and its leaders banned ritual slaughter and the teaching of Torah.

The head of the Berlin Reform community, created a few years later, argued against mention of Jerusalem, Zion or the Land of Israel. He opposed circumcision and the wearing of *kippot* or prayer shawls. In Hungary, travel on Shabbat was permitted, and the *Kol Nidrei* prayer was abolished.

The Reform conference held at Brunswick in 1844 described its philosophy as love of the people among whom one lives, and a desire to be 'patriots, not cosmopolitan'. At the Frankfurt Conference of 1845 it was said that a separate language (Hebrew) was a characteristic of a separate nation, and the hope of national restoration was inconsistent with our feelings for the 'fatherland'. These sentiments were of course not reciprocated when the Nazis came to power, despite the patriotic contribution of German Jewry in the First World War.

The creation of Reform synagogues did not go unopposed. One of the most influential leaders of the resistance was Samson Raphael Hirsch (1808–88) who, after serving as Chief Rabbi of Moravia (one of the largest Jewish constituencies in Europe), returned to Frankfurt to confront the Reformers. His view was summarised in an article he wrote in 1854 entitled 'Religion Allied to Progress'.

His first priority was observance of the Torah, but there was no conflict between Torah and the world, he argued, one does not have to choose. 'Judaism has never remained aloof from true civilisation and progress', he wrote, but his followers in future generations became associated with a less tolerant, more isolationist view of Judaism. He was considered a candidate as Chief Rabbi of Britain in 1845.

Among the moderates who split from the Frankfurt Conference was Zacharias Frankel who founded the Jewish Theological Seminary at Breslaw in1854. He accepted the Torah as the foundational sacred text, and is regarded as the pioneer of Conservative Judaism which became a distinct movement in America, holding the balance between two extremes. The United States had become involved in this dichotomy at an early stage due to the large German Jewish immigration there.

The controversial Pittsburgh Reform Platform of 1885 followed the seemingly important fatherland concept: 'We consider ourselves no longer a nation, but a religious community.'[2] It also declared its belief in 'the Messianic hope for the kingdom of truth, justice and peace', a hope, surely common to all religions! The reformers had not in fact reformed Judaism, but replaced it with a sort of unitarianism, and it was not until as late as 1999 in a statement of principles, that the American Reform movement finally recognised the need for an increased commitment to Judaism, its observance and study.

By contrast, the urge to reform in England was not at all ideological, 'a luke-warm affair',[3] more a matter of convenience! Eighteen Sephardi members of Bevis Marks Synagogue, and six Ashkenazi members of the Great Synagogue, having been rebuffed by their respective leaders, called a public meeting on 15 April 1840 to consider the establishment of a new Synagogue.

Their initial concerns were a far cry from their continental counterparts: the distance of new places of residence from existing synagogues, services to be held at more appropriate times and be moderate in length, services to be conducted with proper decorum and in a manner more calculated to inspire feelings of devotion, sermons in English, abolition of public donations when called up to the Reading of the Torah, the abolition of certain rituals such as the second day of the festivals, and most provocatively, the publication of a revised prayer book.

Chief Rabbi Solomon Herschell (1762–1842) clearly wished to stop the spread of Reform Judaism, and what was seen as rejection of the Oral Law. In May 1841, he asked the Board of Deputies for help to defend the current position against the proposed establishment of a dissenting synagogue. After much discussion, the Board resolved on 9 November that a *cherem* (or ban) be prepared whereby all faithful Jews would be prohibited from having any contact with the new congregation. Raphael Langham[4] quotes the nineteenth century commentator James Picciotto as suggesting that the Chief Rabbi and his Sephardi counterpart were reluctant to take such a step, but were pressed by the lay leadership, perhaps as a deterrent.

If so, it did not prevent the secession, and despite 'regret expressed by the secessionists at the threat of excommunication'[5] and pleas to avoid ill-will, the Chief Rabbi's declaration[6] was promulgated on 27 January 1842, the date on which the West London Synagogue was established, with the Rev. David Woolf Marks (1811–1909) as its first Minister. Banishment and exclusion from the community was a draconian response which failed as a punishment, and offered no hope of compromise. It divided families, and created unnecessary friction and hardship. In regard to Rabbi Herschell, Israel Finestein describes the *cherem* as one of 'the acerbities which clouded the closing years of his tenure'.[7]

The problem was compounded by the fact that his successor Rabbi Nathan Adler felt bound by it, and in 1847 he refused to allow the usual burial service for a member of the Great Synagogue who had supported reform. Its President urged him to desist from implementing 'a decree unsuitable to an enlightened age', and on 7 January 1848 the JC expressed pain at the opportunity lost 'to establish peace and union among a distracted community'.[8] Age and frailty alone (78 years, and in poor health) might well have cast doubt on the merit of Rabbi Herschell's edict.

The role of Sir Moses Montefiore was significant in this as in all matters during his long reign as President of the Board of Deputies. He was faced with the difficulty of accepting a de facto pluralism, and having to deal with a new religious system which was held to be invalid, even subversive.[9] The problem of appearing to grant recognition without doing so is one which has been agonised over in every generation since. Israel Finestein accepted that Montefiore acted out of a sense of what he deemed his duty, and refused to certify the Minister of the new West London Synagogue as a Secretary for marriage purposes as required by Statute, a matter which was only rectified by subsequent legislation.

In August 1853, the proceedings of the Board were adjourned amid 'a scene of the most indescribable uproar'.[10] Four members of the West London Synagogue had attempted to take their seats and were asked to leave. They had been duly elected to represent Orthodox provincial Synagogues, but their personal status as members of a Reform congregation was held to disqualify them, although the Board was evenly divided on this.

The revolt of the four Deputies and their supporters was followed by weeks of bitterness and controversy, and the JC challenged Chief Rabbi Adler to respond. He did so with some statesmanship in a sermon entitled 'Solomon's Judgment':

> We must try to heal the breach which exists between brethren and brethren. Where the breach cannot be healed, let us agree to differ, and let us have peace in our own camp. Why should you diminish your own vitality without real benefit to either party? Let us not lavish our energies on an unprofitable difference. Let us put away all anger and ill-feeling.[11]

But the benefit of his words and the possibility of an olive branch were negated by his observation elsewhere that a *cherem* cannot be annulled until the party concerned has altered the religious position which has caused it to be issued. The Sephardi community had in 1849 removed the *cherem* from those of its members who wished to acknowledge their 'transgression', but there was to be no corresponding reconciliation in the Ashkenazi world. By condoning the original pronouncement against the West London Synagogue, alienation and banishment of those with whom one disagreed were thus approved as instruments of public policy, and cast a long shadow into the future.

Nathan Marcus Adler (1803–90) former senior Rabbi of Hanover, where he was born, scion of a distinguished rabbinic line, university-educated, but with considerable Jewish scholarship, was the overwhelming choice for Chief Rabbi in 1844 following the death of his predecessor. In common with other Orthodox rabbis he had protested against the Brunswick Conference. Moses Montefiore had no formal role in the election, but may well have seen Adler in advance as a potential candidate, having previously asked for a copy of his sermons. Following Adler's arrival, a close bond existed between the two men.[12] Whilst most congregations were entitled to participate in his election, it was the principal London congregations which dominated the outcome, by virtue of their contribution to the Chief Rabbinate Fund.

Rabbi Adler was installed at the Great Synagogue on 9 July 1845. 'He who is an earnest servant of God must stand upon the wall, defend the precious inheritance, and preserve it in its entirety', he declared, knowing that he had arrived in England at a critical juncture. It was necessary to oppose those who would 'pull down existing structures of religious theory and practice'.[13] Quite apart from the issue of Reform, the Emancipation debate was at its height, with ceaseless public discussion involving fundamental issues of considerable importance. He may well have seen it necessary to avoid any perceived dilution of Orthodoxy, such as might be inferred from a revocation of the edict of his predecessor.

When Emancipation came, with the Jewish Relief Act of 1858, it led to a feeling that a 'culmination' had been achieved, that old prejudices would dissolve, and that favourable change would come in time. The western Orthodoxy of the Chief Rabbi, and the conservative style of English reform, could perhaps live in amity. Conventional society conformed to an undemanding religiosity, and a commitment to inherited Judaism which seemed to require no personal view or observance of the enshrined traditions.

'The heirs of the Emancipation wanted above all to uproot the concept that to profess the Jewish religion was to belong to a Jewish nation'.[14] The concept of separateness was downplayed or explained in purely religious terms. Rabbi Adler himself declared that the Jews had no interests which were different from those of the country at large, and he urged his Ministers to avail themselves of every opportunity to address gentile audiences. It was part of a policy to present Judaism as a continuing civilising force, in the van of progress, now as of old.

In the non-Jewish world, the 1858 Act led to 'a great demand for information and literature about the Jews and Judaism. It was a constant theme in the newspapers and periodicals throughout the 1860s. There was a mounting Christian curiosity, and a boom in Spinoza studies. Matthew Arnold's philo-semitism had broadened the appeal of Jewish topics. There was also the enigma of Disraeli and talk of Jewish Restoration, and literature concerning possible British interest in it.'[15]

However, the presentation of the English Jew as a member of a morally elevated, westernised denomination to some extent collided with Rabbi Adler's stated desire to 're-animate, strengthen and confirm the love of Judaism'.[16] In consequence, there were long periods of public discord throughout his Rabbinate, despite the high regard in which he was held.

Rabbi Adler's campaign for better amenities at existing Jewish educational establishments was not supported, nor was his desire for additional Jewish day schools for the children of wealthier families. He had hoped that the 1870 Education Act (over which he had been consulted) would provide funds for denominational education, but it did not do so, and despite pleas from the Chief Rabbi for realistic support, his new Jews College was consistently underfunded.

He was instrumental in the creation of the College inaugurated in 1855, with support from the Sephardi community, but the result was not as he wished in that he had hoped it would remain open to all interested in higher Jewish studies. Its primary purpose was the training of English-speaking

Ministers, but the extent of their training and role was continuously in question, and the curriculum of the College was stripped of anything resembling serious Jewish learning, such as might be available at a corresponding institution abroad. The Rabbinic qualification was not deemed essential in order to present Judaism to the gentiles, and the Rabbinical diploma was not available at the College until the twentieth century.

The new Jewish Englishman wanted to divest the community of any appearance as an alien group with special claims upon benefits or amenities, and this view was 'most graphically demonstrated in the opposition to proposals for the establishment of a specifically Jewish workhouse'.[17] For no doubt similar reasons the Chief Rabbi was challenged as to the wisdom of creating a separate Jewish hospital in London, instead of using the existing Jewish wards. Likewise, there was disapproval of seeking exemption for Jewish marriages from the scope of the newly established Divorce Court. The *get* was and remains a significant feature of Jewish divorce law. Rabbi Adler had hoped to maintain the power of the Beth Din to grant Jewish divorces, but the tide of English law was generally against him.

There were also differences between English and Jewish law as to the prohibited degrees of marriage. Despite strenuous advice from the BOD, clandestine marriages continued to be performed within the immigrant communities, and there was concern as to the position of marriages from within non-Orthodox congregations. Successful representations to Parliament made by Rabbi Adler and the BOD were undermined by the direct intervention of Sir David Salomons (former Lord Mayor of the City of London) who expressed his 'belief that the power of divorce by Jewish ecclesiastical authorities ought to be entirely abrogated.'[18]

Emancipationists it seems were not merely looking for relief from civic disabilities. They were also looking for emancipation from continental-type Orthodox Judaism.[19] A new Jewish world outlook was emerging in England which was to create a tension out of which further demands for reform would inevitably arise. However, Rabbi Adler was staunchly traditional, and was prepared to accept only minor change.

The Chief Rabbi was particularly concerned with the conduct of services, often thought to be too long and indecorous. He introduced regulations urging his constituent congregations to regard their synagogues as miniature sanctuaries, where dignity and solemnity would prevail and foster feelings of devotion. Whilst some local congregations might have bridled at his regulations, they had the long term effect of strengthening the institution of the synagogue, and providing a centralised and coordinated religious administration.

It is not surprising that Rabbi Adler would have sought to bring to an end the rivalry and disunity which existed between the main London Ashkenazi synagogues. The extent of his involvement is not clear, and it has been suggested that he 'button-holed' the respective Wardens at his home during one Succoth. There had already been discussions about union, and it is possible he was 'pushing at an open door', but his personal encouragement for renewed and energetic action is not in question.

Given the reluctance of synagogues to sink their differences, the creation of the United Synagogue (US), must be regarded as an outstanding achievement for all concerned. Five individual congregations were initially involved in the union which was sanctioned by Act of Parliament in 1870. The religious authority of the Chief Rabbi was enshrined in a Deed of Foundation approved at the first meeting of the US Council presided over by Lionel Louis Cohen (1832–87). His father, Louis Cohen, as the senior figure at the Great Synagogue, had in fact presided over the election of Chief Rabbi Adler.

Lionel Louis Cohen[20] was one of the lay leaders most associated with the movement for establishment of the US. He served as Vice President until his death, at which time there were eleven affiliated congregations. There are today more than sixty. He also worked tirelessly for the Board of Guardians, which he helped to create in 1859. Charitable relief had previously been operated in a haphazard manner, and under his leadership the Board of Guardians became the major communal charity for the relief of the poor. Cohen served as its first Honorary Secretary, and in 1869 he was elected President.

'Mingled in his ultimately benign paternalism, was a large dose of an authoritarian spirit, however altruistic his motivation.'[21] Lionel Louis Cohen believed that the ruling Jewish families should remain in some form of control, and was extremely cautious over changes in the communal structure. 'His reserve in such matters was significantly illustrated in his concern lest the establishment of the AJA in 1871 might intrude on the working of the BOD, and he raised this matter at its inaugural meeting.'[22]

The individual members of the AJA were not answerable to 'constituents' whereas the Board 'enjoyed a status within the Jewish community, which was recognised by Parliament.'[23] Clarity of communal purpose and unity in action were essential in his view, and he welcomed the formation of a joint committee in 1878 relating to foreign affairs.

In 1884, Cohen expressed public concern at the humanitarian consequences of further immigration at a time of trade depression and an overcrowded labour market. The plight of Jewish immigrants was so severe that in 1888, Chief Rabbi Adler also addressed the issue with a circular entreating every rabbi in East Europe 'to publicise the evil which is befalling our brethren who have come here, and warn them not to come to the land of Britain.'[24] He elaborated by referring to the poverty and overwork which immigrants might expect, the likely violation of the Sabbath, and the risk of falling into the hands of missionaries. There was also concern that further entry might provoke anti-Semitism by added pressure in the affected areas of Jewish immigration.

One quarter of London Jewry was said to be in receipt of charity at the middle of the century, and of these 95 per cent were 'foreign poor'. 'The communal scene was dominated by poverty, and new Jewish charities sprang up to help meet the needs of the Jewish destitute.'[25] However, the scale of immigration (after 1881) was set to expand considerably for the remainder of the century, and the concerns expressed by Cohen and others 'inevitably encouraged the restrictionist movement, whose agitation culminated in the Aliens Act of 1905'.[26]

East End Jews were well aware of their differences with the West End, which, despite their inner divisiveness, reinforced in many their sense of independence. English Jews were in their eyes as foreign as they themselves might be perceived to be! The Chief Rabbi neither looked nor dressed nor spoke as they expected of a Rabbi, and his successor who publicly discouraged the use of Yiddish, virtually disentitled himself from any serious claim on their attachment![27]

It was Sir Samuel Montagu (1832–1911), rather than Lionel Cohen and the Rothschilds, who was able to bring together some twenty small, quarrelsome and embarrassingly unEnglish East End communities, based largely on their different territorial origins. The result was his creation of the Federation of Synagogues in 1887,[28] with himself as President, avoiding what was headed to be a separatist immigrant community.

Samuel Montagu, later Lord Swaythling, a successful banker, was MP from 1885 until 1900 representing Whitechapel, where the new and impoverished mainly Orthodox Jewish immigrants were congregating. A pious Jew himself, 'he was motivated not only by the desire to curb the proliferation of cramped and sometimes unhygienic places of worship, but also by the ambition to bring to bear upon communal life the religious enthusiasm which those congregations represented'.[29]

Meanwhile a pressing priority for Lionel Cohen was the continued questioning of the traditional forms of synagogual service by many within the Orthodox fold, and an Association was formed in 1873 to campaign for liturgical modifications. There was a desire for more English sermons, and a shortening of the services. Such measures were presented as 'directed to achieving greater sustained attention by congregants' and submitted for consideration by Chief Rabbi Adler. His somewhat reluctant decision to authorise limited change was said to acknowledge the need to impress a new generation.

Nathan Marcus Adler had hoped to see 'a deepening of the orthodox faith, a more wholesome response to the questioning coming from the secularly lettered younger generation, a greater interest in Jewish literature, and a better educated Jewish laity. The lay leadership however was less moved by some of the enthusiasms which stirred him.'[30]

The debate over change at that time did not turn upon the principles of rabbinic authority or upon the validity of the Oral Law. Lionel Louis Cohen was not concerned with theological speculation, or rabbinic rationalisations, but with efficient management of a synagogual system which enshrined the faith of his fathers.

'Had the leadership resisted liturgical change, the campaign would have turned into doctrinal channels.' Even so, by the end of the 1880s, 'religion was moving increasingly into the intellectual sphere, ever more subject to the test of reason and history.'[31] A fresh evaluation of the biblical text was taking place, as well as a questioning of the binding character of rabbinic interpretation. Continental style reform was indeed waiting in the wings!

Notes

1. IF, 'Post Emancipation Jewry: The Anglo-Jewish Experience', Oxford School of Postgraduate Hebrew Studies, Sacks Lecture 1980, *Jewish Society in Victorian England*, p.154.
2. Lawrence Rigal & Rosita Rosenberg, *Liberal Judaism: the First Hundred Years* (London: ULPS, 2004) p. 82, n.2.
3. Meir Persoff, *Faith Against Reason. Religious Reform and the British Chief Rabbinate, 1840–1990* (London and Portland, OR: Vallentine Mitchell, 2008), p.26.
4. Raphael Langham, *250 Years of Convention and Contention: A History of the Board of Deputies of British Jews 1760–2010* (London and Portland, OR: Vallentine Mitchell, 2010), p.45.
5. Persoff, *Faith Against Reason*, p.14.
6. Reproduced ibid., p.16.
7. IF, *Anglo-Jewry in Changing Times, Studies in Diversity 1840–1914* (London and Portland, OR: Vallentine Mitchell, 1999), p.45.
8. Persoff, *Faith Against Reason*, p.29.
9. IF, *Jewish Society in Victorian England* (London and Portland, OR: Vallentine Mitchell, 1993), p.241.
10. Ibid., p.123.
11. Persoff, *Faith Against Reason*, pp.76–7.
12. Ibid., pp.92–3.
13. Rabbi Raymond Apple, 'Nathan Marcus Adler – Chief Rabbi', *OzTorah*, November 1970.
14. IF, *Jewish Society in Victorian England*, p.172.

15. Ibid., p.175.
16. Ibid.
17. IF, *Studies and Profiles in Anglo-Jewish History: From Picciotto to Bermant* (London and Portland, OR: Vallentine Mitchell, 2008), p.92.
18. IF, *Jewish Society in Victorian England*, p.53 n.74, also p.70.
19. Ibid., p.34.
20. For a full appreciation see IF, *Studies and Profiles in Anglo-Jewish History*, Chap. 4.
21. Ibid., p.62.
22. Ibid., p.66.
23. Ibid.
24. Lloyd P. Gartner, *The Jewish Immigrant 1870–1914* (London and Portland, OR: Vallentine Mitchell, 2001, 3rd edn), p.24.
25. IF, *Anglo-Jewry in Changing Times*, p.31.
26. IF, *Studies and Profiles in Anglo-Jewish History*, p.94.
27. Ibid., p.72.
28. IF, *Jewish Society in Victorian England*, p.192.
29. Ibid., p.193.
30. IF, *Anglo-Jewry in Changing Times*, p.14.
31. IF, *Studies and Profiles in Anglo-Jewish History*, pp.14–15.

4

The Watchman

> By 1910, the Anglo-Jewish community had doubled and redoubled in size, especially in the provinces. It was becoming a community of communities, and within each of them there were divisions, dissensions and polemics over Zionism, which were at times especially heated. Everywhere there was an expanding diversity …. existing priorities were now everywhere under enquiry.
>
> Israel Finestein[1]

In addition to inherited divisions exacerbated by the rising tide of Jewish immigration, Rabbi Hermann Adler (1839–1911) presided over the emergence of two major new divisions, as dramatic in effect as any other: Zionism and Liberal Judaism.

Born in Hanover, son of his predecessor, Hermann Adler was well qualified academically, having attended rabbinical college in Prague, and obtained a doctorate in philosophy from Leipsig in 1862. The following year he became principal of Jews' College, and remained associated with the College as Tutor in Theology and later as Chairman of the Council, notwithstanding appointment as Minister at the new Bayswater Synagogue in 1864.

He served as deputy to his father Chief Rabbi Nathan Adler, who delegated some of his duties to him from 1880, on account of ill health. In approval of this arrangement, the United Synagogue Council recorded that 'by his high abilities and conciliatory disposition, he had gained the affection of a large and important congregation'.[2] On his father's death in 1890, Hermann Adler was unanimously elected Chief Rabbi, and served until his own death in 1911. He also served as President of the JHSE, as Vice President of the Anglo-Jewish Association (AJA), and the Jewish Religious Educational Board (JREB), and was active on the Russo-Jewish Committee.

He quickly made his name as a preacher, and it is possible that he had more claim to be considered 'the father of the Anglo-Jewish pulpit' than his father on whom that title was originally bestowed by the historian Cecil Roth. He brought to the Chief Rabbinate an impressive dignity, from which the

Jewish community benefitted in the gentile world. His involvement with royalty and high ranking Christian clergy led (according to Cecil Roth) to 'an inevitable tendency for him to interpret his position in Anglican terms'.[3]

Hermann Adler believed that the Emancipation was a historical achievement, the attainment of which must not be put at risk. Anglicanisation was the order of the day, as expressed by the *Jewish Chronicle* (JC) on the eve of Queen Victoria's Diamond Jubilee: 'We have become Englishmen ... our constant effort is to anglicise our community ... without damage to our religion.'[4]

Anglicanisation was not only expedient, but a matter of moral principle, a communal priority, which included the promotion of secular education, and of English in place of Yiddish. The inculcation of Judaism was associated with good citizenship, and in the event of hostile criticism, Chief Rabbi Adler preached the merits of not attracting attention, and maintaining a low profile.[5]

Hermann Adler urged the importance of the Jewish mission, but only as a doctrine intended to raise the moral standards of mankind, and he did not proceed beyond the ancient imperative of Isaiah (42:6) to be 'a light unto the nations'. He declared that Judaism was entirely compatible with modern sophistication when properly understood, and that the concept of mission was a sufficient explanation of the separateness of the Jews, so long as it was devoid of any national content. Even reference to the Messiah had to be explained so as 'to divest it of any breath of excessive particularism'.[6]

Zionism was alien to the philosophy of the Emancipation, and was represented as offering the enemies of the Jews evidence of alleged international designs and lack of patriotism. We were not 'strangers and sojourners',[7] and Hermann Adler became the principal exponent of the Jewish national idea as part of a religious system only. 'Since the destruction of the Temple, we no longer constitute a nation. We are a religious communion', he declared in April 1909. Theodore Herzl had previously observed that the Gentile has never yet disputed our nationality – that role was reserved for the Jews themselves![8]

Hermann Adler had visited Palestine in 1885, and had no objection to Jewish settlement there. He was obviously aware of the biblical prophecies, and was not averse to the principles of the Chovevei Zion movement which grew out of the worsening position of the Jews in Europe and Russia during the 1880s. However, he was not alone in later dissociating himself from political Zionism. Before 1897, a return to the ancient homeland was fantasy, but after Herzl and the first Zionist Congress, it entered into the real world for those that wished to work towards it, however remote the end result might be.

Zionism was clearly in conflict with the concept of Victorian Jewishness, to which Rabbi Adler was so attached. Addressing the AJA in July 1897, he described the Zionist Congress as an 'egregious blunder' and castigated Herzl's scheme for a Jewish State as mischievous and contrary to Jewish principles.[9] The programme of the new Zionist movement was for him impractical and imprudent, and associated with the advance of radicalism and socialism, with which a proportion of its grass roots supporters were identified.

In a speech given in November 1898, Chief Rabbi Adler saw as appropriate the words of the prophet who advised the Babylonian exiles to settle there, and 'pray for the welfare of the city in which you dwell, for in their peace shall you have peace'.[10] The return to Zion will occur not by our efforts 'but by the hand of Hashem, whenever He decides to send his *moshiach*', he said. Meanwhile the Jewish people must wait silently for the fulfilment of the biblical prophecy and avoid 'intrigues and diplomatic manoeuvres'.

However, there were those in whom the new Zionism awakened a realisation of the significance and purpose of Jewish identity. It proclaimed a cultural, even a spiritual rebirth, not solely linked with a return to the land itself, and there were also those who saw in it the hand of divine providence. The conflict between Zionists of all shades of opinion and their Jewish opponents was thus firmly established, and would remain a major issue of contention for over half a century.

In terms of Halakhah, Hermann Adler continued the tradition of his father as 'the watchman, guardian and preserver of the Holy Law'.[11] He (and the Haham) did not attend the Jubilee service at West London Reform Synagogue in 1892, although many in leading positions did so. He disallowed on grounds of Halakhah the involvement of ladies in a choir at the service to mark the founding of the new Hampstead Synagogue, but acquiesced thereafter 'to secure and retain that congregation within the United Synagogue'.

Like his father, Hermann Adler believed that synagogual music would enhance the impact of services, and by adding a degree of solemnity, would reduce apathy and encourage devotion. A choir was indeed considered a major attraction at the synagogue, but the issue of mixed choirs was divisive, even though it was in fact a mixed choir which performed at the service to mark the Queen's Diamond Jubilee in 1897.

In respect of 'clandestine' marriages or divorces in accordance with Jewish law, but irregular under English Law, the Chief Rabbi supported a draft Bill in 1889 imposing a penalty on foreign rabbis who performed them. The Bill, supported by the BOD, did not proceed, but stern notices were circulated. He was chided for 'unseemly subservience' to lay attitudes. Meanwhile his English placidity[12] towards theological matters was about to be tested.

The establishment of the Hampstead Synagogue in 1892 was preceded by a desire for major changes in the service, but the limited changes which the new Chief Rabbi was prepared to sanction led the more Reform-minded members to plan their own breakaway service on Saturday afternoons. Some 200 people attended the first such service at West Hampstead Town Hall on 22 February 1890.[13] The Rev. Morris Joseph (1848–1930) of the North London Synagogue officiated, and had in fact prepared a new prayer book with a number of radical changes. These included the removal of the prayer for the re-introduction of sacrificial rites in the event that the Temple was restored, a prayer of which he especially disapproved.

Morris Joseph was in fact the preferred ministerial candidate for the new post at Hampstead, but Hermann Adler refused to sanction his appointment declaring that his views (particularly those on sacrifices) were at variance with traditional Judaism. His refusal was widely criticised, but he continued to accept leading members of Reform in prominent positions on educational bodies under his authority. His subsequent denunciation of the Jewish Religious Union (JRU) did not lead him to ask for their withdrawal. Indeed the Rev. David Woolf Marks, Minister of the West London Synagogue, had participated with the Chief Rabbi and the Haham in the service to celebrate the laying of the foundation stone of the new Synagogue at Dennington Park Road.

Responding to his rejection, Morris Joseph regretted that the spiritual life of the new congregation had been starved in obedience to a rigid system. He regarded the accent on unity and uniformity as moribund, and expressed the belief that only an enlightened teaching of it will ensure a living Judaism.[14] He did not espouse reform in the continental style, and his views were relatively moderate by comparison, having served only Orthodox communities until then. However in 1893 he took over from Rev. Marks as Senior Minister at the West London Synagogue, and remained there until his death in 1930. The Rev. Aaron Asher Green (1860–1933) was appointed to Hampstead.

Was an opportunity lost in the light of subsequent events? The rejection of Morris Joseph did not spark a revolution, but was nevertheless a significant moment in the long history of challenges to Orthodoxy. The Hampstead Committee had been evenly divided and the pressure for new services continued. In due course this led to the formation of a society for that purpose, and it was in fact Joseph who proposed that the new Society be called the Jewish Religious Union. Its first service was held at 3.30 p.m. on

Saturday 18 October 1902 with 300 people in attendance.[15] The Rev. Simeon Singer (1846–1906) officiated.

As Minister at the New West End Synagogue since 1878, Singer was a power in the Orthodox community, but in the direction of moderate progress. He had no objection to biblical passages being read in English, and was willing to preach in the Reform Synagogue. He was the author of the well-known Authorised Daily Prayer Book, first published in 1890, and still in use today. It should be noted that after traditional study abroad, Simeon Singer qualified as a rabbi in Vienna in 1890. He might well have been considered as a candidate for the Chief Rabbinate, except that Hermann Adler's succession was hardly in question.

Simeon Singer chose not to make public use of the title of rabbi which was regarded as within the personal prerogative of the Chief Rabbi. He was the first US Minister to go abroad in order to obtain the rabbinical diploma, not available in England, and was followed by Hermann Gollancz, Minister at Bayswater, who obtained ordination in 1897. He however, insisted on the right to be called 'Rabbi' which led in 1901 to rabbinical examinations being held at Jews' College, under the authority of the Chief Rabbi.[16]

Another leading United Synagogue Minister who joined the JRU was the Rev. Joseph Frederick Stern (1865–1934)[17] of the East London Synagogue. He came to be regarded as the archetype Jewish 'clergyman' of the Adlerian school of thought. He wanted to maximise the reverential side of worship and accepted that certain parts of the prayer book might be expendable. He was a pioneer in the provision of special services for children, and repeatedly called for greater expenditure on Jewish education. His influence on communal opinion was considerable, but his association with the Union was divisive within the Orthodox community, as was the involvement of two Honorary Officers of the United Synagogue.

According to Lawrence Rigal's account[18] the service began with a prayer that the new Union would proceed, not in a spirit of rebellion, but with love and reverence for the faith of Israel. Claude Montefiore preached a sermon. There was a mixed choir with harmonium. Men and women sat together. The service was mainly in English. In a subsequent sermon, Chief Rabbi Adler inevitably condemned the service and the JRU for departing too radically from the Sabbath ritual, for promoting 'unJewish irreligious disunion', and for being a denial of divine authority. Stern and Singer withdrew from the JRU soon after.

However by 1909, Claude Montefiore (JRU President) felt that with sufficient support having been achieved, the time had come to establish a separate and independent synagogue, 'built upon our own lines, founded to teach Judaism as we conceive it without creed or dogma'.[19] The heavy bondage of Rabbinic law must be removed. No tinkering was possible. The ivy was killing the tree. Many years later, using the same metaphor, Israel Finestein responded that one cannot maintain the tree without the roots.[20] The ivy was not the issue!

Despite the 'internecine contentions and feuds' (JC) unleashed unwittingly by the 1842 dissidents, they were not true reformers. They simply wanted orthodoxy to be more amenable. By contrast, Montefiore believed that there must be a separate branch of Judaism for Liberal-minded Jews, with its own form of worship, own theology, and its own synagogue. His views were published with the decision of the JRU to set up an independent congregation, and the fundamental principles of what became Liberal Judaism were now spelled out for all to read and discuss. Mere liturgical changes were no longer sufficient. True continental style reform had arrived, and the key players needed for it to take root were in place.

The epic nature of the Liberal confrontation with orthodoxy can be seen from the views which Claude Montefiore set out in 1909 at great length, and which became known as the JRU Manifesto.[21] He disposes of the idea that the Union stands only for certain 'externalities', and makes it clear that his views were more far-reaching than the original objectives of the JRU, which were simply 'to provide means for deepening the religious spirit among those members of the community who are not in sympathy with present Synagogue services, or who are unable to attend them'. A few phrases will suffice to indicate the flavour and extent of the revolt:

> We differ from orthodoxy in our concept of revelation. We have no creed and will have none. Our principles are not dogmas, they can and will receive adjustment. Bring back the drifters to cherish, rather than to obey, and they can rightfully call themselves Jews. We recognise no outside binding authority between us and God. Remove the heavy bondage of Rabbinic law. The authority of the Book and the Code is condemned. We can only accept what reason and conscience tells us to be good. The traditional concept of Judaism is doomed.[22]

The genie was finally out of the bottle, and he continued in the same revolutionary style. 'The erroneous and the obsolete clog and ruin the living and the true. Religious ceremonial must contain a religious quality, suited to the present, or be transformed. The main festivals are to remain, also the Sabbath, despite immense problems of observance.' He considered that circumcision be maintained as desirable, and rejected intermarriage in order to maintain the separate distinctive continuance of Judaism. However,

Judaism was to be regarded as a universal religion, not suited to one race 'with no taint of partiality or national limitations'.

Reaction from the orthodox was swift and damning. 'We cannot trust conscience and reason alone',[23] the Chief Rabbi declared. Whose conscience and whose reason are we to follow once the Code has gone? Who is to decide what 'seems to us good'? Resignations followed as leading members on both sides disentangled themselves, and the new movement was now identifiable for the first time. The name of the JRU was extended: 'for the advancement of Liberal Judaism'.[24]

Claude Montefiore's response[25] to Rabbi Adler's criticism was measured and moving: The issue was one of authority, and the final authority is 'within'. Morality will survive the rejection of the Oral Law. Liberal Judaism has been the salvation of thousands of Jews in America, and can be for Jews and Jewesses in England. He referred to a 'wave of modernism which cannot be combated by medieval denunciations', anticipating the threat to all religion which was to come from secularity. Only we can keep it in Jewish channels, he said, and we mean to try. He pleaded in vain for 'a word of godspeed' from his Orthodox brethren. It was not forthcoming.

At his appointment in 1891, Rabbi Hermann Adler had pleaded for communal harmony, avoidance of 'schisms and divisions, discord and disruption', but the Liberals and the Zionists were not his only problems. In the East End, there were those, mainly immigrants who repudiated the official English style of Judaism because it was not Orthodox enough, and considered that pious Jews should not be associated with it! Chief Rabbi Adler had no real experience of the hardships and turmoil of life in Eastern Europe where every community had its own rabbi. His refusal to allow immigrant rabbis to use such titles, combined with widespread poverty, added insult to injury.

'His ecclesiastical personage attracted little sympathy in the East End',[26] as one might expect in the circumstances, and his 'insistence on being recognised as a unique rabbinical authority contributed much to the erosion of his status and standing'.[27] He did not feel comfortable with the 'noisy, untidy piety' of East End Jews, and complained that they were always quarrelling among themselves. He was not alone in fearing that they would damage the position of the community at large, and urged the establishment of English classes to enable gainful employment to be obtained.

He urged sympathy for the new immigrants who had flooded into England, but these 'denizens of the East' clearly did not see him as one of them, creating yet more division within the Orthodox fold. Chief Rabbi Adler was by temperament unsuited to gain the confidence of the mass of East End Jewry, and 'he never quite lived down his words in a much publicised sermon on Succot 1887 when he said it was necessary to anglicise, humanise and civilise them.[28] His object may have been worthy, but the language was not.

In 1892, the Machzikei Hadath congregation had 'precipitated the bitterest religious conflict for a generation,'[29] and resolved to encourage immigrant Jewry to pursue an independent path. The issue turned on the question of Shechita with claims and counter-claims as to the integrity of kashrut in the respective communities. Lack of finance eventually forced the separatists to recognise the authority of the main Board of Shechita in 1905, and Machzikei Hadath became a constituent part of Samuel Montagu's Federation as part of the settlement.

Despite his efforts, Orthodox discontent with 'Adlerism' continued unabated. In 1910, some thirty rabbis thought to be 'truly representative of the sunken mass of pious immigrants, and not tainted by imitations of Anglican clergy, gathered in Leeds'.[30] However the opportunity to devise an acceptable programme for English Orthodoxy was lost as the conference almost inevitably degenerated into an attack on anything which did not resemble the standard of piety in Eastern Europe from which they came.

The conference appears to have focussed on Halakhic details, but also attacked modern methods of Hebrew education, admonished married women who did not wear the wig, and urged Jews to stay away from theatres and dance halls. The JC, having supported the conference, was clearly disappointed, and complained in strong language of narrow-mindedness and ridiculous proposals. The need to integrate the immigrant community into the communal system was clearly urgent, but remained for Rabbi Adler's successor.

By the end of his Rabbinate, London contained the largest concentration of East European Jews for any city other than New York and Chicago.[31] He expressed concern for 'our brethren who toil in East London', but was adjudged by some to be a tool of the sweatshop employers. His opposition to this practise was deemed to have been half-hearted, whilst others blamed him for failing adequately to respond to an appeal for support from Jewish strikers in Leeds.[32]

Nevertheless, Chief Rabbi Adler attached importance to caring for the poor and infirm. He organised visitations in which practical counselling was to be given, and encouragement towards self-help and training. Such contacts would also attempt to promote loyal allegiance to the faith, and counter any socialist or revolutionary tendencies. He identified Judaism with social reformism, and regularly attacked those who charged excessive rents, but whatever might have been his personal sympathy, he was seen by working-class Jews, as in other areas of discord, as an arch representative of established and over centralised authority.

In an address to the Bayswater congregation in September 1909, following the death of Sir Benjamin Cohen (brother of Lionel Louis Cohen) and no doubt having in mind their example of service and leadership, Chief Rabbi Adler suggested that 'the languid and half-hearted support of the younger generation to the cause of Judaism, its synagogues and charities, constitutes an even greater menace to Anglo-Jewry than the projected Liberal schism'.[33] This unfortunate assessment of the comparative dangers clearly 'had implications and results beyond his contemplation'.

'Devoid of pomposity, he evinced an unfailing awareness of the solemnity of his office. His satisfaction with his role as a cultured English gentleman of eminent Frankfurt lineage was patent.'[34] Chief Rabbi Adler was linked by blood and sentiment to the Anglo-Jewish plutocracy, and was an effective spokesman and ambassador for the community. He believed that the English aversion to extremism and respect for established authority would suffice, but 'was called upon to pronounce on questions whose posing negated his whole outlook'. In the end, 'events outstripped him and his generation'.[35]

Israel Finestein sub-titled his essay on Hermann Adler as a 'Portrait of a Jewish Victorian Extraordinary'.[36] Clearly, he belonged in the nineteenth rather than the twentieth century. He was a child of his own generation, and perhaps even that of his father! His period in office was one of great transition, and at the end of his term, the Jewish world had changed out of all recognition. The widening rift within the communal leadership, the new immigrant communities, and the new preferences for Zionism and Liberalism, meant that the need to 'navigate the shoals of multiple controversy'[37] was greater than ever.

Notes

1. IF, *Anglo-Jewry in Changing Times, Studies in Diversity 1840–1914* (London and Portland, OR: Vallentine Mitchell, 1999), pp.240–2.
2. Rabbi Raymond Apple, 'Hermann Adler – Chief Rabbi' in A.D. Crown (ed.) *Noblesse Oblige: Essays in Honour of David Kessler OBE* (London and Portland, OR: Vallentine Mitchell, 1998) .
3. Ibid.
4. JC, 18 June 1897.
5. IF, *Anglo-Jewry in Changing Times*, p.227.
6. Ibid., p.229.
7. See above p.15 (Emancipation).
8. See IF, *Scenes & Personalities in Anglo-Jewry 1800-2000* (London and Portland, OR: Vallentine Mitchell, 2002) p. 276.
9. IF, *Jewish Society in Victorian England* (London and Portland, OR: Vallentine Mitchell, 1993), p.194.

10. Jeremiah 29:5–7.
11. Meir Persoff, *Faith against Reason* (London: Vallentine Mitchell, 2008), p.101.
12. IF, *Anglo-Jewry in Changing Times*, p.234.
13. Lawrence Rigal & Rosita Rosenberg, *Liberal Judaism: The First Hundred Years* (London:ULPS, 2004), p.7.
14. Matthew Lagrone, 'The "Inhibition" of Morris Joseph', *Jewish Historical Studies*, 2015, 47, pp.147–8.
15. Rigal & Rosenberg, *Liberal Judaism*, pp.22–3.
16. IF, *Anglo-Jewry in Changing Times*, p.248 n.11.
17. See IF, *Jewish Society in Victorian England*, Ch.12.
18. Rigal & Rosenberg, *Liberal Judaism*, p.22.
19. See post p. 153 (Secularity).
20. See p.153 (Secularity).
21. Rigal & Rosenberg, *Liberal Judaism*, pp.314–329.
22. See summary of Manifesto provided in Persoff, *Faith against Reason*, pp.143–5.
23. See Rigal & Rosenberg, *Liberal Judaism*, p.42.
24. Ibid., p.43. See also Geoffrey Alderman, *British Jewry since Emancipation* (University of Buckingham Press, 2014), p.202.
25. Meir Persoff, *Faith Against Reason. Religious Reform and the British Chief Rabbinate, 1840–1990* (London and Portland, OR: Vallentine Mitchell, 2008), pp.439–45.
26. Lloyd P. Gartner, *The Jewish Immigrant in England 1870–1914* (London and Portland, OR: Vallentine Mitchell, 2001, 3rd edn), p.115.
27. Geoffrey Alderman, *British Jewry since Emancipation* (Buckingham: University of Buckingham Press, 2014), p.147.
28. IF, *Jewish Society in Victorian England*, p.177.
29. Gartner, *The Jewish Immigrant in England*, p.209.
30. Ibid., p.218.
31. Ibid., p.17.
32. Ibid., p.115.
33. IF, *Studies and Profiles in Anglo-Jewish History*, p.142.
34. IF, *Anglo-Jewry in Changing Times*, p.218.
35. IF, *Jewish Society in Victorian England*, p.178.
36. See IF, *Anglo-Jewry in Changing Times: From Picciotto to Bermant* (London and Portland, OR: Vallentine Mitchell, 2008), Ch.8.
37. Ibid., p.220.

5

The God Within

Claude Montefiore's thesis was that the Jews were once a nation, but were now a Church, citing with approval Chief Rabbi Adler's statement that the great bond which unites the Jews was not race, but a common religion.

Israel Finestein[1]

It is doubtful whether the Liberals' revolt would have got off the ground in England but for two remarkable and highly placed individuals. Claude Montefiore provided the intellectual content, and Lily Montagu the spiritual content needed, both somewhat lacking in the earlier Reforms of 1842. Those reformers were mainly concerned with matters of convenience, rather than specific theological principles, and had in fact made several overtures at reconciliation with the US. Thus the leaders of the new Liberal Judaism did not see them as a base for further reform.

Claude Joseph Goldsmid Montefiore (1858–1938) was a great-nephew of Sir Moses on his father's side, and a grandson of one of the founders of University College, London on his mother's side. He gained a first class degree in Classics from Balliol College, Oxford where his tutor, Benjamin Jowett (the Master), a liberal Christian thinker, encouraged in him a critical approach to Jewish religious texts. This involved the idea 'that its own truths and treasures might be enriched from the truths and treasures that may be vouchsafed to other than Jewish teachers'.[2]

Some say his thinking was overly influenced by his study of Christianity. Ahad Ha'am, the great Hebrew writer, disapproved of Montefiore's 'infatuation' with Christianity, as quoted by Edward Kessler in his presentation to the JHSE on 15 January 1998.[3] He argued that in fact Montefiore devoted some energy to rejecting Christian criticism of the rabbis, as one who believed that Liberal Judaism was a historical religion with roots in the past.

Claude Montefiore himself chose not to become a rabbi and, being financially secure, devoted himself to scholarship and philanthropy. An effective lay preacher, he spread the 'principle of religious development and religious liberty'. He was by all accounts a gentle, prudent and self-effacing person, deeply concerned with questions of education, welfare and social policy, as well as theology.

The Hon. Lilian Helen (Lily) Montagu (1873–1963) was the daughter of Sir Samuel Montagu,[4] later Lord Swaythling, who was strictly Orthodox in his views. As a young person, Lily received private religious instruction from the Rev. Simeon Singer. It was in fact Claude's mother (Emma, daughter of Sir Isaac Lyon Goldsmid) who had funded the publication of Singer's Prayer Book, as acknowledged in the preface. Claude was also acknowledged there originally, having contributed some of the translation, but his name was removed from subsequent editions, and replaced by 'an accomplished scholar'!

In January 1899, barely 25 years of age, Lily went public with her concerns in an article which appeared in the prestigious *Jewish Quarterly Review*, founded in 1887 and co-edited by Claude Montefiore, who certainly sympathised with her views. The article was entitled 'The Spiritual Possibilities of Judaism Today', and in it she declared a need 'to rediscover our Judaism, and to reformulate our creed'. She wished 'to rally round her the discontented and the weary, to lift Judaism from its desolate position, and together absorb it into our lives. We who are conscious of our great needs must organise ourselves into an association to rediscover our Judaism.'

In the centenary publication of the Liberal Jewish Synagogue (LJS), Lawrence Rigal describes Lily as a 'thoughtful, serious young woman, who believed that prayer was important, and that those whose Judaism was confined to ritual observance were missing something very valuable'.[5] Israel Finestein referred to her 'ceaseless emphasis on the spiritual side of religion' and her 'unmitigated defiance of authority, puzzling an older generation, and enraging her many critics'.[6] Her biographer, Dr Ellen Umansky, referred to an early conviction that it was her destiny to minister to the Jewish community. Apparently Lily also had an unshakeable belief in life after death.

Lily devoted her life to extensive charitable and social work which gained her an OBE. She was concerned for the position of the low paid, and was active in the National Council for Women, and the National Association of Girls' Clubs. Her work with young Jewish people convinced her that they 'were not being inspired to become active and enthusiastic Jews'. Following her address to the inaugural conference of the Union of Jewish Women in 1902, Chief Rabbi Adler praised her devotion to the growing Jewish youth movement, and referred to her lofty spiritual aspirations, regardless of dissension in wider matters. She was among the first three Jewish women to be appointed a JP in 1920 (the others were Nettie Adler and Marion Phillips).[7]

In a biography of her father published in 1913, Lily summarised her disagreement with him on matters of doctrine, and made her position clear beyond doubt. 'Liberal Judaism owes its existence to a different authority – to the God within, as interpreted by the trained conscience.' She is thus a latter day St Joan whose voices spoke to her directly from God, her God, and 'drove her to re-establish the religion on the basis of truth dignity and beauty'.[8]

Any resemblance to established Judaism was thus a matter of intellect and conscience, and although this gives an impression of elitism, Lily's dedication to saving Jewish souls was clearly sincere. She could well have been the prototype for Major Barbara (of Salvation Army fame) brought to the stage by Bernard Shaw in 1905. Yet despite the 'unmitigated defiance' referred to above, one detects in Lily a residual attachment to some of the old ways.[9] In the above address, she emphasised the importance of family worship, and observance of the 'Friday night', and despite fundamental differences with her father, she was buried at her request next to her parents in the Edmonton Federation Synagogue.

Lily Montagu called upon the community to contemplate the future in the light of modern thought, but according to Israel Finestein, she claimed she did not want Judaism to be put in jeopardy. She may well have hoped that the JRU would act as a 'catalyst for change'[10] within established Judaism, but it could not and did not evolve other than as a force leading towards separation. The new Saturday afternoon services alone would not be sufficient to satisfy the reformers, and with the development of a distinct theology, and the rejection of ancient sources of authority and interpretation, schism was indeed inevitable.

Nevertheless, those leading members and ministers from within the United Synagogue whom she persuaded to join the JRU did not regard it as divisive at the time. But whatever they and Lily may have thought, 'the JRU was not to be merely a rather exotic and genteel dilution of US Judaism'[11] and 'for those with eyes to see it, a revolution was in the making'.[12] Meir Persoff describes what Lily and Claude started as a 'seemingly unstoppable bandwagon',[13] and one cannot help but be impressed at the numbers eventually involved.

Following the decision to set up an independent congregation in 1909, and having quickly achieved a sufficient number of seat-holders, premises were obtained in Hill Street, Marylebone. Formerly the Mount Zion Baptist Chapel, it seated over 400 and services began there in 1911. However, within a few years, it was clear that the premises would not be large enough. A site was obtained in St John's Wood, and the foundation stone of the new Liberal

Synagogue with seating for 1,400, was laid by Claude Montefiore on 18 January 1925.

Meanwhile there were efforts to expand elsewhere with new Liberal synagogues in north London, south London and Liverpool in the 1920s, and later in Brighton. In December 1934, some 230 people attended the first Liberal service in Birmingham, and by 1937, they were sufficiently strong to build their own architect-designed synagogue in Sheepcote Street. In 2009, as a result of redevelopment, they moved to an even finer new building, still flourishing.

Many of the German refugees who were able to escape were from a Reform background and found a natural home with the Liberal movement, with some 2,000 people attending Holy Day services at St John's Wood in the late 1930s. It is claimed that during these years Liberal Judaism 'captured the imagination of those within Anglo-Jewry who were searching for something modern in terms of religious experience'.[14] By 1952, there were sixteen Liberal Synagogues in London and the provinces. Today there are forty including the most recent Liberal communities established in Suffolk and York, and the title of the LJS centenary publication in 2002 (*Liberal Judaism: The First Hundred Years*) clearly indicates a movement planning for another hundred years.

There are regular meetings, such as the Shabbaton held on 16 November 2013 to mark the 50th anniversary of Lily's death, attended by her biographer, Dr Ellen Umansky. Celebration Days and Strategy Days, Sunday Seminars and biennial weekends all involve considerable effort, and point to an effective administration, binding together its members with each other and with their movement, creating for them a clear identity as Liberal Jews. Some 300 members attended their biennial conference in 2014.

The bi-monthly newsletter 'LJToday' reports on a multitude of activities, and the reaching out by the movement to new groups in areas not commonly associated with Jewish residence. The LJ publication catalogue is impressive as to the amount of material available to members, and the three-year Torah reading cycle is another experiment interesting for some. Following discussions with the Board of Deputies in 1922, the LJS voted to seek affiliation which was accepted, a clear recognition of its arrival as an independent force within the community, by the lay authority if not the religious.

The success of Liberal Judaism in England owes much to a third person of stature whose surname also began with an 'M'! Rabbi Israel Isidor Mattuck (1883–1954) was born in Lithuania, but had been taken to America as a child, and ordained rabbi in 1910 at the Hebrew Union College. In 1912, whilst serving a community in New Jersey, he agreed to be appointed Minister at Hill Street. It was a brave and difficult decision, knowing that he must help found a new congregation where Liberalism barely existed, and in a strange country with an obsession about communal unity, and where the title of Rabbi was reserved only to the Chief Rabbi. His arrival was greeted with hostility from both the religious and lay leadership.[15]

The Hebrew Union College was founded in 1875 by Rabbi Isaac Mayer Wise, the father of American Reform Judaism. He had come to America from Germany in 1846, and saw a substantial German-speaking community without leadership and at risk from conversion, seen by some Jews in Europe as a means of acquiring or retaining civic status. His theology was that originally advanced by the early European Reformers, for whom the Jews were not a separate nation or race, whereas a universal mission based on the morality at the heart of the Bible was acceptable, especially if presented in a contemporary garb and manner.

Rabbi Mattuck was imbued with the same ideas, which were very much on a par with the views of Claude Montefiore. Such reformers were not afraid that change would cast doubt on the divine origin of Judaism. On the contrary, they thought to protect the divine from the multiplicity of minutiae which have in their view clogged the system, and created the need for 'drifters' to be rescued. They believed that revelation was ongoing, and that the Jewish mission was to disseminate the religious and moral message of Judaism to the world. To that end, the Dispersion of the Jews was seen as a providential act of God, rather than as a misfortune.[16]

In his Inaugural Address given on 20 January 2012, Rabbi Mattuck acknowledged its link with the past but emphasised that Liberal Judaism meant complete freedom of thought and practice, and a focus on the spirit rather than the letter. His attitude to tradition was 'to affirm its value, but deny its authority'. What we cannot accept on present day evidence, we cannot accept on the dictum of tradition. Furthermore, in a theme which continued throughout his Ministry, and reiterated in a sermon towards the end, he declared that, 'Judaism cannot have a message for the world of today if it clings to obsolete beliefs and ideas'.[17]

Almost his first task was to prepare new prayer books for Sabbath services 'which bore little resemblance to traditional liturgy'.[18] In 1923 and 1926 he produced prayer books for all services with revisions in 1937. Their purpose, he said, was 'not to maintain tradition, but to maintain life'.[19] They were well received, and were used throughout the Liberal movement for some forty years.

Other prayer books followed until 1995 when the Siddur 'Lev Chadash' was introduced. Co-edited by Rabbi John Rayner (1924–2005) its name means 'New Heart' and refers to a prophecy of Ezekiel (36:26). Lawrence Rigal mentions five previous generations of prayer books, each introducing some radical reform to Jewish worship. He describes the process as one of 'constructive innovation'[20] as the movement repeatedly struggled with the content and language of the prayers. He believes that the overall result has been to attract back 'apathetic or lapsing Jews' and to deepen the religious experience of Liberal members.

Apart from his duties as Minister, Rabbi Mattuck agreed to be elected Chairman of the Executive Committee of the World Union of Progressive Judaism (WUPJ) founded in 1926 on the initiative of Lily Montagu, with Claude Montefiore as its first President. Rabbi Mattuck proved himself skilled at negotiating through the different shades of opinion and religious belief involved.[21] In addition he was a dynamic and original speaker, capable of inspiring attention. Hugely influential on Liberal Judaism throughout the world, he remained its principal rabbi in Britain until 1947, and Chair of the WUPJ Executive until his death.

His recent biographer Pam Fox refers to Rabbi Mattuck's concern for social reform, having 'declared his support for the working man soon after his arrival'.[22] Although he said he was not concerned with party politics, Rabbi Mattuck considered himself free to explore political issues from a religious viewpoint in his sermons, although Claude Montefiore did not agree.

Rabbi Mattuck was vociferous in his condemnation of anti-Semitism in the 1930s, and extremely concerned at the oppression and potential destruction of German Jewry.[23] He was proactive in his help for refugees, when others were ambivalent, and 'appealed publicly for refugees to be received with friendship and hospitality'.[24] He set an example by helping a number of prominent people to come to England, by sponsoring children, and by taking a child from the Kindertransport into his own home.

He shared the early reformers' antipathy to Zionism which they believed to be incompatible with the universal message of the Jews. And in a sermon given on 9 June 1917 entitled 'The Theory of Zionism', Rabbi Mattuck asserted that 'religion was greater than nationality' which 'apart from its intrinsic error, holds no promise for the future of the Jews'.[25] He considered Zionism as a threat to the religious content of Jewish life. He accepted that persecuted Jews needed a place of refuge, but 'deeply regretted that the British Mandate for Palestine (its 'guardian angel') had proved unworkable'.[26] He never publicly renounced his opposition to the Jewish State.

In the aftermath of the Balfour Declaration (2 November 1917) Claude Montefiore wrote a pamphlet entitled 'The Danger of Zionism'. It is hardly surprising in the circumstances that the Liberal Synagogue became a 'religious refuge for the anti-Zionists in the inter-war years'.[27] Its policy of neutrality towards Zionism, proclaimed by the JRU Council in 1930 led to a negative or at best a half-hearted and conditional support for the Jewish State by some of its adherents. However the tide was turning among others and a major shift in policy by the American Reform movement in 1937 'endorsed both political and cultural Zionism, and affirmed the obligation of all Jewry to assist in developing Palestine as a Jewish homeland'.[28]

The appointment of Maurice Perlzweig in 1924 as associate minister appears to have been somewhat eccentric in that he was a confirmed Zionist, which was bound to create tension. Recognising the problem, Claude Montefiore, himself opposed to Zionism, helped Perlzweig produce a pamphlet indicating that it was possible to be both a Liberal Jew and a Zionist. The document appeared in 1935 as an explanation of and perhaps justification for its policy of neutrality. Perlzweig left the Liberal ministry in 1938 to serve the North Western Reform Synagogue at Alyth Gardens, Golders Green, London.[29]

In 1947, in an address to the Cambridge University Jewish Society, Lily Montagu gave frank expression to her own distaste for the Zionist movement, and was met with vociferous hostility. The creation of a Jewish State hung in the balance at that moment, but she appeared immune to its significance. However, she and Claude Montefiore would doubtless be astonished to learn that if they now wished to visit the headquarters of the World Union of Progressive Judaism today, they would have to go to Jerusalem!

Rigal suggests that 'a corner was turned'[30] in 1951 when the Brighton Liberal congregation wished to insert a prayer for Israel in its services. Whilst declining to grant an official endorsement, the Union of Liberal and Progressive Synagogues (ULPS) agreed that each congregation should be autonomous in this regard. However, Rosita Rosenberg, Rigal's co-author of the centenary publication described the road to the affirmation of commitment to the State of Israel in 1992 as 'long and arduous, and the clash of opinion still reverberates'.[31]

Despite what are now active Liberal and Reform Zionist youth groups, there are perhaps still some in Progressive Judaism for whom the State of Israel remains a question mark, an elephant in the room, inconsistent with a dogged determination not to be held a nation, and not to be held responsible for any of its perceived shortcomings. In the same vein, there are some who feel the need to downplay anti-Semitism since it too implies that Judaism is or might be something other than merely a religion.

However, on a different issue, there is nothing ambivalent about the attitude of Liberal Judaism towards female equality. Claude Montefiore was certainly ahead of his time in acknowledging the need for the emancipation of Jewish women, and Liberal Judaism stands out as a beacon of light in this important area. The elevation of Sara and the other biblical Matriarchs to an equal status with the Patriarchs in the latest Liberal liturgy is highly indicative.

Lily Montagu herself set an example as a lay minister from an early age. She gave her first sermon at an adult service in 1918, prompted by Rabbi Mattuck, and was formally inducted in 1944. In 1903, she had described the segregation of women at services as an 'outmoded oriental custom' which has now been swept away, as Liberal men and women sit and recite prayers together. Women can actively participate in Liberal services if they wish, and indeed can lead them, without the inhibition which has dogged the Orthodox world.[32]

Recognising the importance of Liberal women in social and charitable as well as religious activities, Lily formed the Federation of Women's Societies in 1946, and it was 'for over four decades at the very centre of Liberal Jewish life'.[33] Liberal women were free to put themselves forward for leadership roles, including that of the Liberal Rabbinate. The ordination of women was agreed in principle in 1954, but it was not until 1967 that the Leo Baeck College agreed to accept women for rabbinic training for fear of there being insufficient rabbinic placement after ordination.

Rabbi (later Baroness) Julia Neuberger was not the first to be ordained (in 1977) but was the first woman to be appointed with sole rabbinic charge – at the South London Liberal Synagogue. The challenges facing young women in the rabbinate are immense, with the need to obtain the respect of the male members of their congregations, and that of other (male) rabbis in their locality. Rosita Rosenberg refers to a collection of essays[34] by women rabbis published in 1994 referring to their early struggles to gain recognition and respect, and the perceived need to be like their male colleagues.

Aware of these problems, the vocation of women rabbis is much tested and they undoubtedly serve their communities with great dedication. At the centenary of Liberal Judaism in 2002, some thirty women had been ordained, occupying positions of great responsibility with large congregations such as St John's Wood and Birmingham, and throughout the movement.

The unequivocal Liberal stand on equality of the sexes is reflected in their desire for equilineal descent. In the traditional world, Jewish status is determined by being born of a Jewish mother, whether the father is Jewish or not. There are those who find this unsatisfactory and unfair regardless of gender equality, and the Liberal view is to welcome children of a Jewish father where the mother is not Jewish.

However there is a proviso that the child has a Jewish upbringing and education within the context of the synagogue and the festivals. Such an approach they feel enables difficult cases to be looked at sympathetically, and demonstrates an inclusive attitude to Jewish identity for those with a strong sense of attachment to the Jewish people. Although there is precedent for Jewish descent through the father rather than the mother in ancient times, that is not how personal status is defined today outside the Liberal world, and is therefore communally divisive.

In January 1947, toward the end of his ministry, Rabbi Mattuck was requested by Louis Gluckstein, President of the LJS, to respond to a ruling by the Beth Din that the BOD could not certify Liberal synagogues for the appointment of marriage secretaries. Only intolerance, he said, could explain the refusal of the Beth Din to accept the Liberal Synagogue as a 'congregation of Jews', as required by Statute.[35] He later went on to argue that the Liberal marriage ceremony complied with the spiritual and moral principles of Judaism. However, references to the Torah and the binding authority of divine law, as against the undeserved stigma of adultery, served only to highlight the fundamental and unbridgeable division between Liberal Judaism and Orthodoxy.

Rabbi Leslie Edgar succeeded Rabbi Mattuck (his father-in-law) at the LJS but was obliged to retire due to ill health in 1962. He was succeeded by Rabbi Rayner who inaugurated a more positive phase in English Liberal Judaism, which had become 'out of step with the less universalistic direction taken by Progressive Judaism elsewhere'.[36] Rabbi Rayner recognised that it was no longer a 'rescue operation', based on faith alone. Many Liberal Jews by then had a composite identity which led to the reintroduction of some traditional and historical elements, although the basic theology remained unchanged.[37]

Liberal Judaism has thus continued to evolve, and stresses the importance of broader issues such as 'righteousness in action'. It emphasises justice above technicalities and seeks to mitigate what they see as the harsh rules of Jewish divorce or illegitimacy. It highlights the biblical obligations of employers towards their staff, and the responsibility of Jewish people to work towards a better world on the principle of *Tikkun Olam*. This ancient principle began in Talmudic days as referring to those obligations which were for the public good, but has metamorphosed over the centuries through a wide variety of interpretations.

For many, the idea of 'repairing the world' which is its literal translation, implies the need for social action, care of the disadvantaged, acts of charity and kindness, and the pursuit of social justice. For others, there is a clear link with present environmental problems. Yet others see observance of the *mitzvoth*, both ritual and ethical, as the proper way to perfect the world, whilst the Kabbalists of the sixteenth century saw it as the way to reunite with God, and overcome evil. It was noticeable that the new Chief Rabbi Mirvis, in his inaugural address in 2013, reminded the community that the obligation of *Tikkun Olam* (however interpreted) applied to all Jews, Orthodox as well as Reform.

When Lily Montagu referred to the God within, she was like all reformers appealing to higher authority, and by doing so, dismissed at a stroke much of the unwanted and unobserved Oral Law. Linked to conscience and to man's innate knowledge of right and wrong, and the divine spark in all of us, she replaces the Law with personal choice and personal obligation, freed from the shackles of the past. The object was not simply to enable Jews to please themselves, but to help reinvigorate their individual belief in Judaism through personal autonomy.

Claude Montefiore with his high intellect saw as inescapable the need to cut out what he thought to be the dead wood, which was for him the only remedy. However different they were from the prophets of old, like them, they warned of the dangers facing the Jewish people, and the apparent inability of Orthodoxy to stem the tide of assimilation and defection. The problems they sought to resolve were real indeed, and the wish to evaluate and judge the legacy of the past 'in the court of personal conscience' was one which readily took root in Anglo-Jewry.

Liberal Judaism continues to grow and together with Reform Judaism now claims to represent a third of affiliated Jews. It has been in the forefront of the campaign for the introduction of equal marriage legislation, and has supported movements for the 'living wage' and the environment. It wishes to play its full part in the community, and sees itself as offering a 'Third Way' alternative to Orthodoxy and secularity.[38]

Both Lily Montagu and Claude Montefiore belonged to an extremely well-entrenched Jewish aristocracy, a small privileged group whose personal influence would be surpassed within a generation. However their own legacy lives on, and their actions created hope for Jews who felt that they would otherwise have nowhere to go. Worldwide, the Progressive movement now represents some 1.8 million members of some 1,200 non-Orthodox congregations.

Were Lily and Claude 'dreamers of dreams',[39] false prophets, to be avoided? Some will certainly say so, but others will point to the rise and rise of Progressive Judaism as indicating an important constituency of Jews for whom Orthodoxy holds no attraction. However, its quest for recognition and a seat at the communal table was to become a new and major source of division.

Notes

1. IF, *Scenes and Personalities in Anglo-Jewry 1800–2000* (London and Portland, OR: Vallentine Mitchell, 2002), p.289.
2. Meir Persoff, *Faith Against Reason. Religious Reform and the British Chief Rabbinate, 1840–1990* (London and Portland, OR: Vallentine Mitchell, 2008), p.117.
3. Edward Kessler, 'Claude Montefiore, Defender of Rabbinic Judaism', *Jewish Historical Studies*, 2000, Vol.35, pp.231–8.
4. See above p. 30 (Agree to Differ).
5. Lawrence Rigal and Rosita Rosenberg, *Liberal Judaism: The First Hundred Years* (London: Union of Liberal and Progressive Synagogues, 2004), p.13.
6. IF, *Studies and Profiles in Anglo-Jewish History: From Picciotto to Bermant* (London and Portland, OR: Vallentine Mitchell, 2008), p.176.
7. Ann Ebner, 'The First Jewish Magistrates', *Jewish Historical Studies*, Vol.38, p.71.
8. Rigal and Rosenberg, *Liberal Judaism*, p.16.
9. See Geoffrey Alderman, *British Jewry since Emancipation* (Buckingham: University of Buckingham Press, 2014), p.206.
10. Ibid., p.202.
11. Ibid., p.205.
12. Ibid., p.206.
13. Persoff, *Faith Against Reason*, p.224.
14. Alderman, *British Jewry since Emancipation*, p.356.
15. See ibid., p.206 n.234.
16. Pam Fox, *Israel Isidor Mattuck* (London and Portland, OR: Vallentine Mitchell, 2014), pp.325–6.
17. 5 October 1945, quoted by Rabbi Danny Rich, *Israel Mattuck: The Inspirational Voice of Liberal* Judaism (London: Liberal Judaism, 2014), pp.11/12.
18. Fox, *Israel Isidor Mattuck*, p.111.
19. Ibid., p.150.
20. Rigal and Rosenberg, *Liberal Judaism*, p.125.
21. Fox, *Israel Isidor Mattuck*, p.176.
22. Ibid., p.159.
23. Ibid., pp.206/7, Sermon 30 October 1938.
24. Ibid., p.210.
25. Rabbi Danny Rich, *Israel Mattuck: The Inspirational Voice of Liberal* Judaism (London: Liberal Judaism, 2014), pp.46/7.
26. Ibid., p.259.
27. Alderman, *British Jewry since Emancipation*, p.356.
28. Fox, *Israel Isidor Mattuck*, p.213.
29. Rigal and Rosenberg, *Liberal Judaism*, p.79.
30. Ibid., p.82.
31. Ibid., p.227.
32. See post Chap. 12 (Women of Worth).
33. Rigal and Rosenberg, *Liberal Judaism*, p.240.

34.　Ibid., p.245.

35.　Persoff, *Faith and Reason*, pp.256–8.

36.　Ellen Umansky, 'Review of Israel Isidor Mattuck, Architect of Liberal Judaism', *Jewish Historical Studies*, 2015, Vol.47, p.247.

37.　Fox, *Israel Isidor Mattuck*, p.341.

38.　Lucian Hudson, former Chair of Liberal Judaism, JC, 16 May 2014, p.29.

39.　Deut. 13:2.

6

Bleak Landscape

The inaugural sermon of the new Chief Rabbi Hertz fell barely short of a devastating critique of the utter inadequacy of the Jewish educational system for the mass of children in the community, both in content and in funding.

Israel Finestein[1]

On 19 April 2004, Israel Finestein gave the Cecil Roth Memorial Lecture from which the above quotation is taken. His lecture was entitled 'A Critical Evaluation of Anglo-Jewish Priorities 1860–1930', and he described the period following emancipation as one of 'Educational Minimalism'. He summed up the lack of Jewish education as having created a 'bleak landscape', which fully justified the 'grim analysis' of Chief Rabbi Hertz in his 1913 inaugural address.

He defined the bleak landscape as containing scholars mainly from abroad left without patrons; Jewish scholarship and educational facilities bereft of sufficient funds, notwithstanding social wealth and high living; and inadequate communal interest in and neglect of higher Jewish study and literary effort.

In his 1962 paper entitled 'Educational Abuses and Reforms in Hanoverian England' Cecil Roth criticised the state of Jewish education, as indicating a pattern of inadequacies in substance, system and form. This abysmal situation had been repeatedly referred to as 'evil' by *The Voice of Jacob* since as far back as 1844, blaming incompetent management and diffused responsibility. It advocated as a matter of urgency the need for a Board of Education with sufficient power and reliable judgment. The inadequacy of textbooks, both in suitability, content and numbers available, 'represented a kind of standing challenge and regular communal rebuke'.[2]

It followed that there was an urgent need for more adequately trained preachers in sufficient numbers and quality who would also be able to help with teaching and writing text books. *The Voice of Jacob* promoted the idea of inviting suitable preachers from Germany to consider a career in England, and suitable British candidates to spend time at European seminaries. These proposals 'remained a dead letter'.[3]

Meanwhile, in 1850, a newly established Jewish Literary Society attracted a number of senior academics and preachers keen to publish and promote Jewish literature, and the translation of rare and valuable works. However it failed to acquire sponsors, and 'the society took no root'.[4] Those who might have supported it were mainly involved in the campaign for emancipation, which was by then reaching a critical phase. However, many emancipationists would have given little if any priority to Jewish cultural activity, which they may well have viewed with suspicion in any event.

Morris Raphall (1798–1868), Minister of the Birmingham Hebrew Congregation for eight years, and former Secretary to the Chief Rabbi, was one of the most influential Jewish preachers in the land, and frequently visited other communities. His departure for New York in 1849 can be taken as clear confirmation of the general indifference with which Anglo-Jewry treated its historical, cultural and literary matters.

This apparent complacency was described as 'astounding' and 'shameful' by Abraham Benisch (1811–78) and such criticism remained a regular theme of the JC of which he was Editor from 1864 until 1869 and later from 1875 until his death. His devotion to Hebrew studies and Judaism was much respected, and he was an enthusiastic supporter of the above Literary Society.

In 1856 Marcus Bresslau, a Hamburg-born author, accused the emancipationists of not wanting things too Jewish. He also blamed the rapid advance in commerce and the spread of wealth for diverting attention from Hebrew learning, which had come to be regarded as superfluous, and out of date.[5] In 1860, he sought to revive Raphall's *Hebrew Review and Magazine of Rabbinical Literature* which had failed through lack of support, and began by criticising the low educational standards of Anglo-Jewry, seemingly devoted exclusively to the accumulation of wealth.[6] He was not alone in such public expressions: the realities were common knowledge. Needless to say, his *Magazine* did not survive.

When he took office in 1845, Chief Rabbi Nathan Adler had proposed a scheme for a Jewish college for training Ministers, but there was 'relentless opposition' to the introduction of rabbinic study into the curriculum. The communal leadership failed to appreciate the nature and extent of the problem, or acknowledge their responsibility. Some regarded his scheme as altogether unnecessary, and at the opening of Jews' College in 1855, Rabbi Adler stated that he had often despaired of its attainment.[7]

His school when eventually opened was to be a place from which boys might graduate for ministerial training. Even so, it was greeted with indifference if not outright opposition, combined with a fear of segregation when the prevailing mood was for integration into English society. Benisch was highly critical of those Jewish parents who displayed no preference for

Adler's school, and sent their children 'to grow up under non-Jewish school influences, nursed in an alien atmosphere … still Jews, in spirit few, in practice still less'.[8] The school itself 'languished in the shadow of limited communal encouragement'[9] until it closed in 1879 to Adler's great disappointment.

On 12 August 1881 the JC complained that 'Hebrew instruction among Jewish children in England was little more than a waste of time, as at present conducted'. Inevitably, the *cheder* education of hundreds of immigrant children in shabby, potentially unhealthy conditions was regarded with aversion by native Jewry, who saw the coming generation unable to participate in the process of Anglicisation. The Talmud Torah system, with much longer hours, fared little better, and although it 'slowly earned the approbation of the community, it remained in perpetual financial distress'.[10]

A promising initiative was that of Barnett Abrahams (1831–63), the young principal of Jews College who was behind the Jewish Association for the Diffusion of Religious Knowledge. The inaugural meeting on 6 June 1860 was well attended, and he focussed his opening declaration on the 'hugely necessary' requirement for Jewish Bibles, prayer-books and works of religious instruction. He also expressed the hope that the Association would tend to make the rising generation not ashamed but rather proud of their belief. 'His early death was a damaging blow to those closely concerned to reverse the trends in Jewish knowledge.'[11] The Association, 'ever fragile and virtually impecunious',[12] was in due course succeeded by the Jewish Religious Education Board (JREB).

The wealthier families identifying with emancipation distanced themselves in the main from efforts to raise Jewish intellectual and cultural levels. This largely unreflecting approach was widely accepted, even fashionable, and it is significant that any awakening of the Anglo-Jewish lay leadership to Jewish cultural needs came only after the completion of the struggle for emancipation. Meanwhile the pressure for improvement in learning was thus left to individuals, who generally differed from the emancipationists in origins, social and economic status, and the extent of their influence.

The priorities of the period and the deepest sentiments of those who remembered the emancipation were clearly in evidence, in what Israel Finestein suggests could well have been thought 'the pulpit code' of the Victorian ministry.[13] It was summarised in an address by Chief Rabbi Hermann Adler on Succoth 1902: The Minister should be outspoken against 'irreligion'. Judaism must be shown to be in harmony with the best aspirations of the age. The Minister must be fully abreast with the culture of his day. Cultivation of the character of his congregants was important.

Congregants were not to be troubled by 'instruction of the intellect which was not the only or indeed the main aim of preaching', whose highest object was a moral one.

The leadership of the US was not greatly if at all interested in the continental movement for Jewish enlightenment, and foreign categories of new scholarship (of which there was no shortage of material) would have seemed to them unalterably alien. In 1897 Henry Lucas, a Vice President of the US, defined the aim of the new JREB as primarily to get young Jews off the streets, and counter the efforts of conversionists. To this end, instruction at an elementary level was considered sufficient and with such a minimalist attitude it is not surprising that Jewish educational finances inevitably did not prosper, despite repeated calls and dire warnings.

The middle and upper class Jews did not see themselves as in need of higher learning, and they were not alone in this. Matthew Arnold (1822–88), the widely noted advocate of educational reform, referred to the English middle class as 'philistines', and the aristocracy as 'barbarians'.[14] His brother-in-law William Edward Forster (MP for Bradford from 1861) when introducing the 1870 Education Bill, referred to the national necessity to have a literate and numerate population if Britain was to face commercial competition and retain its position as 'the workshop of the world'.

This was very much the view in Europe, and especially in Germany where educational reform was considered desirable for the social and economic benefit of the State. Hence Leopold Zunz, a pivotal figure in the German Haskalah movement, was able to argue that the Jews should prove their worth through their literature and higher intellectual achievement, which would secure them a greater degree of recognition. He believed that 'the neglect of Jewish scholarship goes hand in hand with civil discrimination'.[15]

Almost the reverse was the view of the Anglo-Jewish community, where Jewish worth was measured in terms of loyalty, philanthropy, sustaining the Jewish poor without dependence on the rates, and an overall sense of duty. The need for Jewish scholarship did not arise in this context, and might even have seemed counter-productive. In England, the need was perceived to disabuse the public of any distorted notions as to Jewish character or civic unworthiness. Philanthropy played a dominant role in this, as well as being an essential aspect of Jewish ethics. However, as late as 1953, the scientist Dr Redcliffe Salaman, giving the Lucien Wolf Memorial Lecture, declared that Anglo-Jewry could not survive indefinitely on its philanthropic achievements alone.[16]

A new Jewish Literary Club was inaugurated in 1869 to promote the study of the Hebrew language, Hebrew Literature, and the translation for publication of classic Hebrew works. Although the Society had the support of Sir David Salomons, the noted emancipationist, as Vice President, and also many Jews of considerable intellectual standing, its creation was opposed. Lionel Louis Cohen was not persuaded of its utility. He attended the inaugural meeting and declared that the stated views of the Society were 'not a priority in the context of Anglo-Jewish life and needs', and that 'its contemplated publications represented a form of unhelpful intellectual luxury'.[17]

He was perhaps rightly more concerned with basic reading skills and an understanding of the liturgy. If so, little was achieved, and in 1901, Solomon Schechter, Professor of Hebrew at University College, London, wrote before his departure for America: 'Ignorance is on the increase among our better situated classes. Very few are capable of reading their prayers, and less are able to understand what they read … the very existence of Judaism depends on the revival of Hebrew learning.'[18]

On the occasion of the Anglo-Jewish Historical Exhibition in 1887, the eminent German-Jewish historian Heinrich Graetz (1817–91) called for the creation of a Jewish Academy whose object would be to provide proof of Jewish continuity. However his hopes did not reflect the priorities of the Anglo-Jewish leadership, or the aspirations of important sections of the community.[19]

Chief Rabbi Hermann Adler drew attention to the effect of immigration on Jewish education since 1880 in a sermon at St John's Wood on 1 December 1894. It meant, he said, that existing Jewish schools were now overfull, classes were too large, and teachers were badly paid. There was no money with which to rent additional premises, and many children went without any organised religious instruction at all. Nevertheless he surprisingly observed that 'there was no absolute need for the erection of new Jewish schools',[20] basing his negative approach on the idea that the 1870 Education Act had been intended to provide ample provision for primary education.

Rabbi Dr Hermann Gollancz (1852–1930) was the first Jew to achieve a doctorate in literature from London University, and the first rabbi to be knighted, in 1923. Speaking at Jews College in October 1915 he referred to 'the proverbial ignorance of the present generation of English Jews, and the amazing want of sympathy with Jewish learning'.[21] He regretted the failure to endow the College adequately, and the seeming failure of Chief Rabbi Adler to secure any substantial endowments despite his connections and the wealth of his friends.

In 1919, Chief Rabbi Hertz referred to 'notorious neglect' and in July 1923, he complained that Jews College 'was still starved and beggared'. At his own Jubilee Dinner in 1938, he felt obliged to complain of the 'short-sighted and disastrous starving of higher theological teaching'. He made it clear that in his view rabbinic scholarship was not a luxury or a dispensable extra. Yet, financial provision by the United Synagogue 'differed little from uncomprehending meanness'.[22]

A glimmer of hope appeared in 1909 with the arrival in Britain of Rabbi Dr Victor Schonfeld (1880–1930), a Hungarian-born charismatic rabbi who wished to stem what he believed to be the steady erosion of whole sections of the community. He promoted the idea of a Jewish secondary school movement which he founded in 1929, but the movement faced severe financial difficulties following his early death. In due course his son Solomon Schonfeld (1910–84) took over as Principal, and successfully expanded the movement with the creation of the Hasmonean School in 1944 and others after the Second World War, aiming for a strong secular as well as religious education.

In 1927, in his 'Affirmations of Judaism', Rabbi Hertz strongly criticised the contempt in which Jewish learning was held in some circles, and in a 'brusque assessment born of painful disappointment' he castigated those 'who for some reason hate Jewish scholarship as something foreign'. The following year, Selig Brodestky and Herbert Loewe collaborated on *The Intellectual Level of Anglo-Jewish Life*, exposing the disengagement on the part of wide sections of the lay leadership from any personal interest in Jewish study. The sense of estrangement was ongoing and became the subject of Israel Finestein's address to the Institute of Jewish Affairs on 12 October 1983.

The absence of Jewish knowledge was not viewed by the lay leadership in the slightest degree as a handicap or an embarrassment, and in February 1946, the Editor of *Jewish Academy*[23] (the IUJF publication) commented that 'the qualification for leading positions in Anglo-Jewry is seen to be success in the material sphere. The success of Jewish organizations is measured by the smooth running of their machinery, rather than by the values which such organizations ostensibly represent.'[24]

Israel Finestein referred to that statement as perhaps having 'a touch of the intemperance of youth' and readily admitted that its strictures have become far less applicable since written. The importance of successful business practice and the role of those with such abilities are not in question today, but until the second half of the twentieth century the rupture between the leadership and Jewish educational endeavour had a depressing effect on the survival of the community.

The low educational attainment of large numbers of Jewish children evacuated in 1939 on the eve of the Second World War is highlighted in the report of Jewish Inspectors at that time. In 1943, the historian Cecil Roth, then President of the JHSE, spoke of 'abandonment' and 'decline' in reference to lack of funding or support for Jewish education and Jewish higher studies. The following year, Nathan Morris, Director of the Committee for Jewish Religious Education, bluntly described the consequences: 'the majority of the present generation of adults are the victims of a system from which they carried away so little as to make hardly any difference to their religious, cultural or social life'.[25]

It was perhaps the shock of these findings, and the need to meet the circumstances of war-time, which led to the creation of the Joint Emergency Committee in which the largest Jewish educational bodies were united. An obsolete and old-fashioned structure was replaced, and the community finally became education conscious. The first ever nationwide Jewish education conference, held in London in November 1945, 'deepened the mood of radical change, and in the wake of the conference, the United Synagogue instituted a levy on seat rentals for the advancement of Jewish education'.[26]

On 31 January 1946, the JC editorialised on the need for 'the unfettered vent of all shades of opinion', and in April of that year, the first meeting of the new London Board of Jewish Religious Education (LBJRE) was held. Honorary Officers were elected, together with an Executive Council to which Israel Finestein (representing IUJF) was elected to serve on its adult education committee.

One important initiative which came to fruition in the post-war period was the formation of the Jewish Youth Study Group movement in 1942. Unlikely to appeal widely, it nevertheless ensured that in the larger communities there would be a core of young people anxious to learn of their uniqueness as Jews, and thus likely to ensure in later life that the knowledge would be passed on. Its members will recall with affection the leading role of Harold Levy, then national inspector of the Central Council for Jewish Religious Education. He was also in 1950 the Editor of *Hebrew for All*, a publication which inspired a proliferation of classes and courses in Hebrew language and literature at many levels.

Other significant developments contributed to what amounted to a mini renaissance. Hebrew seminars run by Levi Gertner, Zionist Federation Director of Education, became almost fashionable among Jewish students in the 1950s and 1960s with the attraction of such outstanding speakers as the philosopher Natan Rotenstreich and the novelist Moshe Shamir. In 1953, Rabbi Dr Alexander Altman, Communal Rabbi of Manchester, founded the Institute of Jewish Studies, later transferred to UCL. 'In widening circles of intellectual opinion there was a heightened sense both of the need for, and the inherent value of, deeper Jewish education.'[27]

In November 1952, the first Jewish Book Week was organised by the Jewish Book Council under the Chairmanship of Dr George Webber, a Barrister and Reader in Law at UCL, who recognised a genuine appetite, previously unmet, for access to Jewish books. This unique annual event attracted widespread support, and continues to do so. The late 1970s saw the beginning of the pioneering educational work of the Spiro Institute, and the Orthodox-based Yakar study centre. More recently there is the outstanding success of Limmud with its 'open lectern' attracting hundreds of speakers and thousands of participants. More recently still a new community centre known as JW3 was established at Hampstead, London with a full range of social and cultural events.

However the negative, even snobbish, attitude to Jewish day schools among some parents continued well into the post-war period, but was gradually reversed as the need became increasingly apparent, and their scholastic success rate made them attractive. Furthermore the Education Act of 1944, long prompted by leaders of all denominations, offered the Jewish community the prospect of significant tangible support for an extension of day school education. On the other hand, it also offered opportunities in the secular world not previously available except to a highly gifted few, with the prospect of freedom from tribe and religion for those who wished it.

An early experiment in the creation of a Jewish public school comparable with those of other faiths was initiated by the hugely talented and charismatic Rabbi Kopul Rosen (1913–62) who founded Carmel College in rural Berkshire in 1948. He was supported by many parents who saw the advantage of a sound secondary education combined with the ethos of an orthodox Jewish environment away from home, but inflation of costs and therefore fees brought the school sadly to a close in 1997. His own early demise was a tragic loss for the community.

It gradually came to be accepted in the words of Kopul Rosen that an educated authentic Jew is better equipped to compete in the outside world with confidence and dignity.[28] Thus 'by stages, in the twentieth century, the Jewish community, sometimes slowly, and at times amid institutional controversy, moved towards an era when the centrality of Jewish education in the communal programme became settled policy'.[29] The Institute of Jewish Policy Research (JPR) now reports that some 63 per cent of Jewish children are attending Jewish schools (an all-time high), and that the number of such schools has also doubled, since the 1992 Worms report[30] gave added impetus to that end.

In the daily recital of our most important prayer, the *Shema*, we are commanded before all else to educate our children. Admittedly the text refers to teaching them the Torah, but in order to do so, it is necessary for them to be able to read and comprehend quite difficult material, and from an early age. It is an idea unique to our people, and Jewish civilisation flourished and continues to flourish as a direct result of this obligation. 'No section of the human family has attached to study and knowledge the same importance as the Jews.'[31]

However the urge to teach our children, or have them taught, never disappeared completely, despite expressions of genuine alarm, and few Jews today would dispute the need for Jewish education for their children or indeed themselves. A plethora of religious and cultural institutions, seminars, schools and courses for all levels now exists, and the amount of Judaica published in Britain now hugely exceeds that of any earlier generation.

The growing awareness of the Holocaust, and the impact of Israel, especially after the 1967 war, all played their part. The bleak landscape finally blossomed, and the Anglo-Jewish community has achieved an unprecedented awakening, and a newfound confidence. However, when one considers the legacy of indifference over such a long period, one might well apply the statement of Kenneth Clark in relation to the survival of western civilisation: 'We got through by the skin of our teeth!'[32]

Notes

1. IF, *Studies and Profiles in Anglo-Jewish History: From Picciotto to Bermant* (London and Portland, OR: Vallentine Mitchell, 2008) p.24.
2. Ibid., p.3.
3. Ibid., p.4.
4. Ibid., p.6.
5. IF, *Anglo-Jewry in Changing Times, Studies in Diversity 1840–1914* (London and Portland, OR: Vallentine Mitchell, 1999), p.18.
6. Ibid., p.178.
7. IF, *Jewish Society in Victorian England* (London and Portland, OR: Vallentine Mitchell, 1993), p.245.
8. Ibid., p.51 n.69.
9. IF, *Studies and Profiles in Anglo-Jewish History*, p.9.
10. Lloyd P. Gartner, *The Jewish Immigrant in England 1870–1914* (London and Portland, OR: Vallentine Mitchell, 2001, 3rd edn), p.237.
11. IF, *Studies and Profiles in Anglo-Jewish History*, p.10.
12. Ibid., p.21.
13. IF, *Jewish Society in Victorian England*, p.334.
14. Matthew Arnold, *Culture and Anarchy* (Oxford World Classics, 1869), esp. chp. 3.
15. IF, *Studies and Profiles in Anglo-Jewish History*, p.13.
16. Ibid., p.18.
17. Ibid., p.76.
18. IF, *Scenes and Personalities in Anglo-Jewry 1800–2000* (London and Portland, OR: Vallentine Mitchell, 2002), p.98.

19. IF, *Studies and Profiles in Anglo-Jewish History*, p.24.
20. Ibid., p.21.
21. Ibid., p.22.
22. IF, *Anglo-Jewry in Changing Times*, p.235.
23. Possibly Israel Finestein himself!
24. IF, *Scenes and Personalities in Anglo-Jewry 1800–2000*, p.100.
25. IF, *Scenes and Personalities in Anglo-Jewry*, p.79.
26. Ibid., p.80.
27. Ibid., p.75.
28. Carmel College Magazine, mid 1954.
29. IF, *Scenes and Personalities in Anglo-Jewry 1800–2000*, p.79.
30. See post pp.94-5 (In Whose Name?).
31. IF, *Scenes and Personalities in Anglo-Jewry 1800–2000*, p.97.
32. Kenneth Clark, *Civilisation* (London: BBC and John Murray, 1969), p.17.

7

Holy War

The enthusiasm that attended the appointment of Dr Joseph Herman Hertz (1872 - 1946) as Chief Rabbi in 1913 was an exercise in hope against a dismal and worsening scene.

Israel Finestein[1]

The period of the Hertz Chief Rabbinate can be categorised in terms of warfare and confrontation, quite apart from two World Wars, the rise of Communism, Fascism and Zionism inevitably involved taking sides.

Torah Judaism itself was beset on both sides, and from within, by powerful forces. It needed a champion, and with uncanny foresight Dr Hertz had declared in his graduation address in 1894 that, 'We may be rejected by the very men we are serving, mocked and heartily abused', but he went on, 'Ours is a resolute band. We are fighting in a holy war.'[2] He remained combative on behalf of orthodoxy all his life. On his death the JC referred to him as a spiritual warrior.

Dr Hertz was born into the world of East European Jewry in Hungary, but in 1884 his family moved to New York where his early education and training took place. He obtained a BA degree from the City College at an incredibly early age, and enrolled in the Jewish Theological Seminary. He was its first graduate Rabbi, and combined his religious studies with a doctorate in philosophy which he was awarded by Columbia University in the same year, a considerable achievement.

The Seminary had been founded by Rabbi Sabato Morais, in order to defend orthodox practices against the threat to traditional Judaism from the American Reform movement, and the young Hertz was clearly inspired to follow his example. The Pittsburg Reform Programme of 1885[3] had been the final straw in convincing Morais that there was no longer any hope of compromise between orthodoxy and the views of those who wished to reconcile it with modern culture. However the pressure for reform was so strong in America that those who supported Morais were eventually outnumbered after his death, and the Seminary then ceased to be the strictly Orthodox stronghold it was at the outset.

Faced with the rejection of Orthodoxy by the majority of American Jewry, Solomon Schechter (1847–1915) believed that Jewish practice (Halakhah) had evolved over time, and could be modified by consensus. However, he was in no doubt that the Torah could not be abandoned, and after a distinguished academic career at Cambridge and London Universities, he succeeded Morais as President of the Seminary in 1902. He concluded that in order to keep Torah Judaism alive, compromise would be necessary, and became in effect the founder of American Conservative Judaism.

But the holy grail of saving orthodoxy, of somehow squaring the circle, was incompatible with a Divine Law which was 'imperative, unchangeable and eternal'. Hertz was as implacable as his teacher in the belief that the law given to Moses at Sinai was immutable. Thus in 1898, after four years at his first Ministry at Syracuse, New York State, he felt he had no choice but to resign, when its lay leadership determined to introduce mixed seating.

What greeted Dr Hertz on arrival in England, after a successful ministry in South Africa, was an attitude of lax observance, when most synagogue members attended rarely, and could barely read the prayers in Hebrew. Torah Judaism was hardly understood by the lay leadership. Assimilation and intermarriage were rife. Jewish scholarship was almost non-existent, and he was faced with a demoralised clergy, ill-paid and poorly regarded.

His knowledge of the English community was limited, but there was a need for someone who could bridge the considerable divide between the immigrants, and those of longer residence. As a notable orator in Yiddish as well as English, and a genuine Talmudic scholar, he was in many ways an ideal candidate, 'as near a perfect fit as could be imagined'.[4] Dr Hertz was not the only candidate, but was supported by Lord Rothschild, President the United Synagogue (US), and Albert Henry Jessel (1864–1917), nephew of Lionel Cohen and a prominent lawyer.[5]

However, the election process lasted for two years following the death of Rabbi Hermann Adler. It was effectively dominated by the US, yet by 1913, the new provincial communities had grown substantially in size, and were clamouring for a greater say in the affairs of the US, and indeed the BOD. With a large proportion of immigrants, they did not want a Chief Rabbi imposed upon them who was not to their liking.

Dr Hertz was inevitably on collision course with Reform and Liberal Judaism, and their repudiation of the Oral Law. Although there was a certain intellectual camaraderie with Claude Montefiore and other leading Liberals, such as Israel Abrahams (1858–1924), Reader in Rabbinics at Cambridge, he regarded their views as subversive, and pursued a vigorous and eloquent attempt throughout his Ministry to stem the tide. For example, he blocked the idea of a joint coronation prayer for George VI in 1937, despite joint participation, and effectively prevented them from access to the BBC at the time.

However 'the lay leadership of the US privately deplored the severity of his language', and he was asked on occasion to redraft some of his sermons in terms less offensive! 'Destructive criticism' of the Liberals, was more likely to be counterproductive to the traditional cause, they said, clearly seeking to maintain a 'broadchurch policy and ethos', and blur the boundaries with the progressives. The ongoing confrontation between Sir Robert Waley Cohen (1877-1952) and Dr Hertz was a depressing feature of his entire Rabbinate.

It cannot be explained simply as the friction generated by two strong and determined personalities, or as an aristocratic refusal to regard Dr Hertz as an equal. Waley Cohen, instrumental in the emergence of Shell Petroleum, was persuaded to become Treasurer of the US in 1913, partly because it needed an affective businessman at the helm, and partly due to family connection. In 1918 he was elected Vice President, and became the dominant personality in the lay leadership, although not elected President until 1942.

Yet this successful non-observant businessman, who might have been expected to remain aloof from religious matters, repeatedly interfered in areas for which the Chief Rabbi had sole responsibility, and on occasion without consultation. Waley Cohen's biographer and nephew, Robert Henriques, appears to suggest that he regarded Orthodox Judaism as 'an alliance of alien dogma, custom, and superstition, which had never before been any part of Judaism except in dark corners inside the ghettos of Eastern European'.[6]

Israel Finestein regarded Waley Cohen as 'impressed and moved by the antiquity of the Jewish tradition, and had a reverence for the wisdom and the heritage of his predecessors',[7] but this was a somewhat sentimental view of Judaism, devoid of observance. It seems by his actions that Waley Cohen wanted to move the US towards the Liberals, with whom he may well have had more in common.

His proposal to move Jews' College to Oxford or Cambridge may be seen in this light. He wanted future religious leaders trained in the atmosphere of one of the ancient universities, where 'the British and Jewish traditions contained elements peculiarly suited to each other'.[8] The plan was opposed by the Principal of Jews' College, and came to nought, but clearly represents a fundamental difference of opinion as to the nature and future of Judaism.

In the same spirit, as Chairman of the War Memorial Council launched in 1919, Waley Cohen wanted funds raised for Jewish education (as a tribute to the fallen) to be used for a dual purpose institution which would serve the needs of the progressives as well as those of Jews College. It was inevitable that Chief Rabbi Hertz would not allow his authority and his responsibility for Jews' College to be diluted in this way, and an attempt by Waley Cohen to muzzle the Chief Rabbi was dismissed by the JC as mean and unworthy.

Prior to the Chief Rabbi's highly successful pastoral world tour of 1920–21, Waley Cohen offensively accused Dr Hertz of wishing to make this arduous trip out of personal ambition! He frequently sought to challenge his status and undermine Chief Rabbi Hertz's authority, although it is said he did not allow others to do so! 'Time and again Waley Cohen adopted the role of Headmaster, guru and father-figure, consumed with self-importance. When in one of those moods Hertz found him insufferable.'[9]

In 1941, Waley Cohen called a meeting with a religious agenda to include Reform and Liberal representatives. The nomination as Chair of Lily Montagu, a founder of Liberal Judaism, gave a clear indication of his intentions. It was inevitably opposed by the Chief Rabbi and the Beth Din, and on this occasion also by the BOD. Chief Rabbi Hertz publicly vetoed the Committee as a serious danger in that Jewish education would be deprived of its Jewish and religious character.

Waley Cohen continued his efforts to muzzle the Chief Rabbi by, for example, initially withholding details of new and scattered communities where Dr Hertz wished to minister during the Second World War. Astonishingly, Waley Cohen refused him permission to give a Passover address to evacuated children, although this was over-ruled, and in 1942, Waley Cohen persuaded the Honorary Officers of the Hampstead Synagogue to destroy copies of the sermon which Dr Hertz had delivered there!

Israel Finestein agreed that Waley Cohen was 'irascible and self-willed' and it seems clear that he inherited the authoritarian tendencies of his uncle, Lionel Louis Cohen.[10] However he considered Waley Cohen entitled to credit for the vast expansion of the US, and the extension of its influence into wide areas of communal life, for the creation of Woburn House as a centre of the community, and for his co-founding with Nathan Morris of the London Board of Jewish Religious Education.[11]

Despite his uncompromising attitude to Orthodoxy, there were those on the right who did not accept the authority of Chief Rabbi Hertz. Among them was a group led by Rabbi Dr Victor Schonfeld with a strict attitude in matters of Halakhah, and deeply imbued with the tradition of Samson Raphael Hirsch.[12] Shortly after his arrival in Britain, he set up the new Adass Yisroel (Congregation of Israel) Synagogue, which led in due course to the creation of the Union of Orthodox Hebrew Congregations (UOHC) in 1926. Chief Rabbi Hertz resented the name as suggesting to the uninformed that only those affiliated to the UOHC were Orthodox.[13]

There were other groups of deeply Orthodox Jews in the north-east of England who did not accept the authority of the Chief Rabbi, and in 1926 with limited funds available, he resisted their efforts to create the Gateshead Yeshiva out of concern for the future of the London Yeshiva Etz Haim.

In 1931 Dr Hertz attempted a definition of the Anglo-Jewish theological position as 'religious advance without loss of traditional values, and without estrangement from the collective consciousness of the house of Israel'. The vagueness of this statement was uncharacteristic, but possibly deliberate 'in order to retain so far as possible the unifying factors in the community'[14] bearing in mind difficult economic circumstances at that time. However Dr Hertz's efforts inevitably produced a backlash from the right, which accused him of 'progressive conservatism', and collaboration with the left.

In 1934, he attended the dedication of an educational centre at the West London Synagogue, a rare event, acclaimed by the JC under the ambitious and somewhat misleading title of 'Burying the Hatchet'.[15] Although his action was not an attempt at congregational conciliation with Reform, it was nevertheless seen as lending support to a movement regarded as antagonistic to Orthodox Judaism. On behalf of the UOHC, he was severely condemned for 'wavering ambiguity' and for 'bringing spiritual standards to a level of lukewarm colourlessness'.[16]

Uniquely, Dr Hertz was Chief Rabbi during two World Wars. In both horrendous conflicts, Jews played a prominent part, either as combatants or victims. Dr Hertz's visit to the Western Front in 1915 not only boosted morale, but provided evidence of the loyalty of the Anglo-Jewish community, and the considerable number of British Jews in the armed forces. Clearly the war effort was to have priority, and he expected Jewish *Cohanim* who had claimed exemption from military service on religious grounds, nevertheless to serve in wartime.

However, Chief Rabbi Hertz's determination to protect Orthodox Judaism was undiminished by the war, and he opposed a proposed link up with the Liberals to meet the educational needs of children during wartime, many of whom were evacuated away from home. He was concerned that such a link would dilute the Jewish and religious character involved, and provide the Liberals with a disproportionate say in such matters after the war. He also opposed the appointment of Leslie Edgar, a Liberal Rabbi, as senior Chaplain to HM Forces. Rabbi Israel Brodie (1895–1979) who had been evacuated from Dunkirk and served in the Middle East, was appointed in his place.

Dr Hertz was a committed Zionist, at a time when the majority of the US lay leadership was hostile to Zionism, and this became another source of conflict with Waley Cohen. Despite his contribution to the establishment of the Haifa oil refinery, and the promotion of industry through the Palestine Economic Corporation, Waley Cohen opposed the prospect of a Jewish homeland there. However the Chief Rabbi believed that Judaism was broader than religion, and wanted to use the influence of the Synagogue to strengthen support for Zionism,[17] an almost revolutionary view in those days.

Opposition in some quarters to the prospect of a Government declaration in favour of a Jewish homeland led to the issuing of a statement to that effect on 24 May 1917[18] by the Conjoint Committee (representing both AJA and BOD). Dr Hertz was present at their meeting, but his objections were ignored, and the issue of Jewish nationality was to remain a major fault-line dividing an already divided community. However, the election in 1939 of the pro-Zionist Professor Selig Brodetsky as President of the BOD might be seen as an important development towards a less timorous and apologetic view of Jewish identity.

Meanwhile, 'the spectre of the cosmopolitan Jew, loyal to international Jewry and to nothing else, haunted Jewish communal leaders'[19] and perhaps inhibited the community from a more positive response to the treatment of German Jews who fell under Nazi control after 1933, and the rising threat from Fascism at home. A proposed Jewish boycott of German goods and services was opposed by Chief Rabbi Hertz as counterproductive, and likely to make matters worse.

Likewise he opposed the public participation of Jews in disturbances with Fascists, whatever the provocation,[20] but reacted robustly to allegations of ritual murder emanating from Germany. The BOD made no official protest on behalf of Anglo-Jewry over the treatment of German Jews until after Kristallnacht (9 November 1938), which represented a major escalation in the Nazi war against the Jews by the destruction of hundreds of synagogues and businesses. However Chief Rabbi Hertz attended a high level public meeting at the Mansion House on 10 December 1938 ostensibly in support of Lord Baldwin's fund for refugees. The meeting was addressed by Cardinal Hinsley who spoke of the need 'to put a stop to this brutal campaign for the extermination of a whole race'.[21]

Before Kristallnacht, the Home Office had agreed a controlled admittance of refugees in conjunction with the newly set up German Jewish Aid Committee. However, they may well have been influenced by a remarkable guarantee to the British Treasury in 1933, by which the BOD undertook that no refugee would become a burden on the State. They may not have realised that the numbers involved would increase dramatically in the short window of opportunity between Kristallnacht and the outbreak of war ten months later. Although horrible in itself, this event may have saved lives by motivating people to escape whilst they still could.

However effective the administration, and however daring the individual initiatives of those such as Rabbi Solomon Schonfeld to rescue Jews from

Europe, the community was quite unable to agree a common approach. 'Jewish organizations fiddled while many central European countries burned with anti-Semitic oppression.'[22] However early in 1938 the Chief Rabbi's Religious Emergency Council was set up, in which Rabbi Schonfeld played a prominent role despite religious differences, and despite reservations by the lay authorities.

Sadly the attitude of the Jewish community to the refugees themselves was ambivalent. There were some who did not welcome the children of the Kindertransport into their homes or communities. Others were shocked at the absence of Jewish observance among refugees from assimilated backgrounds, and some feared that in the post-war period, the refugees might arouse latent anti-Semitism.

Some 60,000 Jews gained admittance to Britain. Many faced poverty, even drudgery, and were obliged to take menial jobs in order to secure entry to Britain. The new arrivals tended to find comfort among each other, as is usual with immigrant groups. A large number of highly gifted individuals such as Freud, Popper, Hamlyn, Weidenfeld and many others contributed enormously to the British cultural scene. However, these great names did not exist in a vacuum, but were the tip of the iceberg of a culturally and intellectually vibrant community, from a mainly middle class and educated background.[23]

Most refugees chose to remain after the war and created their own communal and social identity. Anthony Grenville associates this with differences in origin: 'The socio-cultural orientation proved stronger than any religious or traditionally Jewish allegiance which might have bound them to Anglo-Jewry.'[24] Yet religious allegiance was important for many refugees, and they were as divided as any other group between Liberal Judaism and Orthodoxy.

As vigorously as he opposed Liberal Judaism, Chief Rabbi Hertz equally opposed any challenge to the authority, accuracy and authenticity of the Torah, by then the subject of Biblical scholarship and the cause of considerable contention. The idea that the Law is from Heaven (*Torah min Hashamayim*) is one of the most important yet divisive concepts in Jewish theology. It is as if the entire edifice of Jewish faith and religion rests not only on the truth of this single assertion, but on its literal truth.

The possibility of human authorship, let alone multiple human authorship, creates the greatest challenge for believers. To rebut this idea, and 'augment the faith of the people', Dr Hertz produced his Soncino Pentateuch which has survived the test of time, and remains in use today. First published in 1936, it contained what he described as a 'People's Commentary', intended to reflect 'the beauty and grandeur' of orthodoxy, and to those who for example doubt the antiquity and Mosaic authorship of Deuteronomy, his notes[25] are essential reading, whether or not one agrees.

One of the most controversial events in the pre-war period, the consequences of which have been far-reaching, was the appointment of Rabbi Y.A. Abramsky (1886–1976) as senior Dayan of the London Beth Din in 1935. On arrival in Britain, he was appointed Rabbi of the Machzikei Hadath, a militant Orthodox immigrant community in London. Born in the Vilna region, he had been active in opposition to attempts by the Communist Government to repress Jewish religion, and in 1929 he was arrested and sentenced to five years in Siberia.

The circumstances of Abramsky's release two years later, and permission to leave Soviet Russia, are by no means clear. There had been an international campaign for his release, supported by Chief Rabbi Hertz. The renowned Soviet writer and poet Maxim Gorky, friend of the poet Chaim Nachman Bialik (1873–1923) and other Hebrew writers in Odessa during his self-imposed exile, is thought to have intervened with Joseph Stalin the Soviet leader. However, the offer of the German Chancellor to release six Communists in exchange for Abramsky may have been the deciding factor.

The lay leadership of the US recognised the advantages of having a world ranking authority on Halakhah, but failed to see the divisive nature of the appointment – described by the JC as a blunder and profound disappointment, regretting that 'the opportunity had not been taken for the appointment of an English-speaking Dayan, able to minister to the needs of the younger generation that knows not Yiddish'.[26] Waley Cohen may well have seen the appointment as a possible counterbalance to the status of the Chief Rabbi. Israel Finestein described the appointment as 'an act of statesmanship and courage'.[27]

Chief Rabbi Hertz supported the appointment, intending to strengthen the reputation of the London Beth Din. He also hoped that the appointment would appeal to those who did not accept his authority, such as referred to above. The UOHC welcomed the appointment, and had been pressing for an improvement of the expertise of the London Beth Din since 1929.[28] Dayan Abramsky certainly set a high standard of Halakhic strictness, particularly in relation to Shechita, and in opposition to conversions of convenience.

Shechita was one of the main areas of dispute prior to his appointment. In 1930, Chief Rabbi Hertz had failed in an attempt to have himself made the sole licensing authority, which had been strenuously opposed by the Federation and the UOHC. However, under the 1933 Slaughter of Animals Act, such authority passed to a Rabbinical Commission which comprised representatives of the US, the Federation, the Union and the BOD. However with four Kashrut Commissions in London alone, Shechita remained the 'litmus test of orthodoxy',[29] and an ongoing source of division.

According to Rabbi Dr Louis Jacobs (whose comments may not be acceptable to some) 'prior to the appointment of Rabbi Abramsky as Head of the London Beth Din, that body was as tolerant as any other. Often at loggerheads with Chief Rabbi Hertz, he [Abramsky] brought all the influence of his strong personality to bear on his colleagues who stood in awe of him and his erudition.'[30] Nevertheless, Dr Hertz was concerned to maintain his position as representative of Orthodoxy, and not to leave the right wing as its only voice.

Despite his reputation for strictness, Dayan Abramsky showed a degree of pragmatism when he permitted the 'national wholemeal loaf' (containing 'suspect' milk powder) to be eaten during wartime. It is said that he acceded to the request of a mourner to shave when his employment would otherwise have been at risk.[31] He devised the 'conditional *get*' for soldiers going to war, so that the widow would be deemed divorced and free to remarry in the event that her husband was missing in action.[32] However there was no such solution for survivors of the Holocaust, which presented the Halakhic authorities with serious and unusual problems as to the presumption of death.

The huge problem of anti-Semitism following the rise of Nazism needed to be addressed after the war, and led Chief Rabbi Hertz in 1943 to become, with the Archbishop of Canterbury Dr Geoffrey Fisher, one of the founding Presidents of the Council of Christians and Jews (CCJ). As Christianity eventually began, slowly and imperceptibly, to acknowledge its Jewish origins, and to regret what had been done to the Jews in its name over the centuries, a network of inter-faith dialogue at all levels came into existence under the aegis of the CCJ, with considerable benefit for all concerned.

'Though the fuller realization of Hertz's hopes was to be long deferred, his own contribution played its part in effecting the onset of what became an unmistakable transformation through a shift of communal priorities and structures.'[33] His most important contribution was perhaps in the field of Jewish education, sorely neglected at all levels, as previously discussed.

From the moment of his installation in 1913 when he referred to 'a crying need for improvement', and throughout his Rabbinate, he fought almost single-handedly for improved funding for Jewish education. He strongly supported the idea of religious teaching in schools in the run-up to the 1944 Education Act.[34] His efforts largely bore fruit after his death, when the need became so obvious as could hardly be ignored, and the problem began seriously to be grappled with.

Dr Hertz had been no mere 'watchman', but on his death in 1946, the landscape must have seemed as equally dismal as he had found it, but for different reasons. The war had ravaged all nations involved, and the Jews lost one third of its people. The traditional Anglo-Jewish community was now 'abruptly cut off from the sustaining force' of products and people from Eastern Europe. It was inevitable that religious observance would be minimal, with priority given to rebuilding lives and careers. Last but not least, he was faced with the emergence of religious pluralism, with its consequences for the authority of his office.

Israel Brodie took the difficult helm in 1948. Of other candidates, Rabbi Kopul Rosen was considered, but thought to be too young. Rabbi Brodie was an accomplished preacher, and his quiet, diplomatic and dignified manner appealed to the lay leadership, faced with massive problems of restoring Jewish communal life. In addition, he was to play a significant part in rebuilding the religious life of European Jewry after the Holocaust.

Rabbi Brodie was the first Chief Rabbi to be knighted. In relation to the progressives, he made it clear like all who have occupied his position, that there was 'no room for spiritual co-existence'.[35] However, his last years in office were blighted by a full blown challenge to the very basis of revelation.

Meanwhile before then, the community came together in 1956 to celebrate the tercentenary of Jewish re-settlement in Britain, and perhaps also its emergence from the horrors of the Second World War. An impressive array of events was organised including an exhibition of Anglo-Jewish life in pictures, and some 800 exhibits were brought together at the Victoria & Albert Museum. A service was held at Bevis Marks, and 650 people attended a Banquet at Guildhall addressed by the Duke of Edinburgh and Anthony Eden, the Prime Minister. Both Cecil Roth and Israel Finestein gave lectures.[36] A new generation of young people could look back with pride, and look forward with hope.

Notes

1. IF, *Studies and Profiles in Anglo-Jewish History: From Picciotto to Bermant* (London and Portland, OR: Vallentine Mitchell, 2008) p.227.
2. Meir Persoff, *Faith & Reason, Religious Reform and the British Chief Rabbinate 1840–1990* (London and Portland, OR: Vallentine Mitchell, 2008), p.160.
3. See above p. 24 (Agree to Differ).
4. Geoffrey Alderman, *British Jewry since Emancipation* (Buckingham: University of Buckingham Press, 2014), p.215.
5. IF, *Scenes and Personalities in Anglo-Jewry 1800–2000* (London and Portland, OR: Vallentine Mitchell, 2002), p.185.

6. Derek Taylor, *Chief Rabbi Hertz. The Wars of the Lord* (London and Portland, OR: Vallentine Mitchell, 2015), p.241.
7. IF, *Scenes and Personalities in Anglo-Jewry 1800–2000*, p.193.
8. Robert Henriques, *Sir Robert Waley Cohen 1877–1952. A Biography* (London:Secker & Warburg, 1966), p.17.
9. Taylor, *Chief Rabbi Hertz: The Wars of the Lord*, p.126.
10. IF, *Studies and Profiles in Anglo-Jewish History*, p.97 n.3.
11. IF, *Scenes and Personalities in Anglo-Jewry 1800–2000*, p.193.
12. See above p.23 (Agree to Differ).
13. Taylor, *Chief Rabbi Hertz*, p.157.
14. IF, *Scenes and Personalities in Anglo-Jewry 1800–2000*, p.10.
15. Meir Persoff, *Faith Against Reason. Religious Reform and the British Chief Rabbinate, 1840–1990* (London and Portland, OR: Vallentine Mitchell, 2008), pp.229/30.
16. Ibid., p.231.
17. IF, *Scenes and Personalities in Anglo-Jewry 1800–2000*, p.192.
18. See post p.127 (Peoplehood).
19. Alderman, *British Jewry since Emancipation*, p.279.
20. For the Battle of Cable St. see post p.176 (The Board).
21. Suzanne Brown-Fleming, 'The Kristallnacht Pogrom', *Jewish Historical Studies*, 2014, Vol.46, p.166.
22. Taylor, *Chief Rabbi Hertz*, p.210.
23. Anthony Grenville, *Jewish Refugees from Germany and Austria 1933–1970* (London and Portland, OR: Vallentine Mitchell, 2010), p.xi.
24. Ibid., p.96.
25. Dr J.H. Hertz (ed.), *Soncino Pentateuch* (London: Soncino Press, 1969, 2nd ed.), pp. 937–41.
26. JC, 27 September 1935, p.34.
27. IF, *Scenes and Personalities in Anglo-Jewry 1800–2000*, p.195.
28. Taylor, *Chief Rabbi Hertz*, p.198.
29. Alderman, *British Jewry since Emancipation*, p.359.
30. Louis Jacobs, *Helping with Inquiries: An Autobiography* (London and Portland, OR: Vallentine Mitchell, 1989), p.218.
31. As told by Dr Chaim Goldwater.
32. Taylor, *Chief Rabbi Hertz*, p.188.
33. IF, *Studies and Profiles in Anglo-Jewish History*, p.236.
34. IF, *Scenes and Personalities in Anglo-Jewry 1800–2000*, p.92 n.34.
35. Conference of Anglo-Jewish Preachers, May 1956.
36. See JC Supplement, 27 January 1956, p.35.

8

Helping with Inquiries

The respective proportions of reason and faith in the interpretation of scripture, had for some time lain dormant within the orthodox community. When such questions came sharply and suddenly to the fore, a new type of dispute emerged within Anglo-Jewish orthodoxy.

Israel Finestein[1]

The two main events which precipitated what became known as the 'Jacobs affair' are well documented, and can be simply stated: Rabbi Jacobs was effectively refused appointment as Principal of Jews College in 1961, and in 1964, Chief Rabbi Brodie refused to certify him as Minister for the New West End Synagogue. The significance of these events is far greater than the career of one man, unleashing as it did a challenge to the façade of Orthodox unity, and a new found assertiveness in the questioning of authority.

Rabbi Dr Louis Jacobs (1920–2006), born in Manchester and educated at both yeshiva (Gateshead) and university (UCL), was an international scholar of renown. After some twelve years as a successful Minister, he accepted a tutorial post at Jews College in 1959, pending appointment as Principal, from which post the then incumbent was shortly to retire. There is no doubt that Rabbi Jacobs was well qualified for the post, and indeed seen as a future Chief Rabbi. As Principal of Jews College he would have been very well placed as a contender in due course.

Unfortunately, Rabbi Jacobs had a problem – he suffered from intellectual integrity! It would not allow him to accept that the Torah was written or dictated by God, or indeed by Moses alone. He had come to recognise the possibility of multiple human authorship, but considered that the faithful Jew had nothing to fear from what Israel Finestein characterised as the 'dethronement of the received biblical text in some Jewish quarters'.[2]

Revelation is certainly at the heart of Judaism, but God's message was revealed over time, in Rabbi Jacobs' view, and through divinely inspired individuals. He realised that this view was not reconcilable with strict Orthodox theology, and struggled to find a synthesis between the two. He would have been aware that Chief Rabbi Hertz had reserved his most scathing criticism for modern Biblical scholarship which, in his view, was a perversion of history and a desecration of religion.[3]

In 1957, Rabbi Jacobs published a book entitled *We Have Reason to Believe* in which he discussed his ideas, and tried to demonstrate that his devotion as an Orthodox Rabbi was not compromised by exposure to Biblical criticism: 'God's message is in no way affected in that we can only hear it through the medium of human beings.'[4] Rabbi Jacobs accepted that the Torah was from heaven, but not in a literal sense. He does not doubt its contents as being the word of God; what he doubts is how it arrived among us. But for the Orthodox community this was heretical. Nevertheless, his book was received at the time without demur, and the idea that rationality should be the basis of belief was welcomed by many.

There were of course those who never reconciled themselves to the validity of Rabbi Jacobs' conclusions, or the manner of his reasoning. However, the majority of the Council of Jews College wanted Jacobs to become Principal when the opportunity arose in 1961. Nevertheless, Chief Rabbi Brodie delayed his approval of the appointment to the extent that it became embarrassingly clear to Rabbi Jacobs that he was not acceptable.

Rabbi Jacobs was also concerned that the post itself and the institution would suffer if an appointment was to be made in what was becoming an undignified fashion. One of the concerns ultimately expressed by the Chief Rabbi was his disagreement with the views expressed in Jacobs' book written four years previously, although without criticism at the time. Jacobs' position had thus become untenable, and he resigned from the College.

He was requested to withdraw his resignation by the College Council, which sent three of its members (one of them being Israel Finestein) to present their request and attempt to persuade him, but he could not agree. The Chairman of the Council, Sir Alan Moccatta, and several other Honorary Officers then also resigned. Felix Levy, a joint Treasurer, in a letter to the JC twenty-five years later[5] recalled that his resignation from the Council of Jews College was over 'a catastrophic manifestation of intolerance, whose result has been nearly a quarter of a century of a paucity of adequately trained ministers'.[6]

That might have been the end of the matter, but it was almost inevitable that Rabbi Jacobs would be invited to return to the Ministry sooner or later. Whilst serving as Director of the Society of the Study of Jewish Theology, his former pulpit at the prestigious New West End Synagogue became vacant in 1963. Dr Chaim Pearl, previously the charismatic Chief Minister at the Singers Hill Synagogue, Birmingham, had decided to accept a call from the Conservative Synagogue in Riverdale, New York. His London congregants were reluctant to see him go, but it provided the opportunity to invite Rabbi Jacobs to return and preach there.

Rabbi Jacobs was of course previously certified as fit to serve as a Minister within the jurisdiction of the Chief Rabbi. The question arose as to whether a new certificate was required, in view of his absence from the Ministry. According to Rabbi Jacobs, the then Secretary of the US, 'a stickler for the strictest interpretation of the bye-laws',[7] insisted that the question be put to the Chief Rabbi. His response was that a new certificate was required, and that he would withhold it for the proposed appointment of Rabbi Jacobs at the New West End.

The Synagogue Board was not willing to accept this ruling, and at an Extraordinary General Meeting, the New West End membership gave an 'overwhelming mandate'[8] to the Honorary Officers to contest the Chief Rabbi's refusal to certify Rabbi Jacobs. Efforts to negotiate a settlement failed since they would have involved him declaring that he recanted his views on the nature of divine revelation. Thereupon a special meeting of the US Council on 23 April 1964 exercised its power to oust the local congregational leaders from office, and install managers to administer the Synagogue.

William Frankel (1917–2008), Editor of the Jewish Chronicle, said he was reliably informed that members of the Beth Din might have preferred to turn a blind eye to Jacobs' return to the pulpit, and thus he would have remained at least nominally under their control. In any event, they may have calculated that his views could do little harm to his congregation, already much anglicised![9]

Some of the most influential families in Anglo-Jewry were members of the New West End Congregation, and if their chosen leader was unable to serve within the US, they would set up an independent congregation in which Jacobs could minister free of the authority of the Chief Rabbi. The New London Synagogue came into being at a meeting held on 3 May 1964,[10] with a resolution to create an 'independent orthodox congregation' invoking the concept of 'Progressive Conservatism' referred to in the preamble to the Constitution of the US. The new congregation expressed its wish for the return of the US to its own traditions, but were bound to be disappointed.

'In their unrelenting opposition to Rabbi Jacobs, the Chief Rabbi and the US regarded themselves as upholding the community's traditions, whilst Jacobs and his supporters presented themselves at the time as doing likewise.'[11] The idea that the US had been ambushed by religious extremism, and that it was 'Dr Brodie who had deviated from the United Synagogue tradition, not I'[12] was attractive to many. However the definition of 'Progressive Conservatism', was not the issue. The US and the Chief Rabbi were responsible for the administration of the Halakhah, and could not simply apply what was 'acceptable to the majority of thinking Jews'.

Any doubt about that was surely dispelled by Rabbi Jacobs' subsequent experience in dealing with matters of personal status on behalf of his congregants. As to conversion, he regarded the requirements of the London Beth Din as 'unknown in the Jewish world, or in Anglo-Jewry until the fairly recent ascendancy of the right wing'.[13] He complained that the Orthodox tradition was being interpreted somewhat harshly by the Beth Din due to the dominant influence initially of Rabbi Abramsky, as previously mentioned.[14]

The problem between the Beth Din and Rabbi Jacobs was later described by the JC as 'insoluble'.[15] It had the effect of stimulating an apparent determination to discredit Rabbi Jacobs by whatever means available, and thus hardening the position of the right. His adherence to traditional norms as an Orthodox Rabbi was frequently put in question, and there were in his view unfair accusations of invalid marriage ceremonies which had considerable consequences for those of his congregants involved. He set out his lengthy and detailed rejection of such allegations in his Synagogue journal.[16] However it was not so much his practices, but rather his beliefs which were held to disqualify him.

In due course the New London Synagogue acquired the premises of the former Orthodox Synagogue in St Johns Wood, recently vacated. It had been sold to a successful Jewish developer who had obtained planning permission to convert it into a block of flats. However this remarkable man was nevertheless somewhat reluctant, perhaps superstitious, about demolishing what was in effect a sacred and longstanding place of Jewish worship, and he readily accepted the opportunity for the building to retain its religious purpose.

His willingness to forego the profit he might have made from this investment (or indeed any profit at all) was extremely generous, as was his support for other communal causes. He was not a Jacobs' follower, and perhaps for that reason, his identity was disguised behind various company façades at the time. Nevertheless, Elijah Alec Colman (1903–91), originally from Birmingham, deserves his place in the pantheon of Jewish benefactors.

William Frankel was a personal friend of Rabbi Jacobs, and a leading member of the New West End Synagogue. He believed that Chief Rabbi Brodie was in fear of the Orthodox right wing, and declared in the JC that 'it was no secret that the Chief Rabbi allows himself to be guided by the extremists of the right'.[17] He saw himself as an instrument for change, and was described in his *Guardian* obituary as a crusading editor who brought a high profile to the JC, whose reporting was previously considered 'turgid and anonymous', and perhaps also too deferential.[18]

The JC strongly supported Jacobs' position editorially, and regularly criticised the Chief Rabbi, stating on one occasion that every thinking layman thought the Chief Rabbi to be mistaken. However, setting aside the strength of his editorialising, Frankel maintains that he sought to ensure that the 'affair' was reported as objectively as possible within the pages of the JC, and that its correspondence columns would be available to all shades of opinion.

However he regarded the bulk of the material received against Jacobs as 'illiterate or simply vituperative',[19] and he himself was subject to much vilification. He quotes correspondence with Rabbi Dr Louis Rabinowitz, former Minister at Cricklewood Synagogue, who referred to 'a spirit of fanatical obscurantism'[20] having seized the official Anglo-Jewish community. Frankel felt that Rabbi Rabinowitz should have been considered a potential successor to Chief Rabbi Brodie, but 'the hard liners ganged up on him'.

There is no doubt that Jacobs was himself treated shamefully. Although no *cherem* was pronounced, he was excommunicated or banned from the Orthodox community in every sense. Perhaps the most awful and petty example of this was the refusal to honour him with calling up to the Torah on the Shabbat prior to his granddaughter's wedding. The then Honorary Officers of the Bournemouth Congregation, together with those who may have advised them, must take responsibility for such discourtesy. A strong sense of injustice prevailed for long after.

It was suggested by way of explanation that Rabbi Jacobs could not make the blessings with a clear conscience, but such an attempted justification after the event stretches credulity. The blessings not only refer to the 'giving' of the Torah, but also to the fact that the Jewish people were chosen to receive it. Any Jew who is prepared to make what is a public declaration of faith in the presence of the holy text itself should be allowed to do so, if the occasion is appropriate. It was for Rabbi Jacobs (not his hosts) to decide whether his conscience prevented him from making the declaration.

Was any damage done to the community by the Jacobs affair? The Masorti movement has in fact provided a home for many already disaffected Jews, and for those who defected in consequence of the affair, as well as 'those disturbed at the seemingly relentless move to the religious right'.[21] There have been, of course, many attempts over the years to make sense of the human condition, and to find a rational basis for faith. Whilst we can never know God's will, blind faith is unattractive to many, and Rabbi Jacobs' blend of faith and reason, combined with humility and erudition, together with his rejection of fundamentalism, was an inspiration to those who might otherwise have been lost.

Furthermore he has given a voice to a sophisticated reading of the Torah which deserves to be represented rather than concealed in the spectrum of Jewish faith. His loss to the official Orthodox fold meant that he was no longer available to those whose conscience might be troubled by scholarship, or who would simply have benefited from wider understanding. Such benefit however became available to students at the Leo Baeck College, where he accepted an appointment to teach Talmud. The College was ostensibly designed on non-denominational lines for basic study, before preparation for the Progressive Rabbinate.

In his autobiography published in 1989 under the title of this chapter, Rabbi Jacobs summarised the 'fuss' as 'about whether traditional Judaism could be seen as a quest, rather than as a corpus of dogmas fixed for all time by divine fiat',[22] a venture into the unknown, with faith in the Lord. 'The implications of modern scholarship will not simply vanish because they are ignored', he said, referring to the 'rigidity of the London Beth Din, and the re-fashioning of the orthodox community into a replica from Eastern Europe'.[23]

He commended the analysis of his case by Kenneth (later His Honour Judge) Zucker, a founder member of the New North London Synagogue in 1974. In an article published in November 1964, after praising Jacobs' attempt to reconcile ancient Jewish law with modernity, he concluded 'It is a mark of his opponents' sterility that their only reply was to cast him out as a heretic'.[24] The creation of the New London Synagogue in 1964, and the desire for freedom of study and enquiry, in harmony with modern scholarship, inevitably produced a backlash. However, those who thought that what became the movement for Masorti Judaism[25] would wither away, were to be disappointed.

Other communities copied the New London, each free to fix its own agenda – akin to the Conservative movement in America. It has clearly been successful, and has struck a balance which many find attractive, 'the last bastion of the old Anglo-Jewish tolerance and reasonableness'.[26] There are now eleven UK congregations in the Masorti fold, of which the most prestigious is perhaps the New North London in Finchley founded in 1974 by Ivor (son of Rabbi) Jacobs and Michael Rose. It now has some 2,500 members, and three different types of service held concurrently when required. It should be emphasised that members of the Masorti movement did not retreat from the wider community, but continued to serve in many of its institutions and charitable endeavours.

Of Louis Jacobs, Rabbi Immanuel Jakobovits, Minister of the prestigious Fifth Avenue Synagogue, New York, declared that 'by his increasing detachment from the Orthodox rabbinical world, he showed that whatever his scholarship and sincerity, he represented a trend that could not be accommodated within contemporary Orthodoxy'.[27]

Nevertheless, Rabbi Jakobovits stated that his agreement to becoming Chief Rabbi in 1966 was dependent on bringing about a reconciliation with the Jacobs faction. He clearly thought this was negotiable, when it was not. The idea that Biblical scholarship was a detachment, rather than an enhancement, something to be embraced, made the result inevitable. His attempt to befriend Jacobs did not flourish, and the latter regarded the offer to accept the Chief Rabbi's authority as a surrender to a reactionary view of Judaism.

But Rabbi Jacobs and many others including William Frankel had also misjudged the mood of the times, and did not anticipate the 'sea-change' which was in the making. A widespread indifference towards Judaism over several previous generations had perhaps suggested that it was time for the Orthodox world to move on, but its religious leadership did not agree, and held firm to its core beliefs. The rejection of Jacobs marked the end of the cosy half-hearted largely unobserved nominal Orthodoxy of the US in the early post-war period, and the beginning of a strong 'counter-reformation'.

On 20 May 1965, the New London Synagogue held a dinner to celebrate its first anniversary. It was attended by many distinguished guests, but one in particular came in for praise. Frederic Moses (Freddie) Landau (1905–99) was Treasurer of the US from 1960 to 1971, and a committed supporter of the Chief Rabbi.[28] Some observers were therefore surprised at his attendance, and the New London Chairman commented, 'Most of us wish that his colleagues were all as tolerant and understanding as he is'.[29] Whilst retaining his membership of the US, Freddie Landau became a lifelong member of the Masorti congregation. Prominent in Anglo-Jewry all his life, 'he was no respecter of persons when principle, conscience or fairness was in issue'.[30]

In the year 2000, the AJA held a reception in honour of Rabbi Jacobs' 80th birthday, and among the tributes was one given by Judge Finestein. He was billed as a past President of the BOD, but he was also an unapologetic member of the Orthodox world, of which others might have expected him to stay away. But it was typical of Judge Finestein that he did not feel compromised in any way by his friendship with Rabbi Jacobs, and would wish to pay due respect to a contemporary for whose personal integrity and scholarship he had the highest regard.

The Jacobs 'affair' became a bitter battle for the mind and soul of Anglo-Jewry. For some it was the last opportunity to defeat the fundamentalists and prevent the right wing strangle-hold which was seen to be emerging. It was a uniquely British confrontation, in that American Conservatism had already established itself on similar lines to the new Masorti movement. Pluralism however did not exist in Britain, where the Chief Rabbi and the US regarded themselves as the sole repository of the community's traditions.

The question which Jacobs bequeathed to future generations was nothing less than: whither Orthodoxy? A policy of entrenched rigidity can only lead to more disaffection, and one sees the emergence of another secession within the Orthodox fold under the banner of what is called 'modern' Orthodoxy – traditional in every respect, but unafraid of modernity, and unafraid of the compassion for which Rabbi Jacobs was chided, but which he accepted as 'the nicest compliment'.[31]

In Israel there is opposition if not open rebellion to the monopoly of Halakhic decision-making by a centralised, mainly extreme Chief Rabbinate. The activities and views of Rabbi Shlomo Riskin of Efrat, for example, have laid bare the depths of the conflict within Orthodoxy.[32] Marriage, conversion and Kashrut are all now the subject of dispute in Israel where the credibility of the Chief Rabbinate is at stake.[33]

In America, a group of rabbis have set up religious academies and teach what has become loosely known as 'Open' Orthodoxy. They have been denounced as heretical by the strictly Orthodox American right, and by the Conference of European Rabbis. One of its leaders, Rabbi Katz, speaking at Limmud, described Orthodoxy as 'in a state of flux, locked in a game of musical chairs',[34] a strange and rather depressing metaphor.

'Wherever you look in orthodox life, one sees conflict, which ought to be healthy, but the favoured methods of debate are demonization and humiliation ... power and authority count for more than the pursuit of intellectual truth'. So said Rabbi Dr Jeremy Rosen[35] in his review of *Faith without Fear* by Rabbi Michael Harris, Minister at Hampstead Synagogue. His new book examines some unresolved issues within Modern Orthodoxy, and argues the need to be morally and intellectually fearless in the interpretation of Jewish faith.

In anticipation of the 350th anniversary of the resettlement of the Jews in England (in 2006) the JC conducted a poll among its subscribers for the 'Greatest British Jew' in that period. Some two thousand nominations were made, and Rabbi Jacobs was announced the winner. The result, and indeed the poll itself, were in his own words 'rather daft', but they were nevertheless a recognition by the rank and file of the community of the value to them of his own moral and intellectual courage.

Notes

1. IF, *Scenes and Personalities in Anglo-Jewry 1800–2000* (London and Portland, OR: Vallentine Mitchell, 2002), p.13.

2. Ibid., p.85.
3. Dr J.H. Hertz (ed.), *Soncino Pentateuch* (London: Soncino Press, 1969, 2nd edn), p.vii.
4. Louis Jacobs, *We have Reason to Believe* (London & Portland, OR: Vallentine Mitchell, 1957), pp.80/81.
5. JC, 18 July 1986, p.32.
6. Louis Jacobs, *Helping with Inquiries: An Autobiography* (London and Portland, OR: Vallentine Mitchell, 1989), p.133.
7. Ibid., p.160.
8. JC, 6 March 1964, p.1.
9. William Frankel, *Tea with Einstein and Other Memories* (London: Halban Publishers, 2006), p.165.
10. Jacobs, *Helping with Inquiries*, p.179.
11. IF, *Scenes and Personalities in Anglo-Jewry 1800–2000*, p.13.
12. Meir Persoff, *Faith Against Reason. Religious Reform and the British Chief Rabbinate, 1840–1990* (London and Portland, OR: Vallentine Mitchell, 2008), p.311.
13. Jacobs, *Helping with Inquiries*, p.212.
14. See above p.73 (Holy War).
15. JC, 30 September 1983, p.14.
16. Reproduced in Jacobs, *Helping with Inquiries*, pp.215–17.
17. JC, Editorial, 29 December 1961, p.14.
18. Michael Freedland, Obituary, *The Guardian*, 25 April 2008.
19. Frankel, *Tea with Einstein*, p.164.
20. Ibid., p.167.
21. Geoffrey Alderman, *British Jewry since Emancipation* (Buckingham: University of Buckingham Press, 2014), p.367.
22. Jacobs, *Helping with Inquiries*, p.xii.
23. Ibid., p.270.
24. Ibid., pp.175–6.
25. Meaning 'traditional' from the Hebrew verb 'to transmit'.
26. Jacobs, *Helping with Inquiries*, p.270.
27. Persoff, *Faith Against Reason*, p.319.
28. For a full appreciation, see IF, *Studies and Profiles in Anglo-Jewish History: From Picciotto to Bermant* (London and Portland, OR: Vallentine Mitchell, 2008), Ch.12.
29. Jacobs, *Helping with Inquiries*, p.194.
30. IF, *Studies and Profiles in Anglo-Jewish History*, p.265.
321. Jacobs, *Helping with Inquiries*, p.221.
32. JC, 12 June 2015, p.26.
33. JC, 4 September 2015, p.36.
34. JC, 11 December 2015, p.30.
35. JC, 5 February 2016, p.34.

9

The Mirage of Unity

The general anxiety to stem the tide of assimilation served to arouse a sharpening discord over proposed procedures to achieve that end. No language or structure could satisfy one party without antagonising another.

Israel Finestein[1]

Rabbi Dr Immanuel Jacobovitz (1921-1999) grew up in Berlin where his father served as a Dayan of the Beth Din until fleeing Nazi Germany in 1938. Once in England, he studied at Jews College and Etz Chaim Yeshiva where he received rabbinic ordination. Rabbi Jakobovits also studied at University College, London, where he obtained both BA and PhD, and became a prominent exponent of Jewish medical ethics. He subscribed to the German Orthodox tradition of *Torah im Derech Eretz* in the spirit of Samson Raphael Hirsch.[2]

At the height of the Second World War when graduates from Jews College were no doubt in short supply, his appointment as Minister at Brondesbury Synagogue was criticised 'with incredulity and indignation', not only on account of his youth (being barely 21 years of age) but on account of his coming from Germany, 'a country abhorrent to all right thinking people!'[3] In 1949, still relatively young, he was appointed Chief Rabbi of Ireland, and in 1958 he accepted a call from the prestigious Fifth Avenue Synagogue in New York.

It is possible that Rabbi Jakobovits did not wish to cross the Atlantic in 1966 to become Chief Rabbi, but felt under an obligation to do so when Rabbi Herzog of Israel withdrew for health reasons. He was well aware of the divisions affecting Anglo-Jewry, and that the United Synagogue itself faced 'the grimmest of all crises – deserted Synagogues and staggering losses by defection and assimilation'.[4] These were extremely serious challenges which might have deterred a lesser man.

He arrived at a time when 'the community was leaderless, torn and confused, when knowledge, observance, family cohesiveness, and sense of continuity, were receding', according to the JC.[5] The New London Synagogue had not long seceded, and as Rabbi Jakobovits said later in an address to the

BOD, 'there were still many influential individuals who wanted to keep the kettle of communal dissension and disaffection boiling, and who had written off the future of the Chief Rabbinate altogether'.[6]

Rabbi Jakobovits had been more than scathing of Rabbi Jacobs in a letter to the JC on 19 January 1962. He accused him of a lack of humility, and as one 'who leans more with Conservative Judaism, a religious system which is alien to Orthodox Judaism, a system which will "fragmentise" communal life in Britain, as it has done in America'. Nevertheless, in anticipation of his installation in April 1967, he declared, 'I will stretch out my hand in friendship to all who care to give me theirs, whether they share my belief or not', a bold invitation indeed.[7]

It was well received by the Liberal community, but what they wanted in return was recognition, and not to be treated as second-class Jews, or indeed as non-Jews. Following the appointment of Rabbi Jakobovits, the Liberal and Reform communities had set up a Standing Committee on Relationships Within Anglo-Jewry to work towards better representation for non-Orthodoxy, and to look for areas of cooperation with the Orthodox establishment.

However, they argued, it would not be acceptable for the Chief Rabbi (and the Haham) to hold themselves out as the sole spiritual leaders of Anglo-Jewry, and would be expected to acknowledge the existence of non-Orthodox Judaism. All previous Chief Rabbis had made it clear this was impossible. Rabbi Jakobovits would be no different, and was later to say 'those who regard the integrity of the Law as sacrosanct, can hardly accord legitimacy to those sanctioning its violation'.[8] Initially however, there was heady talk of reconciliation, of partnership and understanding, and looking for ways to 'build bridges'.

In this context, soon after his election Rabbi Jakobovits made a number of decisions in the spirit of compromise. He granted permission to the BOD for the appointment of a marriage secretary at the New London Synagogue, which he could have withheld. He also corrected any misconception as to the legitimacy of children born of parents married in a Liberal synagogue, who would have qualified to be married in an Orthodox one had they so wished.

In 1971, Rabbi Jakobovits founded the Jewish Educational Development Trust (JEDT) and the allocation of funds raised was made available not only to Orthodox educational institutions, but also to support non-Orthodox institutions, such as the Akiva School founded in 1981. The JEDT was not an offshoot of the US, and the Chief Rabbi may therefore have felt more independent in regard to it, especially as among its patrons were members of Progressive Synagogues. Financial support also came from many prominently involved in fund-raising for Israel, and Israel Finestein suggests this may well have led in due course to the idea that the then Joint Israel Appeal (now UJIA) should widen its scope to include allocation of funds for local needs.[9]

In the same year, again in the spirit of accommodation, Rabbi Jakobovits did not oppose an amendment of Clause 43 of the BOD Constitution to the effect that the Board shall 'consult with the respective religious leaders of those congregations' outside his jurisdiction. The Board was previously required to be guided solely by the Chief Rabbi and the Sephardi Haham, and this requirement was a constant source of irritation for the Progressives and their Deputies.

The new formula was in many ways a major concession, a partial acceptance of the fact that there were congregations within Anglo-Jewry which did not follow the Orthodox tradition. When the new formula was approved by the Board, on 24 October 1971, many Deputies on the Orthodox side were unable to follow the statesmanlike lead of Rabbi Jakobovits, and resigned. Some returned, but many did not.[10]

Another example of his approach was in relation to the Council of Christians and Jews (CCJ) where the Chief Rabbi was the only Jewish President, but the varying strands of Christianity were each represented by their own separate co-president. Liberal rabbis and lay persons were much involved in the work of this important inter-faith body, and in a gesture of compromise, Rabbi Jakobovits agreed to the setting up of a Consultative Committee on Jewish-Christian relations, with wide representation. It was regarded as 'a major step forward'[11] and lasted for some twenty years.

Rabbi Jacobovitz was conservative by nature, and believed in individual responsibility such as had been demonstrated by Jewish communities in America and in England in overcoming much poverty by their own efforts, without recourse to help from the host country. Critical of the 'welfare state', and a supporter of law and order, he spoke out against the underlying philosophy of 'Faith in the City', a report by the Commission on Urban Priority Areas in 1985, which denounced what it perceived as harsh economic measures under Margaret Thatcher, British Prime Minister from 1979 to 1990.

The views expressed by Rabbi Jakobovits were his own, and whilst many in the Anglo-Jewish community agreed with them, there were others who had reservations about an apparent policy of 'devil take the hindmost', as Mrs Thatcher charted an uncompromising course of privatisation against a background of high unemployment. However, his views were more than welcome to Mrs Thatcher who made him Baron Jakobovits of Regents Park in 1988, the first Rabbi to become a member of the House of Lords. Had the post been vacant, and had he qualified for it, Mrs Thatcher might well have preferred to appoint him Archbishop of Canterbury in place of the then incumbent, who had commissioned the above report!

Despite his declared wish to embark on a 'peace mission', Rabbi Jakobovits made it clear in his installation address, as one might expect, that he was resolved to preserve the Orthodox tradition, and not to preside over the liquidation of British Judaism. While wishing to serve all sections of the community, he stated that 'the Torah would not be replaced by an umbrella as the symbol of my office'. It was thus clear and inevitable that he and the Liberals 'trod a mutually defiant and difficult path',[12] and examples quickly followed.

Almost the first indication of trouble was the failure of efforts to set up a unified Universities' Chaplaincy service, when Rabbi Jakobovits, as Chair of the organising committee, insisted that the field of chaplaincy should be under his sole jurisdiction. The following year (1968) he refused to hold a joint Independent Day service with the Progressives on the twentieth anniversary of the establishment of Israel.

This contrasted with the events of 1967, when the Jewish State was at war, and both Liberal and Reform bodies responded fully to the call from Rabbi Jakobovits for a cooperative effort. Rosita Rosenberg also points to several precedents for joint rabbinical participation in services such as those held to celebrate the coronation of King George VI (1937) and to celebrate the tercentenary of the resettlement of the Jews in England (1956).[13]

Rabbi Jakobovits later upbraided US leaders for attendance at a significant centenary service at the West London Synagogue, even suggesting that such attendance was a violation of Jewish Law.[14] When the Orthodox Chief Rabbi of Denmark visited London in 1972, he was refused permission to preach at a US Synagogue, on account of his association with the World Council of Synagogues.

And at a memorial meeting for the Israeli victims of the Munich Olympic massacre, Rabbi Jakobovits apparently declined to read a psalm alongside Reform Rabbi Hugo Gryn, senior Minster at West London. Harold Langdon, the former Chair of the Reform Synagogues of Great Britain was prompted to comment, in shock and disappointment, 'the builder of bridges has proved to be a demolition expert'.[15]

Apart from religious dissension, the period in office of Rabbi Jakobovits coincided with the external challenge of three wars in Israel: the Six Day War (1967) the Yom Kippur War (1973) and the Lebanon War (1982). The growing agony of Soviet Jewry was also a matter of considerable concern. Rabbi Jakobovits was a fearless and consistent supporter of the Middle East peace process and a two state solution, and was frequently criticised by some of the less tolerant right wing of the community.

Internally, there was a growing undercurrent of pressure for different priorities, for urgent redistribution of financial resources, for the undoing of central control and for the need of younger elements in administration. On the centenary of the US in 1970, Israel Finestein observed that Salmond Levin (1905–99) an Honorary Officer since 1955, and President 1978–81, had 'caught the growing mood' for change in an article entitled 'Thinking about the Future'.[16] A knowledgeable and devout Jew, Levin referred to 'erosion of the community by secularism, out marriage, low marriage and birth rates, and Aliya, the continuous movement into gentile surroundings, and older congregations left behind by migration',[17] issues which were to cast a long shadow into the future.

This was not the divisive language of legitimacy and authenticity, but of the more important need for communal planning on a large scale, for new style multi-purpose synagogues, for the encouragement of new professionals and businessmen, and for the pre-eminence of Jewish education. The growing threat of secularisation and the issue of Jewish identity now came to the fore in conferences held by the BOD (1977) and the US (in 1979) and in public debate in which Rabbi Dr Jonathan Sacks, as Principal of Jews College and later as Chief Rabbi, sought to stimulate the pursuit of Jewish knowledge.

In his address to the BOD at their 1984 Conference entitled 'The Changing Face of Anglo-Jewry', Rabbi Jakobovits felt able to refer to a 'considerable measure of internal tranquillity', and after seventeen years in office, his comments represented a major assessment of the community at that time. He referred to a 'quiet revolution' in communal thought and action in which Jewish education had 'at last achieved its rightful place at the head of communal concerns'.[18] He was positive in his view of the future of the community, despite demographic trends, and believed that there was now a mutual recognition by both spiritual and lay leadership that Jewish tradition was the cement uniting the diverse strands of the community.

Even so, religious legitimacy and acceptance could not be achieved under the cloak of pluralism. Keeping the Law and ignoring the Law could not be equally valid, in his view, and communal statesmanship was needed to prevent a form of confrontation in which a single section makes demands which cannot be met as a matter of conscience. A form of tolerance was needed which recognised the fact of dissent, but which retained the right of traditional Jews to reject the claim that the beliefs of other segments are equally authentic. There could never be complete mutuality and reciprocity, except in relation to 'common problems'.

However, as if this basic dichotomy was not enough, Rabbi Jakobovits urged his rabbis a short time later, 'not to allow their presence or name to be used for promoting any activity which could be construed as according legitimacy to non-traditional Judaism'.[19] Non-recognition was in any event the practise in Orthodox circles, and Geoffrey Alderman records a somewhat extreme example when in 1982 Rabbi Chanoch Ehrentreu refused to meet the Pope, 'not because he had any objection to shaking the Pope's hand, but because he would have been part of a delegation which included a Reform Jew'.[20]

Rabbi Jakobovits explained his stiffening attitude in an article entitled 'Avoiding the Collision'[21] in which he sought to distinguish between appearing on a joint fund-raising platform, and participation in other events which could be misinterpreted as endorsing Progressive Judaism. He was clearly concerned by criticism of his purported fraternisation with the Progressives from the more hard line rabbis to his right, some of whom barely regarded the Progressives as Jews.

However his Orthodox critics need not have worried, as his position was clear – Judaism based on the Halakhah cannot be expected to legitimise another interpretation, and mutual efforts with the Progressives invariably came to grief when put to the test. Rabbi Jakobovits wanted evidence of a genuine attempt at rapprochement with traditional Judaism, especially in the area of conversion, where the Progressives felt that education in, and knowledge of, traditional Jewish practise was sufficient, regardless of observance. Lengthy discussion over proposals and counter proposals achieved nothing.

One has only to read the extensive correspondence between Rabbi Jakobovits and Sidney Brichto (1936–2009) Executive Director of ULPS, or Rabbi John Rayner (1924–2005) Minister at the Liberal Jewish Synagogue since 1965, to observe the gulf between them. Rabbi Jakobovits had nevertheless tried with some patience over many years to bridge that gulf, but the Progressives could not accept that he (and the Haham) were the sole spiritual leaders of Anglo-Jewry, especially when it had been pointed out by the sociologist Dr Barry Kosmin in 1982 that barely 60 per cent of synagogue members in the United Kingdom (less in London) acknowledged the authority of the Chief Rabbi.[22]

Rabbi Jakobovits had in fact succeeded in generating a climate of personal goodwill with the Progressives, despite an 'on-off relationship',[23] but the tranquillity to which he had referred in 1984 could not survive, and he pleaded for concentration on constructive work without public recrimination. Every assertion of Orthodox belief which differed from the Progressives should not be a cause for war, and he reiterated the century-old formula of 'agreement to disagree'[24] in his desire to avoid communal heartbreak and preserve the cohesion of the community.

It was inevitable however, that in due course, the Reform and Liberal leadership would be denied consultation in the choice of Rabbi Jakobovits' successor. And thus in 1989, at the end of his Rabbinate, the ULPS publicly declared that the authority of his successor would not be accepted, and that he would not be allowed to speak on behalf of their community. The affirmation in that document that the Jewish community was not monolithic, but pluralistic in nature, was a statement of the obvious. What was at issue was the recognition of that fact and what it entailed.

Meanwhile the Orthodox fold was far from unite; it was, in fact, a patchwork of vested interests which took precedence over religious unity. Rabbi Jakobovits had also pursued a policy of painstaking dialogue with their various strands, but had failed to secure any form of rationalisation or cooperation. In a 'frank passage' quoted by Meir Persoff, and reproduced by Israel Finestein,[25] the Chief Rabbi referred to the enormous amount of time spent in tortuous negotiations, trying to ensure harmonious relationships between the Federation of Synagogues, the US and the Sephardim. His sense of frustration is palpable!

During an interview in 1978, Rabbi Jakobovits dismissed the whole notion of unity as 'based on a false premise'.[26] The idea that all British Jews would one day again sing from the same hymn sheet was not essential in his view: 'the unity of our people is not destroyed if we do not all pray together'.[27] What was needed was not unity, but unity of purpose, and looking back in 1997, he referred to the need to put stability before the mirage of unity: 'We must shift our concern from form to substance, to live as fuller and better Jews, rather than seek to gloss over theological differences'.

A mirage it certainly was, an 'Anglo-Jewish fetish' he called it, held out over two centuries as a kind of holy grail, unattained and unattainable in any religious sense. The concept of 'unity' does not exist among the Jews of America or Israel, and exists in Britain perhaps due to the relatively small size of the community, or to the not unworthy urging of the *Jewish Chronicle*, and the not unreasonable desire of the Board of Deputies to present a united front to the outside world. Nevertheless, the constant pressure for unity, and the fear of disunity, became an excuse for mutual recrimination, concealing for a time other important ingredients of Jewish identity.

To the BOD in 1984, Rabbi Jakobovits emphasised the need to prevent a form of confrontation in which a single section will make demands, which as a matter of conscience the rest of the community cannot meet. 'We must uphold a form of tolerance, recognising the fact of dissent, whilst retaining the right of traditional Jews to reject the claim that the beliefs of non-traditional Jews were equally authentic.'[28]

Despite his view that there can be only one authentic Judaism, Rabbi Jakobovits refused to sanction a blanket denunciation of Reform and Liberal Jews, declaring that he could not exclude non-observant Jews from his concern, and could work with them on common problems. His 'peace mission' may have succeeded only in the very limited sense that personal animosity was largely avoided during his Rabbinate, but his concern for the community as a whole, his recognition that all Jews were authentic Jews, and that 'every Jew was an infinitely precious brother',[29] does his memory great credit.

But the battle for pluralism was unending, and sniping continued unabated from both sides.

Notes

1. IF, *Scenes and Personalities in Anglo-Jewry 1800–2000* (London and Portland, OR: Vallentine Mitchell, 2002), p.42.
2. See above p.23 (Agree to Differ).
3. Letter, JC, 2 January 1942, p.18.
4. Rabbi Jakobovits, 'Looking Ahead', Sermon, 26 November 1967.
5. Editorial, JC, 28 May 1965, p.7.
6. Report, JC, 9 November 1984, p.24.
7. JC, 16 December 1966, pp.6–7.
8. The Quiet Revolution, JC 9 November 1984, p.25.
9. IF, *Scenes and Personalities in Anglo-Jewry 1800–2000*, p.30.
10. See post p.173 (The Board).
11. Laurence Rigal and Rosita Rosenberg, *Liberal Judaism: The First Hundred Years* (London: Union of Liberal and Progressive Synagogues, 2004), p.169.
12. Meir Persoff, *Faith Against Reason. Religious Reform and the British Chief Rabbinate, 1840–1990* (London and Portland, OR: Vallentine Mitchell, 2008), p.343.
13. Rigal and Rosenberg, *Liberal Judaism*, p.167.
14. Persoff, *Faith Against Reason*, p.350
15. Rigal and Rosenberg, *Liberal Judaism*, p.168
16. JC Supplement, 17 July 1970, p.19.
17. IF, *Studies and Profiles in Anglo-Jewish History: From Picciotto to Bermant* (London and Portland, OR: Vallentine Mitchell, 2008), p.247.
18. JC, 9 November 1984, p.24.
19. Persoff, *Faith Against Reason*, p.359.
20. Geoffrey Alderman, *British Jewry since Emancipation* (Buckingham: University of Buckingham Press, 2014), p.379.
21. JC, 8 February 1985, p.18.
22. Alderman, *British Jewry since Emancipation*, p.380.
23. Rigal and Rosenberg, *Liberal Judaism*, p.167.
24. See above p.26 (Agree to Differ).
25. IF, *Studies and Profiles in Anglo-Jewish History*, p.249.
26. With David Nathan, JC, 6 January 1978, p.17.
27. Persoff, *Faith Against Reason*, p.357.
28. JC, 9 November 1984, p.25.
29. Ibid.

10

In Whose Name?

Live and let live!

Israel Finestein[1]

On his election as President of the Board of Deputies, Israel Finestein gave a number of interviews to the media, and in one of them he was asked if in one sentence he would summarise his policy for the future of the Anglo-Jewish community. He said he did not need a whole sentence, and replied without hesitation with the four words quoted above.

As always, his words were carefully chosen, and these four were not a clever answer to a difficult question, but a challenge and a clear assertion of what was needed. They represented his core belief in tolerance as the key to overcoming division. The future of the community depended on its various strands living together in peace.

The outcome of the Board Presidential election of 1991 was by no means certain,[2] but there had recently been another election for a quite different post, the outcome of which was a foregone conclusion! The election of Rabbi Dr Jonathan Sacks as the new Chief Rabbi in 1990 was beyond doubt. Although in quite a different mould from his predecessor, he was the obvious candidate to succeed Rabbi Jakobovits.

These two men, Israel Finestein and Jonathan Sacks, stood head and shoulders above their peers, each in his own field. To some extent they were both hampered by office, but their ongoing influence and legacy were not dependent upon office, or restricted by it. They were not partners in any formal or even informal sense, but shared a mutual understanding of the greater issues, and although a generation separated them in age, they became close friends. Israel Finestein lobbied discreetly in favour of Rabbi Sacks, although that was probably unnecessary in the circumstances. More significantly, he remained supportive throughout.

Stanley Kalms (b. 1931) Chairman of the Dixons Group Plc, knighted in 1996, and ennobled in 2004, is credited as having been 'Kingmaker' for the new Chief Rabbi in 1990. He was certainly an enthusiastic patron of Rabbi Sacks, who was an outstanding speaker and intellectual, 'miles ahead of the next guy', but, in an interview with Michael Freedland on 11 October 2011,

Lord Kalms sought to downplay his role: 'I just created the publicity ... He walked it, I just opened the door.'[3] He agreed he was influential in Dr Sacks becoming Principal of Jews College in 1984, which put him at the forefront of modern thinking rabbis.

Jonathan Henry Sacks was born in 1948, and achieved a first class degree in Philosophy at Cambridge. He later attended both Oxford and London Universities where he obtained his Doctorate in 1981. In the same year he achieved rabbinic ordination, having attended Jews College and Etz Chaim Yeshiva. He was appointed Rabbi at Golders Green in 1978, and at Marble Arch in 1983. He was knighted in 2005, and became a Life Peer in 2009.

In his installation address in 1991, the new Chief Rabbi Sacks called for action to ensure Jewish continuity 'in the face of the serious decline in numbers receiving any form of Jewish education, and the growing losses in terms of affiliated or identifiable Jews'. Inevitably on the religious front, he confirmed that his own position would be no different from that of his predecessors. There was need to move away from expectations which could not be satisfied. Equal legitimacy for every interpretation of Judaism was not there to be granted by the Orthodox rabbinate. The Progressive world saw his remarks as justifying their declaration of independence in 1989.[4]

But as always there were mixed messages, as Rabbi Sacks had held out to Sidney Brichto the prospect of a 'genuine way forward' in response to an article by the latter entitled 'Halakhah with Humility'.[5] Needless to say, nothing came of this, and Rabbi Sacks was quickly challenged from the right for any implied suggestion of merit in an alternative belief system, such as might be inferred from his dealings with the Liberal leadership. Ironically, the Brichto article drew considerable fire on himself from his own side!

The economic downturn which had affected the whole community during the 1980s caused increasing financial difficulty for the US and resulted in the Kalms Report of 1992 entitled 'A Time for Change'. Whilst the main thrust of the report related to issues of the management and finance of the US, it was accepted by Rabbi Sacks as a momentous challenge to the rabbinate, and a unique opportunity for renewal, complementing the structural changes envisaged.

He observed that 'the failure of the US to attract had a significance which was less financial than spiritual',[6] and sought to remedy this by developing the communal philosophy of 'inclusivism' which he presented in his book *Community of Faith*. This was published in 1995 to mark the 125th anniversary of the US, and in it he stressed the importance of enlarging the religious and cultural programmes of synagogues beyond the service proper.

Another report of equal significance in 1992 was that of a committee headed by Fred Worms on the state of Jewish education, and was entitled

'Securing our Future'. In the words of Israel Finestein, this report 'sharpened the awareness of the shortcomings of the prevailing system, and contributed much to the innovative spirit, which was undoing the remnants of a besetting complacency'.[7]

The Worms report was commissioned by the JEDT (of which Lord Kalms had been the first Chairman) and it was welcomed by Chief Rabbi Sacks as further demonstrating the urgency for action to ensure Jewish Continuity, which he launched as an organisation in May 1993. He referred to a polarisation in Jewish education 'between those who know, and those who do not'.[8] It was estimated that one third of all Jewish children of school age received no Jewish education at all, and there was clearly an insufficiency of Jewish secondary school places.

The community's priorities had to change, declared Chief Rabbi Sacks in an address to the BOD in March 1996, and more money was needed to be spent on strengthening Jewish identity. And as if to confirm the scale of the problem, a survey of British Jews[9] concluded in the same year that one third of the community as a whole was unaffiliated to a synagogue, and that the rate of intermarriage was over 40 per cent.

Meanwhile, the Chief Rabbi encountered mounting difficulties in holding an acceptable balance between conflicting groups. Both religious left and religious right were concerned about the proportionate extent of allocations to the other side, with the result that the Chief Rabbi handed over responsibility for the Continuity movement to laymen. The readiness of the JIA to contribute to Continuity was also an important development insofar as it became accepted that the needs of Israel and the Diaspora were complementary.[10]

However, 'inclusiveness' eluded Chief Rabbi Sacks. As a practical policy it was doomed to failure. It was based on the idea of dialogue between Orthodox and non-Orthodox members of the community, already highly suspicious of, if not positively antagonistic towards each other. Faced with the rejection of the Halakhah by the majority of Jews, the Jewish people, divided as perhaps never before, seemed destined finally to break apart, and Rabbi Sacks is to be credited with at least trying to do something about it.

His concept of inclusivism was highly sophisticated, and spoke of love, respect and understanding, of leniency in the application of the Halakhah, and of a recognition of the role of the non-Orthodox in Jewish peoplehood. It may not have succeeded in practise, and given our long history of divisiveness, it may indeed well appear to have been an alien concept! It was nevertheless an idea which deserves a place in the history of Jewish theology. With an emphasis on collective responsibility, on rapprochement rather than alienation, and a rejection of exclusivist thinking, it remains an ideal worth striving towards, insofar as neither traditional Judaism nor any of its variations was intended to be compromised.

However, such ideas were well beyond the agenda of those with entrenched views. Right wing elements clearly viewed it with suspicion, and left wing elements regarded themselves as betrayed when it failed. The fight for pluralism by the left would continue, as would resistance by the right to any form of recognition. It was a war of attrition fought anywhere and everywhere, but nowhere more so than over events following the death of Hugo Gryn, when both left and right wound themselves up into a state of indignation, bordering on hysteria. Strong language was used by the right. The left were said to be 'disgusted'[11] and withdrew from the Consultative Committee on Jewish Christian relations.[12]

Rabbi Hugo Gryn (1930–96) was Senior Rabbi of the West London Synagogue for thirty-two years, and an outstanding leader of his community. Israel Finestein refers to him as a 'prominent proponent of communal harmony, a prominent spokesman in every branch of Zionist effort, and an influential advocate of Jewish day school education'.[13] It seems more than likely that Rabbi Gryn would have understood that his friend Rabbi Sacks had a difficult decision to make when he died, and that his decision not to attend the funeral, right or wrong (or inability to do so) should be respected.

Here was a man of such stature that recognition on a personal level could hardly be denied, but on a 'political' level, Chief Rabbi Sacks was in difficulty over whether to recognise the effective head of the Reform establishment. His attempt to redress the balance by taking part in a memorial meeting for Rabbi Gryn on 20 February 1997, sponsored by the CCJ and the BOD, was condemned in an unprecedented manner by right wing elements, and in particular by Rabbi Chanoch Padwa (1908–2000) who had been recruited by Rabbi Solomon Schonfeld in 1955 to lead the UOHC Beth Din. Chief Rabbi Sacks tried to explain himself to Rabbi Padwa, but should perhaps have realised that a private letter containing criticism of Rabbi Gryn would somehow or other find its way into the public domain.

The bad feeling released by these events and comments made public during the period was sadly to continue for a considerable period of years, and may not yet have subsided. In May 2013, Rabbi Gryn's widow sought to lay the matter to rest, confirming that there was never any grievance on her part, and regretting the ongoing 'venomous and divisive comments'.[14]

Writing in 2002, Israel Finestein's version of the above, discreet as always, referred merely to 'acts of omission and commission and responses thereto, which accentuated tension between religious 'right' and 'left' and within the

Orthodox community'.[15] He obviously regretted the publication of Chief Rabbi Sacks' letter, but he understood the pressure under which it was written. He regarded it as an unfortunate incident which reflected badly on all concerned, not merely on Rabbi Sacks, and should not be used to denigrate the office of Chief Rabbi. He was concerned for 'the consequences if any for the communal system or its "ecclesiastical" structure which cannot with certainty be discerned'.[16] After all, the role of the Chief Rabbinate was already weakened by polarisation when Rabbi Sacks inherited it. Did he represent the entire community, or the Orthodox alone, or merely the members of the United Synagogue?

Clearly a low point had been reached in the long history of Anglo-Jewish discord, and efforts needed to be made to prevent further 'infighting and mutual recrimination'. The Progressive movements began to work closer together and, after many months of negotiation with the US, an agreement known as the Stanmore Accord[17] was reached in November 1998. This limited measure accepted the need for mutual courtesy, declaring that 'the absence of recognition did not entail the absence of respect'. It set up a new type of Consultative Committee to explore communal issues, and by so doing, established a modicum of goodwill between the laymen involved. However, although it refers to 'the approval of our religious leaders', those Orthodox rabbis who did not openly condemn it, remained aloof from the document itself.

It has been suggested that Chief Rabbi Sacks should not have tried to accommodate the right wing, and had no need to justify his actions. There were those who criticised him for apparently seeking to appease the ultra-Orthodox or strictly Orthodox unnecessarily. If so, they certainly did not reciprocate! 'The sectarians pursued Sacks relentlessly'[18] on the issue of certifying marriages by Masorti congregations, and efforts to assuage such critics by declarations of his attachment to 'Torah true Judaism' evoked no less severe criticism from the left.

Lord Kalms stated in the interview referred to above that Rabbi Sacks should not have given in to pressure over criticism of his book *The Dignity of Difference* published in 2002 and received with widespread acclaim in a world where multiculturalism seemed then an attractive philosophy. However the implication that all religions were of equal status, or that God spoke to mankind in many languages, or that no one creed had a monopoly of spiritual truth were controversial to say the least, and construed by some as inconsistent with basic Jewish beliefs. They led to accusations of heresy, and he clarified some of his remarks in the second edition.

To a growing extent, Chief Rabbi Sacks was obliged to take note of the unexpected emergence of 'a rightward movement in the approach to

Halakhah and Scripture which was not common in an earlier generation'.[19] Israel Finestein suggests that this was partly in reaction to the lax attitude to Jewish observance in the immediate post-Second-World-War era.

The surge to greater religiosity and observance was noticeable across the board, notwithstanding a decline in synagogue membership, and it was not restricted to traditional or 'middle of the road' Judaism. The emergence and expansion of the Charedi and Ultra-Orthodox communities was a significant development in this period in which they doubled in numbers, and in the number of their synagogues, and after the death of Rabbi Schonfeld in 1984, the balance of power within the UOHC moved significantly to the right.[20]

These communities are not homogenous by any means, and reflected the different strands of their Chassidic and non-Chassidic origins in Eastern Europe, some isolationist, others (such as Lubavitch) dedicated to outreach. The high birth rate among the devoutly religious led to 'a paradox of enormous importance' in that they were becoming a greater proportion of the community, which was itself declining in numbers.[21] Thus they represented a substantial constituency (estimated at 10 per cent) which did not consider itself within the jurisdiction of the Chief Rabbi, and had withdrawn from affiliation to the BOD in 1971.

At the same time, there is some resistance to this rightward trend in the emergence of so-called 'Modern' Orthodoxy[22] which wishes to differentiate itself from Ultra-Orthodoxy, and engage positively with the modern world. However such debates within Orthodoxy are of limited interest for many Jews who look for spiritual content as part of an authentic Jewish life. A new generation wants to believe, to have faith, to see God at the heart of their religion, and have found inspiration in the written and spoken words of Chief Rabbi Sacks, one of his titles being 'The Struggle for Holiness in a Secular Age'.

In his most recent book *Not in God's Name*, he offers a vision of what religion should be like in order to reject violence and accommodate those with whom we disagree. His voice in this area rises above petty differences, stressing morality and social conscience as 'the ingredients of Jewishness in the modern world'. At a time of intense conflict between secularity and faith, he and others like him have given traditional Orthodoxy the opportunity of a new emphasis, attractive to those looking for a new lead.

Meanwhile there could be no compromise as to who was a Jew! The issue came before the British Courts during 2009 as a result of the refusal of the JFS to admit a young man whose mother had converted to Judaism but not through Orthodox channels. To the surprise of many, the Court of Appeal overruled the lower Court and declared that a policy of determining eligibility based on descent rather than religious practice amounted to racial discrimination, in breach of current legislation.

The decision was approved by a majority on appeal to the Supreme Court, and has led to the most convoluted proof of Jewish allegiance by reference to such as the number of certified attendances at synagogue service by the parents and/or the child. The issue could be resolved by appropriate amendment to the relevant legislation, as in fact suggested by some members of the Supreme Court, but no such initiative has yet been taken.

Some welcomed the decision and saw a need to widen the range of pupils to be admitted to faith schools, whilst others felt that the Jewish ethos of such schools could be undermined. Others commented on a certain lack of reasoning by the Court in relation to conversion. How was it possible to convert into or out of an ethnicity?[23] Chief Rabbi Sacks vigorously protested that the principles underlying membership of the Jewish faith had nothing to do with race, and everything to do with religion, and made this the subject of his Lecture on 31 October 2010 in memory of the late Israel Finestein.

On the adult educational front, the highly successful conferences known as Limmud have been the source of criticism of Rabbi Sacks for his failure to attend, although he saw no harm in doing so prior to becoming Chief Rabbi. The willingness of his successor to do so initiated a bout of bitter infighting, and on 2 October 2013, seven Torah scholars advised that no Jew who fears God should attend!

They fear that Limmud 'blurs the distinction between authentic Orthodox Judaism and non-Orthodox beliefs and practises'.[24] However, the sheer weight of the condemnation from the right was largely counter-productive, giving credence (rather than the reverse) to the idea of an alternative view, and providing added publicity to the Limmud enterprise.

Some two thousand Jews and Jewesses of all ages eagerly seize the opportunity to attend the annual cross-communal feast of learning held in the December holiday period. They seek to enhance their Jewish knowledge and identity, or simply to experience the 'buzz' of having to choose from among one thousand or so individual lectures spread over several days. Historical, social and communal issues are presented, of great benefit to those who hear them, and only a small proportion deal with religion or religious texts. But no Orthodox rabbi (with few exceptions) has dared to attend lest he be damned by association.

The involvement of the Torah scholars did nothing to enhance the status or practise of Orthodox Judaism, and mainly acted to silence those rabbis and teachers who could have been working to that end. References to 'pseudo-Judaism' and 'aberration' provoked angry responses in the correspondence columns of the JC, and were denounced as inappropriate. Rabbi Harris of Hampstead expressed his 'shame and distress',[25] and principal lay leaders of the community condemned a 'shocking lack of leadership ... rooted in tactical power play, rather than religious principle'.[26]

As early as 1976, in a letter to the JC, Rabbi Sacks had expressed the view that an informal willingness to share traditional learning should not be confused with formal recognition of Reform Judaism, and that to confuse the two 'does great harm to the cause of Jewish unity'.[27] Had he lived, Israel Finestein would have been dismayed by the public discord over Limmud. Writing in 2008, he referred to the 'ever-mounting numerical success of Limmud and its inclusive consistency as among the challenging signs of the changing times'.[28] As a traditionalist, he regretted the absence there of Orthodox voices, but otherwise approved of what can only be described as a gem of Anglo-Jewry.

Many such as Lord Kalms had high hopes for inclusivism, and were disappointed that it could not be achieved. However Lord Sacks can hardly be responsible for the ongoing antagonism between the different movements within Judaism. Almost utopian in its reach, inclusivism required a coming together of the community, an objective which had defeated all his predecessors. In his valedictory address to the BOD on 19 May 2013, Rabbi Sacks reiterated the well-worn words – 'on matters of religion, we will agree to differ', and perhaps recalling the language of Stanmore, he added significantly on this occasion 'but with respect'.

Agreement to differ implies, however, a degree of tolerance and understanding, a focus on shared values, on common problems, not insignificant in themselves, and on a shared language and history. To live and let live is not a passive doctrine. It requires a positive effort, an avoidance of confrontation, and a putting aside of sterile arguments over legitimacy and recognition.

Only then will the community be able to flourish, and in the words of Rabbi Jakobovits, 'take pride in its enormous achievements with less inclination to highlight petty squabbles and passing scandals'.[29] Or in the words of Rabbi Sacks: 'Not until families can live at peace, can a nation be born'.[30] On accepting the prestigious Templeton Prize, Rabbi Sacks concluded his address: 'We need to reframe the ethics of responsibility in forms suited to the 21st century, and in ways that are uniting rather than divisive'.[31]

The ongoing stresses and strains of his Rabbinate did not inhibit Chief Rabbi Sacks from making a rousing and morale boosting assessment of the community in an address to a crowded public meeting in 2006, to mark the end of the various celebrations of the 350th anniversary of the resettlement of Jews in England. The long and impressive sequence of communal events for that year was successfully coordinated by Marlena Shmool, formerly Community Research Director at the BOD.

As in 1956, there was an Exhibition (at the Jewish Museum), a service of thanksgiving at Bevis Marks (attended by the Prime Minister, Tony Blair), and a Gala Dinner (at the Mansion House). The Queen and Prince Philip hosted a reception at St James' Palace. There was a children's concert at Queen Elizabeth Hall, Southbank. Israel Finestein and the historian Todd Endelman delivered lectures.

It is said that Menasseh ben Israel returned to Amsterdam in the belief that his mission had failed, although he was granted a pension by Cromwell for his pains. However, whilst there was opposition to readmission by some English merchants and churchmen, it seems to be accepted that the lawyers consulted by Cromwell found no impediment to a return. Some historians have pointed out that Cromwell's Whitehall Conference in December 1655 did not produce any document, or specific declaration, formally re-admitting the Jews. However, the fact remains that for several centuries prior to 1656, Jews who wished to practise openly as Jews were excluded from England. After Cromwell's Conference they were not.

Continuous Jewish residence in one place is always a matter for celebration, given our history. However, 350 years puts Britain on a par with the long periods of Jewish residence in Spain (Sephardim) and Poland (Ashkenazim), but without the disabilities and persecution involved in those places from time to time. The Anglo-Jewish experience has been uniquely benign, a liberal and tolerant society providing equality and opportunity, from which the whole community has benefited, as well as the host country.

Chief Rabbi Sacks retired in 2013 at the normal retirement age. There followed the usual debate as to the purpose of his office, and how his successor was to be chosen. There were a number of candidates, and there were those who wanted Rabbi Sacks to remain. However, the name of Rabbi Ephraim Mirvis, highly regarded Minister at Finchley, appeared early and remained to the fore.

One hopes for calmer days under Rabbi Mirvis with some trepidation. He inherited a house divided as ever at home and abroad, anti-Semitism reborn, anti-Israel sentiment at a peak, and the world engulfed by extremism, violence and a callous displacement of humanity on a scale not seen since the Second World War. In whose name?

Notes

1. IF, radio broadcast, 16 June 1991.
2. Contested by Professor Eric Moonman (b. 1929) Senior Vice President BOD, former Labour MP and ZF President.
3. Interview with Michael Freedland, 11 October 2011, in JC 14 October 2011, pp.12/13.
4. See above p.91 (Mirage of Unity).
5. JC, 2 October 1987, p.29.
6. IF, *Scenes and Personalities in Anglo-Jewry 1800–2000* (London and Portland, OR: Vallentine Mitchell, 2002), p.41.
7. Ibid., p.39.
8. Ibid., p.41.
9. IJPR; key findings presented by Stephen Miller, Marlena Shmool and Antony Lerman are discussed in IF, *Scenes & Personalities*, pp.41/2 and p.49, n.26.
10. IF, *Scenes and Personalities in Anglo-Jewry 1800–2000*, p.43.
11. Lawrence Rigal and Rosita Rosenberg, *Liberal Judaism: The First Hundred Years* (London: Union of Liberal and Progressive Synagogues, 2004), p.170.
12. See above p.87 (Mirage of Unity).
13. IF, *Scenes and Personalities in Anglo-Jewry 1800–2000*, p.43.
14. See Mrs Gryn's letter to JC, 10 May 2013, p.27.
15. IF, *Scenes and Personalities in Anglo-Jewry 1800–2000*, p.44.
16. Ibid.
17. Set out in Rigal and Rosenberg, *Liberal Judaism*, pp.335–7.
18. Geoffrey Alderman, *British Jewry since Emancipation* (Buckingham: University of Buckingham Press, 2014), p.401.
19. IF, *Scenes and Personalities in Anglo-Jewry 1800–2000*, p.43.
20. Alderman, *British Jewry since Emancipation*, p.368.
21. Ibid., p.395.
22. See above p.83 (Helping with Inquiries).
23. D. Herman, 'The Wandering Jew has no nation: Jewishness and Race Relations Law', *Jewish Culture and History*, Vol.12, p.152.
24. Quoted in JC 18 October 2013, p.42.
25. JC, 15 November 2013, p.2.
26. JC, 18 October 2013, p.1.
27. JC, 26 November 1976, p.20.
28. IF, *Studies and Profiles in Anglo-Jewish History: From Picciotto to Bermant* (London and Portland, OR: Vallentine Mitchell, 2008) p.29 n.14.
29. 'Trouble and Tradition', JC, 25 September 1992, p.32.
30. Jonathan Sacks, *Not in God's Name: Confronting Religious Violence* (London: Hodder and Stoughton, 2015), p.144.
31. JC, 10 June 2016, p.9.

11

The Velvet Revolution

The rise to unabashed prominence of the Jewish woman in
communal life was among the most marked transformations
within Anglo-Jewry in the course of the twentieth century.

Israel Finestein[1]

The most fundamental division in any society is that between the sexes, and
Israel Finestein addresses this issue with considerable optimism. Previous
reference to Lily Montagu might suggest she was the only outstanding lady
of her time. In fact she was but one of a number of remarkable Jewish women
in Victorian England. As a historian of the period, Israel Finestein was well
acquainted with them, describing their collective impact as a 'velvet
revolution'.

The chapter from which the above quotation comes was entitled 'Step
Forward Ladies', a title which undoubtedly reflects a bygone age. However if
it sounds condescending to some female ears today, that was certainly not
his intention, as is clear from the enthusiasm with which Israel Finestein
greeted the emergence of Jewish women into a male dominated community.
He did not define what he meant by the velvet revolution, except by his focus
on the advancement of women. His only explanation was that 'in velvet, they
(revolutions) sometimes take longer'.[2]

'What women these Jewesses are', wrote Matthew Arnold (1822–88) to
his mother in 1863. 'They are possessed of a force triple that of our western
races.'[3] Son of the famed Headmaster of Rugby School, he did not share his
father's distaste for the Jews, and 'had no doubt as to the meritorious nature
of the Judaic pursuit of what he termed right conduct'.[4] He had a
distinguished literary career, and was elected Professor of Poetry at Oxford
in 1857.

A frequent visitor to the homes of leading families in politics and society,
he regarded his Jewish hostesses as highly gifted representatives of the Jewish
segment of British Society. A genuine personal friendship developed between
himself and Louisa de Rothschild (1821–1910) whom he found to be a
woman of intellect with wide literary tastes. She was the wife of Sir Anthony
who in 1870 became first President of the United Synagogue, and her

financial support made possible the creation of schools for Jewish women and adult girls.

These schools attracted many gifted lady teachers and head teachers, such as Miriam Belisario (1820–85) who with her sisters for many years kept a girls' school for children of members of the Sephardi community. She also compiled a 'Hebrew and English vocabulary', and a guide to Jewish religious practice, which was commended by the well-known scholar David Aaron de Sola, a significant tribute for an educational work by a woman. However 'the Belisario school in Hackney stood high in terms of standards, independently of any association with de Sola's name'.[5]

Louisa de Rothschild was also instrumental in the establishment of evening classes for Jewish women and girls by Mrs Sarah Harris in the 1850s. She was ably assisted by her daughter Emily Harris, who later referred to the palpable need to offer an alternative to the 'streets at night, after long hours in the tailoring and furrier workroom'.[6] Lily Montagu was one of her guest helpers and teachers. The example of the Harris family and others broadened the acceptability of employment-related education for Jewish girls, and led to a distinct form of emancipation and opportunity, especially among the children of immigrants.

There was a considerable intellectual output from highly gifted women throughout the Victorian period. Abigail Lindo (1803–48), whose father was Chairman of the Sephardi Elders, compiled a Hebrew–English dictionary, first published in 1837 and dedicated to her cousin Moses Montefiore. It was directed at preserving the Hebrew language as potentially a language of every day speech, a daring innovation at the time. Israel Finestein noted that there was less reserve in the Sephardi tradition towards the idea of scholarly women.

The 'Jewish Library' was founded and subsidised by Charlotte Montefiore (1818–54) a niece of Sir Moses, and was intended to publish tales of Jewish life. In addition, Charlotte wrote and published proposals for alleviating the conditions of the poor. She urged the 'cure' of poverty, and proposed an industrial school, and a convalescent infirmary, in more salubrious areas. She played an active part in the Jewish Ladies Benevolent Loan and Visiting Society, and in anticipating the urgent need for welfare reform, 'she merits a high place in the gallery of Jewish socially caring women of her day'.[7]

On the literary scene, Grace Aguilar (1816–47) school-teacher, novelist, historian and social commentator, stands out, and although a strong supporter of emancipation, she sensed the danger to Jewish cohesion. She elaborated on the need for adequate Jewish education in 'Spirit of Judaism', although to her annoyance, her publisher added a preface indicating differences of opinion with mainstream Jewish thought. She was much praised by the JC as 'an exemplary Jewish woman, and as a champion of her people',[8] at a time when the JC 'paid scant attention to the presence and interests of Jewish women'.[9]

Among other titles, Grace's *Vale of Cedars* relates to Jewish endurance against the Spanish Inquisition, and her *Women of Israel* was a popular account of biblical and other Jewish heroines. She suffered from ill health throughout her short life, but her output was considerable. Israel Finestein agreed that Grace made no pretence at original scholarship in her historical writing, and has suffered from a bad press over time.[10] Nevertheless, he characterised her as 'distinctively forward looking and uncommonly realistic'.

Ada Maria Ballin (1843–1900) won the prestigious Hollier Prize in Hebrew at University College, London in 1880. Soon after, she and her brother published a new Hebrew grammar in a fresh style, which was regarded as a significant advance in the teaching of Hebrew. However she was informed that the book 'is sold almost entirely to Christians!'[11] Ada studied medicine, and became a specialist in skin treatment. She also studied philosophy and modern languages with considerable success.

Perhaps the most outstanding female Hebraist was Nina Salaman (1877–1925) who translated medieval Hebrew poetry whilst still in her teens. She was encouraged among others by the well-known Jewish writer Israel Zangwill, who provided an introduction to the Jewish Publication Society of America. They later invited her to translate the poetry of Yehudah Halevi (1075–1141), published in 1924. In addition to her translations, Nina also wrote historical essays, book reviews and poetry of her own. She would have been the first woman President of the JHSE in 1922, but for falling seriously ill.[12]

Nina Salaman wanted Jewish women to become literate in order to influence the next generation.[13] Although a traditionalist, she was active in the Jewish League for Woman Suffrage (founded 1912), and also wanted to improve the status of women in the Jewish community, with the right to vote in synagogue elections. Nina and her husband, the physician Redcliffe Nathan Salaman, both supported the Zionist cause, and in honour of the Balfour Declaration they planted the 'Jerusalem Orchard' at their country home.

They lived not far from Cambridge where Nina worked from time to time, and became closely connected with scholars at the University. On 5 December 1919, she daringly preached from the pulpit of the Cambridge Hebrew Congregation which caused a stir, later defused by Chief Rabbi Hertz who argued that the service had already ended when she did so! He delivered the eulogy at her funeral on Rosh Chodesh Adar 1925, a rare tribute.

Henrietta (Nettie) Adler (1868–1950) daughter of Chief Rabbi Hermann Adler, was outstanding in her personal involvement on behalf of the disadvantaged. She was 'a foremost protagonist of children's rights' at a time when children were employed in appalling circumstances. She began social work as a school manager, and served on the governing bodies of several local schools in Dalston and Hackney. 'Wedded to public duty' she attended the Board of Deputies representing the Union of Jewish Women, and served as a Council member of the AJA. She was a metropolitan magistrate for many years, one of the first Jewish women to be appointed.[14]

As a member of the Liberal Party, Nettie was co-opted on to the London Education Committee in 1905, and was elected to it in 1910 following a comfortable victory in the local election for the Central Hackney Division. She served on other London County Council committees relating to public health, child care, and housing, and was Deputy Chair of the LCC in 1922/23. Nettie represented Central Hackney from 1910 until 1925, and from 1928 to 1931. The constituency had a considerable Jewish immigrant population, with all the tensions which that will have created. Her tenure was 'primarily a testament to the remarkable abilities of an outstanding Jewess – the first to achieve national prominence in the political sphere in Britain, and internationally known as a social worker and educationalist'.[15]

Changes were 'unmistakably and progressively taking place in the social standing, aspirations and achievement of women',[16] and a strong sense of injustice pervaded their exclusion from the franchise. After years of bitter struggle, a majority in the House of Commons was finally in favour of votes for women, but it was not until 1918 when their contribution to the First World War effort was widely recognised, that a limited measure was passed. It would be another ten years before restrictions were removed, and all women were granted the same status as men.

In the face of the new post-Victorian era, an older way of life in Jewish society was slowly giving way to a more prominent place for women, as demonstrated by the creation of the Union of Jewish Women in 1902. The JC referred to the well-attended nationwide conference which preceded its formation as 'a notable gathering', and devoted seven pages to reporting its proceedings. Israel Finestein refers to 'two of the most notable women among the impressive galaxy who addressed the conference' as Anna Simmons, well known for her welfare work in Manchester, and Alice Model of Hampstead who was principal founder of the Jewish Maternity Hospital and the Jewish Day Nursery in Whitechapel.

Anna Simmons, widow of the respected Minister at Manchester Reform, was credited with the idea of the conference, and it was generally recognised that the success of the occasion owed much to her. The president of the convening committee, 'an imperious lady', was Julia Matilda Cohen (1853–1917) mother of Sir Robert Waley Cohen (1877–1952) prominent industrialist, and a future leader of Anglo-Jewry. The enthusiasm engendered by the new movement 'set unimpeachable precedents for the public involvement of Jewish women in public office. There could be no turning back!'[17]

Quite apart from those with special skills and aptitudes, many Jewish women had large families and lived in crowded accommodation, but by dint of personality and strength they triumphed over adverse conditions. The historian G.M. Trevelyan once asked, 'Where were the Pilgrim Mothers? Were they not equally heroes?'[18] Professor Lloyd Gartner (1927–2011) formerly of Tel Aviv University, in a lecture to the JHSE, referred to the hardihood, vigour, thrift and devotion to family of women in the Jewish migration to England and America.[19] He concluded that 'It was perhaps not realised at the time that the equal participation of women in the great Jewish migration was the first sign of that momentous process of women's equality'.

It is well known that many immigrant wives of necessity played a dominant role in managing the household economy, often as breadwinner on subsistence wages, and they remained a major influence on their families. The enormity of this burden on the immigrant generation is well documented by Rickie Burman (former Director of the London Jewish Museum) in 'Jewish Women and the Household Economy in Manchester 1890–1920',[20] and further studies. However, with increased prosperity, and a reduction of family size, the economic contribution of women was no longer essential, and for some, their own economic and educational position improved.

The Zionist movement and its various political and charitable organisations provided opportunities for a major contribution by Jewish women at all levels. But special praise must be reserved for those young women (and men) who dedicated their lives to redeem the land of Israel in its infancy. In the main, they gave up the expectation of a comfortable life and prepared themselves for the extreme hardship of an agricultural community. In February 1949 several young Jewish women from Britain[21] helped found Kibbutz Lavi on a barren hilltop in the Gallilee, some ten miles west of Tiberias.

Ambassador to Britain, Yehuda Avner (1928–2015) was also one of the original founders. He described their new home as a 'waterless expanse of hard-hearted acreage', and the work there as a 'backbreaking chore of clearing rocks and stones'.[22] He recounted that one of his tasks was to dig the communal latrine, which to his horror, and that of his new wife, was still in use when he returned in 1954 from a period of duty with Bnei Akiva, the religious Zionist youth movement in England.

The women of Lavi were by no means unique, and Avner refers to the self-sacrifice of his future wife's sister (Esther Cailingold) who almost knowingly gave her life by volunteering to serve in the Jewish quarter of the Old City during the 1948 War of Independence. Completely surrounded, wounded, and with no means of escape, she wrote in her last letter home that she was 'proud and happy to pay the price for the realization of our longings'.[23]

Such dedication was in the tradition of other Jewish heroines such as Hannah Senesh (1921–44) whose voluntary mission behind enemy lines during the Second World War almost inevitably led to her capture, torture and execution. The bravery of Denise Bloch (1916–45) and Muriel Byck (1918–44) who served as agents of the Special Operations Executive behind enemy lines is given special treatment by Martin Sugarman in his detailed account of the military contribution of British Jews in the Second World War.[24]

Another outstanding Jewish heroine in terms of leadership was Golda Meir (1898–1978) who became Prime Minister of Israel unexpectedly in March 1969, ten years before Margaret Thatcher became the first woman Prime Minister of Britain. By contrast, Golda emerged through the Labour tradition, and was one of those pioneers who had immigrated to Palestine in the 1920s to work on the land. Her ability was quickly recognised and she represented her kibbutz at the powerful Histadrut federation. Golda rapidly rose through the ranks of the political left, and eventually served as Minister of Labour. She became Minister of Foreign Affairs in 1956.

Her period in office as Prime Minister was much influenced by the near tragedy of the Yom Kippur War (1973) and the sacrifice involved, and she was instrumental in obtaining urgent additional arms from the American President Nixon, crucial for victory. She was known as the Iron Lady of Israeli politics, and it is said that Ben Gurion described her as the best 'man' in the government. She was described by Avner, who worked closely with her, as 'an epic embodiment of true legends, and legendary truths'.[25]

The corresponding highpoint in Anglo-Jewry in terms of female leadership was the election of women to be Honorary Officers of the Board of Deputies. The first was Rosalind Preston, elected as a Vice President in 1991, and Josephine Wagerman (b.1933) was the first and so far only woman President, elected unopposed in 2000. Mrs Wagerman was previously for some ten years the successful Principal of the old established Jews Free School in North London. She was and remained a strong advocate for female equality, and stated on her election, 'There is a strong feeling that the tide is turning'.[26]

Israel Finestein referred to an increasing number of women who have sought membership of the Board at that time, and 'the steadily advancing role of women in communal life'.[27] A significant improvement began in his view in 1971 with the Women's Campaign for Soviet Jewry. Their success in informing public and Government opinion (sometimes in the face of internal opposition) gave added prestige to Jewish women seeking wider influence in the community. Likewise he quotes the example of Rebecca Sieff (wife of Lord Sieff) and Elsie Janner (wife of Lord Barnet Janner) as eagerly followed by women in various fields of communal effort.

In 2006, as part of the celebrations of the 350th anniversary of the Resettlement of the Jews in England, a 'Question Time' evening was held at the Bevis Marks Synagogue. There were four ex-Presidents of the Board on the panel, which included Jo Wagerman and Israel Finestein. Perhaps because of her presence, they were asked (among other questions) whether an aspiring President should preferably be male if he had any hope of election to the top job. Ms Wagerman's firm response indicated that this was very much a matter of concern to her, in what was still a predominantly patriarchal community.

Five years later, women remained clearly under-represented in the community, and the Commission on Women in Jewish Leadership was established. Its aim was to enable the community to take proper advantage of the high educational and professional achievement of women, and in July 2012 'Women in Jewish Leadership' was formed to implement the recommendations of the Commission. Israel Finestein, who died in 2009, would have supported these initiatives.

'Women in Jewish Leadership' is co-chaired by Laura Marks OBE, founder of Mitzva Day, and Norma Brier OBE, former Chief Executive of Norwood. Laura Marks was elected senior Vice President of the BOD in 2012, and at the triennial elections held in 2015 women were elected to fill two of the three Vice Presidential slots, and are well represented in the various divisional committees of the Board. However, the annual delegation of twelve members of the Jewish Leadership Council to meet with the Prime Minister contained only one woman in the current and previous year. This prompted considerable public comment and disapproval as reported by the JC.[28]

In the secular world in Britain, it took many centuries before women were allowed to own property, and they achieved the vote only after years of bitter struggle, both militant and moderate. Even so, female equality is still considered a long way off, and it should not be as remarkable as it still is when a woman now becomes head of a major company or university. The fact that the current heads of the International Monetary Fund and the

American Federal Reserve are both women should give hope for the future, and it may be significant that for the first time there were more women than men in the 2014 New Year's Honours List.

In the Jewish world, with access to higher education, more women have entered into an ever increasing array of active roles in charitable, educational and welfare endeavours. In the administrative field, women have taken the opportunity to lead regional Representative Councils when these were opened up to them, and likewise now sit on synagogue councils. Equal representation on boards of management is now available, and in November 2013 Chief Rabbi Mirvis agreed that female members could be elected as Trustees of the United Synagogue.

Chief Rabbi Mirvis has now introduced the new post of *ma'ayan* whereby, subject to a course of study, women can qualify as advisers of women on religious matters. This was described by the US President as 'a truly significant development for the United Synagogue and for the future of UK Jewry'.[29] In addition, it should be noted that many wives of rabbis are uniquely qualified to inspire the women of their congregations, and are already making a major contribution in their communities.

Although controversial issues remain, and are discussed in the next chapter, Israel Finestein felt able to conclude that 'the velvet revolution was irreversible in the new age'.[30]

Notes

1. IF, *Studies and Profiles in Anglo-Jewish History: From Picciotto to Bermant* (London and Portland, OR: Vallentine Mitchell, 2008), p.184.
2. Ibid.
3. IF, *Anglo-Jewry in Changing Times, Studies in Diversity 1840–1914* (London & Portland, OR: Vallentine Mitchell, 1999), p.200.
4. IF, *Studies & Profiles*, p. 275.
5. Ibid., p.164.
6. Ibid., p.166.
7. Ibid., p.165.
8. Ibid., p.173.
9. David Cesarani, *The Jewish Chronicle and Anglo-Jewry 1841–1991* (Cambridge: Cambridge University Press, 1994), p.25.
10. IF, *Studies and Profiles in Anglo-Jewish History*, p.172.
11. Ibid., p.169.
12. Obituary written by Herbert M. Loewe, *Jewish Historical* Studies,11 (1924–27).
13. Todd M. Endelman 'Nina Ruth Davis Salaman' in *Jewish Women: A Comprehensive Historical Encyclopaedia* (Jewish Women's Archive, 2009).
14. See above p.44 (The God Within).
15. Geoffrey Alderman, *British Jewry since Emancipation* (Buckingham: University of Buckingham Press, 2014), p.199.

16. IF, *Studies and Profiles in Anglo-Jewish History*, p.180.
17. Ibid., p.182.
18. Ibid., p. 185 n2.
19. Lloyd Gartner, 'Women in the Great Migration', *Jewish Historical Studies*, 40 (2005), pp.129–39.
20. Rickie Burman, 'Jewish Women and the Household Economy in Manchester 1890–1920', in D. Cesarani (ed.), *The Making of Modern Anglo-Jewry* (Oxford: Basil Blackwell, 1990), Ch.4.
21. Among those known to the writer personally were Jean Levinson (Hull), Sheila Oster (London), and Hannah Winter (Harrogate).
22. Yehuda Avner, *The Prime* Ministers: *an Intimate Narrative of Israeli Leadership* (London: The Toby Press, 2010), p.75.
23. Ibid., pp.59/60.
24. Martin Sugarman, *Fighting Back: British Jewry's Military Contribution in the Second World War* (London and Portland, OR: Vallentine Mitchell, 2010), Ch.14.
25. Avner, *The Prime Ministers*, p.256.
26. Interview with *The Telegraph*, 16 July 2000.
27. IF, *Scenes and Personalities in Anglo-Jewry 1800–2000* (London and Portland, OR: Vallentine Mitchell, 2002), p.27.
28. JC, 22 January 2016, p.10.
29. JC, 19 February 2016, p.10.
30. IF, *Studies and Profiles in Anglo-Jewish History*, p.183.

12

Women of Worth

Miriam of old neither needed nor sought male approval for taking independent action.[1] With opportunity and commitment, she famously came forward in historic song. The women of Israel followed her lead, and the people remembered.

Israel Finestein[2]

The success of the 'velvet revolution' in the secular world has not been matched by any comparable success in the traditional world, where men have dominated religious practise since earliest days. Indeed it may well have provoked a resurgence of deeply held resistance to female equality, as normally understood. Some emergence has of course occurred in the Progressive world,[3] but only on strict terms in the Orthodox world, to the dismay perhaps even torment of those Orthodox women who see more to life than wifely duties.

The high status of women, and the respect which should be accorded to them, is illustrated in the Bible with many examples including the song of Miriam quoted above. Man and woman were created equal on the sixth day, although Eve is later placed under Adam's authority. Sara and the other Matriarchs of Genesis were free to act independently and influence their husbands' actions, and did so, often with profound consequences, but always with divine approval. However they should be seen as exceptions to the general rule.

There can be no doubt that Jewish women share with men the benefit and burden of the great Revelation at Sinai, and any suggestion to the contrary[4] is largely offensive in today's world. Yet there are those who would point to some ambiguity in the Exodus account,[5] as suggesting the absence of women at Sinai. However, the Deuteronomy account of Sinai,[6] and of the subsequent septennial covenant,[7] clearly refers to all the people, men women and children. 'The Torah includes everyone, and citizenship is conceived as being universal.'[8]

Nevertheless a bias existed, and Rabbi Akiva famously chided his students for trying to prevent access by his wife, and acknowledged her contribution with the words, 'What is mine and what is yours are all hers'.[9]

Whilst the rabbis of the Mishna sought to enhance women's rights in relation to marriage and divorce, Rabbi Norman Solomon summarises their position as 'Sympathy yes, stretching and bending the law yes, but full equality, no!'[10]

The women of the Talmudic period were outsiders. The oral law was the result of conversations between men, held in synagogues or halls of learning from which women were excluded. With very few exceptions, only men's words were recorded, and like most other societies at that time, women were without a voice and illiterate. The injunction in the *Shema* to teach the law to your children is invariably translated as directed at both sexes, but not everyone of the sages accepted that the use of the masculine gender for collective forms was intended to include the feminine – rather they see the reverse, implying invisibility and otherness to women, and subordination to men.[11]

Teaching the Torah to women was thus frowned upon by some sages – better to burn it, said Rabbi Eliezer, than give it to women![12] Nevertheless there is a strong strand in Halakhah which encourages Torah education for women, and when books became available outside the synagogue in the Middle Ages, women quickly learned to read, and their status improved. The example is quoted by Amos Oz and Fania Oz-Salzberger of the great biblical commentator Rashi (1040–1105) who taught Torah to his three daughters, and in consequence founded an intellectual dynasty.[13] And any purported prohibition against Torah education for women was dismissed by the Chofetz Chaim in 1903 due to changing social conditions, and greater understanding.

'The voice of a woman is naked', is an obscure Talmudic remark,[14] the meaning and purpose of which is far from clear, except that 'naked' is used to indicate lack of chastity, or impropriety, and therefore something prohibited. Other rabbis at the time added that a woman's thigh or hair might also be 'naked'. One possible interpretation from the context of their discussions was the need to avoid distraction whilst reciting the *Shema*, but the purported prohibition has been taken well beyond the area of prayer.

Later commentators have suggested that the original remark means that one should not look at or listen to women, and avoid conversation with them altogether,[15] a view with which Maimonides agreed. This has led some extremists to disrupt air travel, to demand that women walk on a separate pavement and sit at the back when travelling by bus. Such objectionable behaviour may be dismissed as irrelevant for present purposes, but nevertheless indicates the scale of the problem faced by those who would seek to address the issues involved.

Maimonides himself considered it 'unseemly for a woman to be constantly going out abroad and into the streets'. He ruled that that the number of times a woman goes outside her home should be limited to only a very few occasions each month, and only when necessary.[16] His negative view of women is well documented by his biographer, Moshe Halbertal, who referred to the influence of the patriarchal tendencies of the Islamic world in which Maimonides lived, it being customary there to restrict a woman's movement in the public sphere.

Maimonides appears to accept that the original caution about a woman's voice referred to the spoken voice only, but nevertheless extended its jurisdiction to the singing voice. The nineteenth-century rabbi Moshe Sofer took the matter much further by ruling that it is forbidden to listen to a woman singing at any time, whether at prayer or not. This purports to justify the prohibition of mixed choirs in the Orthodox synagogue service, and was almost inevitably extended to purely social occasions.

On 5 September 2011, a small number of observant Israeli officer cadets left the hall when a female soloist began to sing as part of an official military event. Four of them were dismissed from the course for refusing to obey an order to return. Rabbi Professor David Golinkin reviewed the issues in the magazine of the International Association of Jewish Lawyers and Jurists,[17] and expressed doubt as to whether there is any Halakhic objection to the sound of a woman singing. He also refers to the Halakhic principle of respect for others.

The behaviour of those who walked out was insulting not only to the performer, but also to other soldiers present, and to the officers in charge. Nevertheless, the Ashkenazi Chief Rabbi of Israel publicly supported those who walked out, and urged the Army to ensure that only men would sing at military events when observant men where present. The implications of this are far-reaching, and represent a philosophy of segregation which few would find desirable or practical in the modern world.

Is it significant perhaps that the new partnership-*minyan* in Borehamwood was called Kehillat Nashirah, 'the singing community'? Or that a new such congregation established in Jerusalem was called Shira Hadashah, 'a new song', perhaps also a reminder of the old song of Miriam. In such services, both men and women may lead the congregation in prayer, and read from the Torah. Borehamwood was the first community in England to hold such services, followed by Hampstead, and Golders Green in 2015. The services were said to be an attempt to preserve Orthodoxy as a meaningful experience for women.

One of the very few women referred to in the Talmud was one Kimchit[18] who was lucky or virtuous enough to become the mother of a large priestly family. When asked what the secret of her success was, she ascribed it to feminine modesty with the words: 'The walls of my home have not seen the strands of my hair'. A potential source of beauty, it has traditionally been considered modest by some to conceal a woman's hair outside the home. By the same logic, it was considered desirable by others to disguise other parts of the female anatomy or conceal them completely, and in some quarters to avoid published images of women.

Attempts to hide women from view have led to an obsession with dress codes,[19] which are in any event important in every sphere, secular as well as religious. The clothes we wear are a statement of who we are. They are an emblem of identity or aspiration to a particular class and status. Our choices reflect not merely our personal preferences, or employment needs, but also the demands or standards of those with whom we wish to identify. The colour, style, supplier, and even the material itself announces our loyalties, whether imposed or freely given. There are no absolutes. There is only custom and fashion.

Today in the Jewish world a man's hat size, shape, width of brim, or the colour and material of his kippa, can tell of his allegiance to one group or another. Clothes are a badge and a uniform. They have no intrinsic religious significance, except that given or accepted by the wearer, such as the longstanding custom that a Jewish male should cover his head for prayer. Furthermore, the requirements of one group may in fact contradict those of another. Trousers may be worn by women Muslims as a token of modesty, and a means of concealment, but may be a sign of immodesty if worn by a Jewess! Perhaps the latter relates to the injunction that a woman 'shall not wear that which pertaineth to a man'.[20]

The need for women to drive is beyond question today, and essential for many. Yet it has been held 'contrary to the rules of modesty in our camp'[21] by certain extremists. Instead of addressing the causes of the issue, which apparently arose from problems at the school gates, modesty is arbitrarily invoked to justify a blanket ban on women driving. In similar vein, the Iranian religious authorities have banned women from cycling as a contravention of chastity.[22] In such ways is modesty misappropriated and brought into disrepute.

Women's modesty is not compromised by an active participation in public life, and seems to be a wholly inadequate explanation for the demands placed upon them. It may be that concealment avoids unwanted attention but that will not itself deter some men from taking liberties, especially when in positions of authority. Several high profile examples emerged during the recent American election campaign.[23] The treatment of women as second-class citizens, or worse, can quickly descend into serious sexual harassment and abuse, of which sadly there are many examples, especially from the Indian sub-Continent.[24]

Jewish men are not immune from temptation, but the Orthodox tradition appears wedded to the belief that men need protection from the possibility of immoral actions or thoughts. The obligation is thus not upon men to behave responsibly (and be punished if they do not) but upon women to present themselves in such a way so that men cannot claim to be sexually distracted by their mere presence or proximity.

But does this require six hundred pages[25] of regulations by which to determine every possible aspect of women's dress and behaviour in the minutest detail? To convert modesty into a huge legal structure is to lose sight of the larger cultural context in which we now live, and suggests an unhealthy preoccupation with women's bodies, as if no other aspect of the relationship with women existed. The suggestion by Rabbi Falk that the daily practise of modesty by women is in some way equivalent to the study of Torah by men is no doubt well intentioned, but is surely misconceived.

There are of course many women who are quite happy to comply with a strict dress code, and do not appear to do so out of compulsion. Perhaps they feel liberated by their compliance, but there are others who wish to be liberated in a different way, and without any suggestion of immorality or inferiority. Peer pressure will also have a major influence, whether for good or ill, but cannot be legislated against or ignored as if it did not exist.

Furthermore, in some quarters, clothing which is meant to be a symbol of modesty has become fashionable, with head coverings which can be colourful and stylish, and potentially more distracting than what lies beneath, if distraction is indeed the issue. This trend has not gone unnoticed, and Rabbi Falk on behalf of the UOHC, in advance of the Jewish New Year 2016, has warned against bright colours, fitted blouses or short skirts, and the need for Orthodox women to avoid the influence of fashion.

Perhaps we should rather look for guidance from the spontaneous gesture of the young matriarch, Rebecca, who veiled herself when she realised she was about to meet her future husband,[26] or the prophet Micah,[27] who referred to modesty as one of the three cardinal virtues of human life. His concept is generally interpreted in terms of humility and connotes an absence of ostentation and the presence of decency and personal holiness, inward devotion and acts of love.[28] These are subjective matters for each individual woman to consider and apply in her own way.

The underlying problems are perhaps even more intractable in relation to services in the traditional synagogue where segregation of the sexes is the norm and women have no specific role there. A suggestion that the Torah should be handed to a woman and passed through the women's section on its way from and to the Ark, has been rejected and condemned as 'Reform-influenced' by Rabbi Ephraim Padwa, who succeeded his father as rabbinical head of UOHC. Whether it is or not, the emotional impact of the Torah scroll itself can be felt as much by women as by men, and cannot be overemphasised. Treated by all with veneration, enclosed with three layers of protective covering, the document itself untouched by human hand, and carried before us throughout the dispersion, its physical presence proclaims our unique identity.

The yearning of women for religious involvement can be equal to that of their male counterparts, and the introduction of the 'partnership-*minyan*' has taken matters much further. Although prohibited by the present and former Chief Rabbi, they appear to have strong support among women, including young women, and could well become part of the landscape, perhaps in due course to become part of 'modern' Orthodoxy.

The opposition appears to rely not so much on Halakha, as on divergence from established practice, which would be 'in violation of the spirit of the Law'. A Talmudic comment as to 'the dignity of the community' is sometimes quoted, somewhat inappropriately in today's world, to maintain the disallowance of female participation.[29] One might hope for a better reason than sheer longevity or 'normative conduct' at a time when women are certainly more educated and emancipated than in Talmudic days, and one must bear in mind the law of the land which provides for equality of the sexes and the absence of discrimination.

Women may of course recite prayers with the congregation and benefit from attendance, but as at present, they can only watch, often in some discomfort. The current Chief Rabbi Mirvis has expressed concern that women should not be distant from the scene of the action, and wants synagogue buildings to be as inclusive as possible. He has no objection to all-women prayer groups, or to women wishing to recite blessings in public in the presence of a *minyan*, such as after illness or childbirth, or the mourner's *Kaddish* when bereaved. The US has produced a booklet to help women say *Kaddish*, and it is accepted that they should feel supported and comfortable in that regard.

The Jewish Orthodox Feminist Alliance (JOFA) was founded in New York in 1997 and is in some respects a successor to the Rosh Chodesh movement for Orthodox women. JOFA extended its work to the UK in 2013. Its mission is to expand the spiritual, ritual, intellectual and political opportunities for women, and to promote meaningful participation and equality for women in family life, synagogues, houses of learning, and Jewish communal organisations to the full extent possible. Its objectives are stated to be 'within the framework of Halakhah', but differences of interpretation are almost inevitable. They are likely to be strongly contested amid accusations already of an over-heated debate.

Dina Brawer, the UK ambassador of JOFA, points to the frustration which may be caused by the gap between a woman's secular and religious world, and to the potential for disengagement from Judaism which might follow. She wishes to develop effective tools to prevent this possibility, and one of those tools is very much educational. She made this clear in her first appearance as the new Scholar-in-residence at Hampstead Synagogue: 'I am here to teach Torah'.[30] The increased opportunity for women to study Torah is a significant feature of the modern age, and cannot be seen in isolation, or as leading nowhere.

Ms Brawer herself is a student at the New York Yeshivat Maharat which ordains women, contrary to Orthodox practise in America, where the late Rabbi Moshe Feinstein (1895–1986) was the principal authority on Halakhah. He recognised the equal sanctity of women, and their sacred task of bearing and rearing children, but he insisted that there could be no deviation from traditional Halakhah which might compromise belief in the eternal validity of the Torah revealed in the minutest detail.[31] Ms Brawer's present status and future ordination have thus caused concern in Orthodox quarters in Britain, and is thought to be the reason for an undefined warning issued by Chief Rabbi Mirvis against offering a platform to speakers who are 'inappropriate'.[32]

Perhaps the clearest indication of the Orthodox male objection to women at prayer comes from the Western Wall in Jerusalem, where a growing number of women have attempted to hold services, wearing *tallitot, tefilin*, and holding the Torah. In 2013, a Jerusalem Court ruled that women were allowed to read from the Torah at the Western Wall, but they were unable to do so until certain male supporters provided them with a Torah scroll from the men's section.[33]

The women's actions may have been seen by some as provocative, but they were opposed with unseemly confrontation, even with threats of criminal prosecution, sadly reminiscent of the treatment of Jews who tried to pray at the Wall before the State was created. However a separate section of the Wall has been allocated for them to worship there as they wish unhindered. Likewise the Israeli Government has agreed to allocate a further section of the Wall for non-Orthodox Jews, where men and women will be allowed to pray there together.

The original men-only and women-only areas of the existing plaza remain unaffected and under the control of the Ultra-Orthodox, but they and their political party are opposed to the agreement with the Reform and Conservative movements. Their objection may well be that they do not want non-Orthodox streams of Judaism to achieve official recognition, but name-calling will not assist their cause.[34] If there is one location intended for the whole of the Jewish people, it is the Temple Mount, of which only the Western Wall remains. All Jewish men (and women) must be free to come there, and address the Almighty (or not) in whatever way seems best to them.

It is suggested that the *mechitzah* or barrier separating the sexes in the synagogue, and other forms of separation, such as separate entrances to buildings, or separate seating socially, are not disrespectful to women, and that Orthodoxy has always regarded the sexes as having different roles. It is argued in support that there would be a long term impact on the community if existing boundaries were blurred, and men should be kept away from the danger of licentiousness. To avoid distraction at prayer is desirable, but to dismiss the whole female human species as dangerous, wanton and impure seems more than excessive, and suggestive of an irrational, deep-rooted fear.

However it is fair to add that the Jews are not alone in man's long-standing belief in 'the tradition of temptation', as described by Miriam Michelson.[35] She submits that notwithstanding the vagaries of fashion ('high heels or no heels') man's perennial disposition to blame women's clothing or appearance for his own sins remains constant!

Gender separation derives from ancient patriarchal societies where male domination is taken for granted. The lengths to which this may be carried can be seen from recent examples in the Muslim world where a woman may be referred to for electoral purposes by initials only, or by reference to some male relative, and there are instances where the name of the bride is absent from the wedding invitation. Such name obliteration is demeaning and renders the woman invisible, without self-identity, and as such needs to be guarded against.

However, male supremacy existed in Britain until the twentieth century but eventually gave way in the face of the modern developed world where the separation of the sexes is meaningless, except perhaps in sporting competition. There are also leisure activities such as swimming, where both men and women might prefer to have single sex sessions. Nevertheless, one cannot avoid the impression of male domination wishing to be preserved, especially in a community where men have the final say in divorce.[36]

It is surprising that certain Universities appear to have condoned male domination by consenting to segregation when demanded by lecturers with extreme views. One might have expected places of learning to encourage its disappearance in the modern world, rather than appease the extremists. The right to free speech does not carry with it the right to interfere with the freedom of women or others to sit where they like, and the risk of abuse has certainly not been minimised by segregation, rather the opposite.

What of the ideal woman, 'the woman of worth, whose value is far above rubies'?[37] Not only does she speak wisdom, and practise loving kindness, but she makes clothes and tapestry, provides food, buys a field and plants vineyards, helps the poor and needy, makes and sells fine linen, engages in business with the merchant, and never sleeps. Clearly she would have no time for sleep!

This woman is no 'shrinking violet', whose role is restricted to the normal duties of a housewife and mother. The text makes it clear that she will also keep abreast of the property market in order to invest wisely, and will understand the complexities of wine production. She will need to be known to local business men and capable of negotiating with them on equal terms. She will need an abundant knowledge of soft fabrics, their manufacture and sale, and for all of these activities, she would need to go out of doors a great deal, far more than Maimonides would approve of!

One hesitates to quote further from the Charedi world where a rabbi in Brooklyn advised that the popular activity known as Zumba dancing, a form of group relaxation and exercise, should be avoided lest it lead to prostitution! One can easily dismiss this as nonsense, but such views are demeaning of women and cast a baleful influence on Orthodoxy, inhibiting what needs to be addressed.

The emergence of 'modern' Orthodoxy is significant in that it is said to contain a more positive view of women. Rabbi Michael Harris argues in his book *Faith without Fear* that 'the prevalent kinds of apologetics around this issue are unsatisfactory'.[38] The fundamental equality between men and women is, in his view, a central ideal of Judaism, and needs to be provided for in a way faithful to the Halakhic process and without rupture to Torah observance. He believes that there are more opportunities to come for women within Orthodoxy.

The rise to power and prominence of women has inevitably created difficult questions for the religious authorities. The voice of the modern woman is not of itself 'naked' and needs to be accommodated. In the words of Jo Wagerman: 'If you believe in the Almighty, it is difficult to accept that fifty percent of the population, obviously intelligent, competent and devout, cannot serve Him in the same way.'[39]

Sexism in the traditional world remains one of its most difficult challenges, yet one which must be addressed, even if the result cannot please everyone. Step forward women of worth! 'Give her of the fruit of her hands, and let her own works praise her in the gates.'[40]

Notes

1. Exodus 15:20–1.
2. IF, *Studies and Profiles in Anglo-Jewish History: From Picciotto to Bermant* (London and Portland, OR: Vallentine Mitchell, 2008), p.161.
3. See above p.50 (The God Within).

4. Norman Solomon, *Torah from Heaven* (Oxford: The Littman Library, 2012), p.251.

5. See Exodus 19:15.

6. Deut. 29:10.

7. Deut. 31:12.

8. Jonathan Sacks, *Exodus, the Book of Redemption* (London: Maggid Books, 2010), p.154.

9. Binyamin Lau, *The Sages, Character, Context and Creativity* (Jerusalem: Maggid Books, 2011), Vol. II, p.195.

10. Solomon, *Torah from Heaven*, p.256.

11. Ibid., p.253.

12. Amos Oz and Fania Oz-Salzberger, *Jews and Words* (London: Yale University Press, 2012), p.91.

13. Ibid., p.99.

14. By the Amora Samuel c.220 CE.

15. See Ethics of the Fathers 1:5, *Singer's Daily Prayer Book*, p.252.

16. Moshe Halbertal, *Maimonides: Life and Thought* (Princeton, NJ: Princeton University Press, 2014), p.36.

17. David Golinkin, 'Does Jewish Law prohibit women from singing in public?' *Justice*, Vol.51 (The International Association of Jewish Lawyers and Jurists, Fall 2012), pp.30–4.

18. Oz and Oz-Salzberger, *Jews and Words*, p.93.

19. 'We are too obsessed with the way women dress', JC, 10 July 2015, p.31.

20. Deut. 22:5.

21. JC, 12August 2016, p.8.

22. *The Times*, 22 September 2016, p.32.

23. And see 'Israel Riddled with Sex Pests!', *Jewish News*, 3 November 2016, p.14.

24. See, for example, 'Sisters who Fought Back', *The Times*, 2 December 2014, p.40; 'Rape as Punishment', *The Times*, 29 August 2015, p.23.

25. Eliyahu Falk, *Modesty, an Adornment for Life* (New York: Philip Feldheim, 2001).

26. Genesis 24:65.

27. Micah 6:8.

28. Hertz, *Soncino Pentateuch*, p.685.

29. 'A dangerous truth', JC, 12 December 2014, p.46.

30. 'Could this woman lead a revolution in British Jewry?', JC, 30 October 2015, p.12.

31. Solomon, *Torah from Heaven*, p.257.

32. JC, 23 October 2015, p.38.

33. See JC, 24 April 2015, p.30.

34. See report, JC, 11 March 2016, p.31.

35. Miriam Michelson, 'The terrible consequences of clothing with women inside of it', *Sunset Magazine*, February 1915, pp.253–62.

36. See post p.164 (Justice).

37. Proverbs 31:10–31; *Singer's Prayer Book* (new edn 1962), p.168.

38. Rabbi Michael Harris, 'Modern Orthodoxy needs the courage to confront difficult questions', JC, 16 October 2015, p.34.

39. Interview, *The Telegraph*, 16 July 2000.

40. Proverbs 31:31.

13

Peoplehood

Jewish national consciousness and identity are no less real, even though they may sometimes appear submerged … We are a people that dwells alone, yet with a wider purpose.

Israel Finestein[1]

In 1899, Claude Montefiore delivered the Presidential address to the Jewish Historical Society of England, and posed the question: were we a Nation or a Religious community? His answer was clear and unequivocal. The Jews may have once been a nation, but they were now a church. He was an Englishman of the Jewish persuasion!

This issue was debated throughout the Victorian era, especially during the long campaign for emancipation. Thus, for example, the Christian pastor John Mills in a survey of British Jews in 1853 concluded that 'his faith and his nation are synonymous; to profess one is to belong to the other'. The issue raised its head again and with mounting concern over Jewish immigration at the end of the nineteenth century, and in 1905, Lord Balfour referred to 'a people apart … however industrious and patriotic … not merely a different religion'.[2]

Claude Montefiore clearly disagreed! He was a member of a purely religious community, bound solely by a common faith, and many Victorian Jews believed or preferred to believe as he did, that Judaism was a religion no different from any other. They were supported in this view by Chief Rabbi Hermann Adler who stated in a controversial interview with the *Manchester Dispatch*, April 1909, that 'we no longer constitute a nation, we are a religious communion'.[3]

But this communion was in serious danger of fragmentation. Those who belonged to the Jewish Religious Union (of which Claude Montefiore was President) had very little in common with the teeming mass of Jewish refugees recently arrived from Eastern Europe. It would have been difficult indeed to obtain agreement between them as to what precisely this common faith amounted to in terms of belief and religious practice.

Other than belief in one God, what the Jews have in common is not faith or belief, so much as the demands of observance, to which many do not adhere. These observances are the result of interpretation and development which many dispute or ignore. The end result is that the Jews today comprise in fact some four, five or even more quite distinct religious communities, whilst at least one half of all Jews have no religious affiliation whatsoever.

In the 1880s, Claude engaged in a series of public discussions with the celebrated journalist and diplomat Lucien Wolf (1857–1930) on the nature of Jewishness and the Jewish role in society, and the dichotomy between religion and nationality was clearly exposed. Wolf was concerned to preserve and strengthen among Jews the sense of their historical legacy, and in 1893 became co-founder and first President of the JHSE. He represented the view that 'fifty centuries of Jewish history were an essential ingredient of Judaism, in which race and religion were almost indistinguishable'.[4]

Claude Montefiore's view as set out in his presidential address was that the 'mission of Israel' cannot be interpreted in any 'partial, national or non-religious sense'[5] as stated in the JRU Manifesto.[6] The concept of God's Chosen people cannot be tainted with national limitations. This is because he regarded Judaism as essentially a universal religion, 'its doctrines not suited for one race, but might be the common belief of all races, ultimately receiving universal acceptance'.[7]

Wolf's response was that to 'denationalise' Judaism was to lose it. For him, a common history, an enduring kinship, common religious and cultural sources and aspirations 'rendered unreal the contention that the sole bond was religious ... He was at pains to emphasise the continuing impact of the national spirit, independent of this or that form of Zionism'. He saw this spirit 'as an inherent product and quality of the Jewish experience'.[8]

It can indeed be said that all civilised nations, and religions, aspire to the same basic morality, but there is something more in Jewish life. If the mission of the Jews is solely the spread of monotheism, its universal character has been largely accepted, and its mission accomplished. But this is to ignore the major differences which exist between and within the different monotheistic religions, each vastly segmented, often with internecine feuding and persecution.

A universal religion suggests that it is open to all people of the world, and the term is often applied to Christianity and Islam because they have achieved world status, but conversion to Judaism is rare, and there are irreconcilable differences. The rejection of Jesus as Messiah would seem to be one impossible barrier to universality, and the 'chosen' status of the Jews must surely be another.

A universal religion would also suggest a method of joining open to everyone. Subject to appropriate tuition, a few drops of 'holy' water are all that is required to become a Christian, and likewise a declaration of faith in Allah to become a Muslim. It is a matter of personal choice, but (subject to a tiny number of conversions) Jews by contrast are born as Jews and their relationship with other Jews is not dependent purely on their religion.

Thus Judaism will always be 'partial', applying to one particular, very small group of people, the Jews. Almost by definition, and certainly by origin, they are identifiable as a particular group, and indeed one which has an exclusive contract with the Almighty! There is nothing universal about the original Abrahamic covenants, which were furthermore and for the most part conspicuously territorial.[9] Yet the idea persisted that Judaism could have wider appeal than what was considered the artificial limit of race, and that it could even be the means of establishing a common worship among Jews and Gentiles.[10]

Sir John Simon MP (1818–1897) a founder member of the AJA and a supporter of Reform Judaism from the outset, 'was endowed as a young man with an acute religious and historical sensitivity, which predisposed him to respond positively to the pains of Jewish existence. He nurtured a form of patriotic attachment to the ancient national and universalistic aspirations of the Israelitish people.'[11]

His views on the present subject are important because unlike other leaders of the community in his time, he never gave up his belief in the existence of a distinct and distinctive Jewish nationality. Whilst he believed in a Jewish role in the progress of mankind, he expressly rejected any suggestion that the Jewish national idea was incompatible with the rights of Jews in the lands of their emancipation.[12] Again unlike others of his class, he saw no conflict between Zionism and emancipation, and joined the British branch of the Chovevei Zion movement when it opened in 1890, approving of its nationalist agenda as well as its programme for refuge and settlement in the face of anti-Semitism.

Inevitably, Sir John became the principal Jewish spokesman in the House of Commons on the persecution of the Jews in Russia, whose position deteriorated rapidly following the murder of Tzar Alexander II in 1881. Despite severe censorship, news of the subsequent pogroms reached the West causing varying degrees of horror, and he secured widespread support for a protest meeting at the Mansion House on 1 February 1882 attended by many leading public figures.

His son Oswald John Simon (1855–1932), a member of the Council of the AJA for almost fifty years, continued his father's work on behalf of the oppressed Jews abroad and organised a further successful protest meeting held at the Guildhall on 10 December 1890. However, unlike his father, he saw no merit in the ancient nationality of the Jews. He wished to see the active propagation of the Faith of Israel beyond the confines of the Jewish race, and he became a strenuous anti-Zionist.

Oswald Simon's concern for his co-religionists was undoubtedly deep and sincere. However, one is entitled to consider whether his actions were more than purely humanitarian, and that perhaps he recognised some relationship with them, some sense of a common fate or destiny. Despite huge social and indeed religious differences, he nevertheless accepted the persecuted Jews as an integral part of the people to which he and his father belonged.

According to Rabbi Mattuck in a sermon given on 28 October 1916, entitled 'Liberal Judaism and the future of the Jews',[13]

> Ancient life in Biblical times as a nation was merely a preparation for a great mission. Israel's life and religion were not meant for all time to be limited to the boundaries of nationality ... The presence of Jews in the various countries is in accord with Israel's destiny, a means for the performance of Israel's divine task ... to lead humanity to the knowledge of one God.

Yet dispersion was not a new phenomenon following the destruction of the Temple. In the ancient world by that time there were already some one million Jews throughout the Roman Empire. The Jews have always wandered beyond their boundaries. They were and are to be found everywhere, and among them there has always existed a unique bond of kinship, enhanced by, but clearly independent of, the existence of the Temple and the loss of the Holy Land.

The Jews are not only a people, but clearly a people on the move, ready to change their address when the need arises; and the need does arise, frequently. England of all places was the first of many countries (in 1290) to expel them and confiscate their wealth. And like the Jews on the move out of Europe during his lifetime, the various branches of the family of Claude Montefiore were in earlier times part of a similar mass migration, following the expulsion of Jews from the Spanish peninsular.

The Montefiores came from Livorno (Italy) where the original synagogue dates back to 1603, and a bold modern style replacement was erected on the same site in 1962 for those Jews who had survived the Second World War. The Goldsmids had originally settled in Hamburg, before coming to England via Amsterdam. By 1899, their combined families had enjoyed some two hundred years of settlement and prosperity in a free country. Not so, the millions of impoverished and persecuted Jews in Eastern Europe.

Implicit in the Mattuck view is the belief that nationality was unnecessary since it was religion which creates the bond of unity among Jews.

Furthermore nationality was an artificial creation of Zionism needed to emphasise the homelessness of a scattered people. In Rabbi Mattuck's 'Theory of Zionism',[14] from which these comments are taken, the centre of the Jewish problem was in Russia, and Zionism merely provided a channel of escape from a miserable existence. Furthermore, the Jewish sense of being separate was the result of unjust and cruel oppression, rather than of divine 'chosenness'.

By contrast, the thoughts of the American Protestant theologian, Reinhold Niebuhr (1892–1971) are of interest. He asserted in 1941 that the Jews were indeed a nationality, and that they 'render no service to democracy or to their people by giving themselves the illusion that they may dispel all prejudice if only they could prove that they are a purely cultural or religious community'.[15] Niebuhr clearly rejected the vision of Claude Montefiore and his followers in that 'the world was not progressing to a post-ethnic moral universe in which differences would no longer matter and complete integration would become possible'.[16]

Were we no longer a nation in consequence of the destruction of the Temple? Not in the sense that a nation presupposes physical control over an area with recognised geographical boundaries. However, the Irish for example claimed nationhood long before it was granted to them, and the Scots still do, as have other people done around the world in respect of areas under the control of others. But whoever has had de facto control over the Holy Land, it remained an identifiable physical place, with which the Jews never ceased to identify themselves and hope for a return of sovereignty.

If not a nation, did the Jews cease to be a people? Our enemies have had no difficulty in identifying us. The ancient Hebrew language has been preserved – through written use, even if not spoken for some centuries. For the most part we have lived apart among each other. And Claude Montefiore himself recognised the unique nature of the Jews in his Manifesto support for circumcision, and his rejection of intermarriage. These policies were justified in his view in order to 'preserve the distinctive continuance of Judaism', but they also preserved the Jews as an identifiable people.

It is true that a pivotal historical event in Jewish history was undoubtedly the destruction of the Temple in 70 CE, a suitably cataclysmic event to suggest a major change of direction. Temple worship, at the heart of Judaism until then, was brought to an end, but the people remained defiantly separate and identifiable, their relationship with each other reinforced by the memory of a non-existent Temple. In the opinion of Ze'ev Jabotinsky,[17] the right wing Zionist leader, 'belief in God was transformed into belief in the nation, and it was the people's sense of nationhood rather than religion per se, that had allowed them to survive two millennia of persecution'.[18]

The Rev. J.F. Stern[19] contrived an ingenious alternative to nationality. Inspired by the emancipation, he had no particular sympathy for the new cultural or political Zionism, and addressed the issue of nationhood in a sermon given on 28 April 1906. 'The words Jewish nation (so frequently used in the liturgy) imply a recognition of brotherhood, and not of nationalism. The Jews constituted a religious brotherhood.'[20] In this way he pleaded for unity rather than division, and for social obligation within the brotherhood.

'We have not come forth from the ghetto to be again confined by geographical limitations', said Claude Montefiore, President of the AJA. As an Englishman, he could not accept that he belonged to any other nationality. Jewish partiality or nationhood would surely impinge upon his status as an Englishman and a Victorian gentleman who had so much in common, or so it must have seemed, with other Victorian gentlemen.

'As the most effective exponent of the mission of Jewish dispersion, Claude Montefiore was in the van[guard] of anti-Zionism.'[21] He feared that a Jewish homeland would suggest a conflict of loyalty and perhaps imperil the hard-won civil rights that had been achieved. A Jewish homeland can bring no political gain to Jews in other lands, but might cause them harm – political Jewish nationalism was for him bankrupt. His aim for Judaism was to be at home in every land – the Jews cannot be at the same time a people of religion and a political nation.

'The great bulk of the Jewish people have remained faithful to the dream of a restoration of their national life in Judea', observed Lucien Wolf, 'but the growth of toleration and the development of emancipation have provided alternatives to nationalism'.[22] However Chaim Weizmann pointed out in 1916 that in his opinion the Jews would remain alien despite civic acceptance. Moses Gaster (1856–1939), Sephardi Haham and fervent Zionist, went further and condemned the claim to be an Englishman of the Jewish persuasion as 'an absolute delusion'.[23]

In his autobiography, Chaim Weizmann, President of the English Zionist Federation and first President of Israel in due course, referred to the 'extraordinary struggle within English Jewry which probably had no historic parallel' in the run-up to the Balfour Declaration.[24] He expressed 'deep humiliation' that an 'assimilationist handful of upper-class Jews' should dispute the very existence of the Jews as a nation. 'We do not wish to offer to the world a spectacle of a war of brothers', he told a Zionist conference on 20 May 1917, but on 24 May, Claude Montefiore and others countersigned a letter to *The Times* pleading that the Jews were not a homeless people, and had no separate national aspirations.

Four days later, *The Times* published by way of rebuke a remarkable leading article by its editor Wickham Steed, and letters from the Chief Rabbi, the Haham, Lord Rothschild and Dr Weizmann who expressed astonishment that anyone should wish to prevent 'the realization of a hope which has sustained the Jewish nation through 2000 years of exile'. That the Jews constituted a nationality was not a matter of opinion, he asserted, but of fact.

In his book *What are the Jews*, published in 1939 at a time of rising Zionist aspiration, Rabbi Mattuck agreed that the Jews were initially a nation, but after two millennia of dispersion, what remained was merely a memory.[25] He maintained to the end of his Ministry that 'it was neither land nor language that united the Jewish people, but rather its faith which can be expressed and lived anywhere'.[26] He denied any trace of racial homogeneity among Jews, no doubt diluted by time and dispersion, intermarriage and conversion, but our historical emphasis on descent inevitably suggests an ethnic component to Jewish identity.[27]

He expressed the view that 'Jewish nationalism negated the historic character of the Jews as a people of religion, and destroyed the uniqueness of Judaism'.[28] This view is in fact shared with a small number of Jews at the other end of the religious spectrum! The so-called Torah True Jews and some members of the Ultra-Orthodox claim that the creation of Israel was a denial of the fundamental belief in heavenly redemption, and that its purpose is diametrically opposed to the teachings of traditional Judaism.

If anti-Semitism is any guide, it is difficult to see the Nazi attack on Jewish businesses and synagogues on the notorious Kristallnacht (8 November 1938) as solely the result of its faith. And the Nuremberg Laws of 1935 introducing anti-Jewish discrimination were clearly racist in character, based as they were on the notion of Aryan supremacy. Furthermore anti-Semitism in its current metamorphosis on the back of anti-Israel sentiment does not appear to have a particularly religious flavour.

When the author of *Mein Kampf* (first published in English in 1933) referred to the 'Jewish peril' he was surely not referring solely to religious beliefs or practices. Was it their religion which caused the Nazis to portray the Jews as a sub-human species and, at the same time, to accuse these same sub-humans of threatening to dominate the world? The Jews as a people 'who gave the world monotheism, and the idea of righteousness, were picked upon as the personification of evil, and fit only to be rooted out'.[29]

The highly improbable history of Jewish survival in dispersion has in itself been a remarkable phenomenon, for which there is no analogy. The retention of belief in a universal readjustment of values through monotheism was certainly a major strand in that survival, as was faith in an earthly redemption an essential component. However, a return to Zion ceased to be a messianic or theological concept when Theodore Herzl put it firmly on the political stage, and this presented those who believed in Judaism as a purely religious community with a fundamental challenge. The difficulty in coming to terms with the new Zionism is well illustrated by the struggle to this effect within Liberal Judaism.

In 1948, the *Liberal Jewish Monthly* commented that whilst every Jew should pray for a peaceful outcome to the War of Independence, and for the survival of the Jews of Palestine, 'the religious destiny of the House of Israel was far greater and more important than the national destiny of a state of Israel'.[30] Likewise, at the time of the Suez War in 1956, whilst agreeing that there was a duty to support Israel, the *LJ Monthly* also stated that the nationalistic philosophy of Zionism always has been and always will be incompatible with Liberal Judaism.[31]

The Lebanon and Gaza wars, and the occupation of the West Bank, have produced agonising dilemmas for many honourable Jews outside Israel (not only for Liberals) who are genuinely aggrieved by any perceived loss of the moral high ground. At a seminar in February 2014 initiated by the Israel government on its relationship with the Diaspora, there was a clear strand of those whose main concern was not so much for Israel's safety, but that it should 'promote equality, act morally and ethically, and commit to social action'. These are religious precepts which no civilised nation would wish to ignore, especially the one nation which gave them to the world.

The Jews are bound by a common culture, religion, history and language, customs and recollections, even the notion of an ultimate home – all the hallmarks of a separate people. What has always mattered was that these various aspects of Jewish life should be retained and transmitted, and communal effort has become more and more concerned with planning to preserve them and intensify a recognisable Jewish identity.

In 1927, the Frenchman Edmond Fleg (1874–1963) sought to explain *Why I am a Jew*. His work was translated into English by Victor Gollancz, and published by him in 1943 at the height of the Second World War as 'an urgent message of hope and obligation for the Jew'.[32] It was reviewed by Cecil Roth as 'one of very few works which can convey so intimate and so clear an impression of the significance of the great heritage of Judaism'.[33]

Many of his readers will recognise the process of Fleg's adolescent alienation from Jewish tradition (Israel Lost) followed by the shock of anti-Semitism, and the discovery that 'we do not plough as others do, or sow or reap, or build or reckon, eat or pray as others do'[34] (Israel Found Again). He immersed himself in the study of Jewish history and law, and finally became proud 'to be descended from this people' (Israel Everlasting).

It is clear that Fleg's journey contained an intensely spiritual element. However, in his concluding summary of reasons why he was a Jew, he focuses on the idea of continuity, mainly cultural or historical, rather than purely religious. His work is thus a classic depiction of peoplehood – or as Gollancz wrote in his Foreword, 'the noblest expression of Judaism and what is called Jewishness'.

Edmond Fleg attended the third Zionist Congress, and with no prior experience of Zionism he was much influenced by what he heard. Surrounded by contrasting Jewish faces from all over the world, he recounts that 'The inevitable happened: I felt myself a Jew'.[35] To Herzl the Jews were a historical entity composed of many different parts, including both religious and non-religious Jews, and confided to his diary in June 1901: 'in the midst of the deepest degradation of the Jewish people ... I made a flag out of a rag, and turned a miserable rabble into a people'.[36]

The events of the Nazi era have sharpened an inescapable sense of the common fate of the Jewish people, now faced with an increased number of anti-Semitic and anti-Israel incidents. The creation and survival of Israel has clearly added a new dimension to the old debate about nation and religion. It does not answer the question posed by Claude Montefiore, but perhaps it points to an overarching solution, inspiring as it does in innumerable ways the perpetuation of Jewish communal life in all its forms.

The Jews have a special and unusual kind of national consciousness, which includes the wish to preserve and explain Jewish survival. In the words of Israel Finestein, 'The essence of Jewish distinctiveness is bound up with peoplehood, and encompasses both Israel and the Diaspora'.[37] The concept of Judaism without Zion cannot survive, any more than can the concept of Zion without Judaism. Whatever one's preference, they are not in conflict. The one does not trump the other. The Jews are uniquely both a nation and a religious community.

Notes

1. IF, *Scenes and Personalities in Anglo-Jewry 1800–2000* (London and Portland, OR: Vallentine Mitchell, 2002), p.291.
2. Geoffrey Alderman, *British Jewry since Emancipation* (University of Buckingham Press, 2014), p.133.
3. Interview, *Manchester Dispatch*, April 1909, referred to in IF, *Scenes & Personalities*, p.290.
4. IF, *Scenes and Personalities in Anglo-Jewry 1800–2000*, p.209.
5. Lawrence Rigal and Rosita Rosenberg, *Liberal Judaism: The First Hundred Years* (London: Union of Liberal and Progressive Synagogues, 2004), p.325.
6. See above p.38 (The Watchman).
7. Rigal and Rosenberg, *Liberal Judaism*, p.324.
8. IF, *Scenes and Personalities in Anglo-Jewry 1800–2000*, p.217.
9. See, for example, Genesis 15:18.
10. Oswald John Simon, *The Times*, 30 August 1897.
11. IF, *Studies and Profiles in Anglo-Jewish History: From Picciotto to Bermant* (London and Portland, OR: Vallentine Mitchell, 2008), p.99.

12. Ibid., p.117.
13. Rabbi Danny Rich, *Israel Mattuck: The inspirational voice of Liberal Judaism* (London: Liberal Judaism, 2014), p.30.
14. Sermon, 9 June 1917. See above p.48 (The God Within).
15. Reinhold Niebuhr, 'Jews after the War', included in *Love and Justice: Selections from the Shorter Writings of Reinhold Niebuhr*, D.B. Robertson (ed.) (Philadelphia: Westminster Press, 1957), pp.132–41.
16. Arie M. Dubnov, *Isaiah Berlin* (New York: Palgrave Macmillan, 2012), p.163.
17. See post p.147 (Zion).
18. Colin Shindler, *The Rise of the Israeli Right* (New York: Cambridge University Press, 2015), p.3.
19. See above p.37 (The Watchman).
20. IF, *Jewish Society in Victorian England* (London and Portland, OR: Vallentine Mitchell, 1993), p.348 n.5.
21. IF, *Scenes and Personalities in Anglo-Jewry 1800–2000*, p.289.
22. Ibid., p.213.
23. Geoffrey Alderman, *British Jewry since Emancipation* (Buckingham: University of Buckingham Press, 2014), p.244.
24. Chaim Weizmann, *Trial and Error* (London: Hamish Hamilton, 1949), pp.252–4.
25. Pam Fox, *Israel Isidor Mattuck* (London and Portland, OR: Vallentine Mitchell, 2014), p.328.
26. Umansky, 'Review of *Israel Isidor Mattuck*', *Jewish Historical Studies*, Vol.47 (2015), p.247.
27. See above p.98 (In Whose Name?).
28. Fox, *Israel Isidor Mattuck*, p.327.
29. IF, *Scenes and Personalities in Anglo-Jewry 1800–2000*, p.307.
30. Rigal and Rosenberg, *Liberal Judaism*, p.81.
31. Ibid., p.217.
32. Edmund Fleg, *Why I am a Jew* (London: Victor Gollancz, 1943), Foreword, p.5.
33. JC, 21 April 1944, p.15.
34. Edmond Fleg, *Why I am a Jew* (London: Victor Gollancz, 1943), p.37.
35. Ibid., pp.33–4.
36. Shlomo Avineri, *Herzl* (London: Weidenfeld & Nicolson, 2013), p.360.
37. IF, *Scenes and Personalities in Anglo-Jewry 1800–2000*, p.301.

14

Restoration

> It became a matter of self-esteem for well-educated Victorian Englishmen to have an opinion about Jewish restoration to the Holy Land, its feasibility, its relation to Biblical prophecy, and the nature and consequences of any British connection therewith.
>
> Israel Finestein[1]

The above quotation is from a major study by Israel Finestein of the unusual phenomenon in nineteenth-century Britain in which the return of the Jews to the Holy Land was considered to be in accordance with Biblical prophecy. It later became known as Christian Zionism.

Many Christians believed that the return of the Jews from the four corners of the earth would precipitate the 'second' coming, and was perhaps even a pre-requisite. The absence of Jews from England was thus considered a handicap to the great ingathering, and was one of the arguments which Menasseh Ben Israel thought likely to appeal to the Puritan Oliver Cromwell in his application for the readmission of Jews to England in 1656.

The idea of Jewish restoration had not been considered by the Catholic Church as a part of Christian theology, but the idea of assisting in the fulfilment of biblical prophecy appealed to many Protestants and Puritans following the Reformation. In the eighteenth century the poet John Milton, the political philosopher John Locke, and eminent scientists such as Isaac Newton and Joseph Priestley all expressed support for the idea of a Jewish return to the Holy Land.

The great eighteenth-century statesman Edmund Burke, whilst not referring to restoration as such, was well aware of the plight of the Jews, and expressed himself thus in a speech to Parliament during the American War of Independence: 'If Britons are injured, they have armies and laws to fly to for protection and justice. But the Jews have no such power, and no such friend to depend on. Humanity then must become their protector.'[2] Whilst there was no shortage of humanity in Britain, it would not be sufficient in the long run elsewhere, and the Jews would need armies and laws of their own. The Holocaust put paid to any doubt about that.

The nineteenth century saw a huge revival of religion in Britain. 'It pervaded all society, challenged men and women of every level of education, and became fused with the objectives of most political parties, and the hopes of every class.'[3] It is hardly surprising therefore that the Victorians saw signs of divine providence in their national success in commerce and empire, and likened themselves to the 'chosen people'. Their material success was believed to be the result of their godliness, and such self-esteem was encouraged by the English Church, with its Protestant emphasis on the Old Testament.

Emphasis on the sole authority of Scripture reinforced the study of the literal meaning and significance of the Biblical prophesies. The scrutiny of prophecy as a current guide and inspiration was widespread. John Keble (1792-1866), the noted Anglican cleric, warned his congregation against liberalism and secularism in a sermon at Oxford on 14 July 1833, by frequent references to divine retribution in the Old Testament.

Hebraic studies by Christians at the English Universities reflected the special place of biblical study, and demonstrated 'a learned interest in the distinctive history of the Jews, their role in society, and the mystery of their survival and providential purpose'.[4] In this, the influence of the Bible was immense. Its language and imagery were part of the national heritage. The English became the people of the book, and that book was the Bible.

The survival of the Jews was believed to be divinely ordained, and both Evangelical and High Church Christians saw the Return as part of their hoped-for conversion. The Evangelical wing in particular viewed the civic and political emancipation of the Jews as more likely to advance that goal. Jewish restorationism was looked on as part of a broad conversionist scheme, or as part of an early transformation of the world scene, precipitating the ultimate moral improvement of mankind. However, not everyone agreed with the restorationist rhetoric, and some clerics challenged the view that the hope of restoration was justified by the prophesies.

John Henry (later Cardinal) Newman (1801–90) expressed reservations about the mixing of ecclesiastical and political considerations in British policy. Some Christians argued that the rebuilding of Jerusalem was not contemplated in the Gospels. However, others preserved the image or inspiration of Jerusalem in the spiritual sense, whilst decrying its desolate state. Charles Egan, writing in 1848, a legal historian,[5] believed that the Jews would be restored to divine favour only upon their conversion. But whether converted or not, it was felt that 'the Jews had some inscrutable role, which it was moral, righteous, prudent and obligatory for Britain to try to discern and facilitate'.[6]

There was certainly a deep-rooted conviction on the part of leading British politicians that Jewish restoration was at hand, and they could not

remain indifferent to it. Sir Robert Grant MP, in support of his Bill to remove
Jewish disabilities in 1833, declared that the Jews are proceeding to the
ultimate restoration of their former greatness, and compared his era with
that of the Exodus. The Jews, he asserted, carry with them the mighty charter
of Heaven's favour, and divine anger would be aroused against those who
impeded their progress – the welfare of Britain itself was at stake!

In the House of Lords, Lord Bexley said that a large body of Christians
agreed with the Jewish belief that their nation will at some time be restored
to the land of their forefathers. Lord Shaftesbury (1801–85), the Tory social
reformer and committed Christian, opposed Jewish entry to Parliament
but believed that 'the Jews had been chosen for a high purpose, and had
a particular part to play in the inscrutable future'.[7] He firmly believed
that British Government should encourage Jewish residence in the Holy
Land.

The temporary conquest of Greater Syria by Egypt in 1831 opened up
possibilities for European powers in the Near East, and Shaftesbury
successfully urged the creation of a British consulate in Jerusalem in 1838.
To him this served both a political and a religious purpose, and he pleaded
for Jewish settlement in Palestine under the protection of the major powers.
In 1841, he issued a memorandum to Protestant monarchs of Europe in
support of the restoration of the Jews to Palestine.

The Crimean War signalled the possibility of further realignment in the
Near East, and the crumbling Ottoman Empire caused concern for British
interests in the region and beyond. With the fall of Sebastopol in 1855,
Arthur Stanley, Dean of Westminster, captured the sense of momentous
developments by his comment that the fall occurred on the same date as the
siege of Jerusalem ended in 70 CE.[8]

In 1853, Shaftesbury wrote to Prime Minister Aberdeen stating that
Greater Syria 'was a country without a nation, and God in his wisdom now
directs us to a nation without a country'. These vast and fertile regions, he
wrote , 'will soon be without a ruler, and must be assigned to the ancient and
rightful lords of the soil, the Jews'.[9] Lord Shaftesbury's love of the Bible is
reflected in his Presidency of the British and Foreign Bible Society (founded
in 1804) from 1851 until his death.

In the long campaign for Jewish emancipation (1828–58) a common
factor among the Christians, whether for or against, was the assumption that
Jewish restoration was a realistic prospect to be taken into account. Despite
urgent Jewish denials of dual loyalty, it was taken for granted that the Jews
had their eyes on another land, and their ultimate hope was a return to
Palestine. The Jews were seen as a nation whose future was closely identified
with the Holy Land in fulfilment of ancient prophecy.

To advance the cause of Jewish settlement in the Holy Land and to improve the living conditions of local residents thus had religious overtones, as well as potential advantages for the national interest. It became fashionable in Victorian times to travel there, and London society came into contact with local conditions in Palestine. James Buckingham MP noted however that English Jews rarely visited Palestine, even as a matter of curiosity or recreation, although Moses Montefiore and Disraeli (if the latter can be counted among us) were exceptions.

The Middle East was in any event a region of immense concern to British imperial and commercial interests, and the Foreign Office was highly sensitive to Russian designs on Turkey, the Indian frontiers, and British-Eastern communications. Lord Palmerston, as Foreign Secretary, ordered the consulate to extend British protection to the Jews of Palestine. He hoped to persuade the Sultan to approve Jewish settlement and land purchase, from which it was argued that benefits would accrue to the Ottomans in terms of revenue, improved law and order, and international ties.

Whilst his predominant concern was to extend British influence in the area, what was under contemplation was nothing less than the actuality of Jewish settlement. Some enthusiasts went beyond a British protectorate, and anticipated political Zionism by reference to a self-governing Jewish polity allied to Britain. 'With its widening authority and mounting prestige, the British role was perceived as clearly marked out by providence,'[10] but 'the proposal to plant the Jewish people in the land of their fathers with international support'[11] was not pursued by the Anglo-Jewish leadership.

No organised Jewish response to the various schemes and hopes came under discussion, nor any political direction. Whether emancipationist or not, many Jews sought to minimise or were disinterested in the Jewish national idea, and were criticised for appearing not to be ready or willing to foster opportunities in the Holy Land. 'It was as though history was biding its time, whilst travel, exploration, archaeology and Semitic language study were fostered by a continuing examination of Jewish restoration, and the role of the Holy Land in the denouement of history.'[12]

In respect of the future fate of Syria, *The Times* urged the Jews themselves 'to show in some definite form what is desirable to be accomplished for their benefit, how it is to be attained, and in what manner it would be conducive to the security of the neighbouring states and the maintenance of the general peace.'[13] They expressed it as 'unlikely that Scripture alone would move the Great Powers of Europe to establish a new focus of civilisation in that interesting region'. In 1842, the *Voice of Jacob* published a letter 'rebuking the community for its indifference', and on 29 September 1843 it stated to no avail that Jewish restoration was 'no longer a futuristic fictitious abstraction'.

The Damascus blood libel of 1840 reinforced the sense of Jewish need and focussed the mind on the danger of indifference. The accusation that local Jews were implicated in the disappearance of a Catholic priest and his servant aroused coordinated action on behalf of the Jewish cause, and did much to foster an interest in the plight of Jews internationally. It prompted the successful mission of Moses Montefiore, supported by the British Government, and the innocence of the imprisoned Jews was in due course conceded.

Montefiore also visited the Holy Land, in fact seven times between 1827 and 1875. He was the first Englishman to be permitted to buy land, intended for a hospital, and he attempted to improve the extremely harsh conditions of the Jews living there. His windmill still stands (at Yemin Moshe) within sight of the Old City, a lasting tribute to his effort to encourage Jews to move and live outside its walls, with assurance of sufficient food.

Israel Finestein expresses the view that Montefiore's involvement with the development of Jewish Life in the Holy Land, 'for all its emphasis on self-help, was essentially a matter of philanthropy and welfare (rather than Zionism) reflecting Jewish kinship, a sense of religious duty, and an acknowledgement of the place of Jerusalem in Jewish History'. However, he was also of the opinion that Sir Moses, who died in 1885, 'would in fact have followed Herzl's star, and would have expected British support for an initiative with the Sultan over Palestine'.[14] In a modern appreciation of Montefiore, he refers to him as

> an important bridge between the age of Jewish powerlessness, which preceded him, and the age of aspiration to statehood which followed him. His career was rooted in the concept of Jewish peoplehood. If he was never jolted towards statehood, his activities were conducive with many other factors, to the day-to-day growth of the Zionist enterprise.[15]

One of Montefiore's travelling companions was Col. George Gawler, a former Governor of South Australia. He was a frequent contributor to the *Jewish Chronicle*, and wrote, 'Every nation which has participated in the persecution of the Jewish people, owes to that people a heavy debt of retribution. Why should not the first instalment be paid by the opportunity now before us to render a service?'[16] Gawler shared with Disraeli the conviction that British life owed much to Jewish influence, and to the Judaic source of Christianity.

Disraeli visited the East in 1830–31, and 'the impact of his journeys through Palestine and his visit to Jerusalem as a Jewish Christian was considerable and enduring'.[17] In his novel *Tancred, or the New Crusade,*

Disraeli's central character declares that 'The vineyards of Israel have ceased to exist ... but a race that persists in celebrating the vintage (on Succoth) although they have no fruits to gather, will surely regain their vineyards'. He clearly expected such sentiments to strike a chord with the reading public. So indeed did the idea of 'a new Judea, poised between east and west', which inspired Daniel Deronda to find a higher purpose to his life and attract others to the cause of a Jewish homeland.[18]

Arthur Stanley believed that the Jewish past was continued by the Christian present, and both had a direct bearing on the future of mankind. He visited the biblical sites, and is quoted in *The Times* as stating 'there is a land more dear to us from our childhood even than England, and there is a city more sacred even than Rome, Geneva or Westminster. That land is the land of the East, and that city is Jerusalem.'[19] Was there a message here also for the Jews? Would they ever respond to *The Times*'s challenge of 1840?

In some provincial cities, Christian exponents of Jewish restoration acquired considerable influence, such as the Hebraist Thomas Scott who preached that national restoration of the Jews and their ultimate conversion were both based on the fulfilment of biblical prophecy. His son John Scott, Anglican clergyman and Headmaster in Hull,[20] sought verification of the Biblical prophecies in historic events, and believed that conversion should not be delayed since restoration might well be at hand. The link between Restoration and Conversion was a major theme of a special session of the Church Congress which met in Derby in 1882, and otherwise approved of a Jewish Restoration in the East of the Mediterranean.[21]

'This sense of approaching dramatic change was not only retained but also strengthened as the century advanced.'[22] No-one knew how, when and through whose agency this dramatic change would occur, except that it was pending, and that when it came it would radically affect the status of the Jews everywhere, and improve the desolate condition of the Holy Land. 'However disparate the motivations, there remained a common residue of providentiality which gave respectability and social acceptance to Jewish ideas about the Return.'[23]

Faith in the divine providentiality of Zionism is at the heart of *The Zionist Revolution: a New Perspective* by Professor Harold Fisch.[24] Writing in 1978, he anguished over the long and painful travail of his people, and 'wrestled to the end with what he once called their messianic tensions'.[25]

Under the force of unrelenting history, including further persecution in the Russian Empire after 1881, the Jews could no longer afford to wait for the Messiah. Inspired by Herzl, they finally began to take practical measures to foster the Return. 'And out of the welter of Gentile restorationist literature, there emerged the irreversible idea of a link between British policy and Jewish restoration. It was an idea whose longevity made it seem natural.'[26] It was an idea whose consequences would be far-reaching.

Lord Balfour (1848–1930) author of the famous Declaration dated 2 November 1917, clearly believed that Restoration was a good cause in its own right, regardless of the geopolitical implications, and the opposition of such Jewish anti-Zionists as Edwin Montagu, a member of the Cabinet. He had referred in 1916 to 'the many crimes and injustices which now stand on record as a perpetual reproach to Christian civilisation', and in 1919 he responded in some detail to the anti-Zionist case in his introduction to the *History of Zionism 1600–1918* by Nahum Sokolov. In the same year, he defended Zionism on the basis that 'all four great powers supported it, and be it right or wrong, it is rooted in age-long tradition, in present needs, and future hopes'.

A key player in the events leading up to the Balfour Declaration was Sir Mark Sykes (1879–1919), a Secretary to the War Cabinet with considerable knowledge of the Ottoman Empire. He was later to distance himself from the negotiations he conducted with his French counterpart François Georges-Picot as to the apportionment of spheres of influence in the Middle East after the First World War. He became convinced of the need for the British alone to acquire control of Palestine, and that Jewish settlement there was essential to that end. He guided Weizmann and others into the correct channels of communication with the Government, and was described by Weizmann in his autobiography as 'one of our greatest finds'.[27]

Sykes himself was a Catholic who grew up in a milieu hostile to Jews, but was later to say that it was his Catholicism which enabled him to understand the tragedy of the Jewish question.[28] He credited Haham Moses Gaster with opening his eyes to Zionism, and changing his view of Jewry. He was not concerned with biblical prophecy as such, but became a Christian Zionist in all but name. He continued to speak for Zionism after the Declaration, and his premature death in 1919 was genuinely mourned by the Zionist leadership.

It fell to Winston Churchill, as Colonial Secretary, to give effect to the inbuilt ambiguities of the Balfour Declaration with its concern for the 'rights of existing non-Jewish communities in Palestine'. He had strongly supported the Declaration, and opposed attempts to limit immigration in the 1922 Government White Paper which he regarded as a dishonourable retreat from its previous war-time commitment, according to his biographer Martin Gilbert.

At the same time, he admired the Jewish people as 'beyond question the most formidable and remarkable race which has ever appeared in the world',[29] with an extraordinary story of exile and centuries of persecution. Churchill was not a Christian Zionist, or even technically a Zionist, but once said that he was 'wedded to Zionism'.[30] His belief in the restoration was both practical and humanitarian. In 1921, on a visit to Jerusalem, he said that a Jewish National Home in Palestine 'would be a blessing to the whole world, a blessing to the Jewish race scattered all over the world, and a blessing for Great Britain.'

Christian Zionism is much concerned with what the Bible has to say about 'the last days' and the 'millennial age',[31] and the restoration of the Jews to their own land is clearly an essential ingredient of its theology. It is not restricted to Britain. John Nelson Darby, of the Plymouth Brethren, made several visits to America between 1862 and 1877, and is claimed by some to be the founder of American Christian Zionism. Not everyone subscribed to his more extreme notions, but the central theme of Jewish restoration remained, and Christian Zionism inspired a revival of the powerful Evangelical movement in the United States.

They did not see the creation of Israel in 1948 as the end of their mission. On the contrary, the ingathering of the Jews appeared to confirm biblical prophecy, and offered hope for the future. A mutual reverence for biblical text ensured common cause, leading to a powerful American pro-Israel faction. Inevitably their views are somewhat hawkish, and appeal to the more right wing Republican Party, but they are of considerable importance.

In 1980, an International Christian Embassy was established in Jerusalem. Its purpose was to mobilise worldwide support for Israel and raise funds for immigration and settlement. They have remained remarkably true to their core beliefs, and at the third Christian Zionist Congress in 1996, they declared as a fundamental tenet, that 'the descendants of the Patriarchs remain the elect of God, and without the Jewish nation, His redemptive purposes will not be completed'.

The power of this statement cannot be over-estimated, because it transcends those voices (if any) which still point to an ancient incompatibility between a Christian Church essentially universal, and a Jewish people essentially particular. It also clearly contradicts those who would still argue that the dispersion of the Jews is evidence of God's displeasure, and that their covenant is consequently forfeit.

On 28 October 1965, Pope Paul VI proclaimed Nostra Aetate ('In our Time') which decreed that God holds the Jews most dear, and they should not be presented as rejected or accursed. The document repudiated anti-Semitism directed against the Jews at any time by anyone, and refers to the great spiritual patrimony common to Christians and Jews.

The origins of this document go back many years, at least as far as Pope Pius XI (1857–1939) who stated (with full knowledge of the Nazi threat) that,

'It is not possible for Christians to take part in anti-Semitism, which is inadmissible. Spiritually we are all Semites.'[32] He publicly rejected the Nazi claim to racial superiority,[33] and indirectly authorised Cardinal Hinsley to speak out at the London Mansion House meeting of 10 December 1938 following Kristallnacht.[34] The present Pope Francis declared[35] that 'all Christians have Jewish roots' in the course of an address celebrating the fiftieth anniversary of Nostra Aetate.

Whilst Restorationism is no longer a part of mainstream Christian thinking today, it has been replaced, and indeed may have stimulated what is sometimes called philo-Semitism. The role and purpose of the Jews as a significant element of ongoing providence however remains, and reflects the enormous advances which have taken place in theological discourse in recent decades. The optimism of the Victorian Restorationists gave way sadly to the horror of two world wars and the Holocaust, but their belief in the ultimate restoration of the Jews to their ancient land was not misplaced.

Notes

1. IF, 'With Eyes Toward Zion: Nineteenth-century British opinion on Jewish Restoration', in M. Davis (ed.) Vol. II p.72; see also IF, *Anglo-Jewry in Changing Times, Studies in Diversity 1840–1914*, Ch. 5.
2. David Bromwich, *The Intellectual Life of Edmund Burke, from Sublime and Beautiful to American Independence* (Harvard: 2014), pp.425–30.
3. IF, *With Eyes Towards Zion*, p.73.
4. Ibid., p.74.
5. IF, *Anglo-Jewry in Changing Times* (London: Vallentine Mitchell, 1999), p.150.
6. IF, 'With Eyes Towards Zion', p.75.
7. IF, *Anglo-Jewry in Changing Times: Studies in Diversity 1840–1914* (London and Portland, OR: Vallentine Mitchell, 1999), p.202.
8. IF, 'With Eyes Towards Zion', p.82.
9. Cited in Albert Hyamson, 'British Projects for the restoration of the Jews to Palestine', *American Jewish Historical Society Publications*, 26 (1918), p.140.
10. IF, *Anglo-Jewry in Changing Times*, p.144.
11. *The Times*, 17 August 1840.
12. IF, 'With Eyes Towards Zion', p.83.
13. *The Times*, 26 August 1840.
14. IF, 'The uneasy Victorian: Montefiore as Communal Leader' in S. and V.D. Lipman (eds), *The Century of Moses Montefiore*, pp.48–9.
15. IF, *Scenes and Personalities in Anglo-Jewry 1800–2000* (London and Portland, OR: Vallentine Mitchell, 2002), p.176.
16. IF, *Anglo-Jewry in Changing Times, Studies in Diversity 1840–1914* (London & Portland, OR: Vallentine Mitchell, 1999), pp.156/7.
17. IF, *Anglo-Jewry in Changing Times*, p.157.
18. George Eliot, *Daniel Deronda* (London: Penguin Books, 1967).
19. *The Times*, 26 January 1870.

20. See post p. 205 (Robinson Row).
21. IF, *Anglo-Jewry in Changing Times*, p.165, n.12.
22. Ibid., p.160.
23. IF, 'Sir Moses Montefiore: A Modern Appreciation', *Jewish Historical Studies*, 29 (1988), p.202.
24. See above p.20 (Emancipation).
25. IF, *Studies and Profiles in Anglo-Jewish History: From Picciotto to Bermant* (London and Portland, OR: Vallentine Mitchell, 2008), p.279.
26. IF, 'With Eyes Towards Zion', p.98.
27. Chaim Weizmann, *Trial and Error* (London: Hamish Hamilton, 1949), p.229.
28. Cecil Bloom, 'Sir Mark Sykes', *Jewish Historical Studies*, Vol.43 (2011), p.148.
29. 'Churchill and the Jews', JC, 12 December 2014, p.46.
30. Ibid.
31. See, for example, Daniel 12:7.
32. Pope Pius XI addressing a group of Belgian pilgrims, 6 September 1938.
33. Pope Pius XI addressing the world's Catholics, 21 November 1938.
34. See above p.70 (Holy War).
35. Pope Francis to the International Council of Christians and Jews, 30 June 2015.

15

Zion

The State of Israel is no ordinary State. It was too long in the making – a millennium and more – for it to be so. Zionism is concerned with Jewish self-consciousness. It goes beyond politics. It is related to identity, survival and purpose.

Israel Finestein[1]

It is mistakenly thought by some that Zionism began with the arrest of the French Captain Alfred Dreyfus (1859–1935) on false charges of espionage. His subsequent trials and incarceration certainly involved a miscarriage of justice so grotesque and deliberate as to establish the Dreyfus Affair as by any standard a historical landmark of major proportions.

Whether Dreyfus was in fact the victim of an anti-Semitic plot is doubted by many historians, and there were other circumstances, such as monumental incompetence, which may have contributed to his arrest as a spy. However, during the campaign which led to Dreyfus's pardon in 1899 and ultimate acquittal in 1906, the scale of Jew hatred at the heart of the French establishment was clearly revealed. It went as far as proposals from certain quarters in the French Parliament to repeal Jewish civil rights, and confiscate Jewish property, which fortunately were defeated.[2]

In his open letter to the President of the French Republic (13 January 1898) under the banner headline 'J'accuse', the novelist Emile Zola expressed his deep sense of outrage at the injustice perpetrated against Dreyfus. His letter concluded with a list of the generals, hand-writing experts and others, in his view guilty of villainy and illegality. He accused only one of them of religious prejudice, but made no accusation of anti-Semitism as such.

Theodor Herzl (1860–1904) was the Paris correspondent of his Viennese newspaper when he reported the original trial of Captain Dreyfus in December 1894, and his contemporary dispatches apparently made no mention of Dreyfus[3] or that he was a Jew until it emerged after the trial. He attended the public degradation of Dreyfus on 5 January 1895, and despite protestations of innocence, Herzl 'accepted that Dreyfus was a traitor, and that his demeanour was consistent with guilt'.[4]

Shlomo Avineri pointed out that Herzl was already deeply troubled by anti-Semitism in Germany, Austria and other major European countries. His play 'The New Ghetto' was an analysis of the Jewish predicament in which their apparent freedom was illusory, but the contempt towards them was indeed real. The Jews 'would find no salvation in the gentile world, as liberal and enlightened as it might be',[5] and remained imprisoned by the invisible walls of a gilded cage.

The emergence of racist political parties in Europe, and the growth of nationalist movements made the Jewish position even more precarious, but what impressed upon Herzl more was the total failure of European emancipation. 'Educated Jews, who had sought entry into Austria's German speaking culture, now found themselves rejected and excluded.'[6] His conclusion was that the Jew must reinvent himself, and find a home of his own. But where was Zion located?

Herzl was well aware of what he called 'the mighty legend' by which Palestine would have the greatest claim, but it was too close to Europe for his liking, too close to the sick continent with its deep-seated and obsessional dislike of the Jews. It was clear to Herzl (if to no-one else) that there was no future for the Jews in Europe, and had he lived a normal span, he would have seen this confirmed in the worst possible way at the hands of a failed art student[7] from Vienna, his home city.

To escape Europe, Herzl was prepared to consider Argentina, even East Africa, bearing in mind also that Palestine had a difficult climate, and little room for expansion. It was perhaps his ambivalence over Palestine which indicated a lack of attachment to, or knowledge of, Hebraic sources, by which no other location could possibly be regarded as the destination for the return of the Jewish people.

However, the need to reflect the inner life and Hebraic tradition of the Jewish people was not lost on him, and he declared in his opening address to the First Zionist Congress on 29 August 1897, that 'Zionism was a return to Judaism, even before our return to the Land of Israel'.[8] He wanted to bring together the most modern and the most ancient elements of world Jewry, without need of 'concessions which might entail deep spiritual sacrifices'.

An unobservant Jew himself, he nevertheless agreed that Basle should be the location for the Zionist Congress only after he 'had ascertained that there was a Kosher restaurant in the city so that observant Jews would not be deterred from attendance'.[9] 'Anti-Semitism has made Jews of us', he said half in jest to his friend Max Nordau in 1895, and had hoped that it would be the religious leadership, the local rabbis, who would lead the people towards Zion. But religious Zionism took many years to emerge.

Herzl was well aware that the Zionist project involved nothing less than a revival of the Jewish people, and the development of national consciousness, and this was adopted at the 1898 Congress. However, the overwhelming objective remained the creation of a State for the Jews, and in the absence of support from leading Jews and politicians, Herzl published in February 1896, to considerable acclaim, his collected thoughts and ideas in his most famous book *The Jewish State*. It attracted a level of international attention which Herzl had hitherto been unable to achieve, and which he considered essential if the new State was to receive public recognition. However, the Jews were inevitably divided!

Dreyfus, for example, despite his ill-treatment, 'considered Zionism as an anachronism', and it is likely that most French Jews of his generation 'had no wish to move to an obscure and inhospitable province of the Ottoman Empire'.[10] The Reform community had long denied Jewish nationhood, and the Orthodox saw it as heretical. Chief Rabbi Hermann Adler warned against Zionistic affiliations, and the Jewish community of Munich objected to the presence of the First Zionist Congress in their city, which was Herzl's first location of choice.

He tried unsuccessfully to persuade the Chief Rabbi of Vienna to attend the second Zionist Congress, and berated those who 'pray for Zion while at the same time go to war against Zion'.[11] Orthodox Jews have for centuries prayed daily in the *Amida*[12] for the ingathering of the exiles, and for the return of the Lord to Jerusalem, but believed or preferred to believe that these events could only be brought about by the Messiah.

On the other hand, Herzl's plans appealed strongly to the masses of Jews from Eastern Europe, where Jewish settlement in Palestine was promoted by the Chovevei Zion (Lovers of Zion) movement despite overwhelming practical problems. It is estimated that they had some 4,000 members at the time of the First Zionist Congress, and most were willing to become part of the new Zionist Organization.

The new Zionism was also welcomed by many who supported the Jewish Enlightenment (Haskalah) and the mass movement which Herzl was able to create thus bypassed the great and the good, who hesitated in their support. However, from the first Zionist Congress, the Jewish people had a representative body on the world stage, something which the Jews had lacked since ancient times.

One of the founders of Chovevei Zion was Leon Pinsker (1821–91), the Jewish doctor from Odessa, whose message was that 'the Jew is entitled, indeed obligated, to attempt to preserve his individual and group identity, which was bound up with the history of his people'. It followed that a Jewish State could not be an end in itself. It must have 'a wider purpose, to increase and sustain the self-awareness of the Jews – culturally, intellectually and morally'.[13]

Against a lurid background of violent anti-Semitism, Pinsker urged the Jews to become independent in his pamphlet entitled 'Auto-emancipation', published in 1882. He famously described the Jew as 'a wandering corpse', which could find safety, self-esteem and the guarantee of continuity only in political nationhood. These ideas were well entrenched among the two million Jews who fled the Russian Empire between 1880 and 1914. Most who had settled in the West rallied to the Herzl banner, and it was their children and grandchildren who would in due course support and to some extent fulfil the Zionist dream.

The importance of the 'wider purpose' was taken up by Achad Ha'am[14] (Asher Ginsberg, 1856–1927) who believed that Zionism must be a source of regeneration for the whole Jewish world. He regarded Herzl's plans as unworkable, and argued that a national home will not solve the Jewish problem.[15] Nevertheless, he urged the creation of a moral or spiritual centre ('mercaz ruchani') a 'haven not only for Jews but for Judaism'. Zion, in his view, was to be a model for the dispersed Jews to imitate so as to avoid assimilation and fragmentation. His views were perhaps unfairly regarded at the time as a distraction from the essential task of state-building, but he saw Zion 'in a context that was wider than purely political'.[16]

In 1891, Ahad Ha'am wrote an account of his first visit to Palestine. The state of the land and its local inhabitants rendered Palestine seemingly uninhabitable for immigration. Only swamps and rock-hewn hilltops would be available. The land was not uninhabited as commonly thought, and he emphasised the importance of 'not provoking anger among the native people, who are not going to step aside so easily'.[17] He castigated Jewish residents who treated the Arab population without respect or good judgment, warning that they 'will become revengeful like no other'.

In his visit to the Holy Land in 1898, Herzl too was shocked by 'the rotting deposits of two thousand years', and 'the hideous wretched beggary near the Western Wall'.[18] It would be necessary to build a new Jerusalem outside the Old City to provide homes for workers with proper sanitation. In the circumstances, his idea that Jerusalem could one day be 'turned into a jewel' was remarkably prophetic. The reality of Zion at that time seemed far removed from his vision of a modern and successful State.

Herzl spent the remainder of his short life in continuous diplomacy, which yielded little, but kept the cause very much alive. He expressed the wish that when he died he would be reburied in the Jewish State, and could hardly have guessed that his remains would be transferred there in as little as forty-five years – with full military honours by an army, and under the flag of the free commonwealth which he had envisaged.

The end of the First World War in 1918 provided the opportunity, even an impetus, for Jews to depart the Russian Empire, and the fall of the Ottoman Empire enabled the purchase of land by Jewish interests, previously blocked. Such a purchase was that of some 17,000 acres at the eastern end of the fertile Jezreel Valley. Degania was founded there in 1921 by members of Poale Zion (Workers of Zion) a left-wing movement which emphasised practical socialist projects in Palestine. And it was there in 1948 that strategically placed, its members were able successfully but at great cost to halt the invasion of Syrian tanks crossing the River Jordan, south of Lake Tiberias.

Herzl confided to his diary that he felt he had 'created' the Jewish State at Basle. He certainly created the political infrastructure, and promoted the idea internationally. But the State itself was not created in Switzerland – it was 'created' in Poland! There some five million Jews, the largest ever Jewish community to that time, learned to fend for themselves over several centuries, to organise their *kehillot* (communities) and to negotiate with the Polish nobility through intermediaries (*shtadlanim*). There they ignored the ebb and flow of international boundaries as Poland was carved up by her neighbours, and produced numerous newspapers, promoted plays and music, and created representative organisations able to sustain a national administration when the time came.

The historian Simon Dubnow (1860–1941) recognised the great mass of East European Jewry as a deeply rooted and permanent feature of the scene, and as fit a candidate for autonomy as any of the other 'nationalities' seeking recognition or independence at the beginning of the twentieth century.[19] He regarded Zionism as 'a beautiful messianic dream' and somewhat speculative. However, the creation of single nation states after the First World War led to 'an upturn in the strength of the Zionist narrative',[20] and the demise of East European Jewry as an 'integrated sector' of a multi-national empire, insofar as it ever was, given its differing social and political elements.

Two outstanding leaders emerged from the remains of the crumbling Russian Empire. They came from different backgrounds, and held contrasting opinions, but both were to shape the future of Zion.

David Ben-Gurion (1886–1973) was born in Plonsk, His father was a leader in the Chovevei Zion movement, and David joined the new Poale Zion whilst a student in 1905. In 1919, the movement split between those for whom the Bolshevik revolution at home was the major priority, and those like Ben-Gurion for whom the development of Palestine on socialist lines was more important. He was able to put together a strong labour movement, which became the dominant force needed when the State was created. However by the early 1960s the economy was stagnating under the burden of defence, absorption and bureaucracy, and the labour coalition began to disintegrate, as the need for a free market economy emerged.

Ze'ev Jabotinsky (1880–1940) a successful writer, was born into a middle-class assimilated family in Odessa, and became leader of the right-wing Zionist movement, with a strong emphasis on Jewish Self-Defence. He co-founded the Jewish Legion of the British Army in the First World War, and for his services he was awarded the MBE. In 1923 he resigned from the Executive Council of the Zionist Organization due to differences with Weizmann, and founded the Revisionist Party whose objective was a Jewish State on both banks of the River Jordan. He was opposed to the socialist ideology of the Labour Zionists.

In 1936, he envisaged the evacuation of the entire East European Jewish community to Palestine, where considerable land would be required for their resettlement. He was therefore opposed to partition, and what he called 'small scale Zionism'. That would leave the Jews with no opportunity to expand later, except by conquest, and 'only an idiot would believe that a military occupation would be a possibility' he declared in 1938,[21] with considerable foresight.

Meanwhile his plan was opposed by the British, and dismissed by the Zionist Organization, and in 1938 he declared quite rightly that the Jews of Poland in particular were living 'on the edge of a volcano'. The attitude of Germany under the Nazis towards the Jews was known by then, but the full horror of the 'final solution' was not known until 1942 by which time he had died. For a man who believed that the Jews should no longer apologise for their existence, or see themselves as victims, one can only guess at the anger and despair he would have felt (and many still feel) at the wholesale rounding up and transportation of Jews in disgusting circumstances, followed by the mass murder of millions on an industrial scale.

Of the many strands of Zionism, the most fundamental is that Zion is the only place where Jews can be free, and safe from persecution, and any Jew who arrives in Israel for the first time, whether as tourist or settler, will immediately and instinctively understand the significance of Jewish sovereignty, and feel a sense of homecoming and belonging, unique to that place. The ancient connection of the Jews with Zion should have been well known to those who already lived there, and since 1897 it was clear that the Jews intended to return. There was no choice, declared Jabotinsky, the Arabs must make room for the Jews. Sadly a satisfactory accommodation with them still remains to be found, whilst a new generation of Arab children are taught hatred of the Jews.

One would have thought the case for finding living space in Palestine for the survivors of the Holocaust was unassailable, but many were refused entry, and incarcerated on Cyprus and elsewhere. In a decision which 'lacked perceptiveness and humanity',[22] the British authorities apparently decided to 'teach a lesson' to some 4,500 Jewish refugees in the overloaded ship *Exodus* which left France for Palestine on 11 July 1947. They were not incarcerated, but in fact returned to France which refused entry, and then sent in Germany of all places. The 1960 film of the same name, with its evocative theme music, was mainly fictional, but stimulated pride in Israel's early achievements. And the lesson was not lost on Jabotinsky's followers. Zion must be liberated.

In 1929 at the age of 16 years, Menachem Begin, born in Brest now in Belarus, joined the popular Betar youth movement founded by Jabotinsky with military training for future members of the Revisionist Party. He rose rapidly through the ranks, becoming head of the largest branch in Poland in 1937. At the third World Conference of Betar in September 1938, Begin effectively began to take over the movement with a clear call to arms. The doctrine of military Zionism, and the use of force in an armed struggle against the British, was born.

Begin arrived in Palestine in 1942, and in 1944 assumed leadership of the Irgun underground army with a declaration of revolt against the British White Paper of 1939, restricting Jewish immigration. He opposed the dominant Zionist leadership as being too cooperative with the British, who needed to be forced out. Ben-Gurion viewed him and his followers as 'dissidents' who wished to pursue the way of terror, and who should be hunted down.[23] Here was a fundamental clash of policy in which there could be only one victor, and at the beginning of June 1948 Begin agreed to disband the Irgun, except for units operating in Jerusalem.

Open warfare between the Irgun and the official Haganah Defence forces, which had been simmering for some time before the State was declared, came to a head on 22 June 1948 pitching Jew against Jew, barely a month into the new State, still fighting for survival. The ship *Altalena*,[24] grounded off Tel Aviv, contained weapons from France, claimed by the Irgun for their own battalions. On the instructions of Ben Gurion, the ship was fired upon and sank with the loss of most weapons, and eighteen men mostly from Irgun.[25]

Despite pressure on Begin to retaliate and raise the flag of revolt against the provisional Government, he accepted that in the new State, 'any opposition to Ben-Gurion should be confined to the parameters of parliamentary discourse'.[26] In any event a central command of military forces had become essential. Begin was not arrested, a destructive civil war had been averted, and most of his men were redeployed, but dispersed into different units of the new Israel Defence Forces.

Begin was an unusual combination of patriot and democrat. But there are many who remember him only as the terrorist leader during the British Mandate, and the demagogue who stubbornly refused to support negotiations between Israel and Germany, the hated former enemy of the Jews, despite other important economic and diplomatic benefits. Nevertheless, his rhetoric expresses a deep understanding of the historical and emotional attachment of the Jews to the land of Israel, and its ubiquitous biblical connections, creating a unique sense of Jewish identity.

'Our ancient stones are not silent', he wrote in his underground newspaper, after an incident at the Western Wall in 1944. 'They speak of the House that once stood here, of kings that once knelt here in prayer, of prophets who declaimed their message here ... long before Britain was a nation.'[27] And when the Wall was retaken in 1967 after two millennia, it was left to him (then a Cabinet Minister in a Government of National Unity) to give expression to the enormity of the occasion.[28] With arms outstretched as if embracing the stones, and with tears in his eyes, he gave thanks, and referred to the famous prophecy of Jeremiah that 'your children shall return to their borders'.[29]

Love of the land itself, its stones and its soil, is given vivid expression in the poetry of Levi ben Amittai, a founder member of Degania, who in 1937 gave thanks for the Jezreel Valley and the opportunity to 'to drink from your waters and eat of your bread'.[30] It is not surprising that he is included in the canon of patriotic poetry and music which emerged in the period before 1948. Ben-Gurion proudly recorded in his memoirs that his home town of Plonsk was remarkably free from persecution, but nevertheless sent the highest proportion of Jews to Eretz Israel from any town in Poland of comparable size.

There is thus a special place in 'the world to come' for those who go up to Zion out of love, voluntarily, hopeful of finding useful work, and willing to face any hardships involved. As it was told in the Midrash, the *mitzvah* of dwelling in the land of Israel is equivalent to all the other *mitzvoth* put together.[31] The high value thus placed on residence there reflected the dismay and regret of the generation forced into dispersion following the failure of the Bar Kokhba revolt. Clearly, the link between Judaism and the land is of the greatest significance.

According to the eminent American Rabbi Soloveitchik, the Land is a gift from God, a divine intervention in history, a testament to His care for His people.[32] Zionism is thus a means for those who wish it, to put the Torah at the centre of Zion, and to fulfil the obligation to settle the land as required by the Almighty.[33] Rav Abraham Isaac Kook (1865–1935), appointed the first Ashkenazi Chief Rabbi of Palestine in 1921, believed that a Jewish State would be a place of unique holiness with important theological significance. He considered that all Jews who worked to that end (whether secular or even anti-religious) were part of the divine process of redemption.

Rabbi Akiva's religious nationalism finally bore fruit, and was invoked by Rav Kook in his address to the new Bnei Akiva Religious Zionist Youth movement, when founded in 1929.[34] But whether orthodox or not, there is the opportunity to pray at the Wall, and to experience a fuller Jewish life, where the festivals form part of the calendar. There is also the lurking hope that among the thousands of religious students excused from national service and allowed to spend time debating the contents of the Talmud, there may yet emerge another Hillel or Akiva, and solutions found to seemingly intractable problems.

Whether he emerges from the Yeshiva or from academia remains to be seen, and there are those who suggest[35] that it is in the latter that all creative thinking in Judaism is currently taking place. Tension, even hostility between the two predates the State, and efforts to introduce Talmud study into the new Hebrew University or Bar Ilan University were resisted. However, Rav Kook was in no doubt that the Yeshivot must grapple with academic methods. The return of Torah study to the land of its birth has inspired many with new searches for meaning and holiness.

Although the primary objective of Herzl's 1897 Zionist programme was in many ways 'a political solution to a political problem',[36] it is clear that could not be the only objective. To Israel Finestein, 'Zionism is more than a reaction to crisis and tragedy'. To equate it solely with the immigration of refugees fleeing persecution is to disregard the heritage from which it arose, and the wider purposes which it must serve. He considered that post 1948 Zionism needed a reformulation which incorporated the whole Jewish people, and his position was thus more akin to that of Ahad Ha'am, and the importance of a Jewish spiritual and cultural, as well as political, revival.

To some extent the Diaspora has indeed demonstrated its will to survive 'Jewishly' with an historic upsurge of Jewish interest, study and commitment since 1948. This contradicts the highly controversial alternative view presented for example by Arthur Koestler (1905–83), the author and journalist. He saw no likelihood of Jewish survival in the Diaspora, only within the State, for those who wished or needed to go there.[37]

Israel Finestein dismissed this as 'a cult of disappearance', and would have agreed with Isaiah Berlin, who also rejected the Koestler thesis saying: 'The creation of the State of Israel has genuinely transformed the individual problem of the Jew in dispersion'.[38] It was a liberating influence on those who chose to remain, their fate no longer resting solely with the Gentiles. There was thus no conflict between Jewish nationalism and continued Jewish life in the Diaspora.

The Zionist Congress held in Jerusalem in 1968 acknowledged the obvious and continuing need to preserve and strengthen Jewish identity everywhere, and the State itself has begun to address the issue of Jewish distinctiveness. However, different factions have widely differing views as to what that does or should consist of, and there are those so imbued with the long traditions of exile, and wish to preserve them frozen for all time, as if in two parallel Jewish universes. Ironically, the 'wider purposes' of the State, now largely accepted, must once again be subordinated to existential pressures, as the spectacular success of the 1967 Six Day War has not led to greater security, but to new challenges affecting all Jews everywhere.

Nevertheless, Zion continues to inspire the Jewish people in their communities throughout the world, providing a unifying factor, perhaps the only unifying factor to rise above the many existing religious and social differences. Even among those who are impatient with current trends, or disagree with individual policies, or wish to dissociate themselves from it altogether, the pull of Zion cannot be ignored!

Zion is a place towards which the Jewish people have always prayed, a place of aspiration and inspiration. It is a historical landmark (*tziyun* in Hebrew) but more than a physical place, it is an ideal, a striving for achievement, as reflected in the Hebrew word 'to excel' (*l'tzayen*). It is also an idea which encompasses and enhances Jewish identity and purpose as a people.[39]

Zion is older than modern Israel, older than Herzl, older than Zionism! Nurtured in Jewish tradition, with roots in ancient prophecy, the Jewish people are inexorably bound to Zion and what it stands for. We are told that in this place, it was promised to the patriarch Abraham on account of his obedience that in his seed would all the nations of the earth be blessed.[40] Let it be so!

Notes

1. IF, 'An Approach to a New Emphasis', in Moshe Davis (ed.), *Zionism in Transition* (1980), p.302.
2. Shlomo Avineri, *Herzl* (London: Weidenfeld & Nicolson, 2013), p.75.
3. Ibid., p.66.
4. Piers Paul Read, *The Dreyfus Affair* (London: Weidenfeld & Nicolson, 2013), p.115.
5. Avineri, *Herzl*, p.80.
6. Ibid., p.89.
7. A.H.

8. Avineri, *Herzl*, p.156.
9. Ibid., p.154.
10. Read, *The Dreyfus Affair*, p.321.
11. Avineri, *Herzl*, p.160.
12. *Singer's Prayer Book* (new edn 1962), p.50.
13. IF, 'Zionism in Transition: An Approach to a New Emphasis', pp.303–4.
14. Pen-name, meaning 'One of the people'.
15. Achad Ha'am, 'This Is Not The Way', Hamelitz, 1888.
16. IF, 'An Approach to a New Emphasis', p.306.
17. Tony Kushner and Alisa Solomon (eds), *Wrestling with Zion* (Grove Press, 2003), pp.14/15.
18. Avineri, *Herzl*, pp.18–19.
19. IF, *Scenes and Personalities in Anglo-Jewry 1800–2000* (London and Portland, OR: Vallentine Mitchell, 2002), p.308.
20. See Israel Bartal, *The Jews of Eastern Europe 1772–1881* (Philadelphia, PA: University of Pennsylvania Press, 2002), p.167.
21. Colin Shindler, *The Rise of the Israeli Right* (New York: Cambridge University Press, 2015), p.4.
22. Raphael Langham, 'The Bevin Enigma', *Jewish Historical Studies*, 44 (2012), p.176.
23. Shindler, *The Rise of the Israeli Right*, p.208.
24. The pen-name of Jabotinsky!
25. Benny Morris, *1948, a History of the First Arab-Israeli War* (London: Yale University Press, 2008), pp.271–2.
26. Shindler, *The Rise of the Israeli Right*, p.237.
27. Yehuda Avner, *The Prime Ministers* (London: The Toby Press, 2010), pp.11/12.
28. Ibid., pp.160–1.
29. Jeremiah 31:17.
30. Levi ben Amittai, *Fields in the Valley* (Tel Aviv: Am Oved, 1950), p. 9.
31. Binyamin Lau, *The Sages, Character, Context and Creativity* (Jerusalem: Maggid Books, 2011), Vol.II, pp.423–6.
32. Ben Elton, 'Why the State of Israel is a religious blessing', JC, 17 April 2015, p.36.
33. Deut. 1:21.
34. Lau, *The Sages*, Vol.II, p.377.
35. Rabbi Jeremy Rosen, JC, 5 February 2016, p.34.
36. IF, 'An Approach to a New Emphasis', p.302.
37. JC, 5 May 1950, p.15.
38. Quoted by Arie M. Dubnov, *Isaiah Berlin* (New York: Palgrave Macmillan, 2012), p.197.
39. Isaiah 1:27.
40. Genesis 22:18.

16

Secularity

Adept at discarding the shibboleths of the past ... the secular
Jew attempts to maintain the tree without the roots ... and live
off the capital of a tradition which his intellect rejects.

Israel Finestein[1]

Secularity divides those who believe from those who do not. But believe in
what? In the non-Jewish world, the answer is simple – believe in God. But
in the Jewish world, the issue is far from simple, due to the unusual compo-
sition of our identity, with faith, nation and culture intermingled. 'The secular Jew faces quandaries unique to the Jews.'[2]

Since the Enlightenment in the eighteenth century, reason has sought to
replace belief, and secularity is now well established as the main challenge
to religion. As early as 1909, Claude Montefiore drew attention to the danger
and suggested that his movement was best placed to respond. In 1956, Rabbi
Jakobovits expressed his concern in his Victor Schonfeld Memorial Lecture
entitled, 'How Can We Meet the Challenge?'[3]

In 1976, some nineteen leading Jewish thinkers of the time attempted to
address the issue, and their collected thoughts were published in a book
entitled *The Faith of Secular Jews*. The above quotation is taken from an
extended article by Israel Finestein in which he reviews the book, but at the
same time, sets his own seal on the subject by objecting to the secular claim
to faith!

For many, faith is a privilege only available to the Jew who accepts the
existence of God as the basis of his religion. Known as the 'yoke of heaven',
the first sentence of the *Shema*[4] is the fundamental declaration of faith of the
Jewish people in God, defined by Maimonides as infinite and indivisible.
And the commandment above all others is, 'I am the Lord your God'.
Secularity is thus by definition inconsistent with faith in a deity. How can
they be reconciled? They are opposites that cannot coexist, and if so, the
secular Jew must be regarded as a contradiction in terms!

Prior to the Enlightenment, this may well have been so. The ancient
hopes and convictions were a powerful buffer against secularity, and indeed

continue to play a 'quasi-compulsive' role. Even Zionism could not completely divorce itself from the old language or the ideas which had long given meaning to Jewish purpose.

And it is important to remember that Judaism is more than a religion or creed. It is a way of life, which involves itself in everyday matters, beyond the synagogue, beyond prayer, beyond belief. The Jewish calendar provides a constant reminder of our history and unique survival. The Hebrew Bible is the source of the moral law, and social justice, unique in the ancient world.

Furthermore a Jew (or Jewess) is primarily a biological phenomenon![5] He cannot choose whether or not to join. He is not refused membership if he is non-observant or if he adopts a secular, even atheist viewpoint. Even if he intermarries or converts to another religion, he will remain Jewish. The Jews are a people, and many have been martyred by virtue of nothing other than one long-forgotten Jewish grandparent.

The various contributors to the book under review attempted to reconcile their desire to remain Jewish with their lack of faith or observance, in various ways. One of the most persuasive (for the present writer) was for a link between 'religion' and a 'religious attitude'.[6] Thus it was argued that 'when a Jew bets his life on the survival of his people, attempts to inculcate Jewish values, is deeply involved in Jewish cultural activities, these experiences are religious in character'.[7]

To put observance and culture on the same level was indeed bold and only possible in a modern emancipated world, as Judaism has in some quarters felt the need to redefine itself in wider terms than before. Thus a belief in the people, its history and survival is indeed to some a matter of faith. Is the deity so far removed from such thoughts, even if divine revelation itself is denied? Must the secular Jew, by his desire to remain Jewish, be left forever 'yearning for a communion that is irretrievably lost'?[8]

The intensity of belief in a secular culture can for some amount to a form of religion as distinct from a mere pressure group or substitute. And the genuine Jewish secularist has to struggle with the 'treasured assumptions of chosenness and redemption' in seeking the grounds of his belief. Do they not apply to him? A 'tinge of deism'[9] must surely be found in the providential role of the Jews in human history.

Baruch Spinoza (1632–77) was perhaps the first secular Jew! The great philosopher was excommunicated by the elders of the Amsterdam community, keen to stamp out any perceived Christian influence from their Spanish past, but it is said he retained a deep religiosity. It is not surprising that he rejected the God of Maimonides, but he did not banish God altogether and identified Him with the beauty of the Universe.

Albert Einstein (1879–1955) was naturally able to identify with Spinoza's God, who reveals Himself in the harmony of the world of which he, the great scientist, knew more than anyone. He considered morality to be of the highest importance, but only if liberated from fear. To the *New York Times* in 1930 he asserted that, 'It is precisely among the heretics of every age that we find men who are filled with the highest kind of religious feeling'.

A passage from Einstein's writing in 1949 is included in the book under review, and he considered two hereditary (and secular) traits as being in the nature of Jewishness: its democratic ideal of social justice, and its high esteem for intellectual and spiritual effort. But 'more than on its own tradition, the Jewish group matured on the basis of oppression and hatred that it constantly encountered'.[10] The secular Jew almost by definition wishes to survive as a Jew, and therefore anti-Semitism alone cannot explain his continued acceptance of separateness and other positive criteria of Jewish teaching.

Ultimately Israel Finestein felt that the test is one of transmissibility. He feared that the secular Jew 'unaided by faith' cannot ensure Jewish continuity, and has not alighted on any alternative formula. However, in his concluding paragraph, he concedes unexpectedly that the 'chain of faith' is itself no guarantee. And he was right to hesitate, because faith is not the prerogative or even a prerequisite of the Jewish religion, which stresses the value of deeds and observance, rather than belief.

Whilst faith and observance should indeed correspond, all too often they do not, and the deity is conspicuously absent. If confirmation of this were needed, one might refer to the report of Dr Stephen Miller of City University London in 1987 to the effect that 'Jewish secondary schools reinforce the ritual dimension of Judaism, but appear to have a negative effect upon perceptions of faith and spirituality'.[11]

Rabbi Cardozo, whom Lord Sacks has described as 'one of deep faith, attuned to the music of eternity', explained that, 'To be religious is to allow God entry into my thoughts and deeds, to have a constant awareness of being in His presence, to see His fingerprints everywhere, and to be worthy'.[12] Here the emphasis is on awareness rather than observance, and whilst the secular Jew cannot accept this remarkable statement in a literal sense, he may well see much to commend in it as he ponders on his providential survival.

Perhaps the least persuasive definition of the secular Jew in the book under review (to the present writer) was that of the famous Yiddishist, Chaim Zhitlowsky (1865–1943) who was so obsessed with that language that he wanted it declared the national language of the Jews! Nevertheless, it had been a defining attribute of Jewish life in every aspect for so long that in his view anyone so steeped in it was 'without doubt, a member of the Jewish people'.[13] One instinctively rejects this definition, but the secular Jew would certainly regard Hebrew as a defining attribute, much closer to our earliest origins.

The *Maskilim*, followers of the Enlightenment, sought to promote the revival of Hebrew, and replace Yiddish which they regarded as 'a garbled dialect that bore witness to the miserable cultural state of its speakers!'[14] A hybrid language originating out of mediaeval German, Yiddish 'clung to their necks like a heartbroken mother'[15] as the Jews embarked for the new world, but it could not survive more than a generation outside the ghetto. It was spoken by religious and secular Jews alike, and is now fashionably resurrected as a genuine source of study and as a link with an important historical epoch.

The secular Jew is inevitably attracted to language as a major source of identity, and sees the Hebrew language rather than the Hebrew religion as the real engine of Jewish continuity. 'Prime among the cultural assets of our people is the vessel which holds all treasures within it – the language', said David Ben Gurion, the first Prime Minister of Israel, as quoted in a biography of him by (President) Shimon Peres.[16] 'The Jewish bookshelf is the secular Synagogue', declared Fania Oz-Salzberger,[17] co-author of 'Jews and Words' with her father Amos Oz. Words and their interpretation are indeed at the heart of Jewish life, both religious and secular.

As devoted and determined secular Israelis 'with not a religious bone in our bodies', they dissociated themselves from 'the current withdrawal from most things Jewish, and see those who dismiss Bible quoting, Talmudic references, and even an interest in the Jewish past, as misguided'.[18] They quote the famous Israeli writer Yizhar Smilansky (1916–2006): 'Secularism is not permissiveness, nor is it lawless chaos. It does not reject tradition or culture, but offers a different understanding of man and the world.'[19]

The secular Jew is thus not an anti-Jew or a self-hating Jew who would rather be a non-Jew, who sees himself as part of an entirely different tradition, global, intellectual, or anything else so long as it is devoid of Jewish content! Such 'nothing' Jews do not deserve the name secular, or *chiloni* in the Hebrew. It might be thought that the Hebrew term, loosely translated as 'profane', the opposite of 'holy', was a term of abuse, but the *Havdalah* prayer does not suggest there is anything profane in the 'weekday' (without which there would be no Shabbat) or the 'other nations' (without which there would be no Israel). 'Darkness' is merely the absence of light. Holiness is emphasised by its absence, if indeed it is absent. The secular Jew can wear his Hebrew name with pride!

In his article Israel Finestein clearly accepts that the secular Jew exists, his original question having been somewhat rhetorical. But his other question was not: Why does he exist? To which one might add: What is his purpose? What kind of a Jew is he? The historian Y.H. Yerushalmi (1932–2009) asserted that 'we confuse ourselves by using the term secular Jew, a meaningless label, which gives no indication of the richly nuanced variety within the species'.[20]

There is indeed a spectrum of secularity, from outright atheism to a genuine desire to somehow square the circle; from mere nostalgia, habit and pride, to active involvement in the Jewish world. However in general it is safe to say that the secular Jew will not attend religious services or keep festivals out of any sense of obligation, but he may do so for their cultural ethos, or simply because that is what Jews do.

The secular Jew will not be unduly concerned with who created the universe, but he may well prefer the non-scientific (clearly non-literal) account in Genesis to the various mythologies of other peoples. The Hebrew Bible itself is 'a magnificent human creation, which requires neither divine origin nor material proof'.[21] Holy writ or not, the obvious delight of Amos and Fania in its 'magic' and 'splendour' indicate a reverence for the text which they almost imbue with holiness.

Chief Rabbi Hertz[22] attempted to show that the Biblical account of the creation is not inconsistent with the concept of evolution, although there are still some on the extreme right of Orthodoxy who stubbornly refuse to accept evolution, and oppose its being taught. Needless to say, the secular Jew will not wish to belong to a religion which rejects all knowledge with which that religion chooses to disagree.

The secular Jew will instinctively reject the supernatural and is unlikely to accept, for example, that the parting of the Red Sea was on the direct intervention of the Almighty. He is more likely to accept perhaps what is now thought to have been the result of a tsunami created by a volcanic eruption across the Mediterranean. However, the importance of this event does not lay in scientific fact, but in the idea that redemption from slavery, being 'strangers in a strange land', and finding a way to the 'promised' land, are essential aspects of our uniqueness.

It is surely impossible, to take another example, that 'the sun stood still upon Gibeon'. However, Joshua needed the sun to dazzle his enemies, and his comprehensive defeat of the more numerous Amorites may well have seemed to the ancients as if his wish had been granted.[23] And why not, when one considers the odds against the conquest of Canaan, let alone the modern rebirth of Israel and the repeated threats to its existence?

The existence of a deity presupposes the possibility of intervention in the personal as well as the natural world, and the secular Jew will have enormous difficulty with the concept of reward and punishment, clearly enunciated in the *Shema* as a simple matter of cause and effect. If we do as we are told, we will prosper, and otherwise we will not.[24]

However, a deeper meaning may be seen from the stated injunction 'to love' and 'to listen', and the underlying obligation is surely to protect the particularity of His people. The implication of the Lord's wrath for failure to listen is clear, but His negative responses are, in fact, expressly reserved for those who 'turn aside and serve other Gods'. The believer may look for divine explanation for personal misfortune, but the secular Jew knows there are none.

The martyrdom of the six million is beyond human comprehension. To think in terms of punishment is an affront to the victims. They were not murdered because of their sins, but perhaps (some say) on account of Zionism and its refusal to wait for the Messiah! A more likely explanation is that we were not Zionist enough, and failed to get our people out of the cauldron before it was too late. They were in the wrong place at the wrong time as, for example, was the wholly innocent (and Orthodox) Jewish family slaughtered in Mumbai in 2008. Likewise in 2012 the murder of Jewish children in Toulouse, and the attack on Jewish shoppers in Paris in 2015 were horribly random.

'My thoughts are not your thoughts', said the Almighty to Isaiah,[25] and it would be wrong, perhaps even blasphemous, to second guess His motives or intentions, which we can never hope to understand. Many Jews would therefore prefer 'random' to impossible, unknowable and implausible explanations. Furthermore, the secular Jew recognises the insignificance of man, and would agree with the Psalmist, 'What is man that thou art mindful of him?'[26] However, he may nevertheless experience moments of transcendence or awe, and wonder whether there might be 'some mysterious essence which unifies and illuminates the world'.[27]

The development of religion in its infancy provided different groups or tribes with a common cause, as early society congregated in larger units.[28] However it did not provide a reason to be tolerant towards the members of other religions, and history records many wars of conquest and the persecution of others for the greater glory of God. The secular Jew will want no part of that, or of the infighting which often takes place within the same faith, especially his own.

The secular Jew is often not born secular. It catches up on him, and sometimes it endows him with a sense of guilt for which there is no atonement, since he has no 'Father or King to forgive the sins of his people'. Yet not many secularists can resist the call of *Kol Nidrei* when more Jews gather together throughout the world than at any other time of the year. And in the materialistic even hedonistic city of Tel Aviv, where the streets are alive until dawn, they fall silent on that awesome evening preceding the Day of Atonement.

Thus, the secular Jew can never quite rid himself of the idea that he is answerable – to whom, other than society at large, he does not know – not to a deity, but perhaps to his forebears and all those who went before, who carried the deity with them in one form or another, and sacrificed themselves for their separateness on the long road home. To the secular Jew, the land of Israel was not 'divinely' promised,[29] but promised it was, in the sense that history has made it the centre of our existence since the beginning.

It was Rabbi, Lord Sacks who made the astute observation that if you 'scratch' a secular Jew, you will find a believer, and he was not referring to belief in the divine, or a return to observance. The secular Jew is not interested in observance, which he sees as merely one strand of Jewishness, but may well acknowledge its deeper significance for others. Belief and faith are not alien to him, and he needs them more than most, sharing a deep-rooted belief in the Jewish people, waiting and willing to fulfil his Jewish destiny.

In the words of Rabbi Lau, referring to the teachings of Hillel, 'Secularity is not a barrier to holiness, which can be found even within the mundane dimensions of life'.[30] The secular Jew and traditional Judaism are not totally independent of each other. Historically, they have influenced each other in various ways, each contributing to the 'melting pot' of Jewish identity.

Israel was re-established primarily by secular Jews, whilst the religious ones dragged their feet, uncertain and unwilling! The early pioneers, whether in the 1880s or the 1920s were primarily from a socialist background, and yet their love of the land and their wish for the ingathering of the exiles had a deep spiritual content. In concluding his poem 'Fields in the Valley', Levi ben Amittai wrote, 'Gather me unto you like an ear of corn to the harvest'. For someone who professed no religious faith, this was little short of a prayer that he should be part of the harvesting of his people from 'the sadness of death and the cradle of bereavement' which was already overshadowing Jewish life in mainland Europe.[31]

On 14 May 1948, the Declaration of Israel's Independence was pronounced by David Ben Gurion at the Tel Aviv Museum, immediately following the departure of the High Commissioner at the close of the British Mandate. It was done hurriedly, and the ceremony lasted only 37 minutes according to the account of it in the Shimon Peres's biography referred to above.[32] It was a Friday afternoon, and the leading members of the new State did not wish or wish others to transgress the Sabbath, although most were not religious themselves.

Given the war in which the fragile new State was already engaged, some invocation to the Almighty was surely appropriate, but He is mentioned only once in the Declaration, and then only obliquely at the end. Upon signing the document, these mainly hard-headed secular socialist pioneers declared that they were placing their trust in 'the Rock of Israel' – a form of words the result of 'last minute wrangling between religious and agnostic members of the Provisional Government'.[33] And in the true spirit of Jewish secularity, not wishing to close the door entirely on its ancient heritage, the meeting ended with the usual blessing for special occasions from the leader of the religious party.

Since the Enlightenment, Orthodox Judaism has faced repeated secession seemingly impotent. It has been replaced in part by other orthodoxies, but above and beyond these, lies the great mass of our people who are not devoid of faith: far from it – they know their lives are on the line, and they know why. No individual group can claim a monopoly of faith or belief.

Herzl, assimilated and genuinely secular, surprisingly stated, 'We recognise ourselves as a nation through our faith',[34] in answer to the question who is a Jew. Likewise Ben-Gurion had no time for Judaism during his lifetime, but refused to define himself as secular. In an interview two years before his death he asserted, 'I too have a deep faith in the Almighty'.

Secular Jews, like the 'northern tribes' once thought expendable, have become an integral if not an essential component of the House of Israel. They are aware of the cause of their distinctiveness, and wish to remain discernible. The thoughtful among them wish to reclaim what is rightfully theirs. The Talmud is no longer to be found only in the yeshiva. New ways to reconnect with our divine heritage can and will be found. Communion is not lost. God is not forsaken. 'The heaven is still His throne, and the earth His footstool.'[35]

Notes

1. IF, 'The Secular Jew: Does He Exist and Why?', *Jewish Journal of Sociology* (December 1977), pp.194, 190, 189.
2. IF, 'The Secular Jew: Does He Exist and Why?', p.187.
3. JC, 17 February 1956, p.8.
4. Deut. 6:4.
5. See above p. 98 final paragraph (In Whose Name?).
6. John Dewey (1859–1952), an American philosopher, *A Common Faith* (New Haven, Conn.,1934), p.27.
7. IF, 'The Secular Jew: Does he exist and why?', p.186.
8. Ibid., p.187.
9. Ibid., p.188.
10. Ibid., p.191.
11. Stephen Miller, 'Studies in Jewish Education', *The impact of Jewish Education on the religious behaviour and attitudes of British secondary school pupils* (IJPR, 1988).
12. Rabbi Nathan Cardozo, 'I am taking of my Kippah!', *Thoughts to Ponder 244* (Jerusalem: David Cardozo Academy, 2012).

13. IF, 'The Secular Jew: Does He Exist and Why?', p.192.
14. Israel Bartal, *The Jews of Eastern Europe 1772–1881* (Philadelphia, PA: University of Pennsylvania Press, 2002), p.99.
15. Amos Oz and Fania Oz-Salzberger, *Jews and Words* (London: Yale University Press, 2012), p.93.
16. Shimon Peres, *Ben-Gurion, A Political Life*, p.50.
17. Interview, JC, 19 April 2013, p.31.
18. Oz and Oz-Salzberger, *Jews and Words*, p.3.
19. Yizhar Smilansky, essay entitled 'The Courage to be Secular' cited in Amos Oz and Fania Oz-Salzberger, *Jews and Words*, pp.3&4 and Felix Posen, 'Secular education is the way to keep Jews Jewish', JC, July 2011.
20. Arie M. Dubnov, *Isaiah Berlin* (New York: Palgrave Macmillan, 2012), p.18.
21. Oz and Oz-Salzberger, *Jews and Words*, p.4.
22. Soncino Pentateuch, p.194
23. Joshua 10:12.
24. Deut. 11:13–21.
25. Isaiah 55:8–9.
26. Psalm 8:4.
27. See interview with Rabbi Arthur Green, JC 16 December 2016, p.32.
28. See Jonathan Sacks, *Not in God's Name* (London: Hodder and Stoughton, 2015), p.182.
29. Genesis 12:7.
30. Binyamin Lau, *The Sages, Character, Context and Creativity* (Jerusalem: Maggid Books, 2010), Vol.I, pp.217–19.
31. See above p.149 (Zion).
32. Shimon Peres, *Ben Gurion, a Political Life* (New York: Schocken Books, 2011), p.117.
33. Ibid.
34. Shlomo Avineri, *Herzl* (London: Weidenfeld & Nicolson, 2013), p.99.
35. Isaiah 66:1.

17

Justice

> If the historic Hebraic element had not entered Western society, the world's history over two millennia would have been radically different in every respect.
>
> Israel Finestein[1]

It was the Hebrew Bible which spread the idea that the law was to be essentially moral, and that the rules governing individuals or public conduct should not be arbitrary or capricious. As a lawyer and Judge, Israel Finestein has written very little on purely legal topics, but when doing so, it is not surprising that he referred to 'the effect of the Hebrew Bible on the principles and practices of English Law'.[2]

The Jewish concept of justice is linked with righteousness and equality. The oppressor is the enemy of God as well as of man. All human life is created in the image of God, and must therefore be respected, even in the face of wrongdoing. But Justice is more than abstention from wrongdoing. It is the foundation of society, and the biblical text makes it clear that the proper administration of Justice is a condition of Israel's existence as a nation, and indeed the existence of any civilised nation. Chief Rabbi Hertz examined the nature of Justice in some detail[3] quoting Isaiah that 'the work of Justice is peace'.[4]

The ancient Hebrews were commanded 'Justice, Justice shalt thou pursue'.[5] Repetition of any word in the Torah is highly unusual, and requires explanation, since by tradition, no word should be regarded as superfluous. Justice could have been repeated merely to emphasise its fundamental importance, but that would be to overlook a deeper understanding as to what justice consists of. The decision arrived at by a Judge must naturally be just, but quite separately, the process by which the law is administered must also be just. Justice must be even handed between the parties, transparent and available for all. It cannot be the result of coercion or secrecy.

The right to a fair trial was thus envisaged long before it was enshrined in the European Convention on Human Rights (ECHR)[6] established in 1950 to ensure that the abuses of the Nazi era were never repeated. Without the presumption of innocence, the right to cross examine witnesses, full disclosure of evidence, and the many other requirements of due process, Justice is not served, and however just the final judgment, it cannot stand.

In an address to the International Association of Jewish Lawyers on 17 March 1999, Israel Finestein considered the life of Sir Arthur Goodhart QC (1891–1978) and takes a close look at the origins of the English Common Law, of which Goodhart was one of the great exponents. He was described by *The Times* as 'essentially a modernist, though with a deep consciousness of and regard for the traditional common law spirit'.[7]

Professor Goodhart was born in New York, the son of a wealthy Jewish family. After graduating from Yale University, he studied law at Cambridge, and was called to the English Bar in 1919. He was appointed Professor of Jurisprudence at Oxford (1931–51) and then served as Master of University College Oxford until his retirement in 1963. He served as Editor of the prestigious *Law Quarterly Review* (1923–71), the leading legal journal in the English speaking world.[8]

The English Common Law does not arise from any Statute or authority of Parliament or Monarch. It is unwritten law handed down since the Middle Ages, and followed by successive generations of Judges as to what they considered to be right and fair in any given circumstance. Its strength lies in the power of precedent, in ceaseless interpretation and refinement, and in the notion of the 'reasonable man'. It has expanded over the centuries until the complexities of the modern industrial world required Parliament to intervene with appropriate Statutes. The system has been adopted in America, in countries of the British Commonwealth, and in Israel. Its scholars and practitioners have always acknowledged that the authority of the Common Law derives from biblical sources.

The protection afforded the citizen by the ancient writ of 'Habeus Corpus' does not arise from any Statute, but from 'an inherent right to freedom', and it follows from this that the Common Law is able to impose limits on the power of the government and those acting on its behalf. In modern terms that is known as Judicial Review, which can if appropriate strike down decisions of public bodies on the basis of unreasonableness. Some might argue that the standard of what is considered reasonable is set too high or too low, but in any event it is subject to the pressure of the times.

The courts also have power to remedy breaches of natural justice, as offending the ancient belief in the equality of man. Israel Finestein refers to an analogy between Parliament and 'the elders' convened by the kings of ancient Israel.[9] This analogy was used in the seventeenth century to demonstrate the moral evil of any royal failure to respect the law, or failure to summon and heed the voice of Parliament.

Lord Wolf (b. 1933), former Lord Chief Justice, observed that one of the strengths of the common law was that it 'enables the Courts to vary the extent of their intervention to reflect current needs'.[10] This view echoes the sentiment expressed by Goodhart that the law must not 'become bound by fixed categories which will make adjustment to modern needs difficult'.[11] The best of Common Law Judges, he said, must have the intellectual courage to criticise those parts of the law which were no longer consonant with the needs of contemporary society.

A legal system in practice is a living organism which must provide for development. If based on laws thought to be immutable, it must find ways of redressing any hardship which otherwise might occur. This is usually achieved by allowing for exceptions where the need arises, without detriment to the basic principle. It is argued, for example, that the Jewish law of divorce by men only cannot be changed. However, the husband who abuses his wife (and quite possibly his children) surely forfeits his right to keep her chained in marriage. Compassion is meaningless without redress, and courage is needed to annul where common humanity demands.

The Halakhah has always been faced with difficult questions, but the onset of modernity has created many more which were unprecedented. Under the heading 'Modern Responsa: 1800 to the present', David Novak refers to the new contextualisation of Halakhah, and identified the two main but contrasting responses in a process which is ongoing.[12] Some respondents have attempted to stretch the law to make it applicable to new situations, especially where suffering was involved, as referred to above. On the other hand, others see a need to keep the law strict, in order to protect Jews 'from a diminishing of their faith by a cumulative process of accommodation to a non-traditional environment'.

The pendulum appears for the moment to be stuck in one direction only, but even the most fundamental of laws such as the Ten Commandments, or the European Convention on Human Rights, cannot exist without constant interpretation as to their meaning and application. Such basic laws as in relation to murder, for example, cannot be administered fairly without taking into account public perception of self-defence, accident, or the needs of warfare. And punishment provided for in one age or society, such as the death penalty or transportation to the colonies, may seem obnoxious in another. Is there a message here for Jewish law?

The American Constitution has been the subject of litigation throughout its two hundred and more years' existence, and is likely to remain so. The Magna Carta of 1215, with its right to justice for all, has been the inspiration for constitutional documents across the world, but one third of its sixty-three clauses were rewritten within ten years, and all but three have since been repealed or replaced! And where the old Common Law proved inadequate in certain circumstances, Equity Law developed in England, and is a major example of the ongoing process in action.

In determining what is right and fair in any given situation, the training, rationality, independence and character of the Judge is very important. The Hebrew Bible sets a very high standard for judicial conduct, independence and impartiality by making it clear that: Justice requires that the Judge must be appointed as competent, rather than as a result of connection. He must be no respecter of persons. He must not favour the poor because they are poor. He must not to be swayed by the multitude. He should not accept gifts 'for a gift doth blind the eyes of the wise, and perverts the words of the righteous'.[13]

However the Talmud appears to have extended the role of Judges to include the idea that they are rendering justice not for man, but for the Lord, in effect 'participating with God in the act of judging'.[14] If so, the litigant is not regarded as coming to court to claim what is rightfully his, but as one who comes looking for succour, who presents himself as one who is worthy of his claim. However this may lead to extraneous factors being taken into account, such as his mode of behaviour or lack of observance of Jewish law, regardless of entitlement.

The idea that the Judge is thus a divine representative, in effect carrying out a religious duty, leads to obvious difficulties. The inability to decide purely on merit may produce doubt and possible injustice in that the opinion and conduct of the 'losing' party may suggest some element of right on his side also. Furthermore, the introduction of extraneous considerations however desirable may constitute a deviation which future judges may feel obliged to follow.

The Rule of Law, as we know it, does not provide for such external considerations, except perhaps in mitigation, and its object is to provide finality so that members of society know where they stand. However, with a different concept of Justice, tension may well arise between religious and secular courts, which has created particular problems in Israel.

Israel Finestein considered the different views as to why the law should be observed. There have been those who argue expediency, power, mutual convenience or fear of punishment. Goodhart argued in his Hamlyn Lectures (1953) that when an act is accepted as a duty, it is not an imposition or command, but an intuitive response to obligation, and thus the instinct to obey derives from the culture and history of society. He pointed out that 'England has been a nation founded on law for a longer period than any other nation in the history of the world',[15] and considered that in England there was a close bond between law and morals.

He had no illusion about the frailty of the human condition and the tension of competing interests, but was at pains to disagree with those (such as Thomas Hobbes in the seventeenth century) who argued that force or the threat of force is essential for compliance with the law. Sanctions may at times be necessary, and coercion may procure obedience, 'but that does not make the law obligatory'. Good law is not law because the State enforces it.[16] The test of legitimacy is basically moral.

Lord Hailsham (1907–2001),[17] a former Lord Chancellor, agreed that Justice could not be defined purely in terms of reason or utility. The law is not simply 'the command of the ruler' or 'what the Court decides', or the outcome of some 'ancient notional contract'. Its source is the Judaeo-Christian tradition, the Hebrew Bible, 'evoking a spirit of regard for the individual personality, and mutual duties'.[18] The source of this regard is a matter of values, and is ultimately spiritual in his view, rather than pragmatic.

It is indeed the spiritual or moral content of the Mosaic Code which distinguishes it from other legal systems in existence in the ancient world. The most well-known is probably that of King Hammurabi of Babylon, a contemporary of the patriarch Abraham, around 1750 BCE. It resembles the Mosaic Code in reference to 'an eye for an eye', but the Hammurabi concept is one of retribution (known as 'lex talionis') whereby the offender must suffer the same fate as the person he has damaged.

However, that is of no benefit to the injured party, and the Hebrew interpretation emphasises compensation for the victim. He may not be able to have his eye back, but he will receive a monetary amount equal to its worth. It is often extremely difficult for such an amount to be computed, but the Court must do its best, because the Mosaic interpretation also emphasises that such compensation shall be commensurate. In other words, the result must be justice, not vengeance.

There are two other significant differences: the Hammurabi code preserves the Babylonian class system in operation – a different punishment applies depending on whether the damage is inflicted on a property owner, a freed man or a slave. However under the Mosaic code, all injuries are to be valued according to the same standard. Furthermore the extension of the retaliation principle to innocent children is expressly prohibited in the Hebrew Bible[19] where everyone is responsible for his own actions, not those of his parents or his children.

The Hebrew Bible makes it clear that the law is applicable to all equally. The monarch is not exempt,[20] and one is reminded of the celebrated English Judge, Lord Denning (1899–1999) who said, 'Be ye ever so high, you are not above the law'. It follows that though appointed by the monarch or the state, Judges are not their agents, and are not obliged to do their bidding. That way lays the gulag and the concentration camp.

However, the moral basis of the law, indeed the supremacy of the rule of law itself, comes under heavy scrutiny when the security of the State and its citizens is threatened. Acts of terror do not lend themselves to due process, and most Western countries have been and continue to be faced with barbaric acts by those espousing ruthless ideologies. The need to prevent terror and obtain vital information in advance may require stern, even underhand means, including what a normal person might regard as torture, and the rendition of suspects across state boundaries.

Do terrorists or terror suspects have rights nonetheless? Or have they by their actions and intentions forfeit their rights, unlike the common thief or murderer who does not respect another's right to property or to life, but is still entitled to due process? Is a terrorist or even a suspected terrorist entitled to the presumption of innocence? Or do we lock them away indefinitely without charge at places such as Guantanamo Bay, which is technically outside American jurisdiction but under its control? President Obama promised to close it down before he was elected in 2008, but has found that to be extremely difficult out of concern over what those incarcerated might do if released, a fear which many believe is well founded.

When upholding the deportation of one who had exposed state secrets in 1977, Lord Denning recognised that national security could be used (as in other countries) to excuse infringements of individual liberties. Many would agree today that the State must have the right to defend itself from terrorism and aggression with reasonable and appropriate responses. Others regard judicial oversight as necessary in order to protect human rights. The dilemma is obvious and agonising and is compounded by cross border issues such as immigration, data protection and attempts as in Europe to harmonise different jurisdictions.[21]

Freedom of expression is today considered so fundamental to society as to justify the circulation of puerile or offensive material, whilst at the same time we seek to combat racism and impose limits on hate mail. There is a fine line to be drawn, but Article 10 of the ECHR makes it clear that this right is not absolute. It carries with it duties and responsibilities, and is expressly made subject to a number of qualifications such as the interests of national security, the prevention of disorder, the protection of the reputation or rights of others, and the prevention of disclosure of confidential information. If these considerations are overlooked (as they often are) the original purpose of the right as a bulwark of freedom is defeated.

There is no corresponding right in the Hebrew Bible. There are however numerous references to the importance of truth, to the avoidance of gossip or slander or false witness, and to the use of words responsibly. The Hebrew Bible wisely focuses on duties rather than rights, and if its admonitions were observed, the rights of others would follow. We recoil in horror when those offended respond disproportionately, as in the appalling murder of the Charlie Hebdo journalists in Paris in January 2015. But they surely knew they were giving deep offence on a highly sensitive and emotive subject to persons unlikely or unable to respond merely with argument or protest, and more likely to respond with violence.

And what of the biblical imperative of righteous conduct? We can surely hope that the divine sanction takes into account the needs of self-defence, of pre-emption and of responding to provocation. These are of particular relevance in the State of Israel whose existence and way of life have been continuously threatened since its creation on a permanent almost daily basis in a very real form.

In an article published in the *Jewish Journal of Sociology*[22] in 1999, Israel Finestein reviewed a number of contributions on the subject of Criminal Justice in Israel, beginning with the Criminal Law Ordinance of the former British Mandate authorities, adopted in 1948 by the newly independent state. It was however no substitute for a comprehensive new criminal code 'despite the valiant efforts of the Judiciary'.

With a growing population from strikingly different backgrounds, a succession of wars with neighbouring countries, and continuing problems of internal security, it became essential for Israel to achieve a proper balance between freedom and control. However it was inevitable that 'state interests' would predominate, and national security would take precedence over community policing. Assistance to the military is bound to absorb many police resources otherwise intended for the benefit of the civilian population in the normal way.

In 1992, the Knesset enacted that 'the liberty of the person shall not be restricted except by a Statute which benefits the values of the State, and is directed to a worthy purpose, and then only to the extent that it does not exceed what is necessary'.[23] This was clearly intended to impact on the interpretation of existing law, and 'introduced a new era of judicial review'. The above enactment aims high indeed, but the reports of the State Controllers' Office (for example) with the specific right to overview Government actions, could easily be thwarted by a highly divided and powerful political system, which will find one way or another to avoid criticism.

The treatment of all its citizens as equal before the law is clearly the intention, and the Jewish murderer of Prime Minister Rabin for example remains in prison for life. However, the Court must have regard to politically motivated offences or acts of terror, and detention without trial under military or emergency regulations cannot be ruled out.

The Administered Territories present special problems for the Rule of Law, and the Israel Supreme Court has jurisdiction to hear appeals by its inhabitants. Its role is crucial in the essential need for balance between security and justice, and the Court has generated a considerable respect among western jurists. This respect is not shared by some local jurists and legal commentators as the Court appears to struggle for example with issues of personal status at the interface with the religious authorities, and with control over judicial appointments. Nevertheless Professor Goodhart has expressed admiration for the independence of the judiciary of Israel, and after the Six Day War, he gave significant public support to the case for Israel's presence on the West Bank, pending assured security.

The Israel Supreme Court has on occasion, relating to the West Bank, ruled against physical pressure during interrogation, and attempted to adopt humanitarian principles based on traditional Jewish law. However, the Jewish world is inevitably divided between those who, in the face of obvious danger, consider the Court too lenient, and would prefer it to act as an arm of the military, and those who deeply regret any loss of the moral high ground.

Given the emphasis on rights-based law since the end of the Second World War, and the problem of adjudicating between competing rights, one might well ask whether the Judeo-Christian tradition can, or indeed should, continue to influence legal thinking in the West. The continual need to defend itself against totalitarian regimes who claim a monopoly of the truth challenges our basic assumptions and invites us to consider suspension of the Rule of Law, as we understand it, however undesirable that may be. That the threat to the West is today ideological rather than territorial substantially increases the problem.

Human rights must of necessity apply to all. As Israel Finestein stated at the conclusion of his 1999 article: 'Like natural justice, human rights represent values which may be imperilled everywhere, if they are ignored anywhere.' The rights and freedoms of minorities can only exist if they exist for everyone, even the unworthy, but can they exist even for those who demand that the world must live by their vision, and according to their law or not at all?

The answer must lie in the values we have inherited, and it is significant that our modern system of rights and freedoms was designed for a democratic not an autocratic society, to be applied with proportionality, under the Rule of Law, for the benefit of all. Only in those circumstances can we resume the pursuit of 'Justice Justice' without fear.

Notes

1. IF, *Scenes and Personalities in Anglo-Jewry 1800–2000* (London and Portland, OR: Vallentine Mitchell, 2002), p.234.

2. IF, 'Jewish Legal and Political Philosophy', *Jewish Journal of Sociology*, 39 (1997), p.89.
3. Soncino Pentateuch, p.821.
4. Isaiah 32:17.
5. Deut. 16:20.
6. Article 6.
7. IF, *Scenes and Personalities in Anglo-Jewry*, p.234.
8. Ibid., Ch.10, for a fuller appreciation.
9. Ibid., p.235.
10. Ibid., pp.240-1.
11. Ibid., p.243.
12. David Novak, 'Modern Responsa: 1800 to the Present', in N.S. Hecht, B.S. Jackson, S.M. Passamaneck, Daniela Piattelli and Alfredo Rabello (eds), *An Introduction to the History and Sources of Jewish Law* (New York: Oxford University Press, 1996), p.394.
13. Deut. 16:19.
14. Hecht et al., *An Introduction to the History and Sources of Jewish Law*, pp.422–3.
15. IF, *Scenes and Personalities in Anglo-Jewry*, p.237.
16. Ibid., p.238.
17. Formerly Quentin Hogg, of whom Israel Finestein was a pupil when training for the Bar.
18. IF, *Scenes & Personalities*, p.240.
19. Deut. 24:16.
20. See above p. 3 final paragraph (Division).
21. See, for example, Dr Richard Lang 'Third Pillar Developments' in E. Guild and F. Geyer (eds), *Security versus Justice?* (Aldershot: Ashgate Publishing, 2008), Ch.14.
22. IF, 'Criminal Justice in Israel', *Jewish Journal of Sociology*, Vol.41 (1999), pp.109-12.
23. Ibid., p.110.

18

The Board

The Board is the representative body of Anglo-Jewry. Whilst this is a truism to most, to some it is only grudgingly conceded and there are even a few who persist in refusing to recognize the claim.

Israel Finestein[1]

The above quotation is taken from the first of three articles about the Board of Deputies which Israel Finestein wrote during 1948–49 when he was a comparatively new and no doubt impressionable young Deputy.

What follows is not a history of the Board,[2] except insofar as it enables consideration of the truth (or otherwise) of Israel Finestein's 'truism'. The Board is accepted in the non-Jewish world as representing the whole of Anglo-Jewry, but those who disagree point to the fact that there are sections of the community which have not affiliated or have ceased to be affiliated. In fact the Board was hardly representative of the whole community from the start!

Its full name is the Board of Deputies of British Jews (BOD) and is so called because it was established by Jews of Spanish or Portuguese origin, for whom the word 'deputado' means delegate or representative, as in the French Chamber of Deputies. The occasion of its establishment was the accession to the throne of King George III in 1760, and the decision of the Bevis Marks Synagogue to appoint a committee whose first duty was to submit a loyal address to the new monarch.

The BOD evolved from this committee, but initially it did not represent the Ashkenazi community which by then had grown in numbers and in the wealth of its leading families to match the Sephardim. They wished to be associated with the loyal address, which was agreed on the basis that they form their own committee. The two committees never combined, but the Ashkenazim were eventually invited to join forces. However, their representatives were not admitted as Deputies (rather than as mere observers) until 1812. This delay was not entirely surprising given the rivalry which existed between the two communities.

In 1836, a Constitution was adopted on the initiative of Moses Montefiore, by then President. It unilaterally proclaimed the Board as sole representative of the Jewish community, although 'this did not always receive complete acceptance'.[3] The basic unit of representation was to be the synagogue, which would be entitled to elect one or more Deputies according to size. However, only male seat-holders at that time could vote to elect their Deputies, thus excluding the many non-seat-holders and women. Furthermore, no provincial synagogues sent Deputies to the Board originally, and there were smaller London synagogues which chose not to affiliate.

The impact of Reform and Liberal Judaism created the most difficult and intractable problems for the Board in relation to its representative status. The synagogue was defined as 'a community professing the Jewish religion', and the Board was bound under what was then Clause 43 of its Constitution to be guided solely by the Chief Rabbi (or the Haham) as to which synagogues satisfied that condition. In consequence, the Board refused to recognise the West London Synagogue, and in 1853 it refused to allow its members to represent Orthodox communities.[4]

Not until 1874, did the Board lift its opposition in principle to that congregation being represented, and in 1886, a formula was agreed whereby the Board would not purport 'to represent the opinion of any congregation which did not accept the jurisdiction of the Chief Rabbi or the Haham'.[5] This enabled the Reform and most strictly Orthodox synagogues to join the Board, and this formula remained effective for almost eighty years. However, the expansion of the Liberal and Progressive movement in due course led to demands for communal recognition, and if possible, recognition of their religious authorities.

The result of subsequent discussions over the reform of Clause 43 led to objections by the Orthodox group that reference to 'respective religious authorities' would imply recognition of the rabbinic leadership of the Liberal congregations. The amended wording did not achieve the necessary two thirds' majority when debated by the Board on 26 July 1970. There followed a long series of discussions which were sufficiently acrimonious at the time for two influential Deputies, Freddie Landau and Ashe Lincoln, to propose that Clause 43 be scrapped altogether. Although unlikely to be passed, and defeated on 23 May 1971, their proposal may have concentrated the minds of all concerned.

The possible breakup of the Board perhaps led the Orthodox to agree the above form of words, subject however to a statement to be annexed that the religious leaders of the Progressives were not exponents of authentic Judaism. The Progressive deputies then made it clear they would secede if a suitable amendment was not agreed by 31 October 1971, and on 24 October, the Board agreed to recognise 'those designated by such groups of Congregations as their religious leaders in relation to religious matters in any manner whatsoever concerning them'. Some eighty Deputies representing the strictly Orthodox and the Federation of Synagogues then resigned.[6]

Assurances were given that the only religious authorities recognised by the Board were the Chief Rabbi and the Haham, and this satisfied the Federation, whose Deputies returned. However those of the strictly Orthodox group did not, except that some were content to do so when the above assurances were incorporated into a mandatory code of practice in 1984. The Progressives reluctantly but tacitly accepted the Code, and now play a major part in the affairs of the Board. The strictly Orthodox remain absent, but are welcome to attend and have sent observers on several occasions in recent times. The present Board President has reported warm relations with leading organisations and figures in the strictly Orthodox world.

The extent to which individuals or other bodies prefer to act independently of the Board is also a significant indication of representational capacity. The emancipation campaign (1828–58) was an early example, in which Sir Isaac Goldsmid publicly objected to the Board's claim to be the sole conduit with the British Government.[7] Furthermore, the JC at that time was not content with 'the leisurely pace adopted by the Board in pursuit of the advancement of the campaign',[8] and proposed a petition to be signed by all who supported emancipation, regardless of Board membership or affiliation.

Sir David Salomons MP (1797–1873), who had been a member of the Board and indeed its President for several months in 1846 during the temporary absence of Sir Moses Montefiore, considered that Jewish Members of Parliament were quite competent to look after the political welfare of the community. He was probably more influential in Government circles than the Board, having been elected Sheriff of London in 1835, and having served as Lord Mayor of London in 1855–6. In his view, the Board constituted a restraint upon the citizenship rights of the emancipated Jew who should be free to make his own representations to the Government on Jewish public affairs.

In the period following the creation of the United Synagogue (US) in 1870, a conference was proposed by the Board to consider amendments to its Constitution, but there was opposition within the US Council to any involvement. However, Lionel Louis Cohen, Vice President of the US and one of its founding fathers, warned against any action likely to subvert or isolate the Board. He accepted that communal government should be in the hands of the aristocratic families, but placed great store on the fact that the Board was recognised by Parliament, and when the US wished to make representations to the Government, he sought cooperation with the Board.

In 1871, the Anglo-Jewish Association (AJA) was founded to defend Jewish interests abroad by diplomatic means. The Board was largely inactive in foreign affairs and 'was criticised for its insularity and reluctance to co-operate on any extended basis with Jewish bodies overseas'.[9] With the decline of the 'hands-on' approach of Sir Moses, in 1878 the Board effectively delegated its role to what was known as the Conjoint Foreign Committee, a partnership with the AJA.

Following the assassination of Czar Alexander II in 1881 and the atrocities visited upon Jews in Eastern Europe, the Conjoint played a central role faced with Government reluctance to intervene. They initially opposed the calling of a public meeting to publicise the position, but prompted by public outrage, and with support from Arthur Cohen QC MP (1830–1914) who became first Ashkenazi President of the Board in 1880,[10] meetings were held throughout the country.

Arthur Cohen doubted 'whether a non-elected organization such as the AJA could be an effective working partner on a day to day basis with a body such as the Board, whose character and influence sprang from its being an elected and representative body'.[11] On the other hand, he felt in relation to the Conjoint, that the Board had no choice, even though this 'inhibited the growth of the Board as a democratic institution'.[12] He was inevitably criticised for giving away too much power.

Over a century later, Cohen's concerns were echoed in the context of a possible merger between the Board and the Jewish Leadership Council (JLC).[13] It is worth noting that when Cohen resigned as President in 1895 (for personal reasons) there were suggestions to combine the Board and the AJA, or to separate the Home and Foreign functions. Neither body agreed![14]

The English Zionist Federation (EZF) was established in 1899 at a time when the Conjoint led by Claude Montefiore and Lucien Wolf was strenuously opposed to Zionism. It refused Zionist representation, and rejected attempts to formulate a common approach to the Government. The Conjoint was thus at variance with a growing number of pro-Zionist Deputies who were beginning to percolate the Board. Worse still was the fact that the Conjoint functioned behind a veil of secrecy, confirming the impression that the Board itself was not representative of the views of the community.

It became clear to the Zionist faction that the Conjoint must be bypassed and an opportunity presented itself following a letter to *The Times* on 24 May 1917, which was a blatant attempt by the Conjoint to forestall the Balfour

Declaration. By a small margin, the Board voted to censure the President for having countersigned the letter, not so much on account of its contents, but because he had done so without consultation with the Board. Membership of the EZF grew substantially after 1917, as did the number of pro-Zionist Deputies.

The influx of some 150,000 Jewish immigrants from Eastern Europe between 1881 and 1904, many with Zionist tendencies, presented the Board with another major challenge to its representative status. A host of new congregations were created, and provincial centres such as Leeds and Manchester grew rapidly in size. Although their Honorary Officers were invited by the Board to discuss their concerns, the absence of proper representation could hardly be ignored. Even so, 'the leaders of Jewish provincial opinion regarded the Board as essentially a London body, despite the presence there in due course of elected Deputies'.[15]

Mass Jewish immigration also presented the Board with the problem of whether and, if so, how to represent those immigrant communities whose rabbis engaged in 'clandestine' marriages and divorces in breach of English law and procedure. Was it the duty of the Board to represent those who wished to uphold Jewish law, known to be at variance with English law, in particular as to the prohibited degrees of marriage? This would have been contrary to the prevailing philosophy of the Emancipationists who opposed the idea that the Jews needed or should seek for themselves special privileges.

The Board thus came under pressure to support efforts to stamp out irregular practices and to impose penalties which for some years 'remained the guiding principle of the Board'.[16] However over time this approach was reversed, as the Board began to see its duty as representing those who wished to uphold Jewish law by seeking concessions for example in respect of Sabbath observance, employment, Sunday trading, Kashrut and the like.

Inevitably from time to time the Board has failed or been unable to move with the speed or effectiveness demanded by specific groups. The Bnei Brith, for example (their first British Lodge having been founded in 1910), decided to act independently of the Board in respect of assistance for aliens. Likewise the Friendly Societies ignored the Board in an appeal to the Chancellor over National Insurance contributions. Tradesmen in the Jewish East End felt their concerns were not addressed. Independent bodies such as the Jewish Labour Council and the Jewish People's Council against Fascism and anti-Semitism (JPC) were established in the 1930s as Board policy was deemed too passive, and over cautious.

The rise of Nazism presented special problems for the Board which did not wish to embarrass the British Government, then pursuing a policy of appeasement, nor wish to aggravate the position of German Jews abroad. In consequence, there were major differences of opinion within the Board and within the community. The Board's reaction to fascist anti-Semitism was perceived to be feeble, but that is to undervalue the efforts of the then President Neville Laski (1933–39) who attended a fascist meeting in 1936 and was 'horrified and insulted' by what he saw and heard.[17]

Intensive lobbying and meetings with the Home Secretary followed, and these resulted in a stiffer response by the police, and a growing awareness by the Government of the threat posed by the British Union of Fascists to the country as a whole. In its own way, the Board played a key role in the defeat of the Fascists and in preventing its members from gaining election to Parliament.

The shared threat of Fascism drew the Jewish community closer together. The JPC, initially in favour of direct action, and other communal bodies such as the Association of Ex-Servicemen, the Friendly Societies, and the Zionist Federation, eventually came to accept the leadership of the Board in this area. Here was a classic example of the Board working behind the scenes, 'in a measured, comprehensive and effective manner'.[18]

The Board was opposed to direct action on the streets as likely to be counter-productive. Its warnings were spectacularly ignored on 4 October 1936 when the Fascist leader, Oswald Moseley, organised a highly provocative march by his uniformed supporters through the East End, with its large concentration of Jewish residents. What followed was a major confrontation with both marchers and police, in which large numbers of Jews and non-Jews, outraged and defiant, united to erect barricades, and eventually to cause the marchers to disperse. However, what became known as the Battle of Cable Street gave undue publicity to the Fascist cause and its anti-Semitic agenda, as the Board feared.

The 'Battle' did not prevent the 'Blackshirt' meetings going ahead later, or subsequent marches. The fascists were not defeated at Cable Street, and their vote increased in the East End in the Election of 1937. On the other hand, the confrontation led to a speedy introduction of the Public Order Act 1936 which sought to control public marches, and forbid the wearing of uniforms.

Meanwhile Zionism remained a major fault line, but with the unopposed election of Professor Selig Brodetsky as President in 1939, the communal tectonic plates shifted in its favour. He was the first foreign-born Jew to become President, the first East End Jew, and significantly the first committed Zionist.[19] Much credit for his election lies with the skilful lobbying of Lavy Bakstansky, a Deputy, and General Secretary of the Zionist Federation. However, some Deputies may well have been influenced if not outraged by the infamous White Paper of May 1939, by which the

Government sought to restrict immigration into Palestine, an obvious retreat from the Balfour Declaration. David Ben Gurion described the White Paper as a declaration of war on the Jewish people.

It was perhaps to avoid potential domination by the Zionists, as well as potential compromise of its independence, that the Board initially declined to send a delegation to the World Jewish Congress (WJC) established in 1936 to act as future spokesman for the Diaspora. On the other hand, Brodetsky was personally associated with the WJC, and argued that this strengthened his negotiating position. Nevertheless, the WJC was another body which acted independently of the Board and made its own direct approaches to the UK Government. It was not until 1974 that the Board agreed to join forces and became as it is today an effective and active participant.

Zionism continued to be a source of controversy despite Brodetsky's election. A Palestine Memorandum submitted by the AJA was attacked by Bakstansky[20] in the course of a lengthy acrimonious correspondence. The Board elections of 1943 finally provided a Zionist majority committed to the creation of a Jewish State after the war. The AJA nevertheless wanted to have their say, as did others such as (later Sir) Louis Gluckstein KC MP, President of the LJS. Echoing the sentiments expressed a century earlier by Sir David Salomons MP, he considered himself free as an MP to address the Government directly, and would not be inhibited by any resolution of the Board to the contrary.[21]

It is hardly surprising that there were objections by some Deputies to the alleged partiality of the Chair towards the 'Progressive Zionist Group' or caucus. An informal meeting, chaired by former President Neville Laski, was called in 1944 to give consideration to the Board's proceedings. The attendance of some fifty-eight Deputies, with support from a further thirty-five absentees, gives an indication of the strength of feeling of those who considered their views were not adequately represented at that time, and led to the formation of an 'Independent Group'.[22]

Israel Finestein referred to the existence of such distinctive groups which coalesced from time to time around their own leaders and orators. However in his view, they were never allowed to push the Board into a party system, and individual Deputies remained free to vote as they thought best in the interest of their constituents and the community at large. He also felt that the role of the President was 'an important safeguard against the intensification of differences inside the Board'.[23]

With the creation of Israel in 1948, the Board was and remains faced with conflicting approaches as to how support for Israel should be manifest. In 1956, Barnett Janner MP (then President) was criticised by those who felt he should not have voted with his party in Parliament against the British invasion of Suez, which was seen as helpful to Israel. The emergence of biased media reporting, and of attempts at demonization and boycott in more recent times have incensed many Deputies, who have demanded ever increased activism.

On the other hand, with the extension of territory controlled by Israel after 1967, there has developed a growing minority of Deputies with misgivings about some of Israel's policies. They reserve the right to criticise the State publicly, and wish to influence the Board to reflect their concerns. On 16 November 2014 Yachad, a movement perceived rightly or wrongly as critical of Israel, was admitted to affiliation of the Board by the required two thirds majority. However, the preceding discussion of their application, adjourned on the first occasion, was acrimonious reflecting a deeply entrenched division of opinion.

At about the same time, a proposal to enter into a joint project with Oxfam proved equally controversial. It was not the project itself, its purpose being mainly agricultural, but rather the views attributed to Oxfam, considered by some to be negative towards Israel. Others emphasised the opportunity to influence opinion from within Oxfam, and the ensuing debate was heated. However the involvement of the Board was not renewed after the first year. A more recent initiative to link local synagogues and churches to support peace-making between Israel and the Palestinians has again divided the Deputies.

The Gaza wars have produced considerable soul-searching. A strong military response by Israel was inevitable following a spate of rocket attacks from Gaza on civilian targets. Operation Protective Edge, as it was called, began on 8 July 2014, and unleashed a torrent of anti-Israel criticism, which contained an increasingly vocal anti-Semitic component. One response of the Board at that time was to invite the Muslim Council of Britain (MCB) to join in condemnation of anti-Semitism, which they did, but the ensuing joint Declaration was considered by many to be ambiguous and inappropriate. However, it may have succeeded in the short term in reducing the number of incidents.

The community is inevitably divided in its assessment of threat and how to respond, but expects the Board to be vociferous in its defence. It is certainly vigilant, and in recent times has responded robustly to anti-Semitic incidents and hate speech, especially on University Campuses. It has also taken a prominent role in establishing long-term dialogue with other faith groups such as the Methodists and Quakers.

The organisation of the Board has frequently been criticised, and in its early years led to the introduction of Honorary Officers and the delegation of responsibility, together with the creation of Sub-Committees, now known as Divisions. The oversight of Government legislation was introduced. A proper and transparent procedure for the election of Deputies by their constituents was introduced, evidence of which remains a fundamental requirement for membership of the Board. The governance of the Board is currently under review both in terms of structure and procedures to enable best use of resources, and to ensure transparency and accountability expected in modern times.

On the historical evidence, it is possible to argue that in a technical sense, there has never been a time when the Board was truly representative of the 'whole' community, which of course includes the Ultra Orthodox who have sent no Deputies since 1971.[24] There are also a large number of small and very small communities[25] especially in the regions which do not elect Deputies to some extent because they cannot afford the cost involved, overwhelmed perhaps by running costs, or a declining membership, and other very real internal problems.

Furthermore, around 1995, the Board transferred responsibility for security to a specialist body, although it retained a key political role in defending the community against anti-Semitism and in its relations with other groups. At the same time, the Board facilitated the creation of an independent and united body to deal with day to day matters appertaining to Shechita, but remained involved in defence of the practise. The historical background in relation to these two matters will be considered in the next chapter.

In addition, there are a large and increasing number of cultural or secular Jews today who no longer belong to a synagogue, choosing to identify as Jews through charitable or other endeavours or not at all. A proportion of the community is thus unable to choose and elect a Deputy, unless they belong to one of the many non-synagogual bodies which are already affiliated to the Board. All of the above is true, but it is not the whole truth! Representation is a complex issue, not easily defined, and largely in the eye of the beholder.

Those with whom the Board deals do not ask about the number of Deputies or affiliated bodies. They see an organisation which has existed for over 250 years, approved by monarchs, recognised by Parliament, with access to Ministers of the Crown for whom the Board is the first port of call when contemplating relevant legislation. They see a body with robust democratic credentials, however imperfect they may be, and they see what is now a highly nimble body which acts with speed, determination and effectiveness.

The Board engages in fighting anti-Semitism continuously, and in considerable inter-faith activity. It makes frequent representation to

Government Ministers and foreign diplomats, and is active on the international scene. The Board's activity on the educational front is considerable with the increase in the number of Jewish faith schools, and has recently sponsored a definitive guide to Jewish religious education prepared by Clive Lawton OBE, a difficult task given the diverse interpretations of Judaism. The Board ensures that the needs of schools of a religious character are maintained in legislation, and by means of inspection (*pikuach*) it ensures that standards are met.

When it engages in this and other work, when it responds to the challenges of the day, it does so on behalf of the whole Jewish population. If any benefit is achieved, it benefits all. It does not, and does not seek to, exclude unaffiliated Jews or Ultra Orthodox Jews from any such benefit. On the contrary, in respect of the latter, the Board seeks 'to ensure that there are no difficulties for those who wish to practise strict religious observance'.[26] No congregation is prevented from electing Deputies if they wish to do so, and no group is prevented from applying for affiliation, and in their absence, there are other ways in which a particular concern can be communicated to the Board.

Lack of adequate and independent funding has also imposed a permanent brake on the scope of the ever expanding needs of the Board and its effectiveness as a representative body. A major part of its funding comes from a Communal Contribution requested from all members of affiliated synagogues, but being voluntary, many elect not to pay. In his 1949 article, Israel Finestein commented that 'The state of the Board's finances is not only an indignity to the representative body of Anglo-Jewry, but a serious inconvenience'.[27]

This observation remained substantially accurate until the end of 2014 when the situation was much improved with the sale of the Board's office premises in Bloomsbury Square. The capital thus released will be a buffer for the immediate future, and a source of hopefully wise investment, but the struggle to ensure that current income exceeds current expenditure will undoubtedly continue.

Meanwhile the Board holds a mirror to a splintered society with extremes of wealth, education and religion, at the same time loyal but also separatist, divided by seemingly irreconcilable differences of opinion hardly justified in so small a community. Anglo-Jewry would probably be ungovernable if it had to start again! It owes its survival to longstanding institutions, and strong leadership, both inside and outside the Board, each claiming to represent the best interests of the community, whether it did or not in any numerical sense.

Throughout its history, the Board has (however slowly) adapted to changing circumstances, to new and varied constituencies, to new styles of leadership, to new and dramatic controversies, to new and widespread prosperity, as well as economic downturns. It has survived allegations of sham, ineffectiveness and atrophy, and has outlived those who would seek to enforce sectional interests or promote individual issues.

The election of Jonathan Arkush as President in 2015 has opened the way to new initiatives, and a new era. With the assistance of Gillian Merron (a former MP) appointed Chief Executive shortly before him, he leads a team of officers and staff widely seen as having introduced a new dynamism and professionalism to the Board. The process of adapting to present and future needs is ongoing, as the Board actively seeks to defend and represent the Anglo-Jewish community, now somewhat smaller, but more confident, modern and integrated than that which existed in the immediate post-Second World War period, when Israel Finestein was first elected to the Board.

Notes

1. IF, *Scenes and Personalities in Anglo-Jewry 1800–2000* (London and Portland, OR: Vallentine Mitchell, 2002), p.252.
2. For which see Raphael Langham, *250 years of Convention and Contention: A History of the Board of Deputies of British Jews 1760–2010* (London and Portland, OR: Vallentine Mitchell, 2010).
3. Ibid., p.13.
4. See above p. 25 final paragraph (Agree to Differ).
5. Langham, *250 Years of Convention and Contention*, p.232.
6. See above p.87 (Mirage of Unity).
7. See above p.18-19 (Emancipation).
8. IF, *Studies and Profiles in Anglo-Jewish History: From Picciotto to Bermant* (London and Portland, OR: Vallentine Mitchell, 2008), p.65.
9. IF, *Jewish Society in Victorian England* (London and Portland, OR: Vallentine Mitchell, 1993), p.316.
10. For a fuller appreciation see ibid., Ch.11.
11. Ibid., p.316.
12. Ibid., p.315.
13. See post p.191 (Leadership).
14. Langham, *250 Years of Convention and Contention*, p.78.
15. IF, *Studies and Profiles in Anglo-Jewish History*, p.222.
16. Langham, *250 Years of Convention and Contention*, p.97.
17. Daniel Tilles, JC, 19 December 2014, p.41.
18. Ibid.
19. For a fuller appreciation see IF, *Scenes and Personalities in Anglo-Jewry 1800–2000*, Ch.9.
20. JC, 8 December 1944, p.10.

21. Lawrence Rigal and Rosita Rosenberg, *Liberal Judaism: The First Hundred Years* (London: Union of Liberal and Progressive Synagogues, 2004), p.79.
22. IF, *Scenes and Personalities in Anglo-Jewry 1800–2000*, pp.258–9.
23. Ibid., p.257.
24. But see above p.173 (The Board).
25. Jewish Small Communities Network website lists ninety affiliated congregations.
26. Langham, *250 Years of Convention and Contention*, p.260.
27. IF, *Scenes and Personalities in Anglo-Jewry 1800–2000*, p.261.

19

Leadership

> A many-sided process of change has been in progress for half a
> century. The contrasts between the 1940s and the 1990s in styles
> and objectives reflect the major transformations affecting the
> Jewish world – the changing Israel-Diaspora relationship, the
> new (old) meaning of Zionism, the changing patterns of Jewish
> leadership, the yearning for answers concerning Jewish identity
> and purpose.
>
> Israel Finestein[1]

Looking back in 1999 over the fifty years since the Second World War, Israel
Finestein described the Jewish scene in Britain as 'marked by paradox upon
paradox'. There were tell-tale signs of erosion and indifference, but there were
also signs of communal revival, and enthusiasm for Jewish knowledge, in a
complex communal scenario.

At some point during those fifty years, a sea change occurred. In religious
terms, the broad easy-going orthodox synagogual highway eventually
narrowed, as members fell to the left and to the right. The 'middle of the
road' largely ceased to exist, with the rise of the Liberal, Reform and Masorti
movements, and the growth of the Ultra Orthodox communities.

At the same time, many opted for cultural Judaism, or secularity, which
was discussed for the first time at the BOD Conference of 1977 under the
heading of 'The Challenge of Secularisation'. No longer taboo, the subject
had been brought to centre stage as an important issue which could no longer
be ignored, and featured in subsequent high-level public discussions.

Furthermore, the State of Israel and its wars contributed to a reduction
of restraint in the questioning of religious authority by some, whilst at the
same time for others it stimulated a keener sense of attachment. It also
offered another option after 1967, when *aliya* to Israel became attractive to
ever increasing numbers, even to many with no Zionist background. Career
opportunities which had not been available before 1967 became available in
the newly expanding Israeli economy, and an open informal and egalitarian
society contrasted greatly with Anglo-Jewry, still obsessed with financial or
professional success. Anti-Semitism in due course accelerated the process.

Policies pursued by the Government of Israel can have an effect on Jews everywhere, and on Jewish-Gentile relations, especially after 1967. Disproportionate public criticism of Israel by Church bodies and the media appeared to contain an anti-Jewish element of great concern to the community, and the standing of Israel abroad was also felt to be compromised.

As the prospect of peace receded following the failure of the Oslo accord, there emerged a real division of opinion, fuelled by frustration and concern for the future of Israel and world Jewry. Some Jews wished to advocate for Israel, others felt obliged to remain silent, but an increasing number claimed the right to criticise Israel's actions publicly, even though they chose not to live there. How, when and whether to respond to the situation in Israel imposes what might well be regarded as the ultimate test of acceptable Diaspora leadership.

But Anglo-Jewish leadership was changing. Those in positions of authority became the subject of scrutiny and criticism, a world away from the 'somewhat decorous, and apologetic self-lauding'[2] of a previous era. The deference shown to the inter-related aristocratic families (known as the cousinhood) which had governed Anglo-Jewry since the emancipation had already dissipated before the onset of the Second World War. One frustrated Deputy at that time referred to them as a 'miserable minority, solely concerned with their social standing'.[3] However, a new 'cousinhood' was perhaps in the making, based not on family, but on wealth.

In 1962, Sir Isaac Woolfson (1897–1991) Chairman of Great Universal Stores, was elected President of the United Synagogue, confirming the steady rise to major influence on communal affairs by men of new wealth and philanthropic inclination. He and Sir Simon Marks (1888–1964) were enthusiastic Zionists, and their combined influence was greatly enhanced by major fund raising for Israel to which they brought immense organisational skill.

'Woolfson's chairmanship of what became the Joint Israel Appeal (JIA) may be said to have inaugurated a fresh epoch in the history of leadership within Anglo-Jewry.'[4] It set a compelling example for younger Jewish businessmen. The JIA extended across religious divisions. It bridged London and the regional communities. It became a unique unifying force whose success and ubiquity gave special prominence to those who directed it as power brokers in communal life.

There was a growth in the study of genealogy, and of local Jewish history, reflected in the output of the JHSE. A greater frankness emerged in the study of occupational structures and immigration, of the socially vulnerable and the under-privileged, such as that published in 1955 entitled *Minority in Britain: Social Studies of the Anglo-Jewish Community.*[5]

In 1956, the community celebrated three hundred years of the resettlement of the Jews in England. Among the lectures occasioned by that event was one given by Dr Abraham Cohen, President of the BOD, who commented that, 'Anglo-Jewry has reached its numerical peak and a decline is bound to set in. The demographic data points unmistakably to that conclusion.'[6] The changes which this brought to the community were far-reaching.

In 1965, the Board established the Community Research Unit to study facts and trends and assist with essential planning in various fields, reflecting the growing need for disciplined research and expert assessments. A climate of self-enquiry led to an intense period of reports commissioned by other major communal organisations. The Institute for Jewish Policy Research, which evolved out of the Institute of Jewish Affairs, sought to strengthen the cohesion of the community, through their detailed studies.

These reports all pointed to a growing need for rationalisation of communal effort, an awareness of the shortcomings of the prevailing system, and the need to accommodate so many different but often overlapping interests. The Kalms Report into the United Synagogue encouraged 'the growing fashion for structural streamlining' and 'the selection [not election!] of men of proven talent'. Chief Rabbi Sacks also envisaged 'a single body to promote, strategize and resource the many activities which create Jewish continuity'.[7]

In a pivotal address to the 1984 BOD Conference entitled 'The Changing Face of British Jewry' Judge Finestein referred to the realisation of communal decline and the current preoccupation with what was called the community's survival capacity. The pre-war oligarchic system had crumbled, new systems and new leadership were necessary. He pointed to the dramatic impact of inflation which threatened the viability of important causes and projects.

Efficient maintenance and growth within the institutional life of the community was being impeded, and a high value was therefore to be placed on those with the power to command resources, and those with the necessary skills and expertise to use them wisely. There was an urgent need, he continued, to extend and even improve the quality and diversity of the catchment area of potential leaders at all levels, still in its early stages, but duplication must be avoided, and cooperative effort encouraged.

The importance of fund-raising could not be over-stated, and had created its own hierarchy. In his view, the power which derived from success in that area had led to a duality of leadership. 'We have here new dimensions to the exercise of communal authority'.[8] It is clear that as early as 1984, Israel Finestein was contemplating the necessity of a major reshuffle within the leadership of the community. His address showed remarkable foresight, anticipating the formation of the Jewish Leadership Council (JLC) by some twenty years!

From the ranks of major benefactors there had arisen schemes and responses to perceived needs in the fields of welfare, education or defence, and implementation of their schemes through newly created or specially adapted organisations. The new personalities involved had successfully served the community without the need of representative machinery, and many were unwilling to work within the older institutions, such as the Board.

Judge Finestein recognised the desirability of harnessing the talents of these newly prominent and successful individuals, however different the source of their influence. It involved a 'responsible distribution of power', and he proposed to invite them to take an active role within the Board. One way was to co-opt individuals on to appropriate committees, but there were other ways which might have been considered, in any event bypassing the normal channel of election as Deputies.

Setting aside communal demarcation and democratic niceties, and bringing together what Judge Finestein described as 'parallel echelons of authority',[9] reflected the ideals of a man who sought only the common good. That both elected and unelected leaders might work together to that end was and remains a powerful ideal, despite reservations.[10] However his proposals (when President 1991–94) were not supported by a majority of Deputies who presumably did not see, as he did, the emergence of complex issues which the Board alone could not resolve.

One such issue which had clearly outgrown the Board's ability to cope was the need for security, which had been one of its core responsibilities since the formation of its Defence Committee in 1936. There are those who considered that it should have remained 'in-house', but it is difficult to reconcile the representative role of the Board with the provision of guards to the extent necessary. What was now required was a level of manpower, funds and specialist expertise which the Board did not possess. Likewise it was not equipped for the recruitment and training of personnel, the monitoring of anti-Semitic, racist or terrorist incidents, and liaising with local police.

The re-emergence of anti-Semitic incidents after the Second World War reached a peak in 1965, and it became clear that every Jewish school, synagogue, office or other place where Jews congregated would need protection. The Board then agreed to the formation of the Community Security Organization (CSO) 'a separate organization but closely associated with the Board',[11] with regional and local security officers.

The security situation deteriorated in the 1970s with the emergence of the National Front and its racial overtones, with the rise of Holocaust denial, and with increasingly anti-Zionist rhetoric. Attacks on the Israel Embassy and the offices of the JIA in 1994 emphasised the seriousness of the situation. In its Annual Report of 1995, the Board stated that the work of the CSO had been transferred to the Community Security Trust (CST) created for that purpose with considerable financial and personal support from benefactors and charitable Trusts.

Israel Finestein described it as 'an expansion of earlier arrangements under a larger body of Trustees and lay and professional managers ... in association with, but independent of the Board'.[12] The President of the Board and the Chair of its Defence Committee were two of the original Trustees, but the complexity of this work, and indeed the need for confidentiality, even secrecy, meant that it was desirable for the CST to be under the control of its own Trustees. Nevertheless, it was envisaged from the start that 'both bodies acknowledge the imperative need for harmonious co-operation'.[13]

Despite repeated commendation from the police, the dedication of some three thousand volunteer guards, the considerable financial support from individual donors and benefactors, and requests for advice from other faith groups, the CST attracted controversy. Its claim to represent the community was inevitably challenged[14] not only because the Ultra Orthodox preferred to appoint their own guards known as 'shomrim', but also on account of an alleged lack of democratic credentials. This provoked various members of the communal leadership to respond with a letter to the JC in support of the CST under the heading of 'Meaningful Representation'.[15] However no alternative defence structure for the community was on the table, let alone one as effective as the one we now have.

The size of the CST budget has called forth comment, but it must maintain five offices in order to operate nationally, and it must clearly pay the going rate to its executives if it is to be effective. However there are those who believe that the State should be responsible for the security of its citizens, and the cost should not be borne by the Jewish community. This point was made forcefully by Dr Gilbert Khan of Kean University, New Jersey, a Professor of Political Science, who was a guest at the annual CST dinner in 2011.[16] The British Government subsequently responded with substantial sums pledged by David Cameron the Prime Minister, and by Theresa May, then Home Secretary.

These amounts are by no means sufficient to cover the total cost, although Dr Kahn clearly thinks they should be, but whatever the amount, it is doubtful that funds released would become available for other communal needs, as he suggests. Unfortunately other communal causes do not generate the same 'pulling power' with donors as does the need for security. Dr Khan did not impugn the work of the CST which he regards as 'critical to maintaining the welfare of the Jewish community'. It will certainly continue to be needed, the more so in the light of an increase in terrorist attacks across Europe, and if there is one lesson from Jewish history, it is surely that the Jews must be prepared to defend themselves, rather than rely on others.

The CST is clearly an example of a new style of leadership. Its Trustees include men of wealth and business experience, some well-known and others not, but credit is due to those willing to devote time and money to protect the community. In the dark and possibly dangerous world of security, there is inevitably the need for secrecy and a degree of anonymity. Although the CST is affiliated to the Board, it is not subject to any scrutiny from elected Deputies, but as with other security organisations, it is difficult to see what kind of supervision is appropriate without prejudice to its activities. However there are those who consider that nevertheless further transparency or accountability is possible, and should be provided.

Another important issue which had outgrown existing forms of leadership is that of the Jewish method of slaughter known as Shechita, which prior to 2003 had been a continuous source of division and controversy. 'The modern Jewish defence of Shechita in England began in the 1870s and 1880s',[17] with papers submitted to medical journals, and an address by Chief Rabbi Hermann Adler in 1893. Between 1911 and 1930 there were four Bills before Parliament proposing that pre-stunning should be made compulsory. Shechita does not permit pre-stunning which its opponents, whatever their motives, believe to be more humane. The BOD lobbied successfully for the exemption of Shechita from the above Bills, which never became law, and the matter came to rest with the creation of the Rabbinical Commission in 1933.[18]

Attacks on Shechita resumed in the post-war period, and in 1950 the National Council of Shechita Boards was established in an attempt to present a unified platform, thus reducing the involvement of the BOD.[19] It seems to have had little effect, and in 1989 the JC was reporting on Shechita in terms of wars and division among the rabbis.[20] The Slaughter of Animals (Humane Conditions) Regulations 1990 also led to objections by various orthodox groups each acting independently of the Board, and conducting their own negotiations with Whitehall.[21]

The organisation of Shechita was part of the divided world of Kashrut, also referred to by the JC in terms of battles and wars. In 1976, it had referred to the organisation of Kashrut as a 'laughing stock', urging the need for a merger of the various Kashrut authorities.[22] In another issue in 1987, Geoffrey Alderman examined the underlying causes of a dispute which threatened to bring chaos to Kashrut supervision in London.[23] Today the organisation and certification of permitted food is in the hands of some twelve authorities, divided along religious lines.

It should be added that a new collateral challenge arose to both Shechita and Kashrut with discriminatory proposals for the labelling of food products. These were described by Israel Finestein in 1992 (then President of the BOD) as 'thoroughly misguided' in a letter to Neil Kinnock, leader of the Labour Party.

By 2003, it became obvious that an effective defence of Shechita could not be assured if interested parties continued to act independently of each other and of the BOD. A new and independent structure was needed to coordinate their efforts, and the initiative was taken by Henry Grunwald QC (BOD President 2003–09) which led to the creation of Shechita UK. It has become accepted as the sole representative of the community in relation to Shechita, and its lobbying has proved successful to date. The Board is represented on Shechita UK, as is the UOHC, the National Council of Shechita Boards, and all Kashrut authorities in the UK.

The risk of multiple voices was apparent in other areas in the post-Second World War period. The leaders of major communal institutions such as UJIA or Jewish Care were entitled to be concerned and involved with matters of communal policy, and did not see their existing affiliation to the Board as adequate for that purpose.

As envisaged by Judge Finestein, it was clearly necessary to involve them if possible in a combined framework, and avoid mixed messages to Government Ministers. To this end, Henry Grunwald attended meetings which resulted in the formation of the Jewish Leadership Council (JLC) in 2003 with considerable financial backing. It was to be an independent umbrella organisation, 'not to supplant or replace the Board, but to support it and other organizations'.[24]

Judge Finestein believed that the Board and the JLC were 'not divided by any issues of substantive policy',[25] and could thus work together, each drawing on the other's expertise. He and the Board leadership welcomed the creation of the JLC as a body which would enhance the long-term effectiveness of Jewish communal representation, and ensure greater consultation.

With Henry Grunwald at the head of both organisations, the JLC was seen as a valuable partner, not a competitor, and certainly not a usurper! However, after the end of his Presidency in 2009, the stage was set for a separation of the two bodies, as the JLC reorganised itself with power concentrated in the hands of its Trustees, rather than its Council of Members. Although the Board President is invited ex officio to be a Trustee, he is unlikely as things stand to be elected Chairman of the Board of Trustees.

Israel Finestein died in 2009, and therefore did not live to see the consequences of what amounted to a parting of the ways. However what is certain is that he never contemplated the demise of the Board, or its denigration, or indeed its subjugation, or that the Board would one day become merely one of some twenty-five or so organisations affiliated to the JLC. He would have strenuously rejected the idea that the Board had outlived its time.

Writing in 2009 in his history of the Board, Raphael Langham felt it was too soon to determine 'how the relationship would develop, what tensions might rise, and whether the JLC might wish to assert itself in areas that have hitherto been the prerogative and province of the Board'.[26] Five years later, Geoffrey Alderman, who had previously welcomed the need for a new institutional framework to reflect diversity, referred bluntly to the 'stark reality of the new order, based on financial muscle, and the shameless ambition of the JLC to supersede the Board as the major conduit for dialogue with the British State'.[27]

Whether that ambition exists remains to be seen. The JLC is still a relatively young organisation and needs time to evolve. It has brought together the leaders of communal bodies, and their work on community infrastructure, and consideration of strategic and policy issues, does not necessarily overlap with the Board. Likewise its willingness to employ regional officers to promote grass roots advocacy with members of local Councils and MPs is highly commendable. Its financial resources much exceed those available to the Board, and this has enabled it to attract capable people willing to serve in various fields, both locally and nationally.

In an address to the Board on 17 July 2011, the leader of the JLC (now Sir) Mick Davis, confirmed that the two bodies had different roles, and that the role of the JLC was to support and complement the work of the Board. He acknowledged that the Board was the democratically elected representative of the community, and explained that the JLC was an umbrella organisation whose Council of Members was composed of those chosen or elected by the members of each of the affiliated bodies.

It is clear that Mr Davis (as he then was) and his organisation were concerned at a perceived need for the community to 'up its game' in the face of a 'changing political landscape' and 'opponents who were becoming better organized and more vociferous'. However the Board was not unaware of such concerns, which have to some extent been addressed, or are being addressed. Perhaps spurred on by the JLC, it has raised its profile in recent years, and robustly deals with the day to day problems of the community, for which it receives a considerable amount of favourable publicity.

The JLC is altogether different from previous bodies which have acted independently of the Board, usually in order to deal with one specific issue or perceived need. However there seems no reason why the two bodies should not be able in the long run to avoid unnecessary duplication, or doubt as to who speaks for the community. Reports of Government Ministers presented in the past with two sets of representatives have caused dismay to a large number of Deputies and their constituents. However at the time of writing, the two bodies appear to be living side by side, ostensibly at ease.

The idea of uniting the Board and the JLC into a single representative body is attractive to many, but that is to ignore the considerable practical difficulties involved in bringing under one roof two bodies which clearly have a different constitutional structure, with different sources of authority and finance. Typical of the Anglo-Jewish predilection for unattainable unity, such an idea may well be another mirage, and indeed unnecessary. Parallel or joint action with others has never been far from the Board, as is clear from its history, and there seems no reason why both organisations cannot continue to do good work, each serving the community in its own way.

Efforts on both sides to consider the possibility of a formal merger were in fact begun in 2013, but three years later they appear to have stalled. Consultations conducted by outside experts to consider merger did not arouse enthusiasm on the part of many Deputies. Others were clearly opposed, and considered that the Board must preserve its power of independent action on behalf of the community, based on its unique historical status, which once lost or put in doubt, would not easily be regained.

Israel Finestein was concerned that 'too few Deputies report to their constituencies',[28] and this comment remains pertinent today. Thus in February 2014, the Board felt it desirable to publish an impressive leaflet itemising the many issues and initiatives which are undertaken for the benefit of all, including the unaffiliated. Furthermore, its forty page 'Manifesto' prepared for the 2015 UK General Election also confirmed the considerable scale and breadth of Board activities. These and subsequent updates are a major resource available to local leadership, and highly regarded by MPs and Councillors who see them.

At the end of the day, 'the Board depends for its effectiveness on the confidence reposed in it by the community'.[29] Much depends on those elected, who must not only ascertain the often conflicting views of their constituents, but also keep them informed, although there may be action behind the scenes which cannot be disclosed in detail. Regular community briefings by the Board, and newsletters from the JLC do not always penetrate to the local community, preoccupied with local needs. In consequence, especially when major problems occur, members of the local community do not know what effective action has been taken or will be taken on their behalf.

The fact that new bodies such as the CST or Shechita UK have been created is regarded by some as a reflection on the Board. Israel Finestein would disagree! They are important and necessary bodies in their own right, and rightly independent. Given the circumstances, the Board might well be praised for having facilitated their creation. Indeed the existence of other independent bodies over the years is not a mark of the Board's failure, but of communal success. With a small professional staff, and dependent largely on communal funding, the Board cannot do everything for the community, and cannot be expected to.

At its 200th anniversary in 1960, the Duke of Edinburgh paid tribute to the outstanding contribution of the Board to the Jewish and non-Jewish world. Prince Charles made similar, and clearly sincere, comments at the 250th anniversary dinner in 2010. The high status which the Board continues to enjoy in the outside world, notwithstanding differences within the community, is the envy of other minorities.

Modern problems in (for example) education, welfare and public relations, combined with the need for rationalisation and difficult choices in a tight fiscal situation, now require a greater degree of expertise and professionalism than before. Leadership has become increasingly a full-time occupation, given the pressures involved, and may well require a degree of financial independence or support, as well as vocation to serve the community in an open and transparent manner.

'Leadership has to do with pointing the way, and setting the pace. It requires some qualitative input and perception of trends. It must rise above routine dispatch of business', said Israel Finestein in his address to the 1984 Board Conference. And all who claim the mantle of leadership, should be prepared to work together. The alternative is division, duplication and disaffection, which has occurred all too often.

Leadership is not the sole prerogative of the Board or the JLC. It is to be expected from all who head or serve affiliated bodies, as well as the myriad of national and local organisations and synagogues which make up Anglo-Jewry. They also have an obligation to unify their communities, to establish good relations with the civil authorities, with other faiths, and above all, with each other.

Notes

1. IF, *Scenes and Personalities in Anglo-Jewry 1800–2000* (London and Portland, OR: Vallentine Mitchell, 2002), p.45.
2. IF, *Scenes and Personalities in Anglo-Jewry 1800–2000*, p.23.
3. JC, 31 March 1933, p.43.
4. IF, *Scenes and Personalities in Anglo-Jewry 1800–2000*, p.19.

5. Maurice Freedman (ed.), *Minority in Britain: Social Studies of the Anglo-Jewish Community* (London: Vallentine Mitchell, 1955); see also IF, *Scenes & Personalities*, pp.36/7.

6. IF, *Scenes and Personalities in Anglo-Jewry 1800–2000*, p.36.

7. Ibid., p.41.

8. See Conference Report 'Leading Questions', JC, 9 November 1984.

9. IF, *Scenes and Personalities in Anglo-Jewry 1800–2000*, p.22.

10. See above p.174 (The Board).

11. Raphael Langham, *250 years of Convention and Contention: A History of the Board of Deputies of British Jews 1760–2010* (London and Portland, OR: Vallentine Mitchell, 2010), p.242.

12. IF, *Scenes and Personalities in Anglo-Jewry 1800–2000*, p.24.

13. Ibid., p.25.

14. Gerald Ronson, 'CST represents all Jews', JC, 29 April 2011, p.20.

15. Ibid., p.22.

16. JC, 11 March 2011, p.37.

17. IF, *Anglo-Jewry in Changing Times: Studies in Diversity 1840–1914* (London and Portland, OR: Vallentine Mitchell, 1999), p.230.

18. See above p.72 (Holy War).

19. Langham, *250 years of Convention and Contention*, p.244.

20. JC, 11 August 1989, p.40 and 18 August 1989, p.25.

21. Geoffrey Alderman, *British Jewry since Emancipation* (Buckingham: University of Buckingham Press, 2014),.p.430.

22. JC, 30 July 1976, p.6.

23. JC, 2 January 1987, p.23.

24. Geoffrey Alderman, *British Jewry since Emancipation*, p.435.

25. IF, *Scenes and Personalities in Anglo-Jewry 1800–2000*, p.22.

26. Langham, *250 years of Convention and Contention*, p.257.

27. Alderman, *British Jewry since Emancipation*, p.436.

28. IF, *Scenes and Personalities in Anglo-Jewry 1800–2000*, p.262.

29. Ibid., p.255.

20

London and the Regions

> They called it the matzo tax ! No tax is popular. Least of all
> when imposed on Jews by an outside Jewish body on the
> purchase of an essential food required for the observance of the
> family festival of Passover.
>
> Israel Finestein[1]

One of the great divisions in Anglo-Jewry is that between London and the
provincial communities. Prior to their expulsion in 1290, there were many
Jewish communities throughout medieval England. However, when the Jews
were allowed to return after 1656, London became preeminent in terms of
both wealth and numbers, but the families which then emerged as leaders
of the community had little if any interest in the provinces.

Jewish resettlement in the provinces in fact began in the eighteenth
century. The synagogue in Exeter dates back to 1740. The Jewish community
of Hull, once the second largest immigrant port in England, celebrated 250
years of continuous Jewish residence in 2016, and the Birmingham
community is at least 225 years old, with evidence of a synagogue dating
from 1791.

In 1856, the Birmingham community was sufficiently affluent to build
the existing 'cathedral' style synagogue known as 'Singers Hill'. The architect
retained was the same as built the Birmingham Council House. The
synagogue portico records (in marble) donations received from Jews living
as far away as Cheltenham, with its own community founded in 1839. Of
similar vintage is the Middle Street Synagogue, sometimes called Brighton's
second most important historic building, consecrated in 1875 after a century
of Jewish residence in the town.

The provincial communities initially accepted the matzo tax which was
added to the basic price, and they were thus spared the need to arrange
manufacture of their own. London bakeries provided matzo for the London
synagogues, and an additional amount was set aside for the provinces.
Distribution was administered by the Great Synagogue which was accepted
in the provinces, as well as in London, as the leading Ashkenazi community.

The object of the tax was the relief of Jewish poverty in London, and that remained the same under the United Synagogue which took over the supply after 1870. However the provinces had their own Jewish poor, and in growing numbers, especially in Birmingham and the Midlands generally where flourishing industries were a magnet for labour and for business opportunities.[2] Likewise many immigrants made their way to Manchester, Leeds and Bradford to find employment in the cotton and wool industries.

There were local efforts to assist the provincial poor with initiatives such as the Passover Association in Liverpool and Passover Relief in Manchester. In Liverpool, the burden of poverty was greater by reason of the temporary residence of an increasing number of trans-migrants hoping for a passage to America. The Liverpool Board of Guardians was the first radical attempt to organise Jewish poor relief, which was followed in London and elsewhere.

In the circumstances, there was no reason why provincial Jews should provide for the poor of the metropolis, and in 1879, the Birmingham Hebrew Congregation, in response to growing hostility, withdrew from the arrangement and was followed by others. It was not easy for local bakeries to obtain rabbinic sanction, but in 1900, Lloyd Rakusen established a factory in Leeds for kosher food including matzo, and obtained the approval of the London Beth Din.

The scale of poverty in London was certainly greater than in the provinces. However the overall burden on potential donors in the provinces was greater in proportion to the numbers to be assisted. The US could hardly deny the inequity of the situation, and their public acceptance of the Birmingham decision was a telling sign of change. A new era was in process of birth, and the assumption of metropolitan precedence and policy-making was no longer to be taken for granted.[3]

The end of the Napoleonic War in 1815 had enabled a resumption of immigration, and by the early 1850s the Jewish population expanded from some 25,000 to 35,000 with considerable growth of provincial communities in size and number. The death of Chief Rabbi Hirschell in 1842 led to demands that his successor would not be imposed by the metropolitan lay leadership, and that there should be an election, not a privately decided appointment.

'It is quite certain that the Jews in the provinces will never again submit to be governed on any other terms than their having a voice in the election of their Chief', wrote an anonymous correspondent in the *Voice of Jacob* on 11 November 1842.[4] There was clear opposition to any assumption of control from the centre, and the larger provincial communities expected note to be taken of their views by the Great Synagogue in London, whose task it was to organise the choosing of a new Chief Rabbi.

Nineteen provincial congregations participated in the subsequent election on payment of a fee towards the expense involved. Nevertheless 'the non-participating communities tended to view the appointment procedure as unlikely to dislodge the power of the London magnates to determine the outcome. They perceived the election as a London matter, a remote event, even if it might entail consequences relevant to themselves'.[5]

Provincial debate over the appointment led to the argument that the Chief Rabbi's writ did not run in the north, and that issue remained on occasion a matter of controversy. It is therefore not surprising that the new Chief Rabbi Nathan Adler decided to introduce pastoral visits to the regions, a practice which was novel in his day, but one which was considered desirable to be continued by his successors.

One of the great needs of the provincial communities, and indeed elsewhere, was for more teachers and suitably trained ministers. Chief Rabbi Adler had hoped that his proposed Jews' College would become a ministerial training centre, but the inclusion of rabbinic study was opposed, and what started out as a boys' school was not supported.[6] The long impasse prior to its establishment in 1855 clearly reflected a lack of any sense of urgency on this important issue.

Whilst Sir Moses Montefiore and others in the London lay leadership were lukewarm, there was strong support for the scheme in the provinces from such as Jacob Franklin (1809–77) communal activist of Manchester, and Bethel Jacobs (1812–69), silversmith and congregational leader of Hull.[7] Meanwhile, the Liverpool community had already set up the first provincial Jewish day school in 1841, closely followed by the Birmingham Hebrew Congregation in 1843.

The struggle for civic emancipation was primarily a London affair, focussed as it was on access to Parliament, but there were leaders-in-waiting throughout the provinces able and willing to take advantage of the opening of municipal office to professing Jews which was granted in 1845. Henceforward there was no shortage of Jewish mayors, sheriffs, aldermen and magistrates in provincial cities, and the image of the growing involvement and success of provincial Jews in public service reflected their economic and social advance. It also helped reinforce the campaign in London for access to Westminster, which had another thirteen years to run.

The BOD was likewise regarded (and is perhaps still regarded by some!) as essentially a London body, despite the presence of Deputies elected by provincial congregations, the first of which was Sunderland in 1838. The practice was for such Deputies to be resident in London, which led to one of the most contentious issues in 1853 when the President, Sir Moses Montefiore, sought to exclude four members of the West London Synagogue who had been elected to represent the Chatham, Norwich, Portsmouth and Sunderland communities.[8]

The Board was equally divided on the issue, which meant that the regional communities had inflicted a personal rebuff to the authority of the President who was obliged to use his casting vote against admission, effectively disenfranchising the four communities involved. Another indirect consequence of this controversy was the opening of plenary sessions of the Board to the press, which represented a significant advance in the accountability of communal leadership to communal opinion.

With the increased pace of immigration after 1881, the community grew to some 300,000 by 1914, and almost a third of this number resided outside London, 30,000 in Manchester and 20,000 in Leeds. Leaders of opinion in London were clearly 'horrified' at the prospect that the community would be transformed 'if Jews in immigrant localities were to acquire influence commensurate with their numbers.'[9] Lucien Wolf, a member of the Council of the AJA, expressed his anxiety over such a 'dreadful' prospect at a meeting in 1916, when representation from the provinces was already quite inadequate.

Continued expansion in the north was accompanied by an increasing sense of local achievement, and the creation of local centres of influence and power, together with an ever increasing emancipation from any subordination to lay leaders in London. Relations with the new communities were under constant scrutiny, and inadequate collaboration was a standing cause for concern.[10] The provincial tours of the Adlers did little to satisfy long term requirements, and whilst generally accepting the published guidance of Chief Rabbi Nathan Adler, the provinces developed their own synagogual traditions, and their own examples of local intellectual and communal life.

Israel Finestein referred to 'a growing interest in the regions in Jewish culture, notably among the emerging provincial middle classes.'[11] This was reflected in the growing number of Jewish Literary Societies in the major provincial cities ahead of London. Dr Morris Raphall (1798–1868), Minister at Birmingham, scholar, preacher and former Secretary to the Chief Rabbi, was in frequent demand as a visiting speaker on Jewish issues and travelled as far afield as Edinburgh and Belfast. He was a 'brave and lonely protagonist of Jewish learning' and his departure for New York in 1849 was a robust rejoinder to the indifference he felt from the metropolitan leadership.[12]

Another source of irritation between London and the provinces was the refusal of the Chief Rabbi to recognise the unimpeachable rabbinic qualifications gained abroad by foreign born, mostly Yiddish-speaking rabbis. Such rabbis often became familiar and popular local figures in provincial centres, whilst the Chief Rabbi, supported by the leadership of the

US, was regarded as a 'mouthpiece of the London establishment',[13] remote and out of touch, especially over the need for Jewish day schools.

The influence of immigrants tended to grow within the provincial communities at a faster rate than in London, with its aristocratic leadership impervious to the newcomers. In the more populist and democratic areas of the north, leadership was more easily infiltrated, which greatly influenced the distribution of power within the Jewish community as a whole. The rise of political Zionism as a major movement in Anglo-Jewry, reversing the non-Zionist trend in the metropolis, owes much to the strength of Zionist opinion among Jews in positions of influence within the northern communities.

In Manchester the Marks-Seiff-Sacher family combination consistently supported Chaim Weizmann, the future first President of Israel, from his early days as a local university lecturer. His employment by a chemical manufacturer, who happened to be the political agent of Lord Balfour, may also have been significant. The Manchester Zionist Society was one of the first to be established in 1896, and in 1910 that city produced the *Zionist Banner*, the first journal of its kind in Britain.

In Leeds the widespread fashionability of Zionism was reflected in the naming of the local Jewish hospital after Jacob Moser (1839–1922) and his friend Theodor Herzl. Moser was Lord Mayor of nearby Bradford in 1910 and a huge local philanthropist. A noted Zionist, he visited Palestine, and contributed to the building of the Hebrew High School in Tel Aviv where a street is named after him. He also contributed to the Bezalel School of Art in Jerusalem.

In Liverpool, Bertram Benas (1880–1968) was a leading lawyer, scholar and influential Zionist who was part initiator of the Hebrew University in Jerusalem. He is credited with arranging the score of the new Jewish national anthem 'Hatikva', first performed in 1915. He was also concerned for student welfare, and was a founder member of the IUJF in 1918.

Whilst the major provincial centres were clearly active and vibrant, there were many smaller communities which struggled for lack of numbers and facilities. In 1872, the Sheffield Hebrew Congregation appealed for aid for a new synagogue. Many of its founders included members of the Great Synagogue who had moved north for business reasons. Their appeal received support by London Jewry which recognised the desirability of a community located where new labour opportunities existed, as distinct from the overcrowded conditions in London.

Unfortunately the encouragement of northward migration did not succeed in other places such as the Potteries in Staffordshire, which despite some forty Jewish families in Hanley, became 'a Jewishly deprived, and ministerially deserted area'. On 30 May 1884, following an extensive pastoral tour, Rabbi Hermann Adler described the situation outside the major cities as one of 'spiritual destitution'.[14]

One purpose of his visits was to stimulate regional cooperation whereby the larger communities would support a group of smaller ones in their vicinity. However, this was criticised as unworkable, and led to the idea of the establishment of a nationwide United Synagogue. However it was implicit in such a scheme that the London community would in effect be subsidising the provinces, and the United Synagogue showed little enthusiasm for any extension of its Constitution, let alone a nationwide expansion. As Chief Rabbi Adler declared frankly in 1901, 'the average Jew in London pays scant attention to provincial Judaism'.[15]

The small Oxford Hebrew Congregation founded in 1841, without waiting for a nationwide scheme, proposed its own affiliation to the United Synagogue in 1883. The burden of maintaining and improving its synagogue premises, used primarily by students during term time, was too great for the small number of resident families. The proposal was welcomed by the JC as 'the first step to expanding the US into the provinces',[16] but it was a step too far for the US, which rejected the request.

As an alternative, the Oxford congregation asked to be granted burial rights in London, which were ultimately agreed on terms, but the eventual outcome appeared to be a reluctant concession made by an excessively inward-looking state of mind in London. King Henry III (1216–72) was more appreciative of his Oxford Jews, and granted them land for burial close to the river near Magdalen College!

On the other hand, to be fair, the US already had additional responsibilities with a changing and expanding metropolitan scene. It was not considered prudent to expand outside the metropolis where unemployment and overcrowding caused by increased immigration were a major problem towards the end of the nineteenth century, and there were falling contributions to the principal Jewish charities at that time. There were also inherent difficulties in determining and enforcing shared responsibility with provincial communities, the older ones no doubt wishing so far as possible to maintain their own autonomy.

However the Oxford story had a happy ending! The grubby conditions in which food was prepared in a small Victorian scullery and eaten by students in the synagogue, itself in a state of disrepair, finally came to an end in 1973. It was clear that the needs of the growing Jewish undergraduate body were in effect a national rather than a local responsibility, and although the number of Jewish residents was also growing in the post-war years, it was a group of London-based alumni which took the initiative to raise the necessary funds for a new Jewish centre on the same site. This incorporated certain adjoining premises which had meanwhile been acquired by the B'nai Brith Hillel Foundation for the benefit of the students.

It should be added that the Oxford Jewish Centre is open to all strands of Judaism, which appear able to work harmoniously together on behalf of the community as a whole. It is a model which might be considered in other situations with limited means, and sets an example to those who might perpetuate factional discord. However, what emerges is a clear picture of self-help by individuals willing to devote time and money to a particular project, but very few other small communities in the provinces were in a position to recruit such assistance.

It took a truly remarkable person to come to their aid! The Rev. Malcolm Weisman OBE, a former Royal Air Force Chaplain, realised that whilst tending to the needs of scattered Jewish servicemen, the same pastoral care was needed by the many small groups of Jews scattered throughout Britain, often without sufficient funds to pay for a Minister or teacher, and without access to Kosher food. In 1963, he sought the agreement (willingly given) of the then Chief Rabbi Brodie that he become their religious advisor, and has since brought active help and a sense of belonging to outlying communities, at the same time of necessity transcending religious division.

His 'parish' stretches from Aberdeen in the north to Jersey in the south, and somehow, within the confines of his legal practise, and senior appointments within the military Chaplaincy, he has managed to travel thousands of miles to visit his parishioners. 'No community is too small, and no distance too great' for him, said Chief Rabbi Sacks on awarding him 'emeritus' status in 2009.[17] Elkan Levy, a past president of the US, was then appointed Director of the Office for Small Communities (OSC) which Malcolm Weisman had in effect created almost singlehandedly. Originally supported by the Jewish Memorial Council, the OSC is now supported by the UJIA.

Provincial Jewry is no longer concentrated in the major towns and cities, and the 2010 census surprisingly indicated a Jewish presence in almost every Local Authority in Britain. As many as ninety synagogues are now listed as linked through the Jewish Small Communities Network, a major internet resource founded in 2002 by Ed Horwich, having witnessed the decline of his home community in Southport. Other much older communities have fallen into the 'small' category in need of help, whilst at the same time, new small communities spring up in places where opportunities present themselves, and in some places where Jews were previously absent.

Despite apparent indifference from the centre, provincial Jewish communities have survived by their own determination to do so, and by the voluntary efforts of individual Jews able and willing to teach, to lead services, to raise funds and to administer. In the course of doing so, they have produced many high achievers who have impacted on the national scene. To name but a few in addition to those mentioned above: Israel Finestein was born in Hull. Isaac Woolfson came from Glasgow. The Birmingham-born Leopold Greenberg took over editorship of the JC in 1907. The developers Jack Cotton and Alec Colman also came from Birmingham, as did the founder of the Odeon cinema chain, incorporating his own initials – Oscar Deutch Entertains Our Nation!

The provinces have survived in spite of London, but as their numbers decline, or they become more scattered, it will no longer be possible eventually for their old age homes, their schools, synagogues and rabbis to be financed by local residents alone. The age of the closely-knit 'nuclear' communities confined to respective localities within a few large cities is long gone, and there is now a clear need for communal planning and allocation of resources on a national scale. Initially mooted towards the end of the nineteenth century, 'nationwide planning remained largely a theoretical debate, confined at best to the tentative stage. Public calls went unheeded or elicited meagre response.'[18] Has anything changed?

All candidates for Honorary Office at the BOD now emphasise the need to accommodate the provinces, and one plenary meeting of the Board is held in a provincial city each year. Some fifty provincial Deputies meet regularly as a Regional Deputies Assembly. They can of course highlight problems in their constituencies, and readily act as liaison for a growing number of meetings and events taking place in provincial communities. But it is the other fifty or so small unaffiliated communities (listed at the OSC) which may be without assets or sufficient funds, but also need to be part of a national agenda.

There is an active Education Team at the BOD reaching out to the provinces, and the Partnership for Jewish schools is an important initiative of the JLC. Schemes in both organisations for young people, for promotion of women in leadership, for social action and inter-faith, all now serve the needs of the whole community. All the religious strands of Judaism, including the United Synagogue, now look to expand in the provinces and cater for their respective needs.

With twenty-one congregations in 1914, the United Synagogue has successfully expanded to sixty-four congregations today, with several in the Home Counties. However in April 2015, the much reduced Sheffield Jewish community, whose former synagogue was capable of seating almost a thousand, became the first provincial member of the US.

It is understood that the US is currently in conversation with other provincial communities, and in particular with the Birmingham Central Synagogue. However an affiliation with the latter would perpetuate a division with the older established Birmingham Singers Hill Synagogue located barely a mile away. Despite failed efforts at merger in the past, both communities have much to offer, and one hopes that the long awaited expansion of the US outside the metropolis will stimulate further interest.

When the British Government applied a tax on tea shipped to the American colonies, it had the most dramatic consequences! 'No taxation without representation' was the immediate response, and could well have been the cry of the Anglo-Jewish provinces at Passover, not only neglected the rest of the year, but for many years refused an adequate say in the corridors of power.

Israel Finestein described the relationship between London and the Regions in his usual restrained fashion as 'A case of Cordial Unease'.[19] As a historian, he was referring specifically to the period before 1914, when 'an affluent community felt inhibited by the divisions and deficiencies of the communal system from engaging in the necessary action'.[20] However, his assessment remained remarkably accurate well beyond that date, and a hundred years later, there is finally at last evidence of more cordiality and less unease.

Someone, almost certainly a Londoner, once asked 'Is there Jewish life beyond Watford ?' The answer lies above!

Notes

1. IF, *Studies and Profiles in Anglo-Jewish History: From Picciotto to Bermant* (London and Portland, OR: Vallentine Mitchell, 2008), p.209.
2. Birmingham was once known as the city of a thousand trades.
3. IF, *Studies and Profiles in Anglo-Jewish History*, p.210.
4. Ibid., p.212.
5. Ibid.
6. See above p.56 (Bleak Landscape).
7. See post pp.206-7 (Robinson Row).
8. See above p.25 (Agree to Differ).
9. IF, *Scenes and Personalities in Anglo-Jewry 1800–2000* (London and Portland, OR: Vallentine Mitchell, 2002), p.6.
10. IF, *Anglo-Jewry in Changing Times: Studies in Diversity 1840–1914* (London and Portland, OR: Vallentine Mitchell, 1999), pp.240–1.
11. IF, *Studies and Profiles in Anglo-Jewish History*, p.216.
12. See above p.56 (Bleak Landscape).
13. IF, *Studies and Profiles in Anglo-Jewish History*, p.229.
14. Ibid., p.226.
15. Ibid., p.231.
16. JC, 18 July 1884, p.4.
17. JC, 18 June 2009, p.C1.
18. IF, *Studies and Profiles in Anglo-Jewish History*, p.224.
19. Ibid., p.209.
20. Ibid., p.236.

21

Robinson Row

> Among the growing number of Jews who branched out along
> the roads of England, Hull was an attraction for the itinerant
> tradesman, as a thriving port and market town, and in due
> course as a likely place in which to settle.
>
> Israel Finestein[1]

Hull may have seemed an unlikely place for itinerant Jewish traders to settle
in the eighteenth century, situated as it is in the eastern corner of Yorkshire,
but it was its very location which made it a place of rising prosperity. It was
situated at the apex of a huge triangle of eight rivers to the West, feeding into
the River Humber, from the northern dales beyond Rippon to Burton,
Derbyshire in the south. It was these waterways which facilitated the
movement of goods and raw materials in the Industrial Revolution, and the
completion in 1816 of the trans-Pennine canal system widened the area for
which Hull was the most convenient port.

Hull's status as a major trading centre was further enhanced by its
location opposite the Baltic ports across the North Sea to the East. The River
Hull initially provided a harbour and mooring for small ships as it fed into
the Humber, but it was too narrow for the size and volume of the shipping
which was to come. In 1778 one of the largest inland dock facilities of its
time was created, followed by two others in 1809 and 1829, facilitating Hull's
continuous rise in both coastal and foreign trade.

The original old town, which had denied entry to King Charles I,
occupied an area of approximately one mile square, and was protected on
two sides by water, and by walls to the north and west. There were walls on
the eastern bank of the River Hull, protecting the harbour, and a garrison
was located there. The High Street moves north following the line of the
River Hull, and its most prominent resident was perhaps William
Wilberforce MP (1759-1833) who led the successful Parliamentary
campaign for the abolition of slavery.

A significant sight is the equestrian statue of William III erected in 1734,
which still stands near the southern end of the old market place, located at
the eastern end of Holy Trinity Church, built about 1312. The Hull market

was extremely successful in the eighteenth century, with as many as fifty commercial road carriers from as far as forty miles distant jostling for position in and out of a very restricted area. The market also provided food and supplies for the shipping trade, an additional lucrative source of business in a major port.

The development of retailing in Georgian Hull is meticulously documented by Dr Ann Bennett (a niece of Israel Finestein) in her book *Shops, Shambles and the Street Market 1770 to 1810*, and in due course, as business expanded, the Hull Corporation attempted to persuade traders to give up their market stalls and move into shops. Retailing thus became and remained a major industry, and the principal activity of the majority of Jews who settled in Hull.

During the French wars, immigration was greatly impeded by the Aliens Act of 1793, but the Jewish community began to grow again after 1815 when the first steam packet sailed up the Humber: 'a herald of cheaper and quicker access from the Continent, which expanded local business life and the pace of immigration into and through Hull'.[2] In 1836 restrictions on immigration had been finally removed, and in 1840 Hull was linked by train to the main rail network, providing easy access to other towns and cities, especially London. The political upheavals in Europe during 1848 further increased the rate of arrivals.

There is no serious evidence that Hull had a medieval Jewish community, although this possibility has been debated by academics. The first identifiable Jew discovered there was one Israel Benjamin, born in Breslau, Germany. It is recorded that on 2 April 1734 he was given a charitable payment of five shillings by Holy Trinity Church, having previously converted to Christianity in Dublin at the age of 45 years. This payment, worth about a week's manual labour, was considerably more generous than the six pence normally paid to vagrants.

A further charitable payment of five shillings 'to the converted Jew' is recorded in the Churchwardens accounts for St Martins Parish Beverley, near Hull, during 1733–34.[3] It is not known whether this payment was also made to Israel Benjamin, but he could well have travelled through Beverley on his way to Leeds, where he died in 1735 and was buried at St Peter's Church.[4] On 31 May 1743, the account books of the Mayor of Hull record the payment of six pence 'to Jacob Samuel, a converted Jew',[5] and although we know very little of Benjamin and Samuel, their recorded presence in Hull clearly suggests the beginning of the movement of Jews into the area.

It also indicates the attraction of conversion for those in need of financial assistance, and the attraction for the conversionists of a community with an increasing number of immigrants. Organised missionary activity in Hull can be traced back to around 1810, when 'The London Society for promoting

Christianity among the Jews' opened a branch there. Its organising secretary was John Scott, headmaster of the local grammar school, an Anglican clergyman described as 'messianic in inspiration and missionary in purpose'.[6] However, the missionaries were largely resisted, and some Jews with no intention of converting nevertheless took advantage of free food, gifts or medication occasionally on offer. Israel Finestein found evidence of only four Jewish converts in Hull during the middle decades of the nineteenth century.[7]

The earliest known Jew who actually resided in Hull was Isaac Levy. He lived near the present Liberty Lane from at least 1766, thus indicating 250 years of continuous Jewish presence in the town, a rare achievement outside London. One Michael Levy is thought to have traded in Hull as a watchmaker as early as 1770.

In 1788, when the mainly Protestant citizens of Hull 'celebrated the centenary of the "Glorious Revolution" with fervour',[8] the leading figure in the Jewish community was one Aaron Jacobs, a jeweller. It is understood that on behalf of the community, he presented the Corporation with an elegant crown, suspended above the statue of William III, immortal hero of the Protestant victory. A contemporary account makes reference to 'a richly ornamented crown', but ten years later, the local historian John Tickell mentions neither the crown nor Jacobs in his account of the local celebrations!

In 1780, the first of three synagogues was established by a small group of families in a disused Roman Catholic chapel at Posterngate. Tickell stated in 1798 that between twenty and thirty people resorted there for worship. In 1809 another congregation was established nearby in Parade Row by a secessionist group headed by one Joseph Lyon, a pawnbroker. The new synagogue 'became the premier of the two, largely because Lyon maintained a Minister (Samuel Simon) at his own expense'[9] and the Minister officiated at mid-week services, not possible at Posterngate.

Joseph Lyon lived in Hull for some twenty years, and as well as being financially successful, he is described as a man of firm character and initiative. It was said that the leading families of Hull had such confidence in his integrity that they would leave their valuables with him when travelling out of town. The local press referred to him on his death in 1812 as 'greatly respected'. He was one of the last to be buried in the Jewish cemetery located in an area which became known as Villa Place, outside the old town.

Dr David Lewis, local historian and archivist, has estimated that the cemetery contained a maximum of sixty-three graves, of which nothing remains, and after years of neglect the area became part of a development site. Possible exhumation and transfer of remains was considered, but did not proceed, partly on account of cost, and partly so as not to offend religious sensibilities. The site was at one time part of a school playing field, and eventually passed into the hands of the NHS. It is now a fenced meadow within a children's play area.

In 1812, nearby land in Hessle Road was acquired for an alternative cemetery, but it was closed in 1858 following the Burial Acts of 1854. Dr Lewis suggests that no more than seventy-five burials would have taken place there out of an estimated maximum of 100 plots. Some stones remain and can be identified. Several prominent Jewish citizens sought to protect the old cemeteries from development in the post-Second-World-War period, and exerted pressure on the Local Authority.

After Lyon's death, and thanks to the efforts of Solomon Meyer (Posterngate) and Israel Jacobs (Parade Row), the two congregations settled their differences, and amalgamated to form the Hull Hebrew Congregation. Land was procured at 7 Robinson Row, and the foundation stone was laid on 27 February 1826. 'Progress on the construction of the new Synagogue, and its opening on 18 June 1827 were extensively reported in the local press.'[10]

Solomon Meyer, formerly of Sheffield, came to Hull in 1823 and opened premises as a pawnbroker, 'ready to advance money to any amount'.[11] His career is characteristic of many Jewish traders who chose to settle in Hull. He had been a longstanding member of the Great Synagogue in London, which contributed £15 towards the building cost at Robinson Row.

Israel Jacobs lived in Hull since at least 1801; a dealer in clocks and watches, he quickly established himself as a jeweller, goldsmith and silversmith. He became known as 'Gentleman Jacobs of Scarborough' where he also had premises, and lived there in his later years. His death in 1853 'was widely reported in the local regional and Jewish press. He became a venerable figure whose personal authority proved to be an inherited family trait.'[12] His son Bethel married Esther, daughter of Joseph Lyon, and became undisputed leader of the community. He was President of the Synagogue in 1851.

In addition to Bethel's large and fashionable shop, he had by the 1840s a workshop nearby, and conducted an extensive business in silverware, watches and jewellery including by order from London and Paris. A versatile man and excellent musician, he was a prominent member of the Hull Literary and Philosophical Society. He assembled objects to be shown at the Great Exhibition of 1851, and was instrumental in having the annual meeting of the Association for the Advancement of Science come to Hull in 1853, despite strong competition from other cities.

Bethel Jacobs was involved with the building of the Hull Royal Institution, a major social and cultural centre which opened in 1853, and he provided gold plate for the visit of Queen Victoria to Hull in 1854. He championed the formation of the Hull School of Art and Industrial Design which opened in 1861. He clearly played a significant part in the life of the city, and on his early death in 1869, 'he was borne to his final resting place by fellow townsmen of all creeds who sincerely lamented the passing of a good man'.[13] He was buried in the relatively new cemetery at Delhi Street, off Hedon Road to the east of the old town, on land acquired in 1858.

It was estimated that there were forty Jewish families in Hull in 1793, and by 1851, the community had risen to about 330 individuals. The 1838 official register of immigrants lists between eighty and ninety Jews most of whom settled in Hull, mainly from Germany or Poland. A variety of occupations is listed, including an optician from Hanover, a shoe maker (David Davis), an umbrella maker (Elias Hart), and a 'quill and pencil merchant' (Joseph Levi). Other Jewish businesses included the import of cigars, patterns of embroidery, and marine stores.

In 1824, Marcus Bibero was brought to Hull by his father from Cracow. He was a world-class swimmer who, by his advocacy, significantly contributed to the successful movement for the municipal provision of swimming baths. Ellis Davidson (1828–78) was a pioneer in the teaching of techniques for art study. His lectures to the Board of Guardians helped promote apprenticeship schemes outside the more familiar and overcrowded occupations. He moved to Maida Vale in London after his marriage.

Harris Lebus (1852 – 1907), whose name is famously associated with the furniture industry, was born in Hull, son of Lewis Lebus from Breslau. The family left Hull for London where Harris attended the Jews' Free School and began business as a cabinet maker at the age of 20. He became the owner of 'one of the largest furniture factories in the world, with a labour force of nearly four thousand'.[14]

Abraham Barnett (1810–1901) was an early resident who moved to the then socially exclusive Coltman Street, a mile or so to the west of the old town. His son was president of the Hull branch of the Anglo-Jewish Association before settling in London. His daughter married Joseph Joel Duveen 'a travelling salesman of enterprise'[15] who arrived in Hull in 1867 from Holland. He greatly developed the antique business inherited by his brother-in-law, and later opened his soon famous premises in New York and London's Oxford Street. He was knighted in 1908.

His eldest son, also Joseph Joel, later Lord Duveen of Millbank (1869–1939) was born in Hull, and achieved fame and fortune as the preeminent international art dealer of his age. He made many philanthropic donations including the cost of building the Duveen Gallery at the British Museum to house the Elgin Marbles, and a major extension to the Tate Gallery in London, with which he was associated. He was raised to the Peerage in 1933.

He donated paintings to the Hull Ferens Art Gallery, and the Guildhall collection, and was awarded Freedom of the City of Hull in 1929. On his death, the Art Gallery received eighteen items from his estate.

The first Jewish Alderman of Hull was John Symons in 1873. He was also the first Jew to be appointed Sheriff in 1890, and served on the Council for forty-three years. His father Moses was a founder member of the Humber Lodge of Freemasons. Solomon Cohen (1827–1907) served on the Council for thirty-seven years and was appointed Alderman in 1903. He was elected President of the Congregation in 1868.

Of the 126 Jewish marriages in Hull between 1838 and 1870, 40 per cent of the grooms were stated to be jewellers which covered a wide range of businesses. Poor immigrants might engage in hawking if they could obtain a licence, and some might later become travelling jewellers as an agent, perhaps going on to trade on their own account. If successful, this might lead into pawnbroking and a 'jewellery shop' which might additionally stock watches and silverware.

The career of Lewis Holt (c.1824–1903), who came originally from Germany in 1847, is indicative of this trend. He is described in successive census records as a hawker of jewellery (1851) a travelling jeweller (1861) and a jeweller and dealer in watches (1901). He was a founder member of the Hull Old Hebrew Congregation to which he presented for its opening in 1903 'a pair of massive ornamental iron gates, a striking and distinctive feature of the new premises, well remembered by all who saw them'.[16]

The preponderance of clock and watchmakers is likely to have reflected a demand for accurate and cheap time pieces as the industrial revolution and the new railway system required a standardisation of time, introduced at Greenwich in 1847. Hawkers were so closely connected with the clock and watch trade that shoddy watches became known as 'Jews watches', according to Professor Todd Endelman.[17] At the other end of the business spectrum, Israel Finestein refers to continental trading connections which led to the appointment of local Jews as representatives of the countries concerned. Victor Dumoulin was appointed Turkish Consul in 1870.

In 1848, Robinson Row had about sixty-five members, ninety by 1860, rising to 112 in 1870 out of a total Jewish population estimated at 550. Although enlarged under the direction of Bethel Jacobs, and re-consecrated in 1852 with seating capacity for 280, the synagogue was quickly becoming inadequate. 'Such was the rapidity of increase in the number of Jews in Hull, mainly through immigration, that the enlarged premises did not succeed in meeting requirements.'[18]

By the mid-1870s adverse comment over the limited nature of accommodation at Robinson Row grew into a regular feature of communal life, and tension progressively increased. 'No town of similar size has a larger number of foreign Jews direct from foreign climes', reported the JC on 8 September 1871, and as many as 500 people attended additional services for the High Festivals of 1875. In that year, Rabbi Hermann Adler, on a visit to Hull, 'urged in firm language, the need for larger premises', and the need was further emphasised by the fact that Robinson Row situated in the old town was no longer in an area favoured by fashion.

Increased immigration undoubtedly added to local tensions, and the inevitable welfare obligations became an increasingly heavy burden. Throughout the nineteenth century, the community set up a series of Welfare, Friendly or Benefit Societies, with an effective Board of Guardians in place by 1880. However, the problem was unending and there was a chronic shortage of funds, notwithstanding a degree of affluence among the older residents. Many external requests for aid were received, such as from Leeds, Swansea and Southampton, as well as from the Chief Rabbi for the poor Jews of Palestine (1854) and Morocco (1860). The community had great difficulty in meeting these requests, if at all.

The more recent immigrants were the object of benevolence rather than affection, and had no native respect for the existing leadership. Furthermore, they represented traditions with which many in the host community were often unfamiliar. A correspondent in the JC of 31 May 1872 observed that the 'Germans' looked down on and mistrusted the 'Russians', and the 'English' think they are superior to all, although they seldom attend the synagogue! The move away from the old town by the longer established and more well-to-do families also added to social distance and personal tension.

Hull Jewry did not participate in the election of Chief Rabbi Nathan Adler in 1844. It is suggested that the fee and expense of doing so may have been among the reasons, rather than any lack of respect for the authority and status of the office. However, the regulations he wished to introduce for the conduct of services, urging the cultivation of solemnity, may have had the reverse effect, causing friction and unrest, as a result of different incoming traditions. Nevertheless, on the advice of Bethel Jacobs, the Hull community was the first in the provinces to contribute financially to the new Jews' College in London opened in 1855.

In 1853, the proposed admittance of four Reform members to the BOD appears to have 'brought forward longstanding resentments'. Hull was only the fourth provincial community to be represented at the Board, and its Deputy was the son of Solomon Meyer. He voted in favour of admittance, but his action was publicly repudiated by the synagogue committee who preferred exclusion. He did not resign, and when challenged, he claimed the right to vote according to his conscience.

In the 1860s Simeon Mosely, by then a Tory Councillor, sought to give up the Presidency, but was persuaded to stay on. 'Having to attend Court as a witness to an assault in the Synagogue was more than my self-respect could bear',[19] he declared, and for some months in 1864 he and Bethel Jacobs felt it necessary to absent themselves from synagogual meetings on account of persistent disorder.

Israel Finestein refers to 'the Synagogual minutes of the early 1860s as good evidence of the inner turmoil, and a succession of prominent figures declined to accept nomination'.[20] The election of Joel Farbstein as President was disputed and led to a bitter quarrel which was scathingly referred to in the local press on 3 March 1865. 'Social difficulties are in the way of harmony', observed the editor of the JC on 31 May 1872.

There were repeated instances of scuffles in the synagogue, with some elements having an 'incorrigible proclivity to disorder'.[21] This led to appearances before the local magistrates, and the court interpreter (German and Yiddish) appears to have been in so much demand that the magistrates showed their appreciation with a formal presentation! That the Hull Watch Committee received a fee in October 1873 for two constables to attend the synagogue to prevent disorder perhaps sums it up!

Much of the above will certainly be recognisable in the affairs of other communities. Frayed tempers and disputes over the allocation of *mitzvoth* are not unique to Hull, any more than accusations of unfairness or favouritism in the President's allotment of seats, or the existence of disputes between members. Whether this small Jewish community was more fractious than any other, it was extremely varied and vibrant, and despite inner dissension between the older and the newer residents, it had an excellent record in its efforts to cater for the needy, and to provide Jewish education for its young people.

The first published record of a Jewish school in Hull was in 1838, and before that it is likely that Samuel Simon held classes in a room adjoining the Robinson Row premises. In 1863 there were thirty-five boys and some twenty-five girls in attendance. On his visit in 1875, Chief Rabbi Adler is said to have conducted a lengthy and severe examination of both boys and girls, by then forty-five and thirty-five respectively, and pronounced himself satisfied. Shortage of space had led to pressure for a separate Jewish girls' school, which was started in 1872. Its numbers exceeded 130 by 1890, and it continued well into the twentieth century when the present writer's mother (sister of Israel Finestein) was a pupil there.

In the realm of more advanced Jewish education, it is worth noting the presence in Hull of Nathan Harris, a Talmudical scholar of high repute from

Lithuania, and grandfather of Henry Feldman, the first Jew to be elected Mayor in 1906. 'Reb Nahum', as he was called, became the centre of a Talmud study circle which continued after his death in 1880. He was in fact, 'the progenitor of a tradition in Hull for a small coterie to meet for informal rabbinic study'.[22] Israel Finestein in his youth, and his father, were regular members of that coterie.

The JC in October 1874 estimated the Jewish population of Hull at 400 families, and the great immigration brought it to a peak at around 1900. Israel Finestein estimated the Hull Jewish population at that time to be approaching 2,000[23] but Dr Lewis has since made calculations based on marriage statistics, and is confident that it was nearer 3,000. This is consistent with estimates of around 2,500 in the annual Jewish Year Book during the first half of the twentieth century. Dependent on information volunteered, the number is likely to be larger, especially following a period of rapid growth and uncertain fluctuations.

Robinson Row clearly could not cope with the increasing pressure of numbers, but a solution was delayed by disagreement. Eventually the community split and a new breakaway Western Synagogue was opened in 1902 by the more anglicised and long-standing members of the community. Its Foundation Stone was laid by the grandson of Bethel Jacobs, whose father Israel Jacobs had performed the like ceremony at Robinson Row in 1826.

The synagogue which had been at the centre of Hull Jewish life for some seventy-five years, and witnessed its turbulent growth, had finally had its day. The building itself was later used as a piano factory, and eventually demolished in 1928. But the end of Robinson Row as a synagogue heralded the beginning of a new era, as the now divided community put down fresh roots to the west of the old town.

Notes

1. IF, 'The Jews of Hull between1766 and 1880', *Jewish Historical Studies*, 35 (2000), p.33; and see IF, *Scenes and Personalities in Anglo-Jewry 1800–2000* (London and Portland, OR: Vallentine Mitchell, 2002), Ch.4.
2. IF, 'The Jews of Hull between1766 and 1880', p.33.
3. As ascertained by Dr Bennett.
4. Murray Freedman, 'The Leeds Jewish Community – The Early Years', *Shmot*, Vol.1.2 (1993), pp.11/12.
5. Ann Bennett, 'Two Converted Jews in Hull', *Shmot*, Vol.15, 2 (2007), p.12.
6. IF, *Anglo-Jewry in Changing Times: Studies in Diversity 1840–1914* (London and Portland, OR: Vallentine Mitchell, 1999), p.160.
7. IF, 'The Jews of Hull between1766 and 1880', p.85, n.20.
8. Ibid., p.36.
9. Ibid., p.38.

10. Ibid., p.40.
11. Ibid., p.41.
12. Ibid.
13. Inscription on his memorial stone.
14. IF, 'The Jews of Hull between1766 and 1880', p.49.
15. Ibid., p.47.
16. Ibid., p.86 n.27.
17. Todd M. Endelman, *The Jews in Britain 1656–2000* (Berkeley, CA: University of California Press, 2002), p.43.
18. IF, 'The Jews of Hull between1766 and 1880', p.52.
19. Ibid., p.62.
20. Ibid., p.64.
21. Ibid., p.66.
22. Ibid., p.74.
23. Ibid., p.82.

22

The New Community

Within less than half a century of the onset of the great immigration, the enlarged and transformed Anglo-Jewry was again a mainly native-born community, more deeply integrated than the Anglo-Jewish community of the 19th Century, reflecting the release of Jewish energy and ambition in the freer conditions of modern England.

Israel Finestein[1]

The period covered by Israel Finestein's major work of research into the history of Hull Jewry ended with the great immigration, which he dealt with in more general terms in a lecture from which the above quotation is taken. Meanwhile, the Hull community flourished, and in many ways reflected the experience of many other communities in Anglo-Jewry. Its story continues here through the twentieth century.

The scale of the great immigration into Hull may be seen from a plaque at Paragon Station, the main city rail terminal. It was unveiled by the President of the Borough of Brooklyn, New York in 1999, and records that prior to 1914, some 2.2 million people passed through the immigration platform there, as many as a thousand a day at times. Most were headed for Liverpool and a passage to America, the 'goldener medina' (golden country). A large hotel in the centre of Hull (still fashionable in the 1950s) was conspicuously named the 'New York' perhaps in an effort to persuade immigrants that they had already arrived!

Separate facilities, away from the local population, were provided for trans-migrants, and the Lazarus Hotel at Posterngate in the old town was among other emigrant lodging houses licensed by the Town Council. Harry Lazarus (1834–1906), originally from Germany, was the Landlord. It is not thought that he was related to the American poetess Emma Lazarus (1849–87) who in 1883 wrote the immortal words on the Statue of Liberty, which no doubt many of his lodgers were hoping to see.

Give me your tired, your poor, your huddled masses, yearning to breathe free, the wretched refuse of your teeming shore. Send these the homeless, tempest-tossed to me, I lift my lamp beside the golden door!

Some did not make it to America, and settled en route at Leeds or Manchester or Liverpool, but Jeremiah Finestein had no reason to look beyond Hull where his older brother Solomon and two married sisters were already established. He arrived from their small township near Minsk in 1905, almost too late for admittance, given the restrictions on immigration then under serious consideration. Why had he not come sooner?

Jeremiah had married young, and in 1899 (aged 20 years) with his wife already pregnant, he was conscripted into a local unit of the Russian Army. Sadly, his wife died in 1903, and by then with two children, he was transferred to the Reserves, and subsequently given permission to leave the area. But for this unexpected twist of fate, his descendants in Hull would never have existed! He married Rosa Bernstein there on 28 January 1906, and Israel Finestein was the youngest of their six sons and one daughter.

By the time Jeremiah arrived in Hull, tension between the established families and the newcomers had produced a major split in the community, and the new breakaway Western Synagogue had been established at Linnaeus Street, barely a mile from the old town. Benjamin Jacobs, son of Bethel Jacobs, was the Honorary Architect and its first President. The imposing building was consecrated in May 1903 with seating for 600. It was set back from the road behind a large grassed courtyard from which access could be obtained to separate buildings on either side, used for teaching or for meetings, and one of them originally housed the Hull Hebrew School for Girls until 1945.

New premises were clearly needed for those that remained, which included the various branches of the Finestein family, and on a newly acquired site at Osborne Street, mid-way between the old Robinson Row and Linnaeus Street, a large new synagogue was built. It opened on 10 September 1903, and the Hull Hebrew Congregation was renamed the Hull Old Hebrew Congregation. Louis Finestein (Israel's brother) became Honorary Secretary in due course, and served the congregation both before and after the Second World War. Another brother, Jacob Wolf (Jack) Finestein also served on the synagogue council for a time in the post-war period.

'The new congregations each partook of something inherent in the other. Thus it was that each regarded itself as heir to the original united Hebrew Congregation.'[2] Any differences between them were not related to matters of observance, 'more a matter of style, mood, and perhaps language, in connection with which the immigration was a major factor'.[3] The members of the Western may well have had a more anglicised outlook, and initially there would have been a certain awareness of differences in social standing, or economic or professional status. This largely reflected the different circumstances of those who had lived in England before 1880, and those who came after.

Over time, however, such differences as there were became increasingly meaningless, and the Hull community was spared the kind of vehement conflicts which occurred in London over such as the creation of a Jewish Hospital, the wisdom of separate Jewish schools, the liturgical and theological issues raised in the move towards Reform, or the curriculum of Jews College. Nevertheless, the process of integration was delayed by the constant inflow of newcomers until beyond the end of the century, creating 'dislocation to the established structures of British Jewry, which went beyond mere numbers'.[4]

Their residence and occupation in a compact city like Hull went far to assimilate the old and the new, although strains and stresses remained and were inescapable. In terms of occupation, Israel Finestein points out that by 1901, 80 per cent of foreign tailors were Jews, with a like preponderance of cabinet makers and shoe operatives, giving rise to concerns over working conditions, overcrowded living conditions, distortion of the local labour market and Jewish involvement in the Trade Union movement. The resulting problems inevitably caused further resentment of the newcomers, and 'the distinctiveness of the new arrivals in religion, language and dress, accentuated public consciousness of their presence'.[5]

Apart from the two main congregations, there were others which should be recorded. A small Central Synagogue was established outside the old town by a number of new immigrants in 1886 'as though by agreement with the native Synagogue'.[6] Robinson Row had not yet split at that time, but was already overcrowded. In 1914, the Central moved to a former Congregational Chapel (Cogan Street) which was destroyed in the Second World War. Alternative premises at Park Street were found in 1951, and some eighty families continued there as a separate community until 1976. Its cemetery was located at Ella Street, and the earliest legible headstone there is dated 16 November 1889.

In 1928, the New Synagogue was created in a former Methodist Chapel previously used as a Jewish Mission since 1916. It was damaged by bombing in 1941, and although that community was unable to continue, the building was repaired and used by Jewish youth organisations. In 1968, a Reform congregation held its first services in Hull, and in 1981 became a member of the Reform Synagogues of Great Britain.

It was in fact the great immigration which produced the modern provincial communities, and 'by 1900 one half of Anglo-Jewry lived outside

London'.[7] Provincial Jewish leaders in fact played a notable part in the 'dethronement' of the BOD President in 1917 as a result of his anti-Zionism. One might have expected some tension, as in London, over the rise of political Zionism, largely supported by the immigrants, but it proved a cohesive force in the provinces where local Zionist Societies flourished.

No doubt thanks to the presence there of Dr Chaim Weizmann, 'Manchester was in some respects the capital of Zionism in England by 1914'.[8] Sir Mark Sykes, described by Norman Bentwich[9] as 'a godfather of the Balfour Declaration' was MP for Hull Central from 1911. Heir to large estates in East Yorkshire, he became a strong supporter of Zionism,[10] and in the same year as the Declaration (1917) he addressed a large Zionist rally in Hull.

The Hull Zionist Society was widely supported both before, but especially after the Balfour Declaration, and the present writer's father was Chairman of the Society in 1932. Distinguished members of both main synagogues were among the Honorary Presidents and Vice Presidents of the Society, as were several influential non-Jews. Leading members of the Society were actively involved in the resettlement of refugees both before and after the Second World War, and formed a strong nucleus of support and fund-raising for the new State of Israel in due course.

The continued and considerable involvement of Hull Jews in the municipal life of the city was epitomised by Henry Feldman JP (1855–1915) who was the first Jew to be elected Lord Mayor in 1906, and he was twice re-elected. Hull had gained City status in 1897, with about 200,000 inhabitants at that time, and its population ultimately rose to approximately 300,000. Feldman was born in Hull, and became a successful wool merchant.

He was one of the founder members of the Western Synagogue, and its representative at the BOD. He inaugurated civic services, and on his death, leaders of the Hull Corporation gathered at the Synagogue to pay their respects. Synagogue Council minutes record profound sorrow at his untimely death, and refer to him as a Talmudist, with knowledge of Hebrew, French and German. He was buried at the Delhi Street cemetery, off Hedon Road, to the east of the old town, where the Western Synagogue acquired land adjoining that which had been acquired in 1858 and in 1894 by the previously united congregation.

Edward Gosschalk was appointed Sheriff of Hull in 1905. Benno Pearlman (1880–1945), a prominent solicitor, was Sheriff in 1923 and 1932. He was elected Lord Mayor in 1928 when he famously walked to his inauguration on the Sabbath behind his horse-drawn carriage which had been sent to fetch him from the synagogue! As Chairman of the Aerodrome Committee in 1934, he inaugurated the first direct air service between

Europe (Amsterdam) and the north of England. Another outstanding member of the Jewish community was Lionel Rosen OBE LLM (1907–77), a highly respected solicitor who served as Sheriff in 1951, and was elected Lord Mayor in 1972.

It is said of Sir Leo Schultz OBE (1900–91) that he was refused entry to Oxford University (having succeeded on examination) on account of his Jewish background. Whether or not this is true, the City of Hull gained a public servant with considerable talent. A Labour Councillor for fifty years from 1926, and elected Lord Mayor in 1942, he was aware that Hull would be a prime target for enemy bombing and should protect its citizens with adequate shelters. His successful campaign undoubtedly saved many lives. A formidable character, he became known as the 'Lion of Hull' and was knighted in 1966. His contribution to the City was further recognised in 2011, on the 70th anniversary of the blitz, by the rare accolade of a ten-foot statue, unveiled outside the Guildhall.

The interwar years saw the immigrant generation and their offspring largely settled, integrated and welcomed into the wider civic and mercantile community. Many outstanding businesses and benefactions of today originated from that period. Jeremiah Finestein's tailoring business from small beginnings was by then well located in a prominent parade of shops, and his customers included skippers and their crew from the vast fishing fleet then operating out of Hull – if their catch had been successful.

Jeremiah was highly regarded in the community. He said little, but exuded warmth and a caring disposition. As their circumstances improved, the family spent their summer holidays in Harrogate, a genteel place renowned for the therapeutic value of its natural springs. Of greater importance was the existence of an established Jewish community there, and a synagogue dedicated in 1932. However, the family could hardly imagine that their holiday renting of a small property for the month of August 1939 would last for six years!

Israel Finestein thus grew up in a seemingly secure world with rising aspirations, but his story might have ended before it began, when in 1932 on his way to school, he was run over by a bus. He might well have been killed, but sustained a compound leg fracture which eventually healed completely, after many hospital attendances.

As the news of this incident spread, the President of the Synagogue, a man of some wealth, telephoned to say that his car (and chauffeur) would be available to transport Israel to and from hospital or elsewhere at any time – a considerable compliment to Jeremiah and his son, whose early indications of intellectual ability had been noticed. However, a chauffeur in those days (in Hull) was somewhat too ostentatious for Jeremiah, and a small Finestein family car was soon acquired!

One other event of significance in that period was the arrival in Hull in 1934 of the young Rev. Judah Levinson from a small Welsh community. He quickly gained the affection and respect of the members of the Osborne Street Synagogue, and in a quiet way held the community together in the aftermath of the Second World War. He was a caring minister and a teacher to whom the present writer is indebted.

In the run-up to the Second World War, Hull had its share of Fascist activity and Moseley himself came to address a noisy meeting in June 1937. However, as early as April 1933 the citizens of Hull had shown their objection to Nazi persecution of Jews at a Mass Protest Meeting supported by the Bishop of Hull, local clergymen and councillors. A similar protest meeting was held following the Kristallnacht attack on German Jews (9 November 1938). It was attended by some two thousand people, with speeches from leaders of various religious denominations and local MPs.

The Hull Jewish community excelled itself in its hospitality towards Jewish refugees from Nazi Germany. Homes were found for sixty-three unaccompanied children on the Kindertransport, and 120 adult refugees who stayed in or passed through Hull were additionally made welcome. These figures are large relative to the size of the community at a time when 'the treatment of refugees by British Jews was very far from universally benevolent',[11] and in some cases positively hostile.

The war itself brought disruption on a large scale to every family. Some Hull Jews responded to the call for volunteers to train as fire-fighters in an attempt to protect the city from the expected aerial onslaught. Nearly four million children nationwide were evacuated to places of safety in what was the largest and most controversial compulsory movement of civilians in peacetime.[12] Where possible, Hull Jewish children were sent to live with relatives or friends in such places as Harrogate or Buxton. Israel Finestein spent his last year of higher education (before Cambridge) literally encamped near Scarborough, his entire school having moved to this seaside resort to ensure continuity and safety. Kosher provisions were despatched as and when possible!

The Hull Jewish community had its share of heroes of whom two showed astonishing bravery. Captain Wilfred (Billy) Sugarman (1918–76) was in the first wave of allied troops to land at Normandy on D-Day. Despite multiple wounds, he led his men to complete their assigned mission, and was awarded the Military Cross for his gallantry. It is reported that on the eve of battle, he left a note stating that if he fell, he wanted it known that he was a Jew who was proud to fight alongside his fellow non-Jews. He later served in the Far East, and after the war became a respected teacher and headmaster. He is buried at Delhi Street cemetery where his headstone simply records that he was a dear, respected and honourable man.

Captain Isidore Newman MBE (1916–44) volunteered for army service in 1940. A 'handsome, athletic man' with knowledge of French which he had studied at university, he was recruited into the Special Operations Executive (SOE) and sent into France on two clandestine missions. He assisted the local resistance on successful sabotage operations with courage and leadership, and at great personal risk he relayed back countless messages essential to the war effort. In March 1944 he was arrested, probably as a result of betrayal, and was eventually murdered with forty-five other agents at Mauthausen on 6 September. A plaque in his honour can be seen outside the Hull Synagogue, and a full account of the brave teacher from Hull is given by Martin Sugarman in Chapter 18 of his book *Fighting Back*.

In the 1941 blitz, the Osborne Street Synagogue, which had been renovated in 1913, and again in 1932, was substantially destroyed after successive air raids over the city. However, the study area alongside the main building survived and became the core of a newly rebuilt synagogue opened in 1955.

The *bimah* at the heart of the old synagogue, with its shiny traditional wood and two ornate candelabra, surprisingly also survived the bombing intact, as did the distinctive iron gates presented by the Holt family in 1903. Both were incorporated into the new building, and until then, the Salvation Army was good enough to lease its nearby 'Citadel' to the congregation for the Holy days. Ironically, their premises had been used in the nineteenth century as a mission hall, no doubt with a view to conversion.

Without doubt Hull and its docks were a major target for aerial bombardment, as Sir Leo had predicted. Over 400 people died in the first two nights of the Hull blitz in May 1941, and the level of damage remained a wartime secret in order not to affect national morale. A rude shock awaited those who returned from the war, or from evacuation: a moonscape of bombsites, craters and broken buildings in inner city areas. As if paralysed, it took the City more than a generation before a serious revival began, perhaps symbolised by the striking Humber suspension bridge on which work did not commence until 1973.

For many in Hull as elsewhere the war put an end to their embryo businesses or careers, and there was the need to start again. Some Jewish businessmen with considerable foresight were able and willing to raise and provide much needed credit to the numerous returnees to the city, in dire need of clothing and furniture for their families. Before long, the Festival of Britain (1951) effectively promised the population a new era of consumerism, creating further opportunities for businessmen not slow to take advantage.

The commercial life of the Jewish community had its normal share of ups and downs, and the city provided a solid base for expansion after the war. The ancient market in the old town had been a focal point for centuries and was for some a natural place to start. Many who began there went on to commercial success, and as late as the 1960s a high proportion of Hull market traders were Jewish.

Manfred Zerny (1873–1937), having come from Germany as a child, learned to be a dyer and dry cleaner, and went on to launch one of the most successful Jewish businesses with eleven branches in Hull alone when he died, and others around the north of England. The business continued to prosper as part of the Johnson Cleaners Group. Harold Oppel (1917–90) had considerable flair for retailing, and was ahead of his time with the introduction of self-service techniques. He created a successful chain of sixteen stores, and employed 220 people when he sold the business in 1985.

Marcus Segal (1918–96) created a substantial textile company which grew to employ 140 people at its factory, and at its height had eighteen retail outlets. It was described as one of the largest privately owned stores in the city.[13] He served as Sheriff in 1966. One of the oldest and perhaps largest of Jewish employers in Hull was C. Rosen & Sons Ltd, manufacturers of ladies and children's footwear. Founded in 1880, they went on to employ 300.

Another successful entrepreneur was Jack Lennard (1918–95), a cousin of Israel Finestein. Some of his communal views were controversial, but in private he was generous to those in need, and was particularly concerned for the welfare of Soviet Jewry. He made frequent visits to Jewish communities in the Minsk area, and bought an apartment in Mogilev for use as a Jewish community centre. He paid for urgently needed medical treatment and training, and on his death, his nephew Dr Howard Cuckle was told by Dr Zuckerman of Minsk, 'it is impossible to know how much we are indebted to him'.

Yet many Jewish businessmen wished to encourage their children to make careers outside business by taking advantage of the new educational opportunities then becoming available.[14] These would propel their children to heights which had not been open to them, heights which would crown their own achievements. The problem for the Hull community was that a large part of its Jewish youth who could get away to university or to other opportunities for advancement did not return. The Jewish population steadily, sadly and inexorably declined from an estimated 3,000 at its height, to 1,100 by 1990, to 670 in 2001, and is estimated at only 350 in 2011 – an astounding collapse of a once thriving community.

Hull Jewry was certainly not the only provincial community to face decline, which has occurred and continues to occur elsewhere, as new generations of young Jews are attracted mainly to London, Manchester or Israel. The slow and belated regeneration of Hull after the Second World War was a special factor, and one reason why those growing up in the post-war period found Hull an unattractive place compared with other areas not so badly scarred and able to recover quickly. However, there was another reason for its decline, which to some extent the Jewish community brought on itself.

Before the Osborne Street congregation rebuilt its synagogue in 1955, it made repeated and futile attempts at merger with the Western Synagogue, as evidenced in its Annual Report for 1951. The Honorary Secretary Louis Finestein, using uncharacteristically strong language, referred to the past year as having been overshadowed by the failure of wholehearted and sincere attempts at amalgamation, which have been 'met with the short-sighted policy of individuals who fail to realise the advantages of our aspirations'. He went on, with considerable foresight as to the likely damage, 'Let our earnestness be judged by our willingness to sink our identity in furthering this cause. Only future generations will assess the folly of the lack of co-operation between the Synagogues in the present day.'[15]

Osborne Street was at that time led by a successful antique dealer, who also represented the congregation at the BOD. The Western was led by a respected GP. They were both strong personalities, no doubt wanting to do the best for their congregants. However the consequences of two almost identical synagogues so close geographically, trying to provide a full range of the same traditional services in a declining community, and at a time of lax observance, inevitably meant that before long neither could hope to survive. And despite the passing of some fifty years and two world wars, one cannot avoid the suspicion that there was a residue of the attitudes which characterised the original separation.

Faced with total reconstruction of the community, a Representative Council was created in 1946, and the community set about successfully creating a proliferation of charitable and other bodies of all kinds such as one might expect in a much larger community. An active pre-war Judeans Maccabi was revived, Bnei Brith Lodges formed, even (inevitably!) a Jewish golf club. A Friendship Club for over 60s founded in 1953 led to an impressive 'flatlet' scheme for elderly residents, which continued until 2013. And none of this detracted from ongoing wider public service. A.K. Jacobs served as Lord Mayor in 1952, as did Lawrence Science in 1958 and 1959, and Louis Pearlman in 1983.

In 1956, when it became clear that merger was no longer possible, alternative efforts to bridge the gap were made by the appointment of Rabbi E.S. Rabinovitz as Communal Rabbi. He successfully served the community as a whole, as did Rabbi Cooper, his successor. But it was not until 1988 that the synagogues realised that they could not possibly continue alone.

In that year, the Hull Old Hebrew Congregation sold its premises – to a night club, with garish neon lights, a shock to the system when seen for the first time by those who had previously gone there to pray. Only its name – 'Heaven and Hell' – gave some indication of its former usage! However the beautiful *bimah* was saved and transferred to Singers Hill Synagogue in Birmingham, thanks to the generosity of Belinda and David Winroope, formerly of Hull.

Joint services were then held with the Western Synagogue, but it would take until 1994 before the two congregations finally came back together as the original Hull Hebrew Congregation and 'became re-united again after ninety years of separation, much history and change'.[16] The Western Synagogue was sold, and new premises were acquired at Pryme Street in the attractive outer suburb of Anlaby where most Jews then lived, and over four hundred people were present at the opening.

Hull Jews were not alone in their reluctance to merge, and the possibility of an almost identical situation is today developing in Birmingham. Israel Finestein was himself involved in an unsuccessful attempt to mediate over a possible amalgamation of three London synagogues and was well acquainted with the problems. The lack of a guaranteed *minyan*, combined with an intransigent leadership, certainly deter young people and others from staying or settling in an area. However, some consolation for the long-term damage to the local community may be obtained from the benefit to other communities elsewhere.

Though much reduced in size, the Hull Jewish community has nevertheless remained active, and is rightly proud of its history. Under the joint leadership of Howard Levy and Max Gold, it celebrated its 250th anniversary with appropriate lectures, exhibitions and social events, attended by more than 300 visitors from all over Britain and abroad.

The Jewish cemetery at Marfleet Lane, a mile or so beyond Delhi Street, was acquired by the Hull Old Hebrew Congregation in 1930. It is located on rising ground on the eastern edge of the city, originally on open land with a commanding view of the River Humber and its once mighty docks, a mile or so distant. But gradually over the years it has become hemmed in by a rising tide of pallets and other bric-a-brac associated with an unplanned industrial sprawl.

The majestic Humber estuary, widening and curving slowly south to the open sea, is now no longer visible from there, nor are the cranes which marked the point of disembarkation and hope for the immigrant generation. That some of them, including Israel Finestein's parents, are buried so close to their point of entry, might suggest that only a minor bridgehead into this country had been achieved. However, the impact of their descendants locally, nationwide, even worldwide, clearly says otherwise, as exemplified by the life and achievements of Israel Finestein, one of Hull's favourite sons.

Notes

1. IF, 'The New Community 1880–1918', *Jewish Historical Studies*, Vol.20 (1960), p.121.
2. IF, 'The Jews of Hull between 1766 and 1880', *Jewish Historical Studies*, 35 (2000), p.82.
3. Ibid.
4. Geoffrey Alderman, *British Jewry since Emancipation* (Buckingham: University of Buckingham Press, 2014), p.151.
5. IF, 'The New Community 1880–1918', p.112.
6. Lloyd P. Gartner, *The Jewish Immigrant in England 1870–1914* (London and Portland, OR: Vallentine Mitchell, 2001, 3rd edn), p.217.
7. IF, 'The New Community 1880–1918', p.118.
8. Ibid.
9. Attorney General, Palestine, 1922–31.
10. See above p.138 (Restoration).
11. Alderman, *British Jewry since Emancipation*, p.294.
12. See *The Times*, 1 September 2012, p.103.
13. *Hull Daily Mail*, 15 March 1968.
14. R.A. Butler's Education Act 1944.
15. Annual Report and Accounts, 1951, amongst the personal papers of Louis Finestein, at the time, Secretary of the Syn.
16. IF, 'The Jews of Hull between 1766 and 1880', p.82.

23

Children of the Ghetto

> Zangwill's irony and jolting paradox are there, so too his characteristic mischievous phrases. His acerbic asides gleam along the pages, and throughout there is his tenderness for the Jewish plight, allied to a suppressed resentment at the historical processes which produced it.
>
> Israel Finestein[1]

The centenary of Zangwill's birth 'slipped by with hardly a murmur', according to the late great anthologist John Gross (1935–2011), himself born in the East End where his father was a medical practitioner. However the silence was broken in 1976 on the fiftieth anniversary of Zangwill's death, with a new edition of his famous novel *Children of the Ghetto*, originally published in 1892. It prompted a period of renewed interest in Zangwill, and Israel Finestein contributed an article from which the above quotation is taken.

The new edition contained an introduction by the eminent historian Dr Vivian Lipman, 'written with charm and zest, sketching the historical background, the persons, places and periods which Zangwill's sharp observation and deft pen imported from life'.[2] He explained in his introduction that Zangwill wished to demonstrate the problems and virtues of the immigrants, their relationship to the previously established Jews in London, and their aspirations to become accepted into English society.

The modern Jewish world effectively began in the closing years of the nineteenth century, which Israel Finestein describes as:

> mightily full of consequence for the Jews. In every sphere there were eruptions against any semblance of presumed or privilege-bound authority. All the novelties and stresses of the day prevailed in one degree or another in the Jewish fold, which could not be expected to remain immune to all the diverse forces playing upon public life. There was a new self-confidence on the part of the hitherto quiescent, and Zangwill was aware of it all.[3]

Zangwill was born to Russian immigrants from what is now Latvia. His father was typically pious, poor and unworldly, leaving to his wife the essential hard-headed decisions which needed to be made. The East End was not as alien to them as it might have been, but for many of the children of that 'ghetto' the problem of reconciliation with a quite different world outside would set in train a deep-seated ambivalence, familiar to so many, about what it means to be a Jew.

His 'ghetto' was the specific area around Petticoat Lane, and the strangely named Fashion Street, 'presented as a kind of sinister bedlam to outsiders'.[4] Its ambience was recreated without too much sentimentality in the film 'A Kid for two Farthings' starring the late David Kossof. A story of hope amidst hardship, it was adapted from the novel written by Wolf Mankowitz in 1953, and based on his experience of growing up in the East End of London.

The Petticoat Lane district was not in fact unique, and many Jewish communities can 'boast' areas where the butcher, the baker, the cobbler and the deli were all near each other, and near where the Jews lived and prayed. The Osborne Street area in Hull, the Hurst Street area in Birmingham, and Cheetham Hill in Manchester were at one time the chosen location of just such a uniquely concentrated Jewish atmosphere. Likewise, Chapeltown Road in Leeds became the centre of a huge Jewish population, although part of the area close to the city centre was so over-crowded and unhygienic as to be condemned by the Local Authority.

Redolent of a world now long gone, we still remember the tastes, sights and sounds we loved, and regret to have lost, but have not lost entirely. In his novel, Zangwill reminds us of the colourful, almost exotic, life of the immigrants. He also reminds us how sharply this contrasted, even jarred with the established Anglo-Jewish life of those who had already been in England for one or two generations. But the division between the old and the new, the rich and the poor, would be blurred under the influence of emancipation and westernisation.

To Israel Finestein, *Children of the Ghetto* is not a great novel. 'It is discursive, episodic and in part, a collection of impressions, humorous anecdote and social comment.'[5] It is a portrait of a community with a limited future, a symbol of its counterparts elsewhere, 'an epitaph on a place and on an age'.[6] But in spite of being a period piece, 'it is not still life, but life in motion'. Zangwill's heroes all appear to be rebels, who are unable to find peace within or without the ghetto, unable to resolve the double lives which Jews must lead.

Its importance lies not in any literary merit, but in the fact that the ideas discussed by Zangwill's characters are real and fundamental, and have continued to challenge the children and grandchildren of the ghetto in every generation. In the silence which appears to have greeted Zangwill's 150th birthday (in 2014) perhaps it is opportune to look again at this enigmatic author, full of contradictions and inconsistencies, as referred to in the analysis of John Gross: 'Nothing could altogether uproot the tenderness and respect which Zangwill felt for the religion of his childhood', whilst at the same time, he points out that, 'the urge to escape underlies much of his work'.[7]

Countless Jews then and since have agonised over Zangwill's dilemma, so that his work remains of more than passing interest. Liberation from traditional Orthodoxy was not of itself an answer, and some kind of cultural continuity needed to be maintained, or some other justification for Jewish separatism. We are, after all, as prophesied 'a people who will live apart',[8] distinguished, indeed isolated, by virtue of our religious and moral laws, and belief in a divine purpose. But does Zangwill accept any separateness at all?

He speaks as if regretfully of 'the steady silent drift of the new generation away from the old landmarks, groping for a purpose and a destiny, doubtful if the racial isolation they represented were not an anachronism'. Yet he married out of the faith in common with other assimilated Jews and Jewesses of his day, and he went further in a letter to Theodore Herzl on 21 December 1903, justifying his action as a positive duty.

His book contains an assortment of characters who are largely outmoded, all looking for an answer to the problem of being a Jew in the modern world, how to make sense of Judaism as a priceless heritage, and at the same time a millstone round the neck of the modern Jew! Esther Ansell, an intelligent girl from the Whitechapel slums who describes herself as 'a curious mixture', and is described by the author as 'an allegory of Judaism', seems to be his spokesperson. Why, she asks, cannot Judaism take honest pride in its genuine history, instead of building its synagogues on shifting sands? Ultimately, Esther's 'dead ancestors' would not be shaken off. They lived and moved in her, and she could not escape them. Had the Jew come so far, only to break down at last?

To John Gross, despite its defects *Children of the Ghetto* is still worth reading as a slice of social history, providing an unrivalled even unique picture of Jewish life in London during the period of mass immigration from Eastern Europe. 'It has an underlying authenticity for all its staginess', he said 'and although Zangwill's characters are overdrawn or over simplified, they are almost never travestied out of existence'.[9] Who can read 'King of the Schnorrers' without enjoyment? As to Zangwill's style, Gross described it as 'a loose melodramatic affair full of strong situations and wild co-incidences'.[10]

Gross himself testified to Zangwill's lasting memory in the East End as a wit, conversationalist, a tireless spokesman for Jewish causes, and as loyal to his origins. At the same time, he suggests that Zangwill was far less caught up in Jewish culture than popular legend suggests.

Nevertheless, Zangwill came to adulthood during a mini renaissance. Claude Montefiore established his important *Jewish Quarterly Review* in 1888, and the Union of Jewish Literary Societies was created in 1902. The Anglo-Jewish Historical Exhibition of 1887 sparked interest in Jewish history and led to the creation of the Jewish Historical Society of England (JHSE) in June 1893. Zangwill was present at the inaugural meeting, and served as president in 1924. Lucien Wolf, its first president, delivered the tribute to him at its meeting on 26 October 1926 following his death.

Zangwill in fact contributed to the first issue of the *Jewish Quarterly Review* with an article entitled 'English Judaism', which in his opinion 'does not lie in Jewish belief, but in the community's native goodness, and was characterized by intellectual confusion'. It was he submitted 'a unique philanthropic organisation', and whether he realised it or not, philanthropy was indeed 'a defining feature of the Anglo-Jewish scene, perceived to be the mark of an English gentleman, and at the same time proof of attachment to the ancestral faith'.[11]

However, Zangwill was essentially an assimilationist, with vague notions of internationalism and an apparent distaste for the wealthy. He saw Jewish religion itself as outmoded, 'an endless coil of laws' which served no purpose, but Reform Judaism, much in debate in his time, was not the answer for him. He dismissed the United Synagogue as a financial enterprise, and commented in *Children of the Ghetto* that 'long after Judaism had ceased to exist, excellent gentlemen will be found regulating its finances!'[12] Perhaps these were the same financiers and merchants he castigated for wanting 'chariots and fine linen, and municipal importance',[13] indifferent to the 'plight of poor and hungry East enders, forced to wait for their food, and listen to their pompous speeches'.[14]

By contrast, Zangwill praises the Jewish working man whom he regards as morally commendable, and the East End which he regards as the embodiment of Jewish authenticity. And in a community dominated by considerations of public image, it is not surprising that Zangwill's portrait of the 'godless businessmen' did not go down well in the West End. Nor was it fair to characterise in this way those exceptional benefactors such as the Rothschilds who devoted themselves to the education and welfare of the children of the East End.[15]

Children of the Ghetto was not the 'long-awaited antidote to the literary poison' of hitherto unsympathetic writers, which the JC had hoped for.[16] No doubt they had in mind such novels as *Reuben Sachs* by Amy Levy, who in 1888 described 'the undisguised nepotism, and the deep, irreverent materialism of the Jewish middle classes in London'.[17] Her exposé of wealth and its corruption of Jewish values must surely have influenced Zangwill, and his own division of the community into contrasting stereotypes is referred to by Bryan Cheyette in a paper presented to the JHSE in January 1985 entitled 'The Post-emancipation Anglo-Jewish Novel: From Apology to Revolt'.[18]

In a similar study entitled 'Anglo-Jewish Fiction 1875–1905', Bryan Cheyette describes Zangwill's novel as 'an attempt to transcend Jewish particularity',[19] and this might well be taken as the theme of his life. He wished to escape the ghetto, but as is clear from his introduction to the novel, he knew full well that 'they who have won their way beyond its boundaries, must still play their part in tragedies of spiritual struggle, and comedies of material ambition, which are the aftermath of centuries of dominance'.[20]

It is not surprising that Zangwill was interested in exploring the complex identity of Benjamin Disraeli (1804–81) whom he described as 'a dreamer of the Ghetto, a semitic sphinx, who brought to English politics, the Jew's unifying sweep'.[21] He was the only British Prime Minister (so far) of Jewish descent, but his background was hardly that of the ghetto. Disraeli's parents were prosperous members of Bevis Marks Synagogue until 1813 when his father refused to accept the duties of Warden, disqualifying himself as totally unsuited in view of his reformist views. His letter of resignation is quoted by A.L. Shane in his presidential address to the JHSE on 6 November 1986.[22] Isaac D'Israeli lived in a splendid property at the corner of Bloomsbury Square until 1829, a property which from 2001 until 2014 in fact housed the offices of the BOD! He converted his family to Anglicanism when Benjamin was aged 12 years.

It is not that Disraeli had escaped the ghetto, more that he appears to have completely escaped the gravitational pull of Jewish peoplehood and the spiritual struggle referred to above.[23] On the other hand, he never sought to hide or denigrate his origins in his climb to power, and declared through Tancred: 'Vast are the obligations of the whole human family to the Hebrew race.' It was a thought which was to take hold in a future generation.

In his play *The Melting Pot* (1908) Zangwill articulated the idea that the European races would not merely merge, but produce a new breed, a new species, free of racial and religious differences. The idea would have seemed absurd to Disraeli who successfully conducted difficult negotiations with the numerous and argumentative European races at the Congress of Berlin in 1878, but Zangwill was looking across the sea. 'America is God's crucible!' proclaimed his hero, and it is not surprising that the play was well received in the States, where the differences in origin of the 'huddled masses' would be submerged in a new collective endeavour. The idea of a universalised

Judaism which Zangwill hoped would be the future religion of all Americans has (unsurprisingly) not come to pass, and differences of background or custom have not disappeared. They may be submerged, but are accepted, even celebrated without rancour.

Zangwill's view of the 'Melting Pot' complemented his view of Zionism, in which he hoped that a Jewish nation would be created which was non-particularist, 'a people like any other'. Indeed it was one theme of Zionism that it would forge a new breed of Jew, utterly different from those who lived in the ghettos of Eastern Europe. Zangwill supported Zionism, but only as a political movement. He was concerned that it might be captured by the religious party, and become what he called a 'movement of fanatics'.

In the same letter to Herzl referred to above, he made it clear that Zionism to him was subordinate to his grand vision, and he could not allow it 'to dwarf my larger sense of what the world needs, and what perhaps I exist to help to teach'.[24] Nevertheless he remained a supporter of Herzl, whose visit to his home on 21 November 1895 marked the beginning of Zionism in London,[25] and was a major event in the history of the Zionist movement.

In 1901 Zangwill quoted the famous remark of Lord Shaftesbury, that the country without a people be restored to the people without a country who could make the wilderness bloom.[26] However, by 1908 he came to realise that 'Palestine already has its inhabitants', and by giving it two peoples, both would suffer. He foresaw future trouble with the Arab population long before anyone else, and it would take nearly a century before Itzhak Rabin (1922–95), one of Israel's great prime ministers, was prepared to acknowledge publicly that the land had not been 'empty and derelict'. He was assassinated for giving voice to this fact, and for seeking to make peace with his neighbours.

At the Zionist Congress of 1903, the same year as the notorious Kishinev Pogrom, and perhaps influenced by the deteriorating position of the Jews in Eastern Europe, Herzl put forward the British offer of an autonomous region in east Africa for Jewish settlement. It was known as the Uganda programme, and Zangwill supported it as a 'night shelter'. However the plan caused uproar among those for whom Jewish tradition and history regarded Zion as irrevocably linked to the Holy Land, and nowhere else.

When the British offer was declined at the Seventh Zionist Congress in 1905, Zangwill walked out, and founded the Jewish Territorialist Organization whose aim was to create a Jewish homeland in whatever territory was available in the world. The Jews needed a refuge from anti-Semitism, and any port in the storm was better than none. Many lives would have been saved if some such place had existed before the Second World War, and given what we know now, a place of refuge was certainly needed; but almost inevitably his plans came to nothing.

Whilst the above cause was practical and worthwhile even as a temporary solution, Zangwill's support for The Foreign Jews Protection Committee was somewhat quixotic. Its object was to protect unnaturalised Jewish immigrants from conscription into the army or repatriation, whilst at the same time preserving their claim to asylum. These two aims were somewhat inconsistent, and any failure on the part of refugees to support the host country by military service during the First World War was considered damaging to the good name of the Jewish community.

To Gross, Zangwill was ultimately a tragic figure, or at least somewhat 'semi-detached', unable to give lasting expression to his dilemma, a permanent wanderer between two worlds: 'We can only guess at his depths'. Less generous interpretations might suggest that Zangwill was a lost soul, a cockney Jew full of half-baked ideas not truly sourced in Jewish history or culture.

Lucien Wolf agreed that an appraisal of Zangwill should be seen in his relations with Judaism and Jewry, and this was quoted by Joseph Leftwich in his Memorial Lecture to the JHSE on the 25th anniversary of Zangwill's death in 1952. However he was too close a personal friend, and so clearly an admirer, that his reference to Zangwill's 'authentic picture of the London Ghetto, lifted by his genius to the plane of timeless literature'[27] is not entirely objective, and somewhat premature. However, he refers to Zangwill as 'disappointed in all his causes' and sadly burnt out at an early age.

The legacy of obligation brought with them by generations of immigrants from Sinai, refined and enlarged over three millennia, was a legacy from which it is far more difficult if not impossible to escape, whether in America (with Esther) or in Zionism (with Herzl) or in the typical English Sussex village where Zangwill spent the last twenty years of his life! One is reminded of the fourth chapter of his Comedies entitled 'The Sabbath Question in Sudminster', a question of observance, one which remains topical to this day for those who think they are no longer children of the ghetto.

We might escape the physical ghetto, but we remain bound by Esther's 'dead ancestors', and make the return journey to the fold, some willingly, some unwillingly, and some, like Zangwill, seemingly trapped forever in no-man's land. He wanted to become a successful English man of letters, and in this he clearly succeeded, but as so often happens, the freedom achieved was most likely illusory. Did he really escape the contradictions he articulated?

Zangwill's ghetto off Petticoat Lane was not in fact a ghetto at all. It had no walls. Its residents had no protection from outside forces, whether physical or ideological. Nor was there any restriction on those who could escape its economic hardship, or flee a perceived religious straightjacket. Colourful Jewish life with its personal doctrinal or social divisions existed outside the ghetto in one form or another throughout the wider Jewish community.

Whilst Petticoat Lane was undoubtedly the ghetto of the title, could it also be seen perhaps metaphorically as a symbol of a historic ghetto in which Jewish spirituality and culture once flourished? 'All over the world, the old Judaism is breaking down', wrote Zangwill, and the 'children' of every Jewish ghetto, tempted by modernity and emancipation, would be faced forever with the problems highlighted here.

It would no doubt surprise Zangwill that 'the grandchildren of his ghetto are in fact the grandparents in new latter day ghettoes, different perhaps, but unmistakably similar'.[28] His pious father is not consigned to history, but is alive and well and lives on in parts of north London and Manchester! Nor is the wider Jewish community consigned to history, now more dynamic in its own divided way, fortunate to have come to terms with the past through a variety of different religious expressions or cultural and charitable activity.

Zangwill gave his famous novel the sub-title: 'A Story of a Peculiar People'. We are certainly peculiar, prone to create and maintain division among ourselves, despite the obvious dangers. 'Yet it was from Judaism, and the Jewish experience that Zangwill derived his humanism', according to Israel Finestein. His progressive outlook on so many causes was 'conditioned and stimulated by his Jewish instincts for compassion, justice and the inviolable worth of the human personality. He was in the end as at the beginning, a Hebrew, with all its contrariness.'[29]

Notes

1. IF, 'Israel Zangwill in His Day, 1864–1926', *Scenes and Personalities in Anglo-Jewry 1800–2000* (London and Portland, OR: Vallentine Mitchell, 2002), p.197.
2. IF, *Scenes and Personalities in Anglo-Jewry 1800–2000*, p.196.
3. Ibid., p.199.
4. John Gross 'Zangwill in Retrospect', *Commentary*, 38 (December 1964), p.55.
5. Ibid., p.197.
6. Ibid., p.200.
7. Gross, 'Zangwill in Retrospect', pp.54–6; quotation on p.56.
8. Numbers 23:9.
9. Gross, 'Zangwill in Retrospect', p.55.
10. Ibid.
11. IF, *Studies and Profiles in Anglo-Jewish History: From Picciotto to Bermant* (London and Portland, OR: Vallentine Mitchell, 2008), pp.17–18.
12. Geoffrey Alderman, *British Jewry since Emancipation*, (University of Buckingham Press, 2014), pp.211–12.

13. Bryan Cheyette, 'The Post-emancipation Anglo-Jewish novel, from Apology to Revolt', *Jewish Historical Studies*, 29 (1988), p.263.

14. Bryan Cheyette, 'Anglo-Jewish fiction and the Representation of Jews in England, 1875–1905', in David Cesarani (ed.) *The Making of Modern Anglo-Jewry* (Oxford: Basil Blackwell, 1990), p.108.

15. See Jo Wagerman, 'Rothschilds Legacy', letter to *The Times*, 15 June 2015.

16. JC, 20 May 1892, p.9.

17. Geoffrey Alderman, *British Jewry since Emancipation* (Buckingham: University of Buckingham Press, 2014), p.72.

18. Bryan Cheyette, 'From Apology to Revolt: Benjamin Farjeon, Amy Levy, and the Post-emancipation Anglo-Jewish Novel, 1880–1900', *Jewish Historical Studies*, 29 (1982–86), pp.253–65; see also Cheyette, 'Anglo-Jewish fiction', pp.97–111.

19. Bryan Cheyette, 'Anglo-Jewish Fiction 1875–1905', in David Cesarani (ed.), *The Making of Modern Anglo-Jewry* (Oxford: Basil Blackwell, 1990), p.109.

20. IF, *Senes & Personalities*, p.198.

21. Todd M. Endelman and Tony Kushner (eds), *Disraeli's Jewishness* (London and Portland, OR: Vallentine Mitchell, 2002),.p.7.

22. A.L. Shane, 'Isaac D'Israeli and his Quarrel with the Synagogue – A Reassessment', *Jewish Historical Studies*, 29 (1982–86), pp.170-71.

23. See above p.20 (Emancipation) for further comment on Disraeli.

24. Cheyette, 'Anglo-Jewish fiction', p.110.

25. Alderman, *British Jewry since Emancipation*, pp.220–1.

26. See above p.134 (Restoration).

27. Joseph Leftwich, 'Israel Zangwill', *Jewish Historical Studies*, 18 (1958), p.83.

28. IF, *Scenes and Personalities in Anglo-Jewry 1800–2000*, p.196.

29. Ibid., pp.201–2.

24

In Conclusion

> Our history is in conflict with every norm and general rule ever
> thought of by the interpreters of history. There is nowhere the
> remotest kind of comparison. It is an endless tale of the
> unexpected.
>
> Israel Finestein[1]

I set out to pay tribute to a man who set the highest standard of communal leadership, tolerance and intellect. He was a Judge who was not judgmental, an 'outstanding spirit',[2] a man of unwavering faith who understood the Jewish condition better than most, and concerned himself with its twin fundamental issues of survival and identity.

I have not set out to write another history of Anglo-Jewry, but rather to review and update Israel Finestein's own historical and other writings. The patchwork picture that emerges is one of such uncompromising division, and such contrasting views strongly held, as serves to highlight the need to focus on what unites rather than on what divides.

Modern Jewish life began with the Emancipation and the Enlightenment, which gave the Jew choices he did not previously possess. The result is an apparent conflict between those choices, which continues to be played out in every generation. Primarily these choices have led to what Israel Finestein described as the 'dethronement' of the rabbinic tradition, and its replacement with a variety of sects on the left, and the growth on the right of a more severe interpretation of Orthodoxy while traditional Orthodoxy is itself now splintered.

These choices have enabled the Jew to yearn for acceptance and normality in his local (non-Jewish) environment, whilst at the same time retaining Jewish kinship. He has a distinct sense of being different, and the more integrated he becomes, the more he feels the need to extol his Jewish origins. Furthermore, the Jewish condition involves the difficulty of living in two contrasting worlds: one current and one historical; one present and one promised; one dispersed for the spread of morality, the other restored in fulfilment of the prophecies.

Other contrasts aggravate the problem: the inner belief in ancient covenants against the external reality of periodic enmity; the power of Judaism against 'millennial powerlessness'; centuries of Christian domination against a sense of having been chosen for the benefit of mankind; a strong self-consciousness against an acute sensitivity. Our identity is inevitably bound up with these many dualities.

The Jews were and always have been at the confluence of events. We were there at the birth of Christianity and of Islam. We have outlived the Persians, the Greeks, the Romans, the Romanovs and the Hapsburgs, and every other Empire that sought to harm us. In the words of Jabotinsky, 'Nobody is old enough to call on us to account. We came before them, and will leave after them.'[3]

At the same time, we who gave the world monotheism and the concept of righteousness have had to accept the various attempts at our destruction. No other people has been required to present and then defend its existence, as we have. We have contributed to the Enlightenment, to Capitalism and Communism, to revolutions in life and thought, to literature, music and science out of all proportion to our numbers – all in a way somehow connected with and influenced by our special history and heritage.

What has prompted us to accept and perpetuate our separateness with all its problems? Many have expressed the view that they would rather not have been 'chosen' for such a fate as ours, at the same time well aware there is no escape, even for the most assimilated. We are what Jewish history has made us.

'One of the most radical ideas of Judaism is that there is religious meaning in history.'[4] Or putting it another way, 'History is the human role in the unfolding of revelation.'[5] Since our survival is almost impossible to explain, the idea of an underlying purpose is highly attractive. Is history the visible part of a divine plan in which we are all partners? Do the Jews have a special role? Israel Finestein points to an unfathomable cycle of cause and effect.

He referred for example to the incalculable havoc caused upon the Jewish world by the crusading armies. Yet their progress across Europe pushed the Jews eastward, contributing to the creation of a large and fruitful Jewish settlement in Poland where Casimir III confirmed privileges on them in 1334. Subsequent persecution in the seventeenth century led to the growth and expansion of the Chassidic movement. The Damascus Libel of 1840 shocked western emancipationists from their complacency, and caused some to look more favourably on Zionism.

Israel is the only country on earth whose destruction is the declared policy of a member State of the United Nations (Iran) in breach of its most fundamental obligations. Located as ever at the cross-roads of civilisation, home to the mythical Armageddon (Har Megiddo), Israel has reason to be concerned by the policies pursued by the current American (Democratic) administration.

However the new Republican President and, indeed, all contenders for the American Presidency in the 2016 Presidential elections gave strong, even moving, public assurances that Israel has an ally it can rely on. But will the West risk war in the Middle East to protect us? Will Christian blood be spilt to save a Jewish country, already much maligned and divided? During the Second World War with the Holocaust in full swing, the Allied powers apparently could not spare a single bomb to disrupt the transportation and murder of Jews, which they knew to be in progress.

At every turn however, in almost every century, providence has found us a shelter, but only at a huge and terrible cost in terms of individual Jewish suffering for those hounded and persecuted. Our identity is indeed forged by such repeated atrocities. One can only hope that the pattern will never again be repeated, and that 1948 will represent a turning point, but how can one reasonably take that for granted? Israel would already have ceased to exist if the combined Arab armies had succeeded in their various attempts to destroy her, and they nearly did so in 1973, when Israel was militarily unprepared.

Military might however is not the only preparation needed. Strong countries and vast empires have often collapsed from within, from arrogance, from indifference to the consequences of their actions, and from underestimating their enemies. We need to stop calling each other names. We need to show respect for our neighbours, both Jewish and non-Jewish. In the face of our history, we need to stand united, but seemingly cannot overcome our millennial predilection for division. And like the supplicant at the very end of Yom Kippur, we ask for salvation, even though we have nothing to offer.

If fragmentation cannot be avoided, we must learn to live with the consequences, and perhaps remember the maxim of Rabban Gamliel[6] 'that disputes should not proliferate in Israel'.[7] His priority was to re-establish Judaism and Jewish society following the cataclysmic loss of the Temple. The 'Return' poses equally dramatic challenges, and calls for equally great leadership.

The contempt publicly shown by leading members of the Israel Knesser towards large sections of world Jewry, describing them as idolaters, or mentally ill,[8] or as fit only to be thrown out of the camp,[9] is quite disturbing, and cannot fail to go unnoticed on High, or by our enemies below. They can hardly be expected to like us, when we clearly do not like each other, and the consequences may affect us all. A squabbling people has little claim on survival, still less on immortality.

The sovereign Israel Parliament (like the State itself) is a miracle of our time, and needs to be treated as such by those who sit there. It should not be taken for granted, and it is bad enough that a former prime minister and a former president are currently serving prison sentences. However one can at least take pride in a healthy judicial system as compared with other countries, where the activities of high ranking leaders might escape attention!

The gulf between Orthodoxy and non-Orthodoxy clearly cannot be bridged or compromised, but both are part of the House of Israel, and both must be accommodated. Recognition of this simple fact does not imply recognition that there are alternative belief systems of equal validity. Orthodox practising Jews (in a minority worldwide) have disproportionate parliamentary power in Israel due to the coalition system. In consequence, there is no agreement to differ, little if any tolerance, and no agreed method for the resolution of major outstanding issues between the civil and religious authorities. How can Jewish identity be defined in such circumstances?

It cannot be defined solely in terms of religious observance, which regrettably does not unite our people, and our story is rather one of schism, alienation and rigidity of thought, the preservation of power, and sterile arguments over recognition and authenticity. There is no serious theological debate, for fear of granting credence to the other side. All who disagree with 'me' must be banned, and different voices stifled. The result has been unseemly name-calling, and attempted demonization of other Jews with seriously different opinions. A thoughtless conformity seems to be the impossible and indeed undesirable objective.

According to Rabbi Jeremy Rosen,[10] the idea that Judaism can speak and has always spoken with one voice is a delusion, as there has never been unanimity on every issue, and there are many issues for which there may be no single or simple answer. It seems clear from the earliest Talmudic debates that the Halakhah was not a homogenous system, and that a number of different traditions existed simultaneously.[11] Yet such difference did not degenerate into sectarian division.

Amongst the most well-documented of disagreements in ancient times were those between Rabbis Hillel and Shamai, and when the rabbis decided in favour of Hillel (as they usually did) the followers of Shammai did not necessarily change their practices. They were not expected to go home and do so. They were not accused of heresy and excommunicated or vilified if they did not. They were not refused rabbinic courtesies. Their children remained free to intermarry with those of other rabbis. And of the greatest significance, their views were not expunged from the Talmudic text, lest they contain some grain of truth for future generations to consider!

In a well-known story, it is recounted that on one occasion of disagreement they both appealed to the Almighty, and were told that they were both right! How is that possible, they asked? And in one of the most profound and important principles enunciated by the authors of the Talmud, He is said to have replied, 'These and those are both the words of the living God'. They each represented valid but contrasting views of Judaism. Rabbi Lau gives the example of 'those seeking to sever the holy from the secular (Shammai) and those seeking to unite them (Hillel)'.[12] Both sought to serve the Lord, but the one put Him on a pedestal, whilst the other brought Him into everyday life.

Other examples of this dichotomy, evident through the ages, are between those rabbis who embraced change and those who resisted it; between those who preferred wisdom and logic to a sometimes painful reliance on the past; and between those who understood the need to rule leniently rather than stringently.

Attempts to define who is a Jew, other than by birth or conversion (which are complicated enough) are inevitably divisive and exclusive. They may serve a purpose in special situations such as for admission to faith schools, or for distribution of limited funds, but no Jew, however remote or tenuous the connection, or lacking in observance, or proof, should fear exclusion from the only country where Jews will be safe from persecution. Our enemies do not distinguish between one Jew and another.

When asked for his occupation, his origin, his country and his people, Jonah replied with the same answer to all questions, 'I am an Hebrew',[13] and his fellow travellers then knew all they needed to know. Today, our identity is more complicated. It must take account of deep divisions within our society, contrasting interpretations of our heritage, and centuries of suffering as well as centuries of greatness. But over and above our long history of discord the common assets we all share tell us who we are.

Foremost among them, whether as believers or not, is our long association with the 'Guardian who neither slumbers nor sleeps'.[14] The covenants and laws delivered in His name illuminate our unique history and form the basis of civilisation itself. Likewise the long and distinguished tradition of rabbinic interpretation belongs to all, whether observed or not, a permanent reminder of the ideas and ideals which have long given meaning to Jewish purpose and achievement.

The Hebrew language is the language of Moses, the Mishna and the prayers. It has never ceased to exist.[15] However, its natural and spontaneous use as a language spoken today by some ten million people owes much to its modern revival by early pioneers such as Abraham Mapu (1808–67), regarded as the first Hebrew novelist, and Eliezer Ben-Yehuda (1858–1922), author of the first modern Hebrew dictionary.[16] No other living language has a pedigree such as ours.

Our liturgy reminds us (if we need reminding) of our connection with the ancestral home, and recalls our collective yearning for peace from on high. Whether recited or not, whether amended or even replaced, our ancient prayers are a direct link with the sages who wrote them to ensure we remained a religious community in dispersion. Our calendar reminds us of our common ancestry, and a mutual history of adversity and survival, of exile and redemption.

Israel Finestein referred to what he called the unifying element, and defined it as 'born of antiquity, sustained by improbable providence, conscious of hope, unsurpassed by adversity, and cognisant of achievement'.[17] Its purpose is clearly beneficial and, knowingly or unknowingly, we are its agents, for better or for worse. Let us be proud of what we share, and what unites us, and accept that what we have in common is greater than what divides us.

Anglo-Jewry is today a thriving community, largely because the infighting has declined. It has benefitted from individual initiatives which have largely transcended differences, or simply ignored them. Finally we may have learned the lesson of Chief Rabbi Nathan Adler from all those years ago: 'Where the breach cannot be healed, let us agree to differ. Why diminish your own vitality without benefit to either party?'[18]

'We are a people, one people',[19] declared Herzl at the first Zionist Congress. We are bound to each other by a common fate, whether we like it or not. However far we travel from each other, or from our faith, we remain accountable to those who came before us, and to those who came before them, and ultimately to those who stood before Sinai and declared 'we will do and we will hear'.[20]

Argument, debate and division are inevitable, and often worthwhile, but it is the totality of our people, and the totality of our heritage, both religious and secular, which will ensure our survival.

Notes

1. IF, *Scenes and Personalities in Anglo-Jewry 1800–2000* (London and Portland, OR: Vallentine Mitchell, 2002), p.312.
2. See Numbers 14:24 (*ruach acheret*).
3. Ze'ev Jabotinsky, 'Instead of Excessive Apology' (1910), translated by Boris Shusteff and cited by him in 'Giving Moral Ground' (1997).
4. IF, *Scenes and Personalities in Anglo-Jewry 1800–2000*, p.304.

5. Matthew Lagrone, 'The "Inhibition" of Morris Joseph', *Jewish Historical Studies*, 47 (2015), p.144.
6. Acknowledged leader of the Yavne generation c.80–110 CE.
7. Binyamin Lau, *The Sages, Character, Context and Creativity* (Jerusalem: Maggid Books, 2011), Vol. II, p.123.
8. Israel Eichler – use of the Mikve for Reform conversion, JC, 26 February 2016, p.2.
9. Meir Porush – location of prayer at the Western Wall, JC, 12 February 2016, p.37.
10. JC, 5 February 2016, p.34.
11. Peretz Segal, 'Jewish Law during the Tannaitic period' in Hecht & Ors (eds) *An Introduction to the History & Sources of Jewish Law* (Oxford: Oxford University Press, 1996), p.139.
12. Lau, *The Sages, Character, Context and Creativity*, Vol.I, Chapter 13.
13. Jonah 1:8–9.
14. Psalm 121:4.
15. Cecil Roth, 'Was Hebrew Ever a Dead Language?', in *Opportunities that Pass. An Historical Miscellany*, eds IF and Joseph Roth (London and Portland, OR: Vallentine Mitchell, 2005), pp.11-17.
16. See also Benzion Benshalom, *Hebrew Literature Between the Two World Wars* (Jerusalem: Youth & Hechalutz Dept. Zionist Organization, 1953).
17. IF, *Scenes and Personalities in Anglo-Jewry 1800–2000*, p.202.
18. See above p.26 (Agree to Differ).
19. Shlomo Avineri, *Herzl* (London: Weidenfeld & Nicolson, 2013), p.159.
20. Deut. 5:24.

Epilogue

In his chosen fields, few if any have equalled him, and he will
long remain unsurpassed.

Lloyd P. Gartner[1]

Israel Finestein died on 12 October 2009 in his 89th year. He had known he
was living on borrowed time for at least two years, his doctor having told
him that his heart condition had reached the critical stage at which he could
drop at any moment. You might be standing in the Post Office queuing for
stamps, he reported his doctor as saying, and you will not feel a thing.

Even before this, he had known that his condition could not be treated,
but he was adamant that his doctor's diagnosis was mistaken, as his stamps
were purchased for him by his concierge! This dry wit, combined with a
placid nature, enabled him to remain entirely affable and to appear, at least
superficially, indifferent to his fate.

In the result he did not drop, and there were several false alarms deriving
from other ailments in that period. Furthermore, he seemed determined to
put his life on the line on occasion by walking to synagogue for a particular
event, or by braving the cold at the funeral of a close friend – his sense of
duty outweighed any personal considerations.

His beloved wife Marion had died five years previously in 2004, and he
had been overwhelmed by her unexpected loss. Totally devoted to each other,
they were planning how to celebrate their 60th wedding anniversary in 2006,
but it was not to be. In her absence, he received considerable support and
hospitality from her sister, and her sister's family, and stayed with them
frequently. However, he had decided to stay alone at his flat for the last two
days of Succoth, 2009.

The festival ended around 8 p.m., and almost inevitably there were
telephone consultations not only as to his health, but in relation to
communal matters. A particularly awkward disagreement had previously
arisen at the Bevis Marks Synagogue, and he had been trying to assist. Late
into that night, he was in conversation with one of its leaders, until he said
he felt tired and would like to resume the conversation in the morning. He

felt the need to call for an ambulance during the night, and died after reaching the hospital.

The impact on his many friends and admirers was considerable, and the community as a whole publicly and privately mourned the loss of a major figure by any standard. Among many moving tributes, was that of the eminent historian Lloyd Gartner who, in reviewing his historical output, concluded as quoted above.

In conjunction with the family, the St John's Wood Synagogue hosted a *shloshim* memorial evening in his honour, on 19 November 2009. The Chief Rabbi, Lord Sacks, spoke of their strong personal relationship and proposed that the family adopt 'Justice, Justice thou shalt pursue' for his headstone, as one to whom that quotation most appropriately applied.

Dr Lionel Kopelowitz, a former president of the Board, and a lifelong friend since their days at Cambridge, recalled the disappointment of his tutor ('He has been seduced by London!') when the offer of an immediate Fellowship was declined following his outstanding double first degree. Fellow historian Professor David Cesarani spoke of his early awe at Israel Finestein's own historical scholarship. His two nephews, Julian Oster Weinberg and myself, spoke on behalf of the family. I focussed on his early life, the influence of his father Jeremiah, and the early indicators of a formidable intellect. I spoke again at the stone-setting on 11 July 2010. Here is what I said:

Eight months ago, we all suffered a profound loss, with the death of someone we loved and respected. It has not been easy to come to terms with this loss, and some are still grieving. To this day, there are those who tell me how much they continue to miss the comfort of his presence, and refer to him as having been their mentor. It was a very special relationship – we all felt that we were part of his life, and that he was a part of ours.

The poem we say on Erev Shabbat ('Lecha Dodi') wishes us to banish sorrow and suffering, and says, 'You have lived too long in the valley of tears'. I am certain Shmul (as he was known) would not wish any further tears to be shed on his account. On the contrary, he would prefer us to celebrate his life, and take pride in his achievements. So here are a few brief reminders.

He was a successful lawyer, and judge. Many who have appeared before him, whether as counsel, or litigant or even criminal, have commented on his patience, humanity and fairness. As a historian, he was praised by other eminent historians for his objectivity. He wrote five books, co-authored, edited or reviewed others, and has some twenty-five articles (perhaps more) published in various learned journals.

As if this were not enough, he took part in Jewish politics at the highest level, and was involved in most of the major communal events throughout his life. In consequence of these various activities, he mixed with the highest echelons of society, but he never forgot his roots.

I could tell you for example of his meeting with Nelson Mandela, or Ben-Gurion. I was present in 1985 when he hosted the Queen as President of Norwood. He guided her round the reception, introducing guests with that mixture of gravitas and informality which was almost his trademark. He spoke to the Queen of the longstanding connection of the Royal family with Norwood over its 190 years, and in the usual 'thank you' from the Palace it was stated that if invited again, Her Majesty would consider it favourably – an astonishing compliment.

Above all, he was unshakeable in his belief in the Jewish cause. He believed in 'Klal Yisroel', that every Jew can contribute to our future, and our greatness, regardless of religious affinity or observance, and he was thus a major unifying force in the community. He accepted that there were divisions. There always had been! But this was not fatal, so long as we focussed on what we all had in common.

There have been many tributes, which have been of great comfort. Over 200 people attended the *shloshim* memorial meeting at St John's Wood, with speakers on different aspects of his life. The Chief Rabbi has graciously decided to dedicate a lecture in Shmul's memory at the end of October, to correspond with the anniversary of his death.

In February, the Institute of Jewish Studies at UCL (where Shmul had spoken himself many times) dedicated one of its public lectures to his memory. More recently the East London Association of Orthodox Synagogues held a successful memorial meeting at Nelson Street when several leading members of the Board of Deputies and the legal profession spoke of their recollections.

Today, as we consecrate his Stone, we must begin the process of looking forward. Shmul wrote a great deal about the past, but he did not live in the past, and would not want us to do so. We must now let him take his own place in history, and be written about as an important historical figure in his own right.

To some extent this process has already begun – with the recent publication of a History of the Board of Deputies, to celebrate its 250th anniversary. There are various mentions of his involvement in events during the second half of the twentieth century. And in relation to earlier periods, the author credits all of Shmul's books as source material.

I began with a quotation from a sixteenth-century Jewish poet, and will conclude with a nineteenth-century English poet – Alfred Lord Tennyson. It was fashionable in his day to make much of grief, or the loss of a loved one. But his message was that the world goes on, and in this poem he writes about the sea which breaks on the sea-shore, and continues to do so, regardless of any individual sense of loss. His poem ends with the words:

And the stately ships go on, to their haven under the hill;
But O for the touch of a vanished hand, and the sound of a voice that is still!

Shmul's voice does not need to be silent – or still, as the poet says. His written words will continue to speak for themselves. And if we listen to our hearts, and remember his presence, if we try to do the right thing, if we remain loyal to our families, to our communities, and to our people … then his voice will be heard again, and we will rejoice that we were his family and his friend.

Note

1.   Lloyd P. Gartner, 'Israel Finestein, Historian of Anglo-Jewry', *Jewish Historical Studies*, 43 (2011), p.6.

Glossary

aliyah	emigration to Israel
Amora(im)	interpreters of the Mishna
Ashkenazi(m)	Jews of European origin
Beth Din	Jewish ecclesiastical Court
bimah	elevated reading desk in the synagogue
cheder(chedorim)	room(s); old style religious instruction classes, sometimes in makeshift premises
cherem	ban, or form of excommunication
Cohen(anim)	Priest, descendent of Aaron
Get	Jewish Bill of Divorce, given by man.
Haham	Sephardi Rabbinic authority/sage
Halakhah	corpus of Jewish law
har	hill or mountain
Hashem	a term used to refer to the Almighty (lit. the name)
Haskalah	Enlightenment
Havdalah	Ceremony to mark the termination of the Sabbath (lit. meaning. 'separation')
Kabbalah	Jewish mystical tradition
Kaddish	prayer in praise of God and memorial prayer for deceased
Kashrut	Jewish dietary laws
Knesset	Israel Parliament
kippa	head covering for prayer
Kol Nidrei	Opening line of the service on Eve of Day of Atonement
Machzikei Hadath	'Upholders of the Law'. Orthodox synagogue founded 1891; joined Federation of Synagogues 1905
maskil(im)	exponent of the Enlightenment
matzo(th)	unleavened bread required for Passover
minyan	quorum of ten men for public worship
Mishna	codification of Jewish practise c.200BCE
Mitnagdim	opponents of Chassidism
mitzva(voth)	religious obligation, also good deed

Moshiach	the Messiah
Semichah	Rabbinical ordination
Sephardi(m)	Jews of Spanish or Portuguese origin
Shechita	method of slaughter under Jewish law of animals for human consumption
Shema	declaration of faith (Deut 6:4)
shloshim	end of thirty days mourning
Shtadlanim	persons of influence who intervened with gentile authorities on behalf of Jews
Shulchan Aruch	authoritative Code of Jewish Law
Siddur	prayer book
Simchat Torah	Rejoicing of the Law
Succoth	Festival of Tabernacles
tallit(ot)	prayer shawl
Talmud	record of rabbinic discussions, incl. commentary on the Mishna, constituting the Oral Law
tefilin	phylacteries
Tikkun Olam	repairing the world
Torah	Five Books of Moses
yeshiva(vot)	seminary for religious study
Yom Kippur	Day of Atonement

General Bibliography

Alderman, Geoffrey, *British Jewry since Emancipation* (Buckingham: University of Buckingham Press, 2014).

Arnold, Matthew, *Culture and Anarchy* (Oxford World Classics, 1869).

Avineri, Shlomo, *Herzl* (London: Weidenfeld & Nicolson, 2013).

Avner, Yehuda, *The Prime Ministers: An Intimate Narrative of Israeli Leadership* (London: The Toby Press, 2010).

Bartal, Israel, *The Jews of Eastern Europe 1772–1881* (Philadelphia, PA: University of Pennsylvania Press, 2002).

Ben Amittai, Levi, *Fields in the Valley* (Tel Aviv: Am Oved, 1950).

Bennett, Ann, *Retailing in Georgian Hull 1770–1810* (Wetherby: Oblong, 2005).

Bloom, Cecil, 'Sir Mark Sykes', *Jewish Historical Studies*, Vol.43 (2011).

Bromwich, David, *The Intellectual Life of Edmund Burke, from Sublime and Beautiful to American Independence* (Harvard: 2014).

Brown-Fleming, Suzanne, 'The Kristallnacht Pogrom', *Jewish Historical Studies*, 2014, Vol.46.

Cesarani, David (ed.), *The Making of Modern Anglo-Jewry* (Oxford: Basil Blackwell, 1990).

Cesarani, David, *The Jewish Chronicle and Anglo-Jewry 1841–1991* (Cambridge: Cambridge University Press, 1994).

Cesarani, David, *Disraeli, the Novel Politician* (London: Yale University Press, 2016).

Cheyette, Bryan, 'From Apology to Revolt: Benjamin Farjeon, Amy Levy, and the Post-emancipation Anglo-Jewish Novel, 1880–1900', *Jewish Historical Studies*, 29 (1982–86).

Clark, Kenneth, *Civilisation* (London: BBC and John Murray, 1969).

John Dewey, *A Common Faith* (New Haven, Conn.,1934).

Disraeli, Benjamin, *Tancred or the New Crusade* (Middlesex: The Echo Library, 2007).

Dubnov, Arie M., *Isaiah Berlin: The Journey of a Jewish Liberal* (New York: Palgrave Macmillan, 2012).

Ebner, Ann, 'The First Jewish Magistrates', *Jewish Historical Studies*, 2002, Vol.38.

Egan, Charles, *The Status of the Jew in England* (London: 1848).

Eliot, George, *Daniel Deronda* (London: Penguin Books, 1967).

Endelman, Todd M., *The Jews in Britain 1656–2000* (Berkeley, CA: University of California Press, 2002).

Endelman, Todd M., 'Nina Ruth Davis Salaman' in *Jewish Women: A Comprehensive Historical Encyclopaedia* (Jewish Women's Archive, 2009).

Endelman, Todd M. and Kushner, Tony (eds) *Disraeli's Jewishness* (London and Portland, OR: Vallentine Mitchell, 2002).

Falk, Eliyahu, *Modesty, an Adornment for Life* (New York: Philip Feldheim, 2001).

Finestein, Israel, see separate Bibliography.

Fleg, Edmond, *Why I am a Jew* (London: Victor Gollancz, 1943).

Fox, Pam, *Israel Isidor Mattuck: Architect of Liberal Judaism* (London and Portland, OR: Vallentine Mitchell, 2014).

Frankel, William, *Tea with Einstein and Other Memories* (London: Halban Publishers, 2006).

Gartner, Lloyd P., *The Jewish Immigrant in England 1870–1914* (London and Portland, OR: Vallentine Mitchell, 2001, 3rd edn).

Gartner, Lloyd, 'Women in the Great Migration', *Jewish Historical Studies*, 40 (2005), pp.129–39.

Gartner, Lloyd, 'Israel Finestein, Historian of Anglo-Jewry', *Jewish Historical Studies*, 43 (2011), pp.1–6.

Gilbert, Martin, *Atlas of Jewish History* (London: Routledge, 2006, 7th edn).

Gilbert, Martin, *Churchill and the Jews: A Lifelong Friendship* (London: Siomn & Schuster UK Ltd., 2007).

Golinkin, David, 'Does Jewish Law prohibit women from singing in public?' *Justice*, Vol.51 (The International Association of Jewish Lawyers and Jurists, Fall 2012).

Goodman, Martin, *State and Society in Roman Galilee AD 132–212* (London and Portland, OR: Vallentine Mitchell, 2000, 2nd edn).

Grenville, Anthony, *Jewish Refugees from Germany and Austria 1933–1970* (London and Portland, OR: Vallentine Mitchell, 2010).

Gross, John, 'Zangwill in Retrospect', *Commentary*, 38 (December 1964).

Halbertal, Moshe, *Maimonides: Life and Thought* (Princeton, NJ: Princeton University Press, 2014).

Harris, Michael, *Faith without Fear: Unsolved Issues in Modern Orthodoxy* (London and Portland, OR: Vallentine Mitchell, 2016).

Hecht, N.S., Jackson, B.S., Passamaneck, S.M., Piattelli, Daniela and Rabello, Alfredo (eds), *An Introduction to the History and Sources of Jewish Law* (New York: Oxford University Press, 1996).

Henriques, Robert, *Sir Robert Waley Cohen 1877–1952. A Biography* (London:Secker & Warburg, 1966).

Herman, D., 'The Wandering Jew has no nation: Jewishness and Race Relations Law', *Jewish Culture and History*, Vol.12 (London & Portland, OR: Vallentine Mitchell, 2010).

Hertz, J.H. *Soncino Pentateuch* (London: Soncino Press, 1969, 2nd edn).

Israel, Alex, *1 Kings: Torn in Two* (Jerusalem: Maggid Books, 2013).

Jacobs, Louis, *We have Reason to Believe* (London & Portland, OR: Vallentine Mitchell, 1957).

Jacobs, Louis, *Helping with Inquiries: An Autobiography* (London and Portland, OR: Vallentine Mitchell, 1989).

Johnson, Boris, *The Churchill Factor* (London: Hodder and Stoughton, 2014).

Kessler, Edward, 'Claude Montefiore, Defender of Rabbinic Judaism', *Jewish Historical Studies*, 2000, Vol.35.

Kitson Clark, George, *The Making of Victorian England* (London: Routledge, 1962).

Kwall, Roberta Rosenthal, *The Myth of the Cultural Jew: Culture and Law in Jewsih Tradition* (Oxford: Oxford University Press, 2015).

Lang, Richard, 'Third Pillar Developments' in E. Guild and F. Geyer (eds), *Security versus Justice?* (Aldershot: Ashgate Publishing, 2008).

Langham, Raphael, *250 Years of Convention and Contention: A History of the Board of Deputies of British Jews 1760–2010* (London and Portland, OR: Vallentine Mitchell, 2010).

Langham, Raphael, 'The Bevin Enigma', *Jewish Historical Studies*, 44 (2012).

Lagrone, Matthew, 'The "Inhibition" of Morris Joseph', *Jewish Historical Studies*, 47 (2015), pp.137–55.

Lau, Binyamin, *The Sages, Character, Context and Creativity*, Vols I and II (Jerusalem: Maggid Books, 2010 and 2011).

Lau, Binyamin, *Jeremiah, The Fate of a Prophet* (Jerusalem: Maggid Books, 2013).

Lipman, Sonia and Lipman, V.D. (eds), *The Century of Moses Montefiore* (Oxford: Oxford University Press, 1985).

Michelson, Miriam, 'The terrible consequences of clothing with women inside of it', *Sunset Magazine*, February 1915.

Miller, Stephen, 'Studies in Jewish Education', *The impact of Jewish Education on the religious behaviour and attitudes of British secondary school pupils* (IJPR, 1988).

Morris, Benny, *1948, a History of the First Arab-Israeli War* (London: Yale University Press, 2008).

Niebuhr, Reinhold, 'Jews after the War', included in *Love and Justice: Selections from the Shorter Writings of Reinhold Niebuhr*, D.B. Robertson (ed.) (Philadelphia: Westminster Press, 1957).

Oz, Amos and Oz-Salzberger, Fania, *Jews and Words* (London: Yale University Press, 2012).

Peres, Shimon, *Ben Gurion, a Political Life* (New York: Schocken Books, 2011).

Persoff, Meir, *Faith Against Reason. Religious Reform and the British Chief Rabbinate, 1840–1990* (London and Portland, OR: Vallentine Mitchell, 2008).

Read, Piers Paul, *The Dreyfus Affair* (London: Bloomsbury Publishing, 2012).

Rigal, Lawrence and Rosenberg, Rosita, *Liberal Judaism: The First Hundred Years* (London: Union of Liberal and Progressive Synagogues, 2004).

Roth, Cecil (ed.), *Essays in Jewish History* (London: Jewish Historical Society of England, 1934)

Sacks, Jonathan, *Exodus, the Book of Redemption* (London: Maggid Books, 2010).

Sacks, Jonathan, *Not in God's Name: Confronting Religious Violence* (London: Hodder and Stoughton, 2015).

Schama, Simon, *The Story of the Jews, Finding the Words, 1000BCE–1492CE* (London: The Bodley Head, 2013).

Shindler, Colin. *The Rise of the Israeli Right: From Odessa to Hebron* (New York: Cambridge University Press, 2015).

Silver, Eric, *Dateline Jerusalem* (Brighton: Revel Barker Publishing, 2011).

Singer, Simeon, *Daily Prayer Book* (London: Eyre & Spottiswoode, 1962, new edn).

Solomon, Norman, *Torah from Heaven: The Reconstruction of Faith* (Oxford: The Littman Library, 2012).

Stern, Eliyahu, *The Genius: Elijah of Vilna and the Making of Modern Judaism* (London: Yale University Press, 2013).

Sugarman, Martin, *Fighting Back: British Jewry's Military Contribution in the Second World War* (London and Portland, OR: Vallentine Mitchell, 2010).

Taylor, Derek, *Chief Rabbi Hertz. The Wars of the Lord* (London and Portland, OR: Vallentine Mitchell, 2015).

Tilles, Daniel, *British Fascist Anti-Semitism and Jewish Responses 1932–40* (London: Bloomsbury Publishing, 2015).

Umansky, Ellen, 'Review of Israel Isidor Mattuck, Architect of Liberal Judaism', *Jewish Historical Studies*, Vol.47 (2015).

Weizmann, Chaim, *Trial and Error* (London: Hamish Hamilton, 1949).

Zangwill, Israel, *Children of the Ghetto: A Story of a Peculiar People* (Leicester: Leicester University Press, 1977, new edn).

Bibliography of Israel Finestein's Work

Books

Picciotto's Sketches of Anglo-Jewish History (London: Soncino Press, revised and re-edited 1956).

A Short History of Anglo Jewry (London: Lincolns Praeger, 1957).

Essays Presented to Chief Rabbi Israel Brodie (London: Soncino Press, 1968), eds H.J. Zimmels, J. Rabbinowitz and IF.

Jewish Society in Victorian England (London and Portland, OR: Vallentine Mitchell, 1993).

Anglo-Jewry in Changing Times: Studies in Diversity 1840–1914 (London and Portland, OR: Vallentine Mitchell, 1999).

Scenes and Personalities in Anglo-Jewry 1800–2000 (London and Portland, OR: Vallentine Mitchell, 2002).

Opportunities that Pass. An Historical Miscellany by Cecil Roth, eds IF and Joseph Roth (London and Portland, OR: Vallentine Mitchell, 2005).

Studies and Profiles in Anglo-Jewish History: From Picciotto to Bermant (London and Portland, OR: Vallentine Mitchell, 2008)

Published Articles

'Some Conversionists in Hull in the Nineteenth Century', *Gates of Zion*, 11, 4 (1957).

'Sir George Jessel, 1824–1883', *Jewish Historical Studies*, 18 (1958) pp.243–83.

'The New Community 1880–1918', *Jewish Historical Studies*, Vol.20 (1960), pp.107–23.

'Anglo-Jewish Opinion during the Struggle for Emancipation 1828–58', *Jewish Historical Studies*, 20 (1964) pp.113–43.

'Jewish Immigration in British Party Politics in the 1890s', *Jewish Historical Studies*, (1971) pp.128–45 – article delivered by IF to the Anglo-American Jewish Historical Conference in July 1970.

'Matthew Arnold and the Jews', *Jewish Quarterly*, 23, 4 (1975), pp.10–17.

'The Secular Jew: Does He Exist and Why?' *Jewish Journal of Sociology*, (1977). pp.185–95.

'Arthur Sigismund Diamond, 1897–1978', *Jewish Historical Studies*, Vol.26 (1979), pp.111–12.

'An Approach to a New Emphasis', in Moshe Davis (ed.), *Zionism in Transition* (New York: Arno Press, 1980), pp.301–6.

'Post Emancipation Jewry: The Anglo-Jewish Experience', *Oxford Centre for Postgraduate Hebrew Studies* (1980), pp.1–20.

'A Modern Examination of Macaulay's Case for the Civil Emancipation of the Jews', *Jewish Historical Studies*, 28 (1984), pp.39–59.

'The Uneasy Victorian: Montefiore as Communal Leader', in S. and V.D. Lipman (eds), *The Century of Moses Montefiore* (Oxford: Oxford University Press, 1985), pp.45–70.

'Early and Middle 19th Century British Opinion on the Restoration of the Jews: Contrasts with America', in Moshe Davis (ed.), *With Eyes Toward Zion* (New York: Praeger, 1986), Vol.II, pp.72–101.

'The Future of American Jewry', *Jewish Journal of Sociology*, 30 (1988), pp.121–5.

'Sir Moses Montefiore: A Modern Appreciation', *Jewish Historical Studies*, 29 (1988), pp.195–205.

'Cambridge Contrasts: Waley Cohen and Brodetsky' in William Frankel and Harvey Miller (eds) *Gown and Talith* (London: Harvey Miller Publishers, 1989), pp.47–51.

'Radical Assimilation in Anglo-Jewry', *Jewish Journal of Sociology*, 34 (1992), pp.129–35.

'Jewish Legal and Political Philosophy', *Jewish Journal of Sociology*, 39 (1997), pp.87–92.

'Chaim Bermant', *Le'ela*, 2 (1998), pp.53–4.

'Criminal Justice in Israel', *Jewish Journal of Sociology*, 41 (1999), pp.109–12.

'The Jews of Hull between 1766 and 1880', *Jewish Historical Studies*, 35 (2000), pp.33–91.

'Lucien Woolf 1857–1930: A Study in Ambivalence', *Jewish Historical Studies*, 35 (2000), pp.239–54.

'Holocaust and Rescue: Impotent or Indifferent?', *Jewish Historical Studies*, 38 (2003), pp.213–15.

Index

Abraham (Jewish Biblical patriarch), 3, 151
Abrahams, Barnett, 57
Abrahams, Israel, 66
Abramsky, Y.A., Rabbi, 72–3, 79
Adass Yisroel (Congregation of Israel)
    Synagogue, the, 68
Adler, Henrietta (Nettie), 105–6
Adler, Hermann, Chief Rabbi, 33–4, 35–6, 39–
    41, 44, 57–8, 59, 122, 144, 188, 199, 209,
    210
Adler, Nathan, Chief Rabbi, 14, 25–6, 27, 28–30,
    31, 33, 37, 56, 196, 197, 209, 238
Aguilar, Grace, 104–5
AJA (Anglo-Jewish Association), the, 29, 35, 70,
    82, 124, 174, 177, 197, 207
Akiva, Rabbi, 6, 112, 150
Akiva School, the, 86
Alderman, Professor Geoffrey, 90, 190
Alexander II, Tsar, 124
Aliens Act (1793), the, 204
Aliens Act (1905), the, 30
allocation of Mitzvoth, 210
Altman, Dr. Alexander, Rabbi, 61
American Constitution, the, 164
American Judaism, 24, 29, 47, 78, 82, 83; and
    Conservative Judaism, 66, 78
American Reform movement, the, 24, 49, 65
Anglicanisation of the Jewish community, 34
Anglo-Jewish historians, xvi, 33, 59, 60–1, 101,
    104-05, 146, 157, 202, 224, 241
Anglo-Jewish Historical Exhibition (1887), the,
    59, 227
Anglo-Jewish leadership, 184, 188, 189–92
Anglo-Jewish Opinion during the Struggle for
    Emancipation (essay), xvii–xviii
Anglo-Jewish theological position, the, per Chief
    Rabbi Hertz, 69
Anglo-Jewry, x, xi, xv–xvi, 238
anti-Semitism, 49, 124, 129, 142–3, 155, 176,
    178, 186–7, 229; from the Nazis, 48, 70,
    73, 128, 139–40, 147, 175–6, 218
Arkush, Jonathan, 181

Arnold, Matthew, 27, 58, 103
Ashkenazi Jews, 6, 7, 29, 171, 194
Association for the Advancement of Science,
    the, 206
Assyrian annexation of the Northern
    kingdom, 4
attempts to merge synagogues, 221, 222
Authorised Daily Prayer Book, the, 37, 44
Avineri, Shlomo, 143
Avner, Yehuda, 107–8

Baal Shem Tov, the, 10
Babylon, 5
Bakstansky, Lavy, 176
Balfour, Lord, 122, 138, 198
Balfour Declaration, the, 48, 105, 127, 138,
    174–5, 177, 216
Ballin, Ada Maria, 105
Bar Kochba uprising, the, 6, 149
Barnett, Abraham, 207
Battle of Cable Street, the, 176
Begin, Menachem, 7, 148–9
belief in God and divine retribution, 157–8
Belisario, Miriam, 104
ben Amittai, Levi, 149, 159
ben Eleazar, Israel (see Baal Shem Tov, the)
Ben Gurion, David, 2, 108, 146–7, 148, 149, 156,
    159, 160, 177
ben Israel, Menasseh, 7, 119, 132
ben Solomon, Elijah (see Gaon, Vilna)
Ben-Yehuda, Eliezer, 237–8
ben Zakkai, Yohanan, 5
Benas, Bertram, 215
Benisch, Abraham, 18, 56
Benjamin, Israel, 204
Bennett, Dr. Ann, xii, 204
Bentwich, Norman, 216
Berlin, Isaiah, 20, 150
Berlin Reform community of Jews, the, 23
Beth Din, the, 28, 51, 72, 79, 85
Bevis Marks Synagogue, 18, 24, 74, 109, 171,
    228, 240

Bexley, Lord, 134
Bialik, Chaim Nachman, 72
Bibero, Marcus, 207
Biblical prophecy: and Jewish restoration, 132–3, 137, 139; and Jewish settlement in Palestine, 34, 35
Biblical teaching: and the Jewish people, 3–5, 34, 112, 116, 157; and justice, 162, 163, 165, 166–9
Birmingham Jewish community, the, 194, 195, 201, 222
Bloch, Denise, 108
B'nai Brith Hillel Foundation, the, 175, 200
Bnei Akiva Religious Zionist Youth movement, the, 107, 150
Board of Guardians, the, 29, 207, 209
Board of Shechita, the, 40
BOD (Board of Deputies of British Jews), 18–19, 29, 70, 98, 100, 171–81, 188, 191–2, 221; and changes to Jewish identity, 89, 185; and Israel Finestein, 14, 93, 108, 109, 171, 177, 180, 181, 185–6, 189–90, 191, 192, 242; and marriage under Jewish law, 28, 35–6, 51, 86, 87; and non-Orthodox Judaism, 24–5, 46, 51, 86, 87, 91, 93, 96, 209; and possible merger with the JLC, 174, 190–1; and the provincial communities, 66, 196–7, 201, 209, 216; and the representation of women, 108, 109
Brawer, Dina, 117–18
Bresslau, Marcus, 56
Brichto, Sidney, 90, 94
Brier, Norma, 109
British imperial interests in the Middle East, 135, 138–9
British sense of indebtedness to Jewish influence, 136–7
British Union of Fascists, the, 176
Brodestky, Selig, 60, 70, 176, 177
Brodie, Israel, Chief Rabbi, 69, 74, 76, 77, 79, 80, 200
Brunswick Conference of Reform Judaism, the, 23, 26
Buckingham, James, 135
Burial Acts (1854), the, 206
Burke, Edmund, 132
Burman, Rickie, 107
Byck, Muriel, 108

Caesarea massacre, the, 5
Cameron, David, 187
Cardozo, Nathan, Rabbi, 9, 155
Carmel College, 62

Caro, Joseph, 8
Casimir III, King, 234
CCJ (Council of Christians and Jews), the, viii, 73, 96
Cecil Roth Memorial Lecture, the, 55
Central Synagogue, Hull, 215
Cesarani, David, 20, 241
Charedi community, the, 98, 120
charitable relief, 29, 30, 40, 44, 194–5, 209
Charles, HRH Prince, 192
Charles I, King, 203
Charlie Hebdo murders, the, 168
Chasidism, 10
Chassidic movement, the, 234
cherem (ban) on Reform Judaism, 25, 26, 80
Cheyette, Bryan, 228
Children of the Ghetto (book), 224, 225, 227–8
chiloni (secular), 156
Chofetz Chaim, the, 113
Chovevei Zion movement, the, 124, 144–5
Christian criticism of Judaism, 43
Christian Zionism, 138–9
Christianity and its origins, 73
Churchill, Winston, 138–9
Clark, George Kitson, 17
Clark, Kenneth, 63
Clause 43 of the BOD Constitution, 172
Cobbett, William, 15
code of practice of the BOD, 173
codification of Jewish law, the, 8–9
Cohen, Arthur, 174
Cohen, Dr. Abraham, 185
Cohen, Julia Matilda, 106–7
Cohen, Lionel Louis, 29, 30, 31, 59, 68, 173–4
Cohen, Louis, 29
Cohen, Sir Benjamin, 19, 41
Cohen, Sir Robert Waley, 67–8, 69–70, 72, 106–7
Cohen, Solomon, 208
Colman, Elijah Alec, 79, 201
Commission on Women in Jewish Leadership, the, 109
communal harmony amongst Anglo-Jewry, xv–xvi
Community of Faith (book), 94
Conjoint Foreign Committee of the BOD, 174
Conservative Judaism, 24, 86; in America, 66, 78
Consultative Committee on Jewish-Christian relations, 87, 96
Cotton, Jack, 201
Council of the Four Lands, the, 9

Court of Appeal, the, and ruling on eligibility for admission to Jewish schools, 98–9
Crimean War, the, 134
Criminal Law Ordinance of the former British Mandate authorities, the, 168–9
Cromwell, Oliver, 7, 119, 132
CST (Community Security Trust), the, 187–8, 192
Cuckle, Dr. Howard, xii, 220
cultural and literary issues, 56, 58–9, 61–2

Damascus Libel affair, the, 19, 135–6, 234
Danger of Zionism, the (pamphlet), 48–9
Darby, John Nelson, 139
David, King, 3–4
Davidson, Ellis, 207
Davis, Sir Mick, 190
de Rothschild, Baron Lionel, 13, 21
de Rothschild, Louisa, 103–4
de Sola, David Aaron, 104
debate over election of Chief Rabbi 1842-45, 195–6
defence of Orthodox Judaism, 66–9
Degania, 146, 149
demographic trends in Anglo-Jewry, 89, 185
Denning, Lord, 167
Derby, Lord, 20
Deronda, Daniel, 137
Deutch, Oscar, 201
dichotomy in application of Jewish law, 237
Dignity of Difference, The (book), 97
dispersion of Jews worldwide, 6, 7, 47, 125, 127, 128, 130, 150–1
Disraeli, Benjamin, 20, 27, 135, 136–7, 228
divide between established Anglo-Jewry and new immigrants, 225
divisiveness in Judaism, 41, 88, 90–2, 183, 236–7; attempts for inclusiveness and pluralism, 95–7, 99–100; and challenges to Orthodox Judaism, 68–9, 76–7, 79–82, 89–90, 226; and Chasidism, 10, 234; between East End immigrants and settled English Jews, 30, 39–40, 225; managing non-Orthodox Judaism in the BOD, 24–5, 46, 51, 86, 87, 91, 93, 96, 209; in modern Israel, 1, 2, 7, 235–6; and Shechita, 40, 72–3, 188–9; since Biblical times, 2–4; over Zionism, 33; and Liberal Judaism, 33, 38–9 (*see also* provincial-London divide, the)
divorce law, 28
dress codes for Jewish women, 115, 116
Dreyfus, Capt. Alfred, 142, 144
Dreyfus affair, the, 142–3

Dubnow, Simon, 146
Duke of Cambridge, the, 14
Duveen, Joseph Joel, 207
Duveen Gallery, the, 207

East End migrants and Orthodox Judaism, 30, 39–40, 175, 176, 224, 225, 226, 227
East London Association of Orthodox Synagogues, 242
ECHR (European Court of Human Rights), 162, 164, 167
Eden, Anthony, 74
Edgar, Leslie, Rabbi, 51, 69
Edinburgh, Prince Philip, Duke of, 192
Education Act (1870), the, 27, 58, 59
Education Act (1944), the, 62, 73
education for Jews in England, 27–8, 37, 55, 56–63, 73, 89, 94–5, 104, 180, 210–11
Egan, Charles, 133
Egyptian conquest of Greater Syria, the, 134
Ehrentreu, Chanoch, Rabbi, 90
Einstein, Albert, 155
electoral franchise and women, the, 106, 109
Elizabeth II, Queen, 101, 242
Emancipation Apologetics (article), 16
emancipation of the Jews in England, 13, 14–20, 26–7, 34, 57, 122, 173, 196
Endelman, Prof. Todd, 101, 208
English Common Law, 163–5
English perceptions of the Jews, 17, 20, 27
English Zionist Federation, the, (EZF) 127, 174
equality for women, 109, 112–20
equity law, 165
Etz Chaim Yeshiva, 94
Exodus (film), 148
expulsion of Jews from Spain and Portugal, 6
Ezekiel, Biblical prophet, 48

Faith of Secular Jews, The (book), 153
Faith without Fear (book), 120
Falk, Eliyahu, Rabbi, 116
Farbstein, Joel, 210
fascism in England, 176
Federation of Synagogues, the, 30
Federation of Women's Societies, the, 50
Feinstein, Moshe, Rabbi, 118
Feldman, Henry, JP, 210–11, 216
female equality, 50–1,109–10
Festival of Britain, the, 219
Fighting Back (book), 219
Finestein, Israel, ix–xi, 20, 25, 38, 65, 72, 82, 89, 91, 99, 100, 106, 187, 233; and the Board of Deputies, 14, 93, 108, 109, 171, 177,

180, 181, 185–6, 189–90, 191, 192, 242; on Claude Montefiore, 38, 43, 136; death of, 240–3; essays and writings by, ix, xvii, 41, 96–7, 224; and Hull, 201, 203, 205, 208, 210, 211, 213, 214, 215, 217, 218, 222; on Israel Zangwill, 224, 225, 231; on Jewish education, 55, 60, 61; on Jewish emancipation, xviii, 14, 16, 17, 19, 21, 23, 57; on Jewish female scholarship, 44, 103, 104, 105; on Jewish identity, 122, 130, 183, 224, 234, 238; on Jewish observance, 98; and Jewish restoration, 132, 136; on justice and the law, 162, 163, 165, 169; lectures by, 55, 74, 101; on Lily (Montagu), 44, 45; on the unifying element within Judaism, 238; and the provincial-London divide, 194, 197, 201, 202; and Rabbi Jacobs, 76, 77, 92; and Rabbi Jakobovitz, 85, 87; and the representation of Jewish women, 109, 110, 112; on secularism, 153, 155, 156–7; on Waley Cohen, 67, 68; and Zionism, 142, 150 and on the Gryn 'affair', 96–7
Finestein, Jacob Wolf (Jack), 214
Finestein, Jeremiah, 214, 217
Finestein, Louis, 214, 221
Finestein, Marion, 240
Fisch, Prof. Harold, 20, 137
Fisher, Dr. Geoffrey, 73
Fleg, Edmond, 129–30
Foreign Jews Protection Committee, the, 230
foreign provocations of the Jewish people, 5
Forster, William Edward, 58
founding of the state of Israel, the, 7, 70, 107–8, 128, 129, 130, 139, 148, 159–60, 177, 216
Fox, Pam, 48
Francis, Pope, 140
Frankel, William, 78, 79–80, 82
Frankel, Zacharias, 24
Frankfurt Conference of Reform Judaism, the, 23, 24
Franklin, Jacob, 196
freedom of expression, 167–8
'Freedom' party, the, 7

Gamliel, Rabban, 235
Gaon, Vilna, 9, 10
Gartner, Prof. Lloyd P., 107, 240, 241
Gaster, Moses, 127
Gawler, Col. George, 136
Gaza wars, the, 178
gender segregation and the patriarchal society, 119
Genesis, book of, 2, 3

George III, King, 171
George VI, King, 66–7, 88
Georges-Picot, François, 138
German refugees in the 1930s, 46, 48, 70–1, 216, 218
Gertner, Levi, 61
Gilbert, Sir Martin, 6
Gladstone, William, 15
Gluckstein, Sir Louis, 51, 177
Goldsmid, Sir Francis Henry Lyon, 13, 15, 17–19
Goldsmid, Sir Isaac, 173
Golinkin, Prof David, Rabbi, 114
Gollancz, Rabbi Dr. Hermann, 37, 59
Gollancz, Victor, 129-30
Goodhart, Sir Arthur, 163, 164, 165, 169
Gorky, Maxim, 72
Gosschalk, Edward, 216
Graetz, Heinrich, 59
Grant, Sir Robert, 133–4
Great Exhibition (1851), the, 206
Great Synagogue, the, 18, 19, 24, 25, 26, 29, 194, 195–6, 198, 206
Green, Rev. Aaron Asher, 36
Greenberg, Leopold, 201
Grenville, Anthony, 71
Gross, John, 224, 226–7, 230
Grunwald, Henry, 189
Gryn, Hugo, Rabbi, 88, 96
Guantanamo Bay, 167

Ha'am, Ahad, 43, 145, 150
Habeas Corpus, 163
Haganah Defence forces, the, 148
Hailsham, Lord, 166
Halakhah, the, 8, 9, 35, 40, 66, 68, 89, 95, 113, 114, 117, 118, 164
Halbertal, Moshe, 114
Halevi, Yehudah, 105
Hammurabi, King, 166
Hampstead Synagogue, 35, 36
Hannassi, Yehuda, 6
Harris, Emily, 104
Harris, Michael, Rabbi, 83, 100, 120
Harris, Nathan, 210–11
Harris, Sarah, 104
Haskalah (Enlightenment), the, 9, 21, 144, 153, 156
Hasmonean School, the, 60
'Hatikva' (Jewish national anthem), 198
Havdalah (prayer), 2, 156
Hebrew for All (publication), 61
Hebrew instruction, lack of, in the *JC*, 1881, 57

Hebrew language, the, 156, 237–8
Hebrew Review and Magazine of Rabbinical Literature (magazine), 56
Hebrew Union College, the, 47
Henriques, Robert, 67
Henry III, King, 199
Herschell, Solomon, Chief Rabbi, 24–5, 195
Hertz, J.H., Chief Rabbi, xvi, 55, 60, 65, 66–70, 71, 72, 73–4, 105, 157, 162
Herzl, Theodore, 16, 137, 142–3, 145–6, 160, 226; and Zionism, 34, 35, 128, 130, 144, 198, 229, 238
Hezekiah, King, 4
Hinsley, Cardinal, 70, 140
Hirsch, Samson Raphael, 23–4, 68, 85
History of Zionism (book), 138
Hobbes, Thomas, 166
Holland and tolerance for Jews, 6
Hollier Prize, the, 105
Holocaust, the, 158, 235
Holt, Lewis, 208
Hope of Israel, The (book), 7
Horwich, Ed, 200
Hull aerodrome committee, 216
Hull as a commercial and trading centre, 203–4, 219–20
Hull Ferens Art Gallery, 207
Hull Hebrew Congregation, 206, 222
Hull Hebrew School for Girls, 214
Hull Jewish community, 204–11, 213–22
Hull Literary and Philosophical Society, 206
Hull Old Hebrew Congregation, 208, 214–15, 221–2
Hull Royal Institution, 206
Hull School of Art and Industrial Design, 206–7
Hull Zionist Society, 216

immigration and education, 59
immigration of Jews in nineteenth-century England, 21, 29–30, 40, 175, 195, 197, 199, 209, 215–16
inclusiveness and collective responsibility, 95–6, 98, 100
Inglis, Sir Robert, 15
Inquisition, the, 6
Institute for Jewish Policy Research, the, 185
Institute of Jewish Affairs, the, 60, 185
Institute of Jewish Studies, the, 61
intellectual inquiry into spirituality and Judaism, 44, 45
Intellectual Level of Anglo-Jewish Life, The (book), 60
inter-faith consultations, 87

intermarriage, 7, 38, 66, 95, 126, 128
International Christian Embassy, Jerusalem, 139
Irgun underground army, the, 148
Isaiah, Biblical prophet, 34, 158, 160, 162
Israel, state of, 16, 49, 63, 83, 88, 129, 168, 178, 183–4, 234–5; and founding of, 7, 70, 107–8, 128, 129, 130, 139, 148, 159–60, 177, 216 (*see also* restoration of Jews to the Holy Land, the)
Israel Defence Forces, the, 149, 178
Israeli general election (2015), 19
IUJF (Inter-University Jewish Federation), 1, 60, 198

Jabotinsky, Ze'ev, 126, 147, 234
Jacobs, Aaron, 205
Jacobs, Benjamin, 214
Jacobs, Bethel, 196, 206–7, 208, 209, 214
Jacobs, Dr. Louis, Rabbi, 73, 76–8, 79, 80–3, 86
Jacobs, Israel, 206, 211
Jacobs, Ivor, 81
Jakobovits, Dr. Immanuel, Chief Rabbi, xvi, 81–2, 85–6, 87–8, 89, 90–2, 100, 153
Janner, Barnett, 177
Janner, Elsie, 109
JC (*Jewish Chronicle), The* (newspaper), 40, 72, 85, 91, 100, 136, 187, 188, 199, 209, 211, 227; on Dr. Hertz, 65, 69; editors of, 56, 61, 201, 210; on emancipation, 18, 34, 173; on Jewish women, 105, 106, 109; on Rabbi Jacobs, 78, 79–80, 83
JEDT (Jewish Educational Development Trust), the, 86, 95
Jeremiah, prophet, 4–5, 149
Jessel, Albert Henry, 66
Jewish Association for the Diffusion of Religious Knowledge, the, 57
Jewish Book Week and the Jewish Book Council, 62
Jewish cemeteries in Hull, 205–6, 216, 222
Jewish identity and role in English society, 122–3, 225–8, 230–1
Jewish identity and Zionism, 151
Jewish Journal of Sociology (periodical), 168
Jewish Labour Council, the, 175
Jewish Ladies Benevolent Loan and Visiting Society, 104
Jewish League for Woman Suffrage, the, 105
Jewish Legion of the British Army, the, 147
'Jewish Library,' the, 104
Jewish Literary Club, the, 58–9
Jewish Literary Society, the, 56

Jewish marriage and divine law, 51, 73, 79, 83, 175
Jewish Memorial Council, the, 200
Jewish Publication Society of America, the, 105
Jewish Quarterly Review (periodical), 44, 227
Jewish Relief Act (1858), the, 14, 15, 21, 27
Jewish secondary school movement, the, 60
Jewish Small Communities Network, the, 200
Jewish State, The (book), 144
Jewish Territorialist Organization, the, 229
Jewish Theological Seminary, the, 65
Jewish Youth Study Group movement, the, 61
Jews' College, 27–8, 33, 56–7, 59, 67–8, 76, 85, 94, 196
'Jews watches', 208
Jezreel Valley, the, 149
JHSE (Jewish Historical Society of England), 14, 33, 43, 105, 107, 122, 123, 184, 227, 228, 230
JIA (Joint Israel Appeal), the, 184
JLC (Jewish Leadership Council), 174, 186, 189, 190–1, 201
JOFA (Jewish Orthodox Feminist Alliance), 117–18
Joseph, Rev. Morris, 36
Josiah, King, 4
Jowett, Benjamin, 43
JPC (Jewish People's Council against fascism and anti-Semitism), 175, 176
JPR (Institute of Jewish Policy Research), 62
JREB (Jewish Religious Educational Board), 33, 57, 58
JRU (Jewish Religious Union), 36–7, 38, 39, 45, 49, 122
JRU Manifesto, the, 38, 123
Judaism, 154, 155, 233–4, 237–8; and justice, 162–3, 165–9
JW3 (community centre), 62

Kaddish (prayer) by women, 117
Kalms, Lord Stanley, 93–4, 95, 97, 100
Kalms Report, the, 94, 185
Kashrut, 83, 175, 188–9
Keble, John, 133
Kehillat Nashirah, 'the singing community', 114
Kessler, Edward, 43
Khan, Dr. Gilbert, 187–8
Kibbutz Lavi, 107–8
Kid for Two Farthings, A (film), 225
Kimchit, 114–15
Kindertransport, the, 48, 71, 218
Kinnock, Neil, 189
Kishinev Pogrom, the, 229

Knesset, the, 168, 235, 236
knowledge and scholarship lack of, 60–1; re-emergence 62
Koestler, Arthur, 150
Kol Nidrei prayer, the, 23
Kook, Rav Abraham Isac, 150
Kopelowitz, Dr. Lionel, 241
Kosmin, Dr. Barry, 90
Kossof, David, 225
Kristallnacht, 70, 128, 140, 218

Lamb, Charles, 17
land purchases in Palestine by Jewish interests, 146
Landau, Frederic Moses, 82, 172
Langdon, Harold, 88
Langham, Raphael, 25, 190
Laski, Neville, 176, 177
Lawton, Clive, 180
Lazarus, Emma, 213–14
Lazarus, Harry, 213
LBJRE (London Board of Jewish Religious Education), the, 61
LCC (London County Council), 106
Lebanon War, the, 88
Lebus, Harris, 207
Leftwich, Joseph, 230
legal status of Jewish marriages, 28, 35–6
legitimacy of children of non-orthodox marriages, the, 86
Lennard, Jack, 220
Leo Baeck College, 50, 81
'Lev Chadash', (prayerbook) the, 47–8
Levin, Salmond, 89
Levinson, Rev. Judah, 217–18
Levy, Amy, 227–8
Levy, Elkan, 200
Levy, Felix, 77
Levy, Harold, 61
Levy, Isaac, 205
Levy, Michael, 205
Lewis, Dr. David, xii, 205, 206, 211
Liberal Jewish Monthly (magazine), 129
Liberal Judaism, 39, 43, 44, 45–6, 48–50, 67, 68, 69, 71, 88; differences with Orthodox Judaism, 38, 47, 50–3; and efforts for better representation, 86, 90–1, 172
Liberal Judaism: The First Hundred Years, 46
Liberal Party, the, 106
Liberal Synagogue, 45–6
Likud, 19
Limmud conferences, the, 62, 99–100
Lincoln, Ashe, 172

Lindo, Abigail, 104
Lipman, Dr. Vivian D., 224
liturgical modifications to services, 28, 30–1, 35, 36, 37, 47
Liverpool Board of Guardians, 195
Liverpool Jewish community, the, 195, 198
LJS (Liberal Jewish Synagogue), 44, 46, 51, 177
Loewe, Herbert, 60
London Beth Din, the, 72, 79, 81, 195
London Society for promoting Christianity, 204–5
London Yeshiva Etz Haim, 69
Lucas, Henry, 58
Lyon, Joseph, 205

maʾayan post, the, 110
Macaulay, Thomas, 16–17
Machzikei Hadath congregation, the, 40, 72
Magna Carta, 164–5
Maimonides, 8, 113–14, 153
Major Barbara (play), 45
Manchester and Zionism, 216
Manchester Zionist Society, the, 198
Mankowitz, Wolf, 225
Mapu, Abraham, 237
Marks, Laura, 109
Marks, Rev. D.W., 15, 25, 36
Marks, Sir Simon, 184
Maskilim, the, 156
Masorti movement, the, 80, 81, 82, 183
Mattuck, Israel Isidor, Rabbi, 46–7, 48, 50, 51, 125–6, 128
matzo tax, the, 194–5
May, Theresa, 187
MCB (Muslim Council of Britain), 178
Mein Kampf (book), 128
Meir, Golda, 108
Melting Pot, The (play), 228–9
Mendelssohn, Moses, 9
Merron, Gillian, 181
Messiah, the, 7, 34
Meyer, Solomon, 206, 209
Micah, Biblical prophet, 116
Michelson, Miriam, 119
Midrash, the, 149
Millbank, Lord Duveen of, 207–8
Miller, Dr. Stephen, 155
Mills, John, 12
Minority in Britain: Social Studies of the Anglo-Jewish Community (book), 184
Mirvis, Ephraim, Chief Rabbi, 52, 101, 110, 117, 118
Mishna, the, 6

Mishne Torah, the, 8
Mitnagdim, the, 10
Mitzva Day, 109
Moccatta, Sir Alan, 77
Model, Alice, 106
modern Jewish history, xv, 7, 233, 235
monotheism, 123, 128
Montagu, Edwin, 138
Montagu, Lily (Lilian Helen), 43, 44–5, 48, 49, 50, 52–3, 68, 103, 104
Montagu, Sir Samuel, 30, 40, 44, 45
Montefiore, Charlotte, 104
Montefiore, Claude, 50, 52–3, 66, 122, 125, 126, 130, 153, 174, 227; Israel Finestein on, 38, 43, 136; and the JRU, 37–8, 39, 123; opposition to Zionism, 48–9, 127; thinking of, 43–4, 47
Montefiore, Sir Moses, 18, 19, 25, 104, 135, 136, 172, 173, 174, 196–7
Morais, Sabato, Rabbi, 65, 66
moral basis of the law, 167–9
Morris, Nathan, 61, 68
Mosaic Code, the, 166
Moseley, Oswald, 176, 218
Moseley, Simeon, 210
Moser, Jacob, 198
multiculturalism and the status of religions, 97
municipal disabilities, 19

Nachman of Bratslav, 10
National Association of Girls' Clubs, 44
National Council for Women, 44
National Council of Shechita Boards, the, 188, 189
National Front, the, 186
nationalism and the partial nature of Judaism, 123–4
nationalism and Zionism, 125–6, 128–9
nationality and the Jews, 15, 34, 47, 125–9
nationwide planning, 201
Nazis and anti-Semitism, the, 139–40, 147, 175–6, 218
Neuberger, Julia, Rabbi, 50
New London Synagogue, the, 78, 79, 81, 82, 85, 86
New North London Synagogue, the, 81
New Synagogue, Hull, 215
New West End Synagogue, 37, 76, 77, 78; and refusal to certify Rabbi Jacobs, 76–8
New York Yeshivat Maharat, 118
Newman, Capt. Isidore, 218–19
Newman, Cardinal John Henry, 133
Niebuhr, Reinhold, 126

Nixon, Richard, 108
North Western Reform Synagogue, 49
Nostra Aetate (papal decree), 139–40
Not in God's Name (book), 98
Novak, David, 164

'Open' Orthodoxy in America, 83
Operation Protective Edge, 178
Oppel, Harold, 220
'Oral Law', the, 10, 24, 31, 39, 52, 66, 113
Orthodox Judaism, 38, 65, 71–3, 82–8, 91, 144,
    160, 172–3; affect of Emancipation on, 27,
    28; challenges to, 36, 38, 68–9, 76–7, 79–
    82, 89–90, 226; and East End immigrants,
    30, 39–40, 175, 176, 224, 225, 226, 227;
    tensions between 'right' and 'left', 96–7, 98,
    99; and women, 114, 115–16, 118, 119,
    120
Osborne Street Synagogue, Hull, 218, 219, 221
OSC (Office for Small Communities), 200, 201
Oslo accords, the, 184
Ottoman Empire, the, 146
Oxfam, 178
Oxford Hebrew Congregation, 199
Oxford Jewish Centre, 199–200
Oz, Amos, 113, 156
Oz-Salzberger, Fania, 113, 156, 174

Padwa, Chanoch, Rabbi, 96
Padwa, Ephraim, Rabbi, 116
Palmerston, Lord, 135
partnership-*minyan* in Borehamwood, the, 114,
    117
Passover Association, the Liverpool, 195
Passover Relief, Manchester, 195
patriarchal societies and gender separation, 119
Paul VI, Pope, 139
Pearl, Dr. Chaim, 77–8
Pearlman, Benno, 216
Peel, Sir Robert, 19
Peres, Shimon, 156
Perlzweig, Maurice, 49
Persoff, Meir, 45, 91
Petticoat Lane 'ghetto' of East End immigrants,
    225, 230–1 (*see also Children of the Ghetto*
    (book))
philanthropy and Jewish worthiness, 58
Picciotto, James, 25
Pinkser, Leon, 144–5
Pittsbugh Reform Platform, the, 24, 65
Pius XI, Pope, 139–40
Poale Zion (Workers of Zion), 146
Poland and Judaism, 9, 234

Polish Jews, the, 146, 147, 149
political system in Israel, the, 1–2
practice or descent for membership of Jewish
    faith, 98-9
prayer books (Liberal), 47–8
Preston, Rosalind, 108
'Progressive Conservatism,' 78
Progressive Judaism, 90, 172–3
promotion of Jewish literature, 56, 58–9
provincial-London divide, the, 194–202
public school experiment, 62

Rabin, Yitzhak, 168, 229
Rabinovitz, E.S., Rabbi, 221
Rabinowitz, Dr. Louis, Rabbi, 80
Rakusen, Lloyd, 195
Raphall, Dr. Morris, 56, 197
Rashi, biblical commentator, 113
Rayner, John, Rabbi, 47–8, 51, 90
reaction by Orthodox Judaism to emergence of
    Liberal Judaism, 39
recognition of foreign-born rabbis, 197-8
recognition of non-Orthodox Anglo-Jewry,
    86–92
Reform Judaism, 23–6, 31, 36–8, 86, 124, 144,
    172, 183, 209, 215, 227; and the American
    Reform movement, 24, 49, 65; *cherem*
    (ban) on, 25, 26, 80; concerns of Moses
    Montefiore, 19; relations with Rabbi
    Jakobovits, 86, 88, 90–1
regulations on the conduct of services, by Chief
    Rabbi Nathan Adler, 28
religious liberty in England, 7, 14, 15–16, 101
religious pluralism, 73, 82–3, 89, 96
religious revival in Britain, 133
Representative Council, Hull, 221
Resettlement of Jews in England in 1656, 7, 13,
    194
resettlement of refugees, the, 46, 48, 70–1, 216,
    218, 229–30
restoration of Jews to the Holy Land, the, 132,
    133–6, 137–40, 146–9, 229, 235; and
    Biblical prophecy, 132–3, 137, 139; and
    Emancipation, the,16; and Zionism,
    143–51, 229
retaliation principle, the, 166
Reuben Sachs (book), 227
Revelation at Sinai, the, 112
revelation in Judaism, 76–7
Revisionist Party, the, 148
Rigal, Lawrence, 44, 48, 49
right to a fair trial, the, 162–3

Riskin, Shlomo, Rabbi, 83
Robinson Row synagogue, Hull, 208–10, 211, 215
roles for the sexes in Orthodox Judaism, 118–19
Rose, Michael, 81
Rosen C. & Sons Ltd., 220
Rosen, Dr. Jeremy, Rabbi, 83, 236
Rosen, Kopul, Rabbi, 62, 74
Rosen, Lionel, 216–17
Rosenberg, Rosita, 49, 50, 88
Rotenstreich, Natan, 61
Roth, Cecil, 20, 33, 55, 60–1, 74, 129
Rothschild, Lord, 66
Russian Empire, the, 146

Sacks, Dr. Jonathan, Chief Rabbi, 89, 93–4, 95–7, 98, 99, 100–1, 155, 159, 185, 200, 241
Salaman, Dr. Redcliffe, 58, 105
Salaman, Nina, 105
Salisbury, Lord, 15
Salomons, Sir David, 13, 19, 21, 28, 59, 173, 177
Samuel, Jacob, 204
Samuel, Moses, 14
sanctity of life and Biblical teaching, the, 3
Saul, King, 4
Schechter, Solomon, 59, 66
Schonfeld, Dr. Victor, 60, 68
Schonfeld, Solomon, Rabbi, 60, 70–1, 96
Schultz, Sir Leo, 217, 219
Scott, John, 137, 205
Scott, Thomas, 137
secularism, 89, 98
secularity and Judaism, 153–60, 179, 183
security concerns, 186–8
Segal, Marcus, 220
Senesh, Hannah, 108
Sephardi Jews, 6, 7, 20, 24, 25, 26, 87, 171
Seventh Zionist Congress, the, 229
Shaftesbury, Lord, 14–15, 134, 229
Shamir, Moshe, 61
Shane, A.L., 228
Shaw, George Bernard, 45
Shechita, 40, 72–3, 179, 188–9
Shechita UK, 192
Sheffield Hebrew Congregation, 198, 201
Shema (prayer), 62–3, 113, 153, 157
Shira Hadashah, 114
Shmool, Marlena, 100–1
Shmul (*see* Finestein, Israel)
Shops, Shambles and the Street Market 1770 to 1810 (book), 204
Shulchan Aruch (book), 8–9

Sieff, Rebecca, 109
Simmons, Anna, 106
Simon, Oswald John, 124–5
Simon, Samuel, 210
Simon, Sir John, 124
Singer, Rev. Simeon, 37, 44
Singers Hill Synagogue, Birmingham, 194, 201–2, 222
singing at public events, 35, 114
Six Day War, the, 88, 151, 169
Slaughter of Animals Act (1933), 72
Slaughter of Animals (Humane Conditions) Regulations (1990), 188
Smilansky, Yizhar, 156
social classes of London Jews, 18, 30
social conformity, 27
SOE (Special Operations Executive), the, 219
Sofer, Moshe, 114
Sokolov, Nahum, 138
Solomon, King, 4
Solomon, Norman, Rabbi, 113
Soloveitchik, Rabbi, 149
Soncino Pentateuch, 71–2
song of Miriam, the, 112, 114
Soviet Jewry, 88
Spinoza, Baruch, 154
Spiro Institute, the, 62
St Johns Wood Orthodox Synagogue, 79, 241, 242
Stalin, Joseph, 72
Standing Committee on Relationships Within Anglo-Jewry, 86
Stanley, Arthur, 134, 137
Statue of Liberty, the, 213–14
Steed, Wickham, 127
Stern, Rev. Joseph Frederick, 37, 126–7
Sugarman, Capt. Wilfred (Billy), 218
Sugarman, Martin, 108, 219
survival mechanisms amongst Jews across the world, 5, 6, 9–10
Sykes, Sir Mark, 138, 216
Symons, John, 208
Symons, Moses, 208
synagogual music, 35

Talmud, the, 8, 150, 160, 165, 236, 237
Tancred, or the New Crusade (book), 136–7, 228
Temple, the, 36, 125, 126
Temple Mount, the, 118–19
Templeton Prize, the, 100
Ten Commandments, the, 164
Tennyson, Alfred Lord, 242–3

tercentenary of the resettlement of Jews in England, the, 88, 100–1, 109, 185
terrorists and moral rights, 167
Thatcher, Margaret, 87–8, 105
Theory of Zionism, The (sermon), 48
Thirteen Principles of Faith, the, 8
Tickell, John, 205
Tikkun Olam, 51–2
Times, The (newspaper), 127, 135, 137, 163, 174
Torah, the, 23, 24, 46, 51, 63, 66, 80, 81, 88, 162; divine authority of, 7, 71, 77; teaching of to women, 112, 113, 116–17, 118
Torah im Derech Eretz, 85
Torah Judaism, 66
Trevelyan, G.M., xvii, 107

Uganda programme, the, 229
UJIA (Joint Israel Appeal), 87, 184, 189
ULPS (Union of Liberal and Progressive Synagogues), 49, 91
Ultra-Orthodox Judaism, 18, 98, 128, 179, 183, 187
Umansky, Dr. Ellen, 44, 46
unifying element, 238
Union of Jewish Literary Societies, the, 227
Union of Jewish Women, the, 44, 106
United Synagogue Council, 33
universalism and Judaism, 123–4
Universities' Chaplaincy service, 88
UOHC (Union of Orthodox Hebrew Congregations), the, 68, 69, 72, 96, 98, 116, 189
US (United Synagogue), the, 29, 35, 45, 103, 173–4, 184, 195, 199, 201–2, 227; financial difficulties of, 94, 97; inclusiveness for women, 110, 117; and Jewish education, 60, 61; and the Kalms Report, 94, 185; loss of congregation, 85, 94 (*see also* Sacks, Dr. Jonathan, Chief Rabbi)

Vale of Cedars (book), 105
Van Oven, Barnard, 16
Vespasian, Emperor, 5
Victor Schonfeld Memorial Lecture, 153
Victoria, Queen, 35, 206
Victoria & Albert Museum exhibition, 74
Voice of Jacob, The (newspaper), 18, 55, 135, 195
voting rights, 18; for women, 109

Wagerman, Josephine, 108, 109, 120
Walpole, Spencer, 15
We Have Reason to Believe (book), 77

Webber, Dr. George, 80
Weinberg, Julian Oster, 241
Weisman, Rev. Malcolm, 200
Weizmann, Dr. Chaim, 1–2, 127–8, 138, 147, 198, 216
welfare and charitable work by Jewish women, 106–7
West London Synagogue, the, 25, 26, 35, 88, 96, 172
Western Synagogue, Hull, 211, 214, 216, 221, 222
Western Wall, Jerusalem, 118, 145, 149, 196–7
What are the Jews (book), 128
White Paper on Jewish immigration to Palestine, 176–7
Whitehall Conference, the, 7, 101
Why I am a Jew (book), 129–30
William III statue, Hull, 203, 205
Winroope, Belinda and David, 222
Wise, Isaac Mayer, Rabbi, 47
WJC (World Jewish Congress), 177
Wolf, Lord, 163
Wolf, Lucien, 17, 19, 123, 127, 174, 197, 227, 230
women and Jewish scholarship and education, 103–6, 110
women as breadwinner, 107
women as pioneers, 107 (see also Kibbutz Lavi)
women in politics, 108
women in public and modesty, 113–16, 120
women in the rabbinate, 50
Women of Israel (book), 105
Women's Campaign for Soviet Jewry, 109
women's rights and Biblical teaching, 112–13, 116
Woolfson, Sir Isaac, 184, 201
works on Hebrew grammar and language, 104, 105
World War II, 218–19; and Jewish women, 107–8
Worms, Fred, 94
WUPJ (World Union of Progressive Judaism), 48

Yachad, 178
Yakar Study centre, the, 62
Yerushalmi, Y.H., 157
Yom Kippur War, the, 88, 108

Zalman, Shneur, 10
Zangwill, Israel, 105, 224–30, 231
Zerny, Manfred, 220

Zhitlowsky, Chaim, 155–6
Zionism, 69–70, 123, 124, 138, 157, 174–5, 176–7, 216; and Claude Montefiore, 48–9, 127; divisions with Liberal Judaism, 33, 38–9; Israel Finestein on, 142, 150; and nationalism, 125–6, 128–9; and the restoration of Jews to the Holy Land, 143–51, 229; and Theodore Herzl, 34, 35, 128, 130, 144, 198, 229, 238

Zionist Banner (journal), 198
Zionist Congress, the 1897, 35
Zionist Federation, the, 61
Zionist Revolution: a New Perspective, The (book), 137
Zola, Emile, 142
Zucker, Judge Kenneth, 81
Zunz, Leopold, 58
Zvi, Shabbetai, 10

Thank you for reading this Vallentine Mitchell Publishers book.

Vallentine Mitchell serves both the academic community and the educated lay-reader, and promotes learning and scholarship to a global audience. Our staff is committed to publishing to the highest standards across a range of disciplines of interest to the Jewish and wider community in the Humanities and Social Sciences. We support authors through strong editorial, marketing and production skills, and are committed to serving international scholarship by promoting our authors' writing and research so that they make the maximum impact on, and gain the widest possible, readership.

Vallentine Mitchell's publishing programme primarily covers Jewish History, Culture and Heritage; Jewish Thought; Middle Eastern History, Politics and Culture; Religion and the Holocaust.

Full details of our publishing programme can be found at our website:

www.vmbooks.com

E-books are available via Ebrary and ProQuest and from mid 2017 via our website